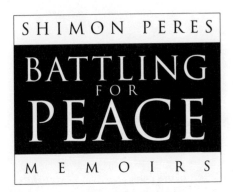

SHIMON PERES

BATTLING
FOR
PEACE

MEMOIRS

Edited by

DAVID LANDAU

Weidenfeld & Nicolson
LONDON

First published in Great Britain in 1995 by
Weidenfeld & Nicolson

The Orion Publishing Group Ltd
Orion House
5 Upper Saint Martin's Lane
London WC2H 9EA

A catalogue record for this book is available from the British Library

ISBN 0 297 81222 X

Typeset by Selwood Systems, Midsomer Norton
Printed by Butler & Tanner Ltd, Frome and London

CONTENTS

ILLUSTRATIONS

The Peres family, 1945. Left to right, standing: Peres's wife Sonia, brother Gershon and his wife, Carmella. Seated: Shimon Peres, his mother and father.

With Ben-Gurion during the Sèvres Conference, 1956 (© Interphoto).

With Sonia after receiving the *Légion d'Honneur*, 1957 (© P. Goldman).

The family in 1955. Left to right, son Hemi, father Yitzhak, mother Sara, son Yoni, Sonia, niece Ruthi, daughter Zikki, Shimon Peres, Gershon and Carmella.

With two political comrades in Rafi, 1969; Moshe Dayan (left) and Teddy Kollek (© Newsphot).

On an Israeli navy missile boat when he was Minister of Defence, 1976.

A press conference after the Entebbe rescue, with Brigadier General Dan Shomron who headed the commando seated left, July 1976 (© Rex Features).

With President Sadat and former Prime Minister Golda Meir at the Knesset during Sadat's historic visit to Jerusalem, November 1977.

In the cockpit of an Israel-made Kfir jet fighter, 1980 (© Israel Aircraft Industries).

Election night, June 1981. Early euphoria gave way to disappointment as the returns showed Peres's Labour Party and its rival, the Likud, almost tied. Likud formed the new Government (© Rex Features).

A handshake between Peres and Yitzhak Shamir, leader of the Likud bloc, after a meeting to 'consider the possibility' of forming a government of national unity, August 1984 (© Rex Features).

As Prime Minister in 1985, meeting President Reagan to discuss beginning peace negotiations with Jordan (© Rex Features).

Meeting Ethiopian Jews, recently arrived in Israel, in Eilat, 1985 (© Rex Features).

With King Hassan II of Morocco, 1986 (© Rex Features).

The secret signing ceremony in Oslo, August 1993. Johan Holst sits in front of Shimon Peres with Abu Ala'a (on his right) and Uri Savir.

A more relaxed moment in Oslo. Left to right, Terje Larsen, Shimon Peres, Johan Holst and Abu Ala'a.

INTRODUCTION

From the beginning, the State of Israel has commanded a disproportionate share of the world's attention. Despite its modest size, United Nations' statistics place Israel third on the list of international news producers, preceded only by the United States and the Commonwealth of Independent States. For Israel is judged not by its size, but by its uniqueness. It came into being against the odds, and it survives against the odds. It has always existed as a turbulent reality on the one hand, and as a bold and fantastic dream on the other.

The reality has been harsh: Israel is a small, desolate stretch of land. 'Greater Israel', the whole of Western Palestine, is only 24,000 square kilometres in area; and Israel, in its pre-1967 borders, covers 16,000 square kilometres. The land, moreover, has always suffered from a chronic shortage of water. The River Jordan is famous, but not for the volume of its waters (in fact, it is merely a meandering stream), and the Sea of Galilee is a frustratingly volatile lake: its level sinks disastrously at the merest hint of drought.

Half of the land – the Negev, in the south – is desert. The more fertile north was plagued by malaria when the first Zionist pioneers tried to settle it. Today, a century later, it is reeling from the drastic ecological effects of over-intensive drainage, irrigation and cultivation. The climate, both in the north and in the south, is harsh, demanding and uncomfortable.

But it was not only the land and the elements that joined forces to resist the Jewish dreamers who came to settle here; the people of the region also did their utmost to extirpate them. The Arab states and the Arab inhabitants of Palestine sought to prevent the creation of a Jewish state, attacked it the moment it was born, and refused for decades thereafter to accept its existence.

This was the reality with which the Palestinian and Jewish youngsters of my generation grew to adulthood and responsibility. Like many others in the pioneering movements, I knew material hardship; I wrestled with the stony soil, guarding at night, working and worrying by day. We lived our life in a constant state of tension, in an electric atmosphere of national awareness. We were always conscious – sometimes self-consciously so – that Jewish history was being made, and that we were actively involved in making it.

Reality for us – for me at any rate – was not what objectively existed or happened; it was what was going to happen, what could still be shaped and fashioned by people. I was trained to work the land and to love it, but what I really loved was working with people. Fortune offered me the opportunity to work alongside men of vision, and I seized it. In the final analysis, I believed that the saga of the Jewish nation and its homeland would not be merely, or even mainly, a story of a land, a state or a faith, but that it would be a story of people, of exceptional individuals. Many of them swam against the tide in order to reach their destination. Some forfeited their lives in the battle to shape reality. A few attained monumental achievements.

I lived and worked in the shadow of those few, and I was swept along with them to soaring heights. They were the ones who guided me into politics – that word which incorporates such a multitude of contradictions. If politics is the down-to-earth application of lofty ideals, then Israel is the political society *par excellence*. During the state's formative decades, the collective political 'we' always took precedence over the individual 'I'. That was the source of the young nation's strength, but also the cause of its internal weaknesses, as highly motivated groups, fired by conflicting myths and memories, clashed and grappled for power.

Israel's collective consciousness is built out of millennia of pent-up memories: the memory of the exodus of the Jewish slaves from Egypt; of the Giving of the Law in the wilderness; of martial valour under King David; of the wisdom of Solomon; of stern, unflinching prophets and compromising priests; of judges, rabbis and rebels; of honest shepherds and duplicitous traitors. The memories of two temples destroyed by foreign conquerors pulsate in the national psyche, as does the painful remembrance of the Holocaust, which threatened to annihilate our people for ever. Israelis absorb and relive all these memories in their school-books. They mark them each year in fasts, festivals and solemn ceremonies.

Moreover, each component of the nation brought its own memories from their far-flung diasporas. Immigrants poured in from a hundred countries, speaking a hundred languages, each group with its own dress, traditions and beliefs, its own tastes and fragrances. They had internalized the culture and the folklore of their home countries, and they brought these with them to the Promised Land. The cultural differences made for divisions within the new nation, some obvious and articulated, others latent but potent beneath the surface of Israeli society. The land itself was the strongest uniting factor: they had all yearned for it. But the myths and memories fomented disharmony.

Nor did they bring with them only Jewish myths and memories. Some of the young pioneers had grown to political maturity during the Russian Revolution, and were permanently and profoundly affected by that experience. Others hailed from France and had adopted French culture as their own. Still others were heavily influenced by British-style democracy, as practised in England and the United States.

The immigrants from Germany brought the music, the philosophy and the literature of the Germany into which their parents, and they too, had sought to assimilate, and which had spewed them out and then destroyed those unable to flee. They had studied at German universities, discriminated against but nevertheless imbibing the political thought and culture that had evolved over centuries of war, revolution and social ferment. They had taken a leading role in the poignant disputes that raged through Jewry: where could the Jew turn to escape the pervasive menace of anti-Semitism? What realistically could be done to rescue the Jews as a nation, or at least individual Jews as human beings? The world hated Jews. Must the world, therefore, be changed in order to save Jews? Or should the Jews change their own world, or change their individual selves, in order to change the attitude of the world towards them?

Some of the greatest scions of Jewry had grappled with these existential challenges: Marx and Trotsky, Freud and Einstein, Disraeli and Blum, Heine and Herzl. They all recognized the massive, historic injustice, but most of them looked to the world at large to rectify it. They despised the Jewish faith as an anachronism. The modern world, they believed, was still tainted by religious fanaticism, which was the cause of its abiding hatred of the Jews. It was corrupted by class exploitation, with the Jews trapped between the exploiting upper class and the downtrodden masses, assailed on both sides. It was perverted by strident nationalism, which bred intolerance. The Jews, as a nation without a state, whose nationhood was their religion, were the first victims.

For these thinkers and leaders, God had failed to alleviate the world's injustice, so He should be discarded. And for many young Jews, the answer lay in those movements aspiring to build a new world order, a communist or socialist Utopia, a cosmopolitan Mankind.

But there were also those who reached a radically different conclusion – the Zionist conclusion. This posited that we Jews must first change our own destiny by becoming a nation, like other nations, with its own state, language, government, army and economy; a nation returning to its roots, to the sources of its strength.

With time, this historic dispute reached its inexorable resolution. Hitler annihilated the assimilationist option. In the Soviet empire, Stalin destroyed the mirage of cosmopolitanism, subjecting that part of the Jewish people under his control to a sustained spiritual and cultural holocaust. Today's exodus of hundreds of thousands of Jews from Russia and its former satellites is one part of the verdict of history; the other is their destination. The State of Israel is the demonstrable vindication of the thesis that advocated changing the Jewish reality. The Jews are returning to their Land, and to their senses.

The Zionist thesis itself was beset by discord from within. The Jewish immigrants had fled from the depredations of right and left in the world outside, but they split into a Jewish right and left, both in *Eretz Yisrael* (the Land of Israel) and in the Diaspora. The right was given to declarative dramatics. Its most prominent leaders, Ze'ev Jabotinsky and later Menachem Begin, were considered great orators; but with them, ringing rhetoric often took the place of practical deeds. They were influenced by the Poland of Pilsudski, and by the Italy of Garibaldi and of Mussolini. For a long time, members of the right-wing Zionist youth movement, Betar, paraded in paramilitary uniforms.

The Zionist right always placed its political and ideological emphasis on the territorial issue. The territory – or a declarative assertion that we control the territory – was its overriding goal. The left, by contrast, believed in pragmatism, in the slow, patient building of its brave new world. Its motto, 'another goat, another dunam', expressed the dogged and unflamboyant approach of pioneering Zionism. It sought lasting achievement, rather than fleeting accolades. The left meticulously built the underpinnings of what was to become the Jewish state: the Histadrut trades-union movement, the kibbutzim and moshavim,* public health services, the school system and a fledgling army. It revitalized the land and aimed at creating a revitalized Jew – a Jew who lived on the fruits of his labour, whether manual or cerebral.

But the Zionist left was itself riven by ideological strife. Some of its leaders had broken away from the communist revolution in their youth, but they had not made a clean break: they still saw Soviet Russia as the world of the future, and they still believed in the doctrines of Marx and Engels – in Leninist determinism, in the dictatorship of the proletariat, even in 'ideological collectivism', which they rigidly applied in order to maintain disciplined solidarity in their kibbutzim.

Opposing them stood the mainstream Zionist-socialist party, Mapai,† led by David Ben-Gurion and Berl Katznelson, both of whom were firmly anti-Marxist, anti-communist and anti-Stalinist. They set out to fashion a new form of socialism that was neither imported from the outside nor translated from foreign sources. They believed that the original heralds of socialist morality had been the prophets of ancient Israel: Amos, who tongue-lashed those who 'swallow up the needy ... [and] ... buy the poor for silver' (Amos 8: 4–6), and Isaiah, whose sublime vision of a peaceful and just society has rarely been surpassed in world literature. Ben-Gurion regarded the biblical injunction, 'Thou shalt love thy neighbour as thyself' (Leviticus 19: 18), as the essence of Judaism.

The political movement which he headed for decades was propelled by the genuine desire to turn the vision of the prophets into modern-day reality. Its vision was of a revived Hebrew language and a revitalized Israeli homeland, in which the moral message of the prophets would once again mould the national ethos.

Throughout his life, and regardless of the changing political circumstances, Ben-Gurion always remained, in my eyes, a statesman and leader of genius. He was one of those rare figures in history whose policy and personality were inseparably melded into one consistent whole. His

* The moshav is a farming co-operative, where each family owns its own farm, whereas the kibbutz is a fully fledged collective. Marketing in the moshav, however, is conducted collectively.
† The Hebrew acronym for the Party of the Workers of *Eretz Yisraeli*, forerunner of today's Labour Party.

policy focused on one central purpose: to restore the Jewish People to its own proper place in history, the place from where, 2,000 years earlier, it had been severed from its land, and hence from its political existence. Diaspora existence appeared to Ben-Gurion an inherently sick and diseased environment in which national spirit and talent were ineluctably warped and eroded. Eventually, he believed, that existence was doomed.

Ben-Gurion sought political independence for the Jews not only so that they could become a nation like any other, but also so that they could fulfil their historic mission as an 'eternal nation' by setting a universal example to the whole of mankind. The biblical phrases 'a light unto the nations' and 'precious people' were his watchwords.

The leadership of this people, and indeed statesmanship in general, meant, for Ben-Gurion, an integrated world-view, embracing strategy and economics, politics and morality. The moral consideration, he insisted, must always be dominant; but the dominant moral consideration, for him, was the physical survival of the people. 'Even Albert Einstein's head, containing his great brain, is not impervious to an assassin's bullet,' he would sometimes remark.

For Ben-Gurion, restoring the Jews to history meant both a physical restoration – a return to the Land – and a spiritual restoration – a return to the Bible. He strove to attain this dual goal with a singleminded enthusiasm that knew no let-up. His personality – forged of willpower, courage, determination and wisdom – was an integral part of that political and national striving. He never shrank back from the challenges of life, however forbidding, and never surrendered to ill fortune. He was always prepared to reconsider even the ostensibly most obvious questions, instinctively bridling at run-of-the-mill or unimaginative answers. He was an inveterate innovator, but also an indefatigably hard worker. He was in command of every detail, deciding, remembering, recording, following through with unflagging self-discipline. His great intellectual gifts gave him the consistent ability to cut through to the heart of an issue, to subject it to penetrating analysis, and to express his conclusions and decisions in the most cogent and persuasive way.

Israeli politics, then, has been concerned not only with building a new land but a new national spirit. It did not set out merely to change an existing reality, which is normally the purpose of politics and politicians, but rather to create – or recreate, after a two-millennia lapse – a new national entity out of a people fractured and scattered across space and time. I have always felt, therefore, throughout my political career, that Israeli political leaders represent more than just a particular electoral constituency: we also represent constituencies that do not exist. Some have died, but their heritage lives within us; others are still unborn. For them, our task is to provide a secure setting for their future lives.

1 *SHTETL* BOY

For my mother, at least, my birth was something of a miracle: I weighed more than five kilograms, and she almost died in childbirth.

I was born as night turned to day on 21 August 1923, into a world in transition. My childhood embraced the old-style piety of my grand-parents' home, the modern culture and Zionism of my parents' gen-eration, and the blue skies and citrus orchards of *Eretz Yisrael*, which filled my own imagination from my earliest years. I could smell orange blossom and see the glistening muscles of the young kibbutzniks almost as vividly as I saw and smelt the forests surrounding our *shtetl*, Vishneva, in the heart of White Russia.

Vishneva's wooden houses lay strung out along three roughly parallel roads. Life for Vishneva's 1,500 Jews revolved around its main public institutions: the two synagogues, the bath-house and the village market. The latter came to life each Wednesday, when the peasants from the surrounding hamlets came to sell their farm produce, and the Jews of the village offered the products of their own cottage industries in exchange. My grandmother, for instance, made woollen boots for wearing indoors during the winter. She had a shed built alongside her home, and this housed a large, round machine which produced the boots. Christmas was her busy season; all the Gentiles in the district wanted her warm boots to wear for midnight mass.

Apart from market day, we children knew little or nothing of the Gentile world. We felt as though we lived on a Jewish island, surrounded by a sea of thick and threatening forests. We knew that there were great cities beyond the forest, full of excitement and novelty, but our horizons stopped at the tops of the graceful, swaying birches and at the banks of the River Olshanky. The river, which bounded our village on one side,

9

teemed with traffic through the summer and froze in silent splendour during the long, winter months.

My own life revolved around school and around Bogdunov station, which was three bumpy miles through the woods by horse and cart from our village, or by horse-drawn sledge in the winter. From there, I knew, we would one day start on our *real* lives, our *aliya* or 'ascent' to *Eretz Yisrael*. Whenever people from our village went on *aliya*, all their friends and relatives would crowd round them at Bogdunov station, laughing and crying in a tumultuous leave-taking. My father, a well-to-do young merchant, owned warehouses near the station, so I was sometimes present at other peoples' leave-taking, wishing that we too were going, while sharing in the sadness of those staying behind. I remember my breathless excitement as the train appeared through the trees, an iron giant belching smoke – the only horseless locomotion I saw in my childhood.

The 'Tarbut' school* to which I was sent taught its pupils in modern Hebrew, as well as in our native Yiddish. The law also required that we be taught in Polish, but the Polish language, like the Polish people, was distinctly unloved in our district – both by Jews and by Gentiles. Vishneva and its environs were geographically part of White Russia; indeed, they had been under Russian rule until 1921 (and would return to it in 1939). Poland seized the area in the aftermath of the First World War, but the Poles were regarded as occupiers and anti-Semites, and as an alien, transient presence unlikely to remain for long.

My Hebrew teacher, the leading light in the Vishneva 'cell' of Hash-omer Hatzair, the Zionist-socialist youth movement, was Yehoshua Rabinowitz, a son of one of the village's most distinguished families. Like me, he was among the lucky ones who managed to realize their Zionist dream before the Nazis destroyed Vishneva for ever. He became Mayor of Tel Aviv and, in 1974, Minister of Finance in the Government in which I served as Minister of Defence. Then, as in the classroom back in Vishneva, I felt his stern eyes upon me, always ready to rein in any exorbitance on my part.

My parents' home, which was spacious and comfortable by Vishneva standards – but which, like all the others in the village, had no electricity or running water – stood behind my grandparents' house, where my

---

* Lit. culture; a network of these Zionist schools existed throughout Poland between the world wars. Vishneva also had a traditional Talmud Torah or religious school, and a state-run public school

mother and her two brothers and five sisters had been born. My grand-father, Reb* Zvi Meltzer, was the final and absolute authority in the family. His word was law, and none of his children or grandchildren would ever dare to defy him. He was a stocky man of average height with a square-cut white beard, which gave him a distinguished appearance in keeping with his standing in the community. His eyebrows, unlike his beard, were still black, and they accentuated his deep-set eyes, full of life's wisdom.

My mother's parents, and my paternal grandparents too, hailed from the township of Volozhin, some twenty kilometres from Vishneva. Whereas Vishneva was just another nondescript *shtetl*, Volozhin was a household name throughout the Jewish world because of its famous Yeshiva (Talmudic academy), founded early in the nineteenth century. Zvi Meltzer, my maternal grandfather, studied at the Yeshiva, sharing a room with Chaim Nachman Bialik, who was to become the national poet of the Israeli state. Bialik described the Volozhiner Yeshiva as 'the place where the soul of the nation was moulded'. My father's father, Reb Zalman Persky, not only studied at the great Yeshiva but was a direct descendant of its founder, Rabbi Chaim Volozhiner (1749–1821), foremost disciple of the *Gaon* (sage) Rabbi Elijah of Vilna (1722–97). Perskys were among the ranking scholars of Volozhin throughout the Yeshiva's existence.

Zalman Persky lived to the age of ninety-six, but I was still a baby when he died and have no recollection of him. My '*Zeide*', Zvi Meltzer, on the other hand, was an intimate and formative influence on me throughout my childhood. I loved him dearly, and I believe, looking back, that he must have singled me out among his grandchildren for special attention. It was he who first introduced me to the Bible and the history of our people, albeit by way of children's stories, but with didactic care and academic precision.

As I grew older, he would draw me into the study of the Talmud, teaching me each day a few lines of the esoteric text and explaining the details of complex legal arguments. I grew up imbued with the conviction that nothing is more precious than intellectual acumen. When someone was referred to as an '*iluy*' (a genius), it was as though he were pronounced to be a world champion in every field of endeavour. A man's brain, I believed from earliest childhood, was his most vital asset. I remember

---

* The traditional title denoting respect for a learned layman.

gazing at people's heads, trying to assess their inner capacity from their external appearance. A high forehead, I knew, was a gift of God, the gift of wisdom. When the adults came home from a public event – a sermon at the synagogue or a political meeting – they would invariably begin their report with a description of the speaker's head, paying special attention to the height of his forehead.

Learning the Talmud with my grandfather also taught me, at a young age, that nothing in the world is one-sided. If you see only one side of an issue, he drummed into me, you have not studied it properly. Without studying properly, a boy grows up blind to the multifaceted quality of life.

I also grew up imbued with the deep conviction that Man is created to serve his Maker by observing his commandments. Woe betide anyone who violates the holy Sabbath, or succumbs to the temptation to eat unkosher food, or prays without concentrating on the words and their meaning. I was thus filled with righteous indignation when one Saturday I came upon my parents switching on a radio which my father had brought back with him from one of his frequent business trips. I grabbed the sinful instrument and hurled it to the ground. My parents had probably only turned it on out of excitement: it was the first wireless ever seen in Vishneva. While they themselves, like many of their con- temporaries, no longer observed the minutiae of the religion, while in Vishneva – out of respect for my grandfather – they would never deliberately flout the ancient laws and customs. My mother's kitchen, for instance, was always scrupulously kosher.

As for me, I would zealously accompany *Zeide* to the synagogue every *Shabbat* (Sabbath). The high point of the year for me was Yom Kippur, when my grandfather, who was blessed with a strong and mellifluous voice, would serve as cantor, an honour traditionally reserved for a respected elder of the community. On Yom Kippur everyone went to synagogue. An other-worldly stillness lay over the village as the Jews of Vishneva, dressed in white, hurried along to their annual appointment with Destiny: 'Who will live and who will die; who by fire and who by water...' The men stood bowed beneath their prayer-shawls as my grandfather intoned the words of the prayer. I presumed that each of them was communicating directly with God himself, pleading for a year of life. I knew that if the tally of his sins was longer than his list of good deeds, he was doomed. From the moment my grandfather strode to the reader's lectern on the eve of the fast and began the poignant, gripping melody of '*Kol Nidre*', I was filled with a tingling sense of awe. Indeed, his voice still seems to ring in my ears, and every year, at Yom Kippur, that same sense of awe still sends a shudder deep inside me.

My grandfather, for all his piety, was not a narrow-minded man. One of his accomplishments, rare for someone of his background and way of life – and especially attractive to me – was the violin. He also read widely, particularly the Russian classics, and in this, too, he exercised an abiding influence on me. I remember reasoning that Dostoevsky, Gogol and Tolstoy somehow enhanced my grandfather's mind, which I venerated, and that, therefore, until I too delved into them, I would remain ignorant and limited. By the age of nine, I was struggling through *Crime and Punishment*, reading by day and reliving the book in restless, fearful dreams at night. I was also reading, with varying degrees of comprehension, the poetry of Yehuda Leib Gordon (1830–92), of Bialik and of Shaul Tchernichovsky (1875–1943). My mother would read to me aloud from Sholom Aleichem, the great Yiddish-language novelist and short-story writer.

The Meltzer family was among the largest in the village. Grandfather Zvi and Grandmother Rivka had eight children, seven of whom lived to adulthood. My mother, Sarah, was the oldest of the five daughters, four of whom eventually went on *aliya*. My youngest aunt, Itka, an enthusiastic member of the Vishneva Hashomer Hatzair 'cell', settled in Rehovot, south of Tel Aviv, where she still lives today, a vivacious and much-loved member of our family.

My mother was considered a particularly successful daughter, blessed with both intelligence and good sense. She inherited both my grand-father's voice and his love of books. She had completed her schooling before the Polish takeover and was, therefore, steeped in Russian litera-ture. She always seemed to be reading, in Russian or in Yiddish. When she was not reading, she was singing.

I was particularly drawn to my Uncle Yosef, even though he was the head of the local Betar – the right-wing Zionist youth movement – whereas I, like most of the youngsters, had joined the socialist Hashomer Hatzair. Yosef had been sent to study at a yeshiva, where he received rabbinical ordination and was thought of as something of an '*iluy*'. I was entranced by his gentle, pensive manner, and lapped up the legends and stories with which he would regale us children. When he was struck by cancer, before the age of thirty, we all knew that he was dying. He would lie on a hammock strung out between two cherry trees in his garden, pale and weak. I would gaze at my beloved uncle, lying there helpless, and wonder why even someone who prayed to God as regularly as I myself did nevertheless had to suffer. God could be cruel and unfair, or at least unfathomable. I never forgave the cherries, whose redness I came to associate with the colour draining, day by day, from my uncle's cheeks.

While my grandfather and my uncle 'spoilt' me with intellectual treats, my parents, more practical people, indulged my material longings: skis in the winter, ice-cream after school. I was often required to repay these prizes with imitations of teachers or of other pillars of our community. My mimickry was especially popular when my father, a strong and energetic man, brought guests home. The assembled company was unfailingly impressed and would predict 'a great future' for my parents' adored first-born.

One of my parents' less successful presents was a mandolin, with which I was supposed to join the school band. Sadly, the family's musical genes seemed to have stopped at my mother; I never could reproduce the notes on the score. At one stage, I tried to write my own notes, claiming that these, at least, I would be able to play. Privately, I filled little notebooks with rhymes and songs written for their author's ear alone.

Economic conditions at home were relatively good throughout my childhood, and I was surrounded by love and security. Nevertheless, I was for ever restless and worried. There was so much I did not understand; and some of what I did understand left me bitter and frustrated. I knew of human suffering from the little I had seen around me, and from my intensive and eclectic reading, and I was constantly troubled by the apparent success of evil and injustice. Reading Mapu's* *Sin of Samaria* and *Love of Zion*, I was grateful that he, at least, divided his world into good men and bad, as I believed the world ought to be divided.

The forces of evil struck close to home one day in 1933, when one of our villagers was found murdered in the woods, by anti-Semitic thugs as it later turned out. The whole village was plunged into grief and terror. For me, as a highly impressionable ten-year-old, the episode was a profound trauma. For the first time in my life, I saw a press photographer, sent to photograph the body of the victim. The Warsaw Yiddish daily, *Moment*, carried the story and the gruesome picture. For

* The Hebrew writer, Avraham Mapu (1808–67).

weeks after, life in Vishneva was muted, subdued under a pall of mourning and anxiety.

By then, the world of my imagination, of *Eretz Yisrael*, had become the focus of my life. I felt as if I belonged there already, and my impatience was fuelled by a constant stream of postcards, letters, stamps, pictures, songs and trinkets mailed by my three aunts and their families who had already settled in Palestine. Everything depicted on the postcards – the buildings, the people, the streets and farms – seemed to me so bright and sunny. Every letter was a cause for rejoicing, but when a case of oranges arrived the whole family took part in the long and delectable celebration. Each exotic fruit came wrapped in pink tissue-paper and stamped with the magic legend, 'Jaffa'. We did not rush to peel and eat them; rather, we savoured their aroma and sniffed these spice-boxes exuding the heady perfumes of the beloved Land.

Remote and protected though I was from the Gentile world outside our village, I was always vaguely aware that Jews in Poland were treated badly and discriminated against. Jews were unfairly and onerously taxed, my father among them. My father, Yitzhak (or, in Yiddish, Getzl) Persky, like his father before him, was a lumber merchant, renting areas of forest and processing the logs into boards and beams for shipment to the city. Later, he branched out into grain, sugar, beer and other commodities, selling in bulk to the army and to shops throughout the district from his warehouses at Bogdunov.

I sensed all the time that this prosperity was ephemeral. It was. Father was virtually forced out of business by blatantly outrageous tax assessments. In any case, he was determined that we would one day leave for Palestine. He decided that he would go first, set up a new timber business in Tel Aviv, find an apartment, and then bring the rest of us over – my mother, my brother Gershon and me. As a 'capitalist' – defined by the British mandatory regulations as someone bringing at least £1,000 into Palestine – neither he nor his dependants required immigrant visas, for which, after Hitler's accession to power in Germany, demand began to exceed supply.

He left in 1932, and for the next two years our contact with him was by letter. He wrote in a bold, confident hand, his letters full of the sweeping optimism that characterized him. Sometimes he enclosed snapshots of himself and his partner, Kabak, both decked out in light summer suits, my father tall and sun-tanned, the other man shorter, but also relaxed and confident-looking.

Eventually, we followed: by train to Istanbul and then aboard a Polish steamship to Jaffa, where our vessel was instantly besieged by a bustling maelstrom of small boats and barges, with longshoremen in red tarbushes and broad pantaloons offering everything from palm branches to green-coloured iced lemonade. But Father was at hand, in a boat of his own, and he smoothly shepherded us through customs and immigration and on to our new home in what was then the centre of Tel Aviv.

Rehov Ha'Avoda, or Work Street – our apartment was at no. 8 – was a turning off King George Street, one of the main thoroughfares of the new Jewish city. The two street names seemed to symbolize our new condition: the main street named in honour of the British colonial ruler, and the side street articulating the Zionist vision of the future Jewish state.

2 NEW WORLD

The transition from Vishneva to Tel Aviv was more than just a move from one place to another; it was a change of worlds. A few days after we arrived, my Auntie Breinke and Uncle Mendl invited us to stay with them for a while at their home in Rehovot. Uncle Mendl, a relaxed, warm-hearted man, was a carpenter by trade. He took a keen interest in politics and read voraciously in Hebrew, Yiddish and Russian. His wife, my mother's sister, was a typical Jewish mother: always welcoming, always anxious. Their house, a pretty little bungalow, stood on a low hill surrounded by citrus groves. When the trees blossomed, it was like living in a perfume factory.

Rehovot itself was a large village rather than a town. We children were free to roam at will through its streets, most of which were still unpaved, and to play in the orchards, green and fertile, which symbolized for us the new Israel.

At Auntie Breinke's, we first tasted the fresh vegetable salads and curdled milk which were national dishes in Palestine but new for us, and the luscious fruits we had read and dreamed about in Poland.

We felt that we had not merely come to a new place, but had become new and different people. Grandfather Zvi's stern authority had suddenly vanished from my life. Synagogue on Saturday mornings was no longer part of my weekly schedule, as dialogue with the distant Deity was now replaced by the intimate touch of the warm sand and sea. And I was no longer buttoned up in jacket and tie, with long sleeves and long trousers. In my loose, short-sleeved shirt and khaki shorts, everything felt airy, sunny and free.

'The *goyim*' (Gentiles), moreover, were no longer the subject of hushed

17

and anxious conversation; their place was now taken by 'the Arabs', who, though our enemies, were not our rulers.

There was an atmosphere of urgent anticipation, which everyone felt and shared in. Soon we would have our own port, our own factories. Our farming settlements were growing all the time. We would even have our own military force. Everything seemed to be moving forwards, breaking new ground, reaching new heights, striving and achieving.

Everything and everybody seemed wonderfully right and brave to me. Everyone was sun-tanned, and sun-tanned people, I assumed, were happy people. And they were right to be happy, I reasoned: they were making the formerly arid soil bloom and recreating with their own labour the land of Jewish destiny.

After a few weeks of 'acclimatization' in Rehovot, we returned to Tel Aviv, or 'Little Paris' as its residents grandly designated it. I remember thinking to myself that Tel Aviv was probably finer, in some respects at least, than Paris itself. Paris, after all, was old, like a wrinkled old woman, while Tel Aviv (Hebrew for Hill of Spring), founded just twenty-five years before, was the lovely, spring-like maiden of the Jewish renaissance. The buildings gleamed white and new against the sea, and the sky never seemed cloudy. (There were none of the man-made smoke clouds of today, at any rate, to obscure my childhood horizons.)

We grew up together with the city. Life in Tel Aviv had something new to offer every day: a building going up, a book just out, a new play at the national theatre, the Habimah, or the Ohel or the Matateh. We youngsters knew all of their repertoires, and their stars – Hanna Rovina, Aharon Maskin, Yehoshua Bertonov and Meir Margalit – were our boyhood heroes.

But our horizons were not limited to Tel Aviv. We were all deeply proud of the kibbutzim, which were, as we knew, the very embodiment of the just life, where true equality and freedom were to be found. The moshavim were also producing a new breed of Hebrew yeoman, who was proving to be a skilled and successful farmer. The moshavniks worked their land themselves and build up village communities based on mutual aid. Even beyond the kibbutzim and moshavim, an egalitarian ethos prevailed in much of the economy. In the Histadrut trades-union movement, for instance, there were no pay grades at that time. Everyone, from the Secretary-General to the tea-lady, was on the same grade. The size of the their pay-packet was determined by the size of their families.

Everything in Jewish Palestine, in the appreciative eyes of the young

Zionist immigrant, was fair, promising and progressive. Modern factories made heavenly fruit juices, and others manufactured false teeth, which were even exported to foreign countries. In Jerusalem, as I knew, the Hebrew University was attracting the finest minds from around the world. And in our own Tel Aviv, a full-scale symphony orchestra was formed by Bronislaw Huberman and soon reached a high enough standard to be conducted by the great maestro, Toscanini.

Of course there were dangers. We were aware of them, too. Among Arabs whom we saw coming in from nearby Jaffa, and those from Zarnuga, close to Rehovot, were people who wanted to destroy this wonderful homeland we were building. They walked around with *keffiyehs* wound round their faces, accentuating their piercing, threatening eyes. Some wore red tarbushes and baggy pantaloons that could easily conceal a *shabriya*, a vicious curved blade made for murder. It was impossible to compromise with them, as everyone knew. There was no point in even trying. There was no choice for us Jews. We would have to keep up our guard, and defend ourselves when need be, until the Arabs accepted our stake in the Land.

Another perceived source of danger, albeit more vague and distant, was the British Mandate. We were constantly reminded of British rule in our everyday lives. It was imprinted on our currency, which proclaimed us to be 'Palestine (EI)'; in other words, neither the one nor the other, neither Palestine nor *Eretz Ysrael*, but rather a hybrid device conceived for the convenience of some far-off bureaucrat in a foreign land. The banknote carried the portrait of His Majesty King George V, after whom the nearest main thoroughfare to our home was named.

Sometimes we would see a British officer from close to, his uniform crisply starched, a small swagger stick stuck firmly under his arm, and polished leather belts girding his waist and crossing his chest. The bearing and demeanour of these grand personages were the palpable evidence, even to our young eyes, of where the source of power truly resided.

We Palestinian Jews suspected the British of perfidious double-talk. Ostensibly, they were committed to our 'National Home in Palestine',★ but in practice they sided with the Arabs. And little wonder. For, as we all knew, the Arabs – and especially the Bedouin – were famous for their

---

★ The key phrase used in the Balfour Declaration, which was issued by the British Government in 1917.

hospitality and winning ways. They had been wooing and winning the hearts of British imperial officialdom for decades; centuries, even. Against such wiles we had no chance.

My parents bought me a bicycle, on which I would assiduously patrol the streets of the city. Each ride, I would count the number of buildings on each street, to make sure that none had disappeared and to keep track of what was being built and where. I would inspect the towering sycamores on the corner of King George Street to make sure that they were properly watered. On the beach, I would bare my pale skin to the sun, anxious to take on the tanned look of the local youngsters.

At the Balfour High School, where my father registered me, there was basketball, and after school we would go round to the local Maccabi sports club to watch older youths playing tennis. We were gravely conscious that sport was an element of the national struggle to revolutionize Jewish society and eventually attain Jewish independence. It was important, therefore, not to lose – whatever sport one was playing, and whomever one was playing against.

In the evenings, we would wander round the local branches of the various youth movements. Some of them were fairly similar to what we had known back in the old country. The Scouts (in Hebrew, Tsofim), for instance, wore similar uniforms and preached the same sort of ideology. The uniforms were supposed to express the movement's belief in order and discipline, while the ideology required members to be prepared, at all times, to help anyone in need. But there was no requirement to analyse the reasons for that need, or commitment to build a new and more just social system.

That, at any rate, was my theoretical critique of the Scouts. On a more practical plane, I would peek through the windows of their clubhouse with all the bashfulness of a gauche and introverted young teenager, as the boys and girls within, perhaps insufficiently ideological but certainly having a good time, would twirl and whirl in intricate polkas. I would watch with rapt but disguised attention as each boy boldly placed one hand on a girl's waist, grabbed her free hand, and flung them both into the tempo without, I marvelled, tripping over his feet or kicking hers.

Some of the youth movements were original and indigenous to Palestine, such as Hanoar Haoved (Working Youth), a socialist group to which I felt strongly attracted. On the other side of the political divide was Betar, the youth movement of the right-wing Revisionist Zionists. There, the kids wore brown shirts and peaked caps, which we, for our part, already knew that we hated. Betar seemed to us in those years a riddle, dark and dangerous. Its members appeared bewitched by a totally alien value-system.

Hanoar Haoved seemed to me the most authentically Palestinian of the movements, and the most attractive ideologically. It represented that most worthy and yet weakest element in society: working youth. Its club-houses were tumble-down shacks. Its uniform was both original and deliberately egalitarian: a blue shirt tied at the neck with a red cord, and khaki shorts. Its membership, too, was eclectic and egalitarian, from exotic Yemenite immigrants to brawny moshav kids. Everyone was imbued with the sense that together we were building a new homeland and a new workers' society. Hanoar Haoved had already set up an impressive number of kibbutzim around the country and had produced several prominent writers and poets, as well as key officers in the unofficial Haganah defence force (the pre-state underground army).

We would do all the things that youngsters in youth movements do: camp out, play pranks (I vividly remember the delightful sensation of smearing one's friends' sleeping faces with thick, black shoe-polish), and sing around bonfires. But right from the start, we were consciously preparing for the day when we would be admitted to the ranks of the Haganah, and then, later, when we would 'embark on our self-fulfilment' – in other words, join an existing kibbutz or help found a new one. To these ends, we were taught night-navigation (by means of the stars) and hand-to-hand combat. We held endless ideological discussions on class warfare, the trades-union movement and the basic structures of kibbutz life. The kibbutz, the solution to the evils of urban, industrialized society, was always the ultimate goal.

My first three years in *Eretz Yisrael* were spent in Tel Aviv. I was an independent child, experiencing life very intensely, but at the same time very privately. Looking back on those years now, I see myself living in three concentric spheres. The first of them, already fully fashioned by my early childhood influences, was that of my own mind and imagination – a world of books and poems. I had, by then, already developed an abiding passion for the Hebrew language, and I indulged this passion with eclectic vigour. The second sphere was school life, or at any rate those aspects of it which captured my enthusiasm. I was made editor of the class newspaper, and conducted in its pages endless debates with other pupils who also fancied themselves as men of letters. I excelled at history and literature, and was apathetic towards mathematics and chemistry, with the attendant consequences.

I changed schools three times in three years. After one year at the Balfour High School (or Gymnasium, as it was called), my parents' deteriorating economic circumstances forced them to transfer my brother and me to the Balfour Elementary School, which was less expensive but not necessarily inferior academically. When I graduated, I won a bursary to the High School for Commerce (this was called the Geula Gymnasium), an exclusive institution for the sons and daughters of the well-to-do. Most of the pupils were strongly rightist in their political affiliations and belonged to Betar or the Scouts. I was the only member of Hanoar Haoved. Thus, in every ideological debate at school, I found myself in splendid isolation, hotly defending positions which left most of the pupils stone-cold.

The teaching staff included a number of noted writers: Asher Barash, Natan Greenblatt, whose stories I remembered reading while still in Vishneva, and Noah Stern, who had come to Palestine from the United States and tried to teach us English. Barash came across as stern, with his thick moustache, but he could be warm and humorous. I remember once persuading him to buy a copy of the class newspaper. 'Did you read it, Sir?' I asked him eagerly the next day. 'What,' he replied, 'you expect me to pay for it and to read it, too?'

Stern wrote Hebrew poetry which we could not understand. He was a tall, gaunt-looking bachelor, a lonely and strange soul. One day, we were told that he had committed suicide. It was only years later that I discovered the depth and power of his verse, and to the present day I regret that we mocked his poetry, and thereby probably deepened his misery.

The third sphere in which my life increasingly revolved was that of the youth movement. In school, we studied; in the movement, we dreamed. I dreamed of my future as a brawny, sunburned kibbutz-farmer, ploughing the fields of the fertile Jezreel Valley by day, singing lustily in the common dining-room at supper-time, guarding the perimeter fearlessly by night, on a fleet-footed horse. The kibbutz would break new ground, literally; it would make the parched earth bloom and beat back the attacks of Arab marauders who sought to destroy our pioneering lives. This was not just my personal dream; it was shared by most of the youngsters in our movement. Nor was it unrealistic: it reflected the movement's ideology and its practical experience over the previous few years. It reflected, too, the real needs of the Jewish *Yishuv*★ in Palestine at that period. We were as much the pragmatic products of our time as the disciples of our particular ideological doctrines.

But doctrine was always important. I remember our earnest celebration of the First of May, the workers' holiday, when the socialist youth movements joined in the adult processions along the city streets. One year, when I was fourteen, we went to hear the author, Sholem Asch, and the socialist leader, Berl Katznelson, address thousands of Tel Aviv workers at the exhibition grounds to the north of the city. The crowd listened in reverent silence as the silver-haired writer delivered his speech in ringing Yiddish. The fate of the Jewish People, he asserted, was in the hands of its working classes. No other element must be allowed to wrest this power and responsibility from the workers. At that time, Asch was considered one of the great intellectuals of the Jewish national revival. His waxen face, adorned with a bushy white moustache, left a lasting impression on me.

Katznelson was much shorter than Asch, his handsome head covered with a shock of black curls. His eyes seemed on fire. He spoke in a pure and stylish Hebrew, and called for unity within the Zionist-socialist movement. He condemned the fighting and factionalism that were plaguing the movement, and insisted that if we socialists could only stand together there would be no limit to what we could achieve. I can hardly exaggerate the effect that these two leaders had on me. I was certain that I had discovered the keys to solving all the problems of our nation. I had been fortunate to be at the right place at the right time – and had absorbed profound and momentous ideas.

My *madrich* (group-leader) in the movement was Elchanan Yishai, who had graduated from the Ben-Shemen youth village and joined a group that founded Kibbutz Alumot in the Lower Galilee. With his steel-blue eyes, expressive face and rippling muscles, he was idolized by all of us. He was a riveting storyteller and an unquenchable optimist, with boundless concern for the lives and problems of each young member of our group.

Another dominating influence on our lives at that time was David

★ Lit. settlement; this was the name by which the pre-state Jewish community in Palestine was known.

Cohen, the founding-father of Hanoar Haoved, a tall, charismatic figure who could hold a young audience spellbound by telling poignant Hassidic tales in a warm, hoarse whisper. Every tale, of course, had a proletarian moral to it. Rabbi Nachman of Breslav and Karl Marx somehow co-existed in didactic harmony within Cohen's order of things. For a youngster growing up in the new Israel, Cohen's collection of tales and morals provided a meaningful link between my own world and the Diaspora world that was steadily fading from my consciousness.

David Cohen's son, Mulla, was a member of my group in the youth movement, and we became firm friends. I began to spend long hours at the Cohens' home, a modest but charming house close to the sea-front in north Tel Aviv, and lined from floor to ceiling with books. It was there that I received my first in-depth induction into the history and philosophy of the Zionist-labour movement.

At the end of ninth grade, Elchanan Yishai approached me with the proposal that I quit my school in Tel Aviv and enrol in the Ben-Shemen agricultural boarding-school instead. Elchanan's brother, Akiva, ran the youth programme at Ben-Shemen, channelling a steady stream of idealistic young graduates – myself among them – to Kibbutz Alumot. At that stage, the youth village was taking in immigrant youngsters, mainly refugees from Hitler's Germany. The idea was that two local lads from the movement live and study with the newcomers, and help them adjust to life in Israel. Elchanan suggested that Mulla and I were suitable candidates. I agreed at once, informed my parents, and prepared to leave the 'big city'.

Ben-Shemen was only a few miles away. The bus route passed through the all-Arab town of Lydda, and the vehicle's windows were covered with netting to protect the passengers from flying stones. I bought my ticket and embarked on what was to be one of the happiest periods of my life.

3 YOUTH VILLAGE

The move from Tel Aviv to Ben-Shemen signalled a return to country life. Ben-Shemen was surrounded both by verdant fields and virulent hostility. The lush greenery was the fruit of the painstaking labour of pupils and teachers. The hatred seemed to grow by itself, bearing down on us from the neighbouring Arab villages and from the bands of armed marauders who would frequently shoot at the school buildings at night. I was only fifteen when I arrived there, but I was a mature youngster, not dependent emotionally on my family.

The founder and headmaster of Ben-Shemen, Dr Siegfried Lehmann, was another magnetic individual who exercised a powerful influence over our young lives. He was very different from the pioneering Yishai brothers. A 'Yekke' (the half-affectionate, half-disdainful sobriquet given to the pedantic, intellectual refugee immigrants from Germany), Lehmann had brought over an entire orphanage from Lithuania, which formed the first nucleus of Ben-Shemen. Educated at German universities, he saw himself as a professional pedagogue embarking on a novel educational experiment, and he applied himself to his task with tireless vigour.

He was never quite comfortable with our rough-and-ready Hebrew, but he succeeded in instilling into us a solid appreciation of music, art and literature. Every Friday afternoon, the entire student body would be assembled on the grass to hear the village youth orchestra – mainly flutes and mandolins – perform *Eine Kleine Nachtmusik* under the baton of our music teacher, Hanan. Lehmann loved Chinese and Japanese painting, and whenever we visited his home he would instruct us in the subtleties of this delicate art form. He was a refined and cultured humanist, and insisted that his pupils take in the best of European literature, as well, of course, as the modern Hebrew classics.

Despite the atmosphere of Arab hostility which pervaded every corner of the village and every facet of our lives, Lehmann was a committed political dove who believed that Zionism should and must offer far-reaching concessions to the Arabs in order to achieve an understanding with them. He was active in Brit Shalom (the Covenant of Peace), a group of ultra-moderates led by such prominent academics as Martin Buber and Judah Magnes, and supported by Professor Albert Einstein.

Einstein once visited Ben-Shemen and presented the youth village with a metal model of the solar system, which became our most prized possession, proudly displayed for years thereafter. Buber was a fairly frequent visitor, undeterred apparently by an impudent harangue to which he was once subjected by none other than myself – and about which I remain mortified to the present day. I had written an article in the student newspaper contending that the teachers were not imparting the 'true Bible', but rather a Bible which they concocted to suit their pet theories and explanations. Lehmann was furious and asked Buber to put the young upstart in his rightful place. I was all of sixteen at the time, and I am ashamed to record that I invoked all the *chutzpah* of that intemperate age in remonstrating with the eminent savant.

Despite this rude outburst, our education at Ben-Shemen schooled us in social norms and relationships in a wonderfully natural way. We lived three boys to a wooden cabin, and my particular cabin earned, for some reason, the nickname 'the Arab doghouse'. We were given a broad measure of independence, both as individuals and as groups of youngsters, and the experience stood us in good stead for the rest of our lives.

Our devotion to the bucolic life was almost fanatical. We would be up before dawn to milk the cows, spent long hours sharpening scythes before the wheat harvest, and meticulously watered each plant in the cucumber patch. On Saturdays, we went on hikes through the surrounding countryside, in the foothills of the Jerusalem range. The same Arabs who took pot-shots at us by night would welcome us during these outings, in the best tradition of Semitic hospitality. Perhaps Dr Lehmann's reputation as a peace activist, which was well known throughout the area, secured at least the daytime truce.

At night, however, there could be no such carefree relaxation, and the older pupils took an active part in guarding the village. Soon after I arrived at Ben-Shemen, I swore my oath of allegiance to the Haganah, by the light of a candle, with a Bible and a revolver on the table before me. Soon after that, I started weapons training, and within a short time I had been appointed commander of one of the guard-posts.

This was not, in fact, an especially high-ranking assignment, but for me it was fateful. My guard-post was just beyond the home of Gelman, the carpentry teacher, from which emerged a barefoot young girl with long, brown plaits and a face of Grecian grace. I was instantly totally smitten. Her name was Sonia, and she was eventually to become my wife. I sought to impress her by reading to her, sometimes by the light of the moon, selected passages from Marx's *Das Kapital*.

I read widely and eclectically, in both prose and verse, and even had the audacity to organize a literary circle, in which I would expound on authors and poets who especially impressed me, from Zalman Schneur to Heinrich Heine. A group of boys and girls in the village who intended to build a kibbutz together elected me as their secretary – this was, I suppose, the formal start of my political career.

America, that vast and distant land, was often the subject of our breathless admiration as children, but as pioneering, idealistic youngsters, it was the Soviet Union that held a special fascination for us – both as the country of origin of most of the Jews then in Palestine, and as the homeland of communism, the ideology that promised to heal all the ills of the world. Culturally and politically, the Russian influence on the evolving ethos of Jewish Palestine was profound. Many of the rousing Hebrew songs we sang around our bonfires were, in fact, Russian melodies. The leading actors of the Habimah theatre, and the leading politicians in our national executive, almost all pronounced their Hebrew with a heavy Russian accent. Our favourite books were mainly the Russian classics, translated into Hebrew: Tolstoy and Dostoevsky, Gogol, Pushkin and Chekhov. Even the Russian penchant for heroic speech-making and interminable arguments was faithfully emulated in our fledgling institutions, until they became part of our national character.

Communism, too, had a deep and lasting impact on our public life and private beliefs. The Communist Party as such was always small, mainly because it was a mixed Jewish–Arab party. The notion that a single party could embrace people from both communities captured relatively few adherents from either side – especially during the war years, when relations between Jews and Arabs in Palestine were at a hate-filled low. But the communist ideology permeated two of the major Zionist parties – Mapam and Ahdut Haavoda.

Mapam, which created some of the most successful kibbutzim in the country, was, in its heyday, a rigidly doctrinaire Marxist party. It preached 'ideological collectivism' and believed in 'the dictatorship of the proletariat'. It used classic Marxist dialectics to interpret world events.

Its leaders were Meir Yaari and Yaacov Hazan. Yaari, whose father was a Hassidic *rebbe* (rabbi and sect leader), was anything but a dictator, proletarian or other. Rather, he looked and behaved like a religious man, an ascetic of slight build surrounded by his idolizing disciples. A brilliant intellectual, he trained himself through self-discipline and austerity, and imbued his movement with the same puritanical values. Its members neither drank nor smoked. They tried to live by the highest ideals of the pioneering life.

Hazan had the outward attributes that Yaari lacked: a handsome face, a commanding physical presence and a thunderous voice. Intellectually, though, he was by no means Yaari's equal. They worked together for decades, usually in co-operation and public harmony, but sometimes in private conflict and jealousy.

Mapam thus offered an imported and adapted sort of Marxism, a Marxism that was suffused, in spite of itself, with Hassidism. When these Marxist *rebbes* sought to stress their complete alienation from their religious heritage, they would use the forms of that heritage itself to make their point. 'Hear, my son, the instruction of thy father,' it is written in Proverbs, 'and do not forsake the teaching of thy mother.' Yaari's rallying cry was, 'Do not hear the instruction of thy father, and do forsake the teaching of thy mother.'

Ahdut Haavoda, the rival Marxist party, also had a *rebbe*-like leader in the figure of Yitzhak Tabenkin. He, too, was respected to the point of veneration by his movement, which, like Mapam, established flourishing kibbutzim throughout the country, in the finest spirit of pioneering Zionism. Like Mapam, Ahdut Haavoda sought a synthesis between Zionism and communism. But unlike Mapam, Tabenkin's movement did not preach 'the brotherhood of nations' – a shorthand for Jewish–Arab brotherhood. Rather, Ahdut Haavoda advocated a strong Jewish defence force, capable of defeating the Arabs once the British had left. Tabenkin was a firm and passionate believer in Greater Israel. He bitterly opposed the concept of partition, which appeared in the various political proposals before and during the war. The movement's kibbutz sector, Hakibbutz Hameuhad, created the Palmach, the elite units of the Haganah, which, in effect, were semi-independent of the Haganah high command and retained a close nexus with the Hakibbutz Hameuhad leadership.

Despite his 'hawkishness', Tabenkin was strongly Marxist in his political outlook and believed in the Soviet Union as the force of the future. His was a strange blend of intense Jewish nationalism and airy Marxist idealism.

Some of the Mapam and Ahdut Haavoda kibbutzim had pictures of Stalin, the 'Sun of the Nations' as they called him, hanging in a place of honour in their dining-rooms. Imagine, then, their cataclysmic sense of being let down when news of the Ribbentrop–Molotov pact came through in 1939. In fact, all the parties of the left, including Mapai (despite its strongly anti-Marxist identity), felt betrayed by that act of defilement. It was only after Germany violated the pact and invaded Russia that we of the left could raise our heads again.

Politics and political strife were very much a part of our day-to-day life in Ben-Shemen. One day in 1939, we awoke to find the entire village surrounded by British soldiers, with plain-clothes CID men looking down at us from perches in the trees around the central courtyard. The rumour soon went round that they were looking for illegal Haganah weapons. We pupils were quickly instructed to assemble in a building called 'the store', where we were to pretend to be deeply engrossed in our studies. In fact, our role was to conceal an arms 'slick' hidden beneath the floor of the building. The tactic worked: the soldiers did not interrupt our 'lesson' to search the place, and the arms there were not found.

But that was the only 'slick' that remained undiscovered. The British unearthed substantial stores of rifles, machine-guns and hand-grenades, and carted the whole lot off with them, along with Dr Lehmann and two or three of the senior staff.

We were both shocked and proud. On the one hand, the 'siege' and search had left us somewhat traumatized, but on the other, we were pleased that so much weaponry should have been hidden in our little village, and that our Dr Lehmann wasn't quite so naïve a peacenik as we had thought. Clearly, he took his responsibility for the security of the village very seriously indeed.

The Arab Rebellion (1936–9) was also very much a part of our lives. We would work and study by day, and at night we would guard. The pupils were deployed in concrete pill-boxes on the village perimeter, where we spent the hours of darkness clutching British-made rifles and firing back into the night whenever we were fired on. I remember watching, fascinated, as tracer-bullets cut through the sky, like fireflies lost in the night.

I remember, too, the heavy sadness that descended over the village when our first victim fell to the Arab attackers. He was Haim, the watchman in the 'Herzl Forest' near the village. We used to go there during the daytime to pick mushrooms and at night to train with live ammunition. He was ambushed in the forest by an Arab gang and shot dead.

My ideological baptism of fire took the form of a seminar organized at Ben-Shemen by a rival socialist youth movement, Mahanot Olim. I was invited as the sole representative of Hanoar Haoved, and as such was considered both alien and in some ways inferior to the other participants, who were all rising stars in the youth wing of Mapai.

The central issue addressed in the seminar was what form of socialism the movement in Palestine ought to adopt. Most Zionist-socialist young-sters at that time tended either to favour the extreme left, extolling Marxism and even Leninism, or the extreme right, advocating the Greater Israel dogma, which meant no territorial compromise with the Arabs. To many of my contemporaries at that time, Russia seemed to be the world of the future. Communism appeared, to them, to hold out the protest of a just and egalitarian society no longer riven by national or class barriers. Such change required a revolution, and revolutions were never a picnic. In the view of these friends and ideological rivals of mine, this justified the violence that came in the wake of the socialist revolution.

The older pupils at Ben-Shemen were divided into four groups, according to the youth movements they each belonged to. Group A was attached to Hashomer Hatzair; Group B to Dror Habonim (which was itself affiliated to the Hakibbutz Hameuhad organization); Group C to Gordonia (the youth movement of Hever Hakvutzot, another kibbutz organization); and Group D, of which I was a member, was an open and heterogeneous grouping which included members of Hanoar Haoved and of Mahanot Olim.

This division into groups reflected differences both over what sort of kibbutz the youngsters proposed to live in after they graduated, and over broader questions of political ideology and orientation. Hashomer Hatzair believed in a rigidly ideological type of kibbutz, based on principles of 'ideological collectivism'. They had no room in their ranks for anyone holding different views. The Hakibbutz Hameuhad school advocated larger, more open kibbutzim concerned with the wider community and intent on influencing the community by political action. Hever Hakvutzot argued for small and intimate kibbutzim, in which the individual member's needs and welfare were the values to be nurtured. It spurned any doctrinaire discipline within its kibbutzim.

As for the political differences between the various organizations and youth movements, Hashomer Hatzair was basically Marxist-Leninist, preaching class warfare and the dictatorship of the proletariat. Their political platform in Palestine, in addition to its strange Marxist-Leninist orientation, advocated Arab–Jewish compromise – at a price which seemed too high to the majority of Jews, because it meant agreeing to a bi-national state, in which Jews and Arabs were to share sovereignty over Palestine. The true distance between Meir Yaari, who was the Secretary-General of Hashomer Hatzair and the leader of its mother-movement, Mapam, and Josef Stalin, Secretary-General of the Soviet Communist Party, was as great as that between Gandhi and Genghis Khan. Nevertheless, Yaari's warm and generous heart was captivated by the rhetorical power of Stalinism, which, in his later years, he profoundly regretted. On the personal level, people related to Yaari the man, rather than the ideologue. He was treated with respect, even admiration. But the attitude towards his ideological baggage, at least in the circles in which I later moved, was one of uncompromising and vehement rejection. The Hakibbutz Hameuhad leader, Yitzhak Tabenkin, was a hard and stubborn man but he was also powerfully charismatic. His speeches would last for hours on end, and his frequent flashes of brilliance would hold his disciples enthralled. He, too, believed in Marxism and tended towards the Soviet Union, but his energies were mainly devoted to building up Hakibbutz Hameuhad's kibbutzim (the largest in Israel), and in creating Ahdut Haavoda, the political party that evolved out of the kibbutz organization.

The leader of Gordonia at the time was Pinhas Lavon, a man of striking looks, a gifted speaker and brilliant polemicist. He was totally opposed to Marxism and Leninism, in fact to any doctrinaire social dogma. Thus, Gordonia rejected the First of May, with its red flags and imported observances. The movement was named after A. D. Gordon (1856–1922), an early Zionist settler who looked like a prophet with his long, flowing beard, wrote like a philosopher and worked like a pioneer. He kept working in the fields of Degania (the first kibbutz) right up to his death, developing what he called the 'Theory of Labour', which saw manual work as a sublime value. Gordon felt that every man should live from the fruits of his own toil, and bring out the best in his individual personality by living close to nature and close to other people in a just social structure. He became a figure of legendary inspiration to the younger generation. His ideas were regarded as a new, original and indigenous Israeli *weltanschauung*.

Beyond the particular ideologies of the kibbutz organizations, there was the broad Zionist-socialist ideology of Mapai, led by David Ben-Gurion and Berl Katznelson. At the end of the day, they were the real victors in the various battles for the heart and mind of Zionist-socialism. They were implacably anti-Marxist and anti-Leninist. They opposed every kind of imported value-system, and rejected efforts to translate and adapt alien ideas. Instead, they based their own ideology firmly on the Book of Books, the Bible.

I came to know Katznelson long before Ben-Gurion. I felt drawn to him after attending his series of lectures at the Mahanot Olim's seminar in Ben-Shemen. Of course I had known about him, as about Ben-Gurion, from my earliest boyhood. He was considered the paramount teacher of the socialist movement in Palestine, the 'intellectual power-house of Mapai'.

His formal position was editor of the party's daily paper, *Davar*, and founder and editor-in-chief of the Am Oved publishing house. But Katznelson was much more than that. He was a friend and confidant of all the leading Jewish writers and thinkers of the day. And, at the same time, he was the political mentor of the younger generation of the party. The rising Haganah commanders would turn to him for guidance, as would senior officials of the Histadrut and of the Jewish Agency. He was considered second only to Ben-Gurion. Indeed, in some respects he was thought of as equal to Ben-Gurion, though he never sought any executive position for himself, preferring the role of party pedagogue.

Katznelson, like Ben-Gurion, appeared even shorter in real life than his photographs. His black curls, tinged by then with grey, framed his handsome, sharply chiselled face. His wise and penetrating black eyes seemed to follow one's every movement and to absorb every word one uttered in his presence. By the time I first had contact with him, he was forty-five and already a veritable legend. His articles and lectures invariably aroused intense and passionate interest. Katznelson never had much of a formal education. As with Maxim Gorky (with whom, he once told me, he had written a booklet on Zionism), Katznelson learned at the university of life.

In fact, he never stopped teaching himself. He picked up several languages, and his knowledge of philosophy and literature was wide-ranging, spanning from Russian and Yiddish to English and Hebrew, which was his great love. His curiosity knew no bounds. Every new thing that he came across – a person, a book or a poem – aroused his intense interest.

The seminar at Ben-Shemen took place soon after Katznelson had published two articles that had had a major impact. In the first, which he called 'Even in Laughter, the Heart Hurts' (Proverbs 14:13), he took issue with the Marxist dogmas of Meir Yaari's Hashomer Hatzair – and ground them to pulp. In the second, 'In Praise of Perplexity, and in Denunciation of Denial', he passed severe censure on his own political camp, arguing that it was far better to admit that one did not have all the answers to the problems of the times than to pretend, to oneself and to others, that one did. He preferred honest doubt to disingenuous dogma. Both articles powerfully influenced my own evolving political outlook.

The two main lecturers at the Ben-Shemen seminar were Yoske Rabinowitz of Hakibbutz Hameuhad (a member of Kibbutz Naan) and Katznelson. Rabinowitz, pale and aristocratic looking, was a confirmed Marxist, and a brilliant and persuasive speaker. He tried to convince the audience throughout the seminar that he was younger and more 'with it' than Katznelson. He had recently visited the Rodin Museum in Paris, for instance, and told us how he had been captivated by the sculpture entitled *Eternal Springtime*. Even the way the legs of the young lovers were intertwined, he asserted with passion, expressed the theme of spring. Doubtless some of the Ben-Shemen students were duly impressed by this display of cosmopolitan culture and erudition.

Rabinowitz's political polemics were standard Marxist stuff. Marxism, he argued, was an empirical science which asked the right questions and, through the process of Hegelian dialectics, came up with the right answers. These were based on the proper synthesis, he explained, of the capitalist thesis and the socialist antithesis. He spoke with all the self-confidence of a man who firmly believed that he was the spokesman and advocate of the most promising and potent force in the world. In his opinion, the great Marxist revolution in the Soviet Union was marching inexorably forwards to a bright tomorrow because it was solidly grounded in pure and incontrovertible scientific doctrine. Most of the pupils were with him.

Katznelson spoke for some forty hours in all. For two whole weeks, he lectured every day for three hours. He would bring with him to his lectures a voluminous card-index, from which he produced ringing quotations, little-known historical facts and amusing anecdotes. He talked rather than lectured and encouraged people to chime in with questions, though in practice hardly anyone did. His relaxed but incisive style held us riveted. We followed his every sentence as he chipped away at the Marxist edifice, hour after hour, until he had brought the entire structure tumbling to the ground.

He compared Stalin to a Pharaoh, and the Soviet socialist paradise to the biblical house of bondage. Many of the economic projects being launched in Russia, he said, were similar to the Egyptian pyramids: their primary purpose was to make a huge impression, and the question of whether they would benefit anyone appeared to be irrelevant.

He showed how the communists had betrayed every promise they had ever made: national freedom, religious freedom, intellectual freedom, the abolition of capital punishment, open diplomacy, a classless society – all of these had been pledged, but none was in fact permitted in the USSR. Stalin was a despot who ruled through fear. Lies, murder and impoverishment were the instruments with which the Soviet system maintained itself in power, and the personality cult surrounding Stalin was designed as a massive cover-up to conceal the truth from the people. They had driven out God, said Katznelson, and replaced Him with a new god of flesh and blood, a cruel and murderous tyrant. It was impossible, he argued, to achieve 'freedom through unfreedom', to obtain 'non-violence through violence'.

I was totally and unreservedly convinced by everything he said. I promised myself then and there that I would fight with all my strength against Marxism, communism and the Stalinist dictatorship. It was in the wake of the seminar that my relationship with Katznelson began. This relationship was to leave a profound imprint on the course of my future life.

Katznelson would invite me over to his home in Tel Aviv every Sunday night. Actually, the apartment on Mazeh Street was more like a library than a home: every wall of every room, including his bedroom, was covered from floor to ceiling with books. Katznelson would spend a great deal of the time prostrate on a couch, even during conversations, because he suffered from debilitating headaches. I would stay an hour or two (depending on his headache), with most of our sessions devoted to the subject he considered most important of all: Hebrew literature. Am

Oved was in the process of publishing a series of new titles which Katznelson felt were basic books in the evolution of modern Hebrew literature. One was *On the Narrow Path* by Aharon Avraham Kabbak, a treatment of the life of Jesus, in which Jesus was depicted as a modern-day young man grappling with the same spiritual dilemmas that were troubling us.

Another work which aroused much interest at the time was Haim Hazazz's *Bronze Doors*. Hazazz was considered one of the most gifted talents among the modern Hebrew writers, and everything he produced was read with much enthusiasm. Like Katznelson, he was an iconoclast and an original, never afraid to speak his mind. His style was sharp and provocative, but, at the same time, he could be unexpectedly lyrical. Hazazz had spent a year living in a Yemenite immigrant quarter. *Bronze Doors* led the reader into this unknown world, peopled by men and women who had made their journey across vast expanses of space and time. Hazzaz portrayed their powerful emotions, their foibles and the special charm of their Hebrew dialect. He was able to depict the contrasts between the ancient conservatism of this community and its surprising adaptation to modernity.

A third contemporary work which Katznelson strongly recommended was a book of verse by the poetess Yocheved Bat Miriam. She wrote on the female figures in the Bible, which she treated with originality, and with a richness of taste and colour that were hitherto unknown in modern Hebrew literature. Bat Miriam was a tiny, fragile woman, who always wore black and spoke to everyone in the third person, an archaic mode of respectful address. She seemed herself to have walked out of the pages of the Bible. Katznelson deeply respected her, both as a poet and as a woman of great fineness and delicacy.

He would read passages from these and other books out loud, analyse them, and illustrate various references and associations – and, at our next meeting, he would indirectly examine me to see whether I had fully understood his arguments. I was expected, in the interim, to have read the rest of the book. He would also want to know whether I had been trying to work up interest among my schoolfriends in new books and current literary developments. He was always on the look-out for bright young people and often asked me about those who seemed promising. Did they have good minds? Were they leadership material? I myself was one of the youngsters whom Katznelson was grooming. Decades after his death in 1944, the ideas and values he instilled in me continue to shape my attitudes to the challenges facing our movement.

While still at Ben-Shemen I was elected a delegate to a national convention of Hanoar Haoved. I even plucked up the courage to speak, and to my complete surprise I was elected a member of the Secretariat. I daresay my candidacy was assisted by the impressively low bass voice that I had been blessed with, even at that tender age.

4 KIBBUTZ POLITICS

My Ben-Shemen days soon began drawing to an end, and with them my youth. That, at any rate, is how I remember feeling at the time. I regarded myself as a fully mature young man, experienced and responsible, who henceforth would be giving to society rather than taking from it. I was proficient, for instance, in saddling mules, in reaping with a sickle, in milking cows, in handling a rifle, in expressing myself articulately in speech and in writing, and in organizing and leading groups of young people. What I needed was the right framework in which to use these skills.

After graduating from Ben-Shemen, our *gar'in*, or core-group for a new kibbutz, was sent for training to Kibbutz Geva in the Jezreel Valley. Geva, like Ben-Shemen, had its cowsheds, chicken-runs, cornfields, orchards, tractors and haycarts. But this was no children's paradise; it was an adults' world, stern and puritanical. Smiles were few and far between. Mistakes were seldom glossed over with a wink and a nod. Here each person was under constant collective scrutiny and was required to measure up to rigidly demanding criteria. Woe betide anyone leaving for work in the fields after the sun had risen, and woe betide him if he returned before it had set. That would be to bluff the day and defraud the field. Our labour, as A. D. Gordon had taught us, was the essence of our life. Anyone wielding his scythe without the requisite energy, anyone betraying a careless slip during milking, could be certain of being censured by the entire kibbutz, a small and closely knit unit in which each individual faced the judgment of his peers all day and every day.

The kibbutz general meetings were the forum for all major decisions. They were also the locus of public opinion. The kibbutz leaders were hard, harsh men, idealists who were difficult to please. Yet these same men could also be warm and welcoming. At the end of the working day, one could visit them in their homes or sit with them on the grass and engage them in relaxed and friendly conversation. Some had a lifetime of interesting experiences behind them.

Geva itself was a thriving kibbutz, its orchards laden with fruit, its fields ploughed straight and true. Geva cows were given the finest feed, and they responded by producing the highest and richest milk yields in the country. The kibbutz also paid careful attention to its human resources, developing first-rate educational and sporting facilities for its children, so that Geva youngsters grew up both brawny and book-learned. In the evenings, we would hear them singing, mainly Russian ballads (which was the repertoire that most of their parents had brought with them to Palestine). To this day, Geva's choir, the Gevatron, is considered the finest vocal ensemble in Israel.

Life for us at Geva was disciplined, though we managed to maintain our harmony and cohesion as a group. However, we were considered a case apart since we were not true Geva youth. We had not enjoyed that special Geva education, nor were we imbued with those special Geva qualities. We were regarded by the members of Geva as somehow inferior, people on whom they could rightly look down. Even though we ostensibly held joint evening activities with the Geva youngsters – songs and discussions around a camp fire – there could be no ignoring the invisible but ever-present barrier that divided them from us. As a result, our group grew more tightly knit, each of us driven by an urge to show that we could do our work as well as any of them.

My job at Geva was to work in the cornfields, but Hanoar Haoved was anxious that I work for the movement too, organizing our own group at Geva and helping similar groups of youngsters at kibbutzim in the Jezreel and Jordan Valleys. To this end, I was provided with a large and brutish Triumph motor-cycle, with which I wrestled manfully on the roads of the area, often ending up in a ditch – the victim of a passing truck-driver's idea of a practical joke. My memory of those roadside ditches is as vivid, all these years later, as the exhilarating sensation of tearing along the roads on my black mechanical beast.

My work for the movement began once my working day on the kibbutz was over: no one on Geva would dream of reducing one's agricultural workload. In the evenings, then, I would ride from group to group of Hanoar Haoved, holding meetings, organizing seminars, and arguing with everyone and anyone who did not accept my view of how the movement ought to develop. I soon made many friends, and many rivals too. Sometimes, we would arrange public debates with kibbutz youth belonging to other youth movements. These proved a fine training ground for developing our polemical and rhetorical skills, and to be quite frank, I rarely ended these evenings as the loser.

I had plunged into this new world of mine with such total enthusiasm that the old world, the world of my grandparents, virtually faded from my consciousness. The Arab riots of 1936–9 in Palestine, and then the outbreak of the Second World War, seemed to sever my mind from the old country. I stopped thinking about Vishneva.

The war dried up the flow of mail between the family in Palestine and those still in Europe. My parents recalled that in the First World War the family had also been separated, with some relatives cut off and not heard from for years. After the war, all were reunited. My parents – and presumably others of their generation – were therefore not totally disheartened by the curtain of fire and darkness that descended over the old world. They lived in the hope that, after it was all over, they would see their loved ones again.

For me, a thoughtful teenager who believed that he understood the world around him, the war seemed both mad and maddening. The mad part was Nazism with its racial theories. How could an entire nation be led astray by such obscene and lunatic doctrines? I knew about Nietzsche's teachings and about Wagner's sympathies, but I also knew that Germany was a nation of scholars, philosophers, artists and poets. How could all of these have been swept away? I felt humiliated by Nazism as a human being, not just as a Jew.

The maddening thoughts during the early years of the war centred on Germany's military successes. I followed, awe-struck, as the German armoured columns trampled across Europe. How could Poland have fallen like a house of cards? How was France cracked and shattered like an empty shell, despite its size, its cultural tradition and its famous army? The German advance seemed unstoppable. It was not only sweeping all before it on the battlefields, but seemed to be exposing something soft and effete in the spirit of the democratic countries. The whole world seemed doomed to fall under the thrall of Nazism, which with Italian fascism and Japanese militarism, had formed an all-powerful coalition. It seemed only a matter of time before the momentum of the German conquests reached the Middle East. The Germans took Greece and

landed in North Africa. Pro-German sentiment swept the Arab countries, which, as I knew, were usually quick to back the winning side.

I remember to this day the feeling of hope, relieving my bleak
trepidations, upon hearing from Yitzhak Tabenkin, the Hakibbutz
Hameuhad leader, that 'Hitler will be destroyed.' The tyrant would fall,
Tabenkin declared, 'because, ultimately, he offers no message of hope to
Europe as a whole, but only to Germany. And even in Germany, his
promises are made not to the whole German people, but only to the
Nazis. And even among the Nazis, only those close to the leadership
can look forward to a share of the spoils. But even they will come to see
that Hitler ultimately serves just one man – himself. All the bloodshed
is designed to gratify the whims of one man . . .'

Our feelings towards the British Mandate were naturally ambivalent.
On the one hand, we regarded it as a foreign power, occupying our land
and manifestly pro-Arab in the way it administered it. We accused the
British of deliberately ignoring Arab attacks on Jewish settlements. These
occurred almost daily, carried out by armed gangs controlled by the
Mufti of Jerusalem, Haj Amin el-Husseini, who was openly siding with
the Nazis. On the other hand, we were full of admiration for the way in
which the British people were standing up to Hitler, alone and exposed
on their beleaguered island. Winston Churchill was the great hero of
our lives. London, bombed but defiant, was the symbol we looked to in
our own determination to fight the Germans.

This determination took two forms among young Jewish Palestinians.
Some sought to enlist in the British army, to fight the Nazis wherever
they were sent. My father was among these; however, he soon fell
prisoner in Greece and we lost contact with him. Others chose to stay
in Palestine, training in the underground, fighting the Arab gangs – and
preparing to fight the Germans if they invaded. The leadership supported
both of these alternatives. Ben-Gurion expressed this position in his
famous statement: 'We shall help the British army as though there were
no White Paper* and we shall fight the British White Paper as though
there were no war.'

As my mother's three sisters had all immigrated to Palestine and built
their homes there, only my grandparents and my uncle Michael were left
in Vishneva – which had reverted to Byelorussia under the Ribbentrop–

* The British Government issued a White Paper in May 1939 severely limiting Jewish
immigration to Palestine and Jewish land purchase in Palestine.

Molotov pact. Michael, their sole remaining son after Yosef's death, had stayed behind in order to care for them.

Vishneva suffered the fate of countless other Jewish communities. The Germans, aided by local collaborators, herded all the Jews into the wooden synagogue, my grandfather at their head. They put on their prayer-shawls as the Germans barred the doors and set the place alight, and they died the age-old death of Jewish martyrs. We heard this account only after the war, from the handful of Vishneva Jews who had managed to flee to the forests and were taken in by the partisans. I imagined my grandfather offering his last prayer to God, in that sweet voice of his which still sings hauntingly in my memory.

In 1992, as Foreign Minister, I paid an official visit to Belarus, as it is now called. I asked the Government in Minsk to arrange for me to visit my own birthplace, Vishneva, and that of my father, Volozhin. They agreed willingly, and Foreign Minister Piotr Kravchenko, a professor of history and a particularly pleasant man, insisted on accompanying me personally on my journey into the past.

He turned out to be remarkably well read in Jewish history and culture. He told me that he was inclined to accept the theory that much of Russia was ruled for a short period by the Kuzars – the Central Asian tribe that is said to have adopted Judaism in the eighth century.★ He said that Belarus was proud of its great Jewish sons and listed among them the painter Marc Chagall, and the Jewish writers Sholom Aleichem and Chaim Nachman Bialik. Local scholars, he said, were currently trans-lating Bialik's works in the Belarussian language, which was undergoing a revival following the country's achievement of full independence as one of the Commonwealth of Independent States. They had also published a charming little book of poems by Chagall, translated into Belarussian and illustrated with his paintings.

Kravchenko proposed that we visit the greatest living Belarussian sculptor, Az-Gor, in his atelier. I politely agreed. Az-Gor, in a classical artist's cap and smock, welcomed us at his gate. 'I am a communist in mind and a Jew at heart,' he declared, and ushered me into a vast hall full of statues of the Soviet leaders, past and present. Lenin and Stalin towered up to the ceiling. Nearby stood a huge Beria. Even Gorbachev

★ The *Kuzari*, a major theological treatise written by the Spanish scholar and poet Rabbi Yehuda Halevi (1075–1145), purports to be dialogue between the Kuzar king and a Jewish sage.

was larger than life. Hidden among these stone giants I spied two busts sculpted in a less heroic style. One was Kant, the artist explained proudly, and the other Rabbi Yehuda Halevi. 'My heart is in the East, and I am in the farthermost West,' he recited the great medieval Jewish poet's famous lines in passable Hebrew. It all seemed so strange and ana-chronistic – a fitting prelude, I mused, to my visit to Vishneva, where we now set out for in our shining black motorcade.

All the way – the village is about a hundred kilometres from Minsk – I compared the actual scenery to what was embedded in my memory. Everything seemed bigger in real life. The trees looked leafier, the river wider. The sky was greyer than I remembered. In Vishneva, the whole village turned out to welcome us, some of the young girls wearing the national costume. We were greeted with bread and salt. The girls sang local folk-songs in my honour. The tunes were catchy and cheerful, but to me they sounded distant, other-worldly.

There are no Jews left in Vishneva today. By the town hall, a pile of stones stands on the site of the collective grave where the remains of the synagogue victims were buried. Among those remains, under those stones, are my grandparents. The stones seemed silent and uncaring, but in my heart I felt I heard their cry.

The old wooden houses are almost all gone. New ones have been built of bricks and concrete. The streets are also different. I walked slowly along what I thought had been the street on which our house had stood. Suddenly, I saw it. It had been rebuilt and is now overgrown with ivy, but I recognized it by the well that still stands outside. The fires of war had consumed everything, but not the well. We let down the bucket and brought it up, full of clear water. I put it to my lips – and it tasted the same. I was overwhelmed. Standing beside the house where I was born, I recited *Kaddish* (the prayer for the dead). Deep inside me, I wept.

From Vishneva we continued to Volozhin. There, too, the local people came out to welcome us, among them a few elderly Jews who had survived the war years. They said that they remembered my father and my grandfather, but their accounts were so woolly and confused that I tended to doubt them.

We visited the building that was the home of the Volozhiner Yeshiva;* today, it is a bakery. On the back wall, we found a bas-relief of the Ten Commandments with the legend, 'Volozhiner Yeshiva, founded 1803'.

* See page 11.

From the Yeshiva, we went to the cemetery. The gravestones there were scattered haphazardly. Most have fallen on to their sides; a few still stand, bent over as though pushed. On eight of them I found my name, Persky.

One of the local Jews said that he knew the house that had belonged to my mother's family, the Meltzers. We walked up an unpaved street and eventually reached it. It was painted green. We walked into the yard; there were a few fruit trees, a cucumber patch and a couple of chickens scratching about. A peasant woman approached, her face wrinkled and scorched by the sun. 'My husband is sick,' she said. 'The price of vegetables has sunk to rock-bottom. We've got nothing. Please, *Nachilnik* [manager], help us a little.' I was touched by the bitter irony of the situation. She apparently thought that I was some government official or foreign dignitary, but in my own eyes I was a local boy who had come back to visit his family's graves. Nothing was left of the family home or of any of Volozhin's illustrious past. But the present seemed bleak, too, for the people of Volozhin.

I left the dollars that I had with me, on the understanding that they would be used to restore the cemetery. Some time later, I was officially informed by the Government of Belarus that the bakery was going to be moved and that the Yeshiva building was being turned into a museum. I understand that the gravestones have been repaired, too.

When the Second World War broke out, my father had signed up for the sappers and my brother had joined a Palmach training course at Kibbutz Yagur, near Haifa,★ so my mother was on her own in Tel Aviv. As her part in the war effort, she took a job in the munition factories which the British had set up at the exhibition grounds in Tel Aviv.

Around the same time, our training period at Geva ended and our kibbutz movement, Ihud Hakibbutzim, decided to send our group further north, to reinforce Kibbutz Alumot. This was no surprise, since most of the members of Alumot were Ben-Shemen graduates. Politically, they were 'Ben-Gurionites', just as we were.

Alumot was situated at Poriya, a desolate hilltop with a breathtaking view of the Kinneret (Sea of Galilee) below it. Two or three grey basalt buildings stood there, the remnants of an earlier attempt to settle the site. They had long lost their roofs: the howling winter winds carried off virtually everything. There was no electricity, and we passed our evenings

---

★ Both he and his wife were injured in the battle for Jerusalem in 1948.

in the eerie light of paraffin lamps. There was no running water either; supplies had to be trucked up in barrels from the Kinneret.

Nor was there much by way of gainful employment, so most of us had to hire ourselves out as farm labourers in the flourishing kibbutzim of the Jordan Valley. I worked for a long time in the rose gardens of Kibbutz Ashdot Yaacov, where one of my co-workers was the mother of the future army Chief of Staff, Dan Shomron. I would get up at 4 a.m., wrap myself up in the warmest coat I could find, and set off on the ten kilometre tramp down the hill to the valley.

Our compensation for these various hardships was the view. Every morning and every evening, we were stunned anew by the breathtaking sights we could take in from our hilltop. To the north-east lay the Kinneret, deep blue and mysterious, serene yet beckoning, its waters playing with the sun's rays or the shadows of the clouds. To the north was the snow-capped peak of Mount Hermon; and to the west, the fields of Yavniel, a village of weather-beaten farmers, every one a tough and crotchety individualist. Farther south, the River Jordan wound like a silver serpent through the green fields and banana groves of the valley, dotted with red-roofed kibbutzim. Our closest neighbour, Kibbutz Kinneret, stood out in this majestic panorama, its rows of lofty palm trees deployed like a guard of honour at the entrance to the settlement. Also nearby was the village of Kinneret (as distinct from the kibbutz); between us there stretched bleak and barren slopes, punctuated with outcrops of grey and forbidding basalt rock.

Gradually, these slopes surrendered to us and to the other farmers of the district. The rocks were cleared, terraces were sculpted into the hillsides, and eventually even these unpromising tracts began to yield crops of vegetables and wheat. One elderly Kinneret farmer named Yizreeli remains particularly vivid in my memory. He would literally stretch out at full length on the stony soil and drive the seeds or saplings into the stubborn ground. Over the years, I got to know him well (his son, Emmanuel, was a member of our kibbutz and a good friend of mine) and discovered that he was not only a good farmer but also a fine musician. He composed rousing melodies to be sung to biblical verses. A record was eventually made of his best works, and it won warm praise in musical circles. I still remember his haunting theme to the words from Isaiah (63:1): 'Who is that who comes from Edom, his clothes stained ...' One could almost see the battle-weary, sweat-streaked soldiers making their way home.

Eventually, we worked our own fields. As we walked behind the straining tractor, we were able to imbue new and vivid meaning into the verse in Judges (5:18): '... and Naphtali ... in the high places of the field'. These particular fields, situated in the territory of the tribe of Naphtali, certainly qualified for that description.

My own job in our little agricultural collective was that of shepherd-cum-cowherd. I would get up long before dawn, strap on an enormous wooden-handled Mauser, and open the sheep pen for the animals to head downhill to the open pastures in the wadis below. The paths down were dangerously steep, and the wadis themselves were also considered danger-ous because of the occasional attempts by bands of Arab rustlers to ambush Jewish shepherds and make off with their flocks. I never had such an encounter, and, as far as I was concerned, nothing seemed to exist on those long, dark nights save the stars, the sheep and their dreamy-eyed shepherd.

I had a much better time with sheep than with cows. I found sheep to be moderate and good-tempered animals, and their short legs meant that they could not get too far too fast. Our cows, on the other hand, were a breed called Damascene, which are noted for their long legs and short tempers. They also seemed to lack any sense of solidarity what-soever, deliberately not following each other but wandering off at indi-vidual tangents to the perpetual exasperation of the would-be cowherd. The worst time was just before dawn, when swarms of irritating stinging fleas would descend on the herd. The cows raised their tails as though at a prearranged signal – and then galloped off in every direction. Often I spent whole days rounding up stray members of the herd.

Nor was rounding them up necessarily simple. Some of them headed for the fields of Yavniel, knowing that they could find juicy corn or at least rich stubble there. The first cow approaching these fields would set off a general alarm throughout the village, whereupon the farmers all grabbed their cudgels and sallied forth to drive back the beasts – and thrash their owners, if they could catch them.

Not even these altercations could cool my enthusiasm. I loved my job for the freedom it gave me to roam around for hours on end, not answerable to a soul, at liberty to dream.

Our kibbutz was perennially hard up. The soil was saturated with salts, and the crops were consequently meagre and of poor quality. Our outlay on farming quickly surpassed our income. Accordingly, our meals were uniformly modest and economical; usually a main course of chopped or fried aubergines, which were cheap and plentiful. For breakfast, though, we would have hearty salads, made of tomatoes and cucumbers, with great hunks of good black bread, fuel for the rigours of the day ahead.

Our 'wardrobe' was similarly Spartan. Everyone was issued with two pairs of khaki trousers – one for work and one for *Shabbat* – and two shirts. As for shoes, we had just one pair of work boots each. The kibbutz as a whole was the proud owner of one pair of grey flannel trousers, one white shirt and one British army-issue battle-dress jacket, which were kept in the store-room for special occasions. One such occasion, for instance, was my wedding. I wore the shirt and trousers, and of course the battle-dress, which the kibbutz decided to have dyed black, to lend more distinction to my appearance.

While our material conditions were harsh and demanding, our social life at Poriya was wonderfully happy. Each Friday evening, everyone would gather to sing and dance long into the night. On weekday evenings, there would be study circles in literature, history and psychology. Saturday evenings were reserved for our weekly general meeting, at which the assembled membership heard reports on the progress of its various ventures – both agricultural and cultural – and made its collective decisions.

One day, entirely unannounced, Levi Eshkol turned up at Alumot. He was a member of Kibbutz Degania Bet, which was nearby, and was considered Ben-Gurion's right-hand man. The purpose of his visit was to persuade the kibbutz to let me work full-time for Hanoar Haoved. Young people were being drawn to the far left, Eshkol warned the assembled company, and Mapai was losing the younger generation – soon it would not have the groups of youngsters it needed to set up new kibbutzim and reinforce existing ones.

The general meeting pondered the question, and eventually agreed to *Haver* (Comrade) Eshkol's request. I was to be allowed to work five days a week at the Hanoar Haoved head offices in Tel Aviv.

I moved in with my mother, who was living alone in a small apartment in the north of the city. On my salary of five pounds a month, I could afford to buy myself a portion of felafel for lunch each day and a hunk of watermelon.

Hanoar Haoved's Secretariat consisted of eleven members of Siah Bet (Faction B), which was later to break away and form Ahdut Haavoda, and one member of Mapai – me.* The Siah Bet leaders, Yitzhak

* Later, I was joined on the Secretariat by three kindred spirits: Eviatar Berg of Kibbutz Dovrat, Nahman Raz of Kibbutz Geva and Amos Degani from Kfar Vitkin.

Tabenkin and Yisrael Galili, in effect ran the youth movement, much to the impotent frustration of Mapai's leadership. My appearance on the scene was naturally received with suspicion and reservation. I quickly realized that there was nothing I could usefully contribute to Secretariat meetings – any proposal I made was invariably shot down by an 11–1 majority. I decided, therefore, that the best thing I could do would be to work 'in the field' – that is, with the ordinary members around the country.

I travelled all over, setting up new branches and strengthening existing one, enlisting new *madrichim* and encouraging the youngsters to take part in hikes, summer camps and seminars, which I managed to organize on a shoestring budget.

One of these hikes turned into something of a *cause célèbre* at the time. A group of us, half from the Palmach and half from Hanoar Haoved, undertook a three-week fact-finding and map-making trek through the Negev, paid for by Ben-Gurion and by the Palmach commander, Yitzhak Sadeh. Also joining us were the noted zoologist, Dr Mendelsson, the Palmach's senior scout, Haim Ron, and the well-known archaeologist, Shmarya Gutman of Kibbutz Naan.

We had twelve camels, on which we piled our gear, and took turns to ride them. We also had revolvers and hand-grenades concealed under the false bottoms of our water canisters. We headed south towards the former Turkish border point, Umm Rashrash (today's Eilat), but before we got there we began to be followed by a Bedouin camel patrol, commanded by a British officer named Lord Asquith (the son of the former Prime Minister). Since the Negev was a closed military area in which trekking was forbidden without a formal permit from the Mandatory Government – which, of course, we did not have – we naturally aroused their suspicions. In the end, we were arrested, piled into an army truck and taken back to Beersheba – then a wholly Arab town – where we found ourselves incarcerated in the local jail.

It was during this trek that I obtained my Hebrew name. I spied a large bird's nest on a not-too-high tree, and shinned up to see it at closer range – thereby disturbing a large eagle, which took to its wings. 'That's a Peres,' Dr Mendelsson explained, using a modern Hebrew ornithological term borrowed from the Bible (Leviticus 11:13). An immediate consensus evolved that as my 'Diaspora-sounding' name Persky was close to the name of this bird, I ought to adopt it henceforth as my new, Hebraicized name.

In Beersheba, we were arraigned before a magistrate and sentenced to two weeks in prison. I, as leader of the illicit expedition, was additionally sentenced to pay a substantial fine. The escapade made newspaper headlines at the time as a daredevil sort of prank. But it was to prove its value during the War of Independence, when Ben-Gurion asked me for the maps we had drawn up – and asked Sadeh and me to plan a route for the army units sent southwards to take Umm Rashrash.

Another memorable trek – memorable to me, at any rate – took us to the top of Masada by the famous Snake Path. I nearly lost my life during this expedition, when I missed a foothold and slid down the slope. Desperately, I tried to dig into the soft sandy earth with my heels, while my friends watched transfixed from above. Eventually, they organized themselves into a human chain, lowering themselves from the top of the fortress-mountain, each holding on to the feet of the man above, until they reached me. I then clung to the heels of the lowest 'rung' and gingerly we all scrambled back up.

A love of the Land and an intimate familiarity with it were considered to be important values which the leaders were expected to impart to all members of the youth movement. But I did not neglect the ideological side of my work either. In the seminars I organized, and in my talks at the branches of Hanoar Haoved, I doggedly advocated my own political views – Jewish statehood now, rather than holding out for Greater Israel – in the full knowledge that this was not the position of the majority of the movement's leadership. This persistence eventually developed into a fully fledged showdown at a national convention of Hanoar Haoved held at the Mugrabi cinema hall in Tel Aviv. Apart from the delegates themselves, this event was attended by all the national leaders of the Zionist-socialist movement. Right at the outset, the convention was presented with a choice of two platforms: 'Binyamin's proposal' – submitted by Binyamin Chochlovkin, the Secretary of Hanoar Haoved and one of the leaders of Ahdut Haavoda; and 'Shimon's proposal' – submitted by me.

To everyone's surprise, 'Shimon's proposal' won by a considerable margin. The ensuing pandemonium is difficult to describe. Neither side had been prepared for this sort of upset, and the Mapai leaders could barely believe their eyes. But the fact was that I emerged from this convention with a solid majority of our movement behind me. I had to think carefully about how to play my hand now. I could easily, and legitimately, have 'taken control' of the movement, but I knew instinctively that it would be premature to do so and might create a split. In the end, I heeded the more moderate advice of Hanoar Haoved's 'father figure', David Cohen, and of Berl Katznelson, my own mentor, and proposed a compromise solution whereby the movement's Secretariat henceforth comprise equal numbers from the two 'schools' of political thought. I decided to forgo pressing home my victory in the interests of unity – and have never regretted that early political decision. But the victory itself continued to dog me throughout my subsequent political career. Ahdut Haavoda never forgot it nor forgave it. Its members attributed to me powers I never had, and regarded everything I did or said with suspicion. Mapai, for its part, treated me like a hero. I was co-opted on to the policy-making bodies of the party, and my name would be suggested for almost every appointment that became available.

The lesson which I myself learned from this experience, and which I was to apply many times in my later career, was not to be overly impressed by titles or by membership of Secretariats and similar institutions. What was important in politics, in the final analysis, was working 'in the field' with the grass-roots membership, getting to know them and their concerns and thoughts, and never despairing of the possibility of changing the overall situation through such steady and relentless 'field work'. There is no substitute for believing – and working.

This episode opened a rift between me and several of my comrades in the movement, which I obviously would have preferred to avoid. But looking back, I still believe that I had no real choice. I could either follow the line that I believed in, or 'follow the party line', which I was convinced was wrong. Ben-Gurion and Katznelson had saved us from the claws of communism; I saw myself as their disciple and their emissary in the youth movement. They imbued in me an uncompromising antipathy to every form of dictatorship and political coercion, including blind obedience and 'line-toeing'. I believed, with them, that man must be free; not just physically, but spiritually. The values which they instilled in me I sought to instil in the thousands of young people with whom I came into contact in my work for the movement.

That work completed, at least for the moment, I returned to Alumot to resume my previous employment with the sheep and cows. By now, we were building our permanent homes, on a hill just to the south of Poriya, so I also learned to carry a hod. Soon, I was elected kibbutz secretary, which entailed spending one day a week in Tel Aviv, doing the rounds of banks and offices in a ceaseless quest for credits and for raw materials with which to continue our building work and develop our agricultural projects.

Sonia was a year younger than I, and she had therefore not come with me and my class to Poriya. She had hoped to go to nursing school, but when that did not work out, she enlisted in the British army, serving mainly in Egypt. We kept in touch and met during her furloughs. When the war drew to an end, she decided to join me at Alumot, and we set our wedding day for 1 May 1945, which was expected to be VE Day. (In point of fact, the war in Europe continued for another week.) The First of May was also Lag Ba'Omer in the Jewish calendar – traditionally a propitious day for a wedding – as well, of course, as being the workers' holiday.

We hoped our joy might be complete by the return of my father in time for the wedding, although we did not know exactly where he was. We knew that he had fallen into German captivity early in the war – we had received letters from him written in prisoner-of-war camps – and we understood, from between the lines, that he had escaped and been recaptured. But beyond that, his fate was unclear, and we waited anxiously for a sign of life once the war ended.

We arranged our wedding at Ben-Shemen, where Sonia had grown up and where I had spent my formative years. The youth village management prepared food-laden tables and a picturesque white *huppa** alongside the swimming-pool. I was decked out in the grey flannels and dyed battle-dress, and both of us were desperately nervous and deliriously happy.

Sonia was twenty-one and I was nearly twenty-two. She loved the bucolic life of the kibbutz, and I loved her. At Alumot, we were now provided with our own tent, although for part of the time we had to share it with Shulamit Aloni, later to become a prominent Knesset Member and Cabinet Minister.

Our 'honeymoon' was enchantingly beautiful. We spent it on the bank of the Jordan, at Bitaniya. Our kibbutz comrades rigged up a shaded bower between two towering eucalyptuses, and this became our love-nest for a week. Each morning, we awoke to the birds' singing – and shared their tree-top view of the surrounding scenery. We would climb down to bathe in the limpid river, and then tear away on my faithful old

---

* The bridal canopy under which the religious ceremony takes place.

Triumph to some beautiful spot in the Upper Galilee or down the Jordan Valley.

A few weeks later, the long-awaited news arrived that my father was alive and well, that he was in England and would shortly embark for Palestine. His cable from Egypt detailing his arrival time preceded his train by just a few hours. Sonia and I climbed on the Triumph and raced down to Lydda – in time to see him, in his crisp British uniform complete with safari helmet, step off the train looking as strong and optimistic as ever, hardly showing the signs of five long years of captivity, danger and adventure. We all went back together to Tel Aviv, hardly able to speak for excitement and emotion. After all, we had not seen Father for close to six years. I had the strange sensation that a new father had been 'born' into our family.

He brought back with him a medal awarded in recognition of his bravery. He had twice escaped and twice been recaptured, but his full story came out slowly – some of it only years later. He was essentially a very modest man, not given to recounting his adventures, and certainly not to boasting – even to his close family. It wasn't really until my children began bombarding him with demands to hear his tale that he gave in – he never could resist them – and we learned parts of his story vicariously through them.

He had first fallen into captivity in Greece. He escaped and managed to spend a year hidden alone in a succession of secluded monasteries. Later, the Greek underground brought him to a small village near Mount Olympus, where eighteen other British and Empire escapees were hiding. Among these was Charles (Charlie) Coward, who was later to be awarded the Victoria Cross for his gallantry. His book, *The Password is Courage*, became a bestseller and was made into a successful film. Led by Coward, the group managed to commandeer a boat in which they set out for Turkey. On the voyage, a New Zealand soldier died from cold and exposure, and Coward decided that my father must adopt the dead man's identity instead of his own Jewish one, in case they were caught again.

They were indeed caught by a German flying-boat, which dragged them back to the Greek coast. Coward made everyone aboard swear that they would not reveal my father's true origins. They were taken from camp to camp throughout occupied Europe, and in each new camp Coward began planning another escape. Once, four of them managed to slip away. They split into two pairs: Coward with a Scottish soldier;

my father with an Australian. But all four were recaptured; in my father's case, because his Australian partner lost his nerve just as the train they were on was about to cross the Czech border.

A third escape attempt almost resulted in tragedy. Coward and his friends, my father among them, succeeded in sawing through the bars of a prison-train. But again they were caught before they had got very far; this time, my father and a New Zealand soldier were accused of organizing the break-out and were peremptorily sentenced to death by the German officer commanding the transport. They were ordered to strip and stand at the side of the train, where the sentence was to be carried out forthwith by firing squad.

Fortunately, Coward did not lose his resourcefulness. As the senior British serviceman present – he held the rank of sergeant-major – he approached the German officer and demanded that the condemned men be given the services of a chaplain, as international law required. Coward warned the startled German that if he failed to comply, the prisoners of war would surely remember his behaviour, and he would be brought to trial after the war as a war criminal. This admonition had the desired effect: a pastor was summoned from among the prisoners of war. Somehow Coward managed to signal to the cleric that one of the two men was a Jew, and that he must not reveal this.

The pastor played his role brilliantly. He also urged the German officer to postpone the execution until the transport reached its destination, where a more thorough inquiry could be held – as international law required. He informed the German that if the shooting went ahead, he would have no option but to interpose himself between the firing squad and the condemned men. 'You'll have to kill me first,' he declared.

This did the trick. Everyone was bundled back into the train. When they eventually reached the designated prison camp, my father and the New Zealander were formally tried, convicted and sentenced to lengthy periods in solitary confinement. The pastor, an Australian, had saved my father's life. Years later, I tried hard to locate him, but never succeeded.

The new prison camp was close to Auschwitz, and the indefatigable Coward started organizing food- and clothes-parcels to be smuggled to the Jewish inmates there. He became known among the Jews, and among the British prisoners of war, as 'The Angel of Auschwitz'. He was directly responsible, according to my father and to other accounts, for saving the lives of a number of Jews.

Coward's final escape, together with my father, was successful: they grabbed a horse and cart and galloped towards General Patton's lines. It was probably the most foolhardy of all their attempts – only a miracle saved them from being shot by the Americans – but it was typical of my father's incurable optimism. He bellowed 'We're British!' as they hurtled towards the GIS – and somehow they made it. I like to think that I inherited from my father something of his flat refusal to be daunted by ostensibly unfavourable odds.

Eight years later, as Director-General of the Ministry of Defence, I received a telephone call from the British Immigrants Association informing me that they had invited 'The Angel of Auschwitz' to Israel as a token of gratitude for what he had done to save Jews during the war, and he had mentioned someone called Persky who had been with him in captivity. They knew that my former name was Persky; was I related?

I phoned my father, who was ecstatic. He organized a family dinner that same evening in Coward's honour. We all fell under the spell of this extraordinary man, at once vivacious and modest, and plentifully endowed with original British humour.

But life had not treated him well since the war, despite his decoration for gallantry. He had returned to his pre-war job as a guard at a timber company, but was soon sacked as part of a retrenchment programme. His autobiography had sold more than a million copies, but Coward had parted with his rights for a mere £250, and with the film rights for another £50! 'My dear wife helped me dispose of that quickly enough,' he told us dryly. The bottom line was that they were penniless and living on unemployment benefits and a meagre army pension. My father, who never asked me for any favours in all my years in government, indicated that this was a special case – and I phoned a friend in England, Chaim Morrison, who immediately agreed to find Coward a job in his company.

5 NEW DUTIES

In 1946, our family had another event to celebrate: our daughter, Zviya, was born at the Scottish Hospital in Tiberias. Meanwhile, our kibbutz began moving to its permanent site, and for the first time we enjoyed the feeling of a solid roof over our heads and the luxuries of running water and electricity.

Before long, I was informed that Mapai had decided to add two younger members to its delegation to the Zionist Congress, which was to convene in Basel, Switzerland – Moshe Dayan, who was thirty-one at the time, and me, who was twenty-three years old. We knew each other vaguely, as I was friendly with his younger brother Zorik, who was later killed in the War of Independence. Now we were to meet for a 'co-ordinating conference' in Tel Aviv.

The 'conference' lasted for several hours, with the two conferees circling Dizengoff Circus time after time, engrossed in conversation. We found ourselves wholly in agreement: we would support Ben-Gurion to the hilt; we would support an 'activist' approach (ie. fighting the British, by force of arms if necessary, in order to achieve Jewish independence); and we would support the unfettered continuation of 'illegal' immigration to Palestine. Dayan even suggested that we propose setting fire to all the detention camps in Cyprus (where the British held all the 'illegals' caught trying to reach the shores of Palestine). This meeting laid the foundations of a deep and almost lifelong friendship.

The delegation embarked on a smallish steamer, which was nevertheless the height of luxury for an impoverished kibbutz member like me. Almost the entire Zionist leadership was aboard. Cabins were allocated by lottery, and I found myself sharing a room with Levi Eshkol and Pinhas Lavon, two of the most eminent leaders in the movement. The lottery also determined who had which bunk, and I found to my enormous embarrassment that I had drawn the 'good' bunk, the one beneath the porthole. The other two were a two-tier arrangement, placed against the inner wall of the cabin. Of course I immediately offered my bunk to Eshkol, who firmly refused it. 'Luck is luck,' he insisted. Lavon then suggested that he would take it instead, whereupon an enraged Eshkol virtually threw himself upon Lavon. This was not to be the last conflict between these two men.

Other notable passengers on the voyage included Zalman Shazar, who was later to be President of the State, Yisrael Yeshayahu, later a Speaker of the Knesset, and the poet Avraham Shlonsky. Most of our time was spent arguing or singing. For me, it was my first opportunity to watch our national leaders from close to – not always an edifying experience.

Just before we left, the Mapai young guard had decided to set up its own newspaper, *Ashmoret* (Night Watch). I was selected to be one of its editors. In that capacity, I undertook to cable news reports and articles from the Congress in Basel. The party's long-established evening paper, *Yediot Hadashot*, also commissioned me to file a daily column, and so I sailed bearing journalistic as well as political credentials.

The Congress itself opened with a moving and impressive ceremony, in the very same hall where Theodor Herzl had convened the first Zionist Congress in 1897. The entire Jewish leadership was represented on the platform: Chaim Weizmann,* Abba Hillel Silver, Nahum Gold-mann, and our own leaders David Ben-Gurion, Berl Katznelson, Eliezer Kaplan, Golda Meir, Levi Eshkol, Zalman Shazar, Yosef Sprinzak, Avraham Hartzfeld, Moshe Sneh, Yitzhak Tabenkin, Meir Yaari, Pinhas Lavon and Yisrael Galili.

For the first time, I realized how divided this Jewish leadership was on a whole range of issues. Firstly, Weizmann's continued primacy was under sharp attack. He was blamed for having failed to prevent the adoption by Britain of its White Paper policy, which cruelly limited immigration and Jewish land purchasing. The broader issue was whether to embark on an all-out struggle against the British – the 'activist' approach, as it was called – or to try to preserve a modicum of dialogue with London. The future of 'illegal' immigration was another facet of the same dilemma: were we to continue with it, or to demand the right

---

* Professor Chaim Weizmann (1874–1952), chemist and leader of the Zionist movement, became the first President of Israel in 1948.

to legal immigration of Jews to Palestine? The most crucial debate centred on the 'Biltmore Programme', which called for independence immediately, even at the expense of partitioning Palestine, and which was vigorously supported by Ben-Gurion.

Weizmann made a memorable speech, defending himself from his detractors. He stood on the platform, tall and pale, and, in his vivid Yiddish, he bewailed the holocaust that had mutilated the Jewish People. His voice shook. Many people in the hall sobbed openly. He spoke out forcefully against the British Government, but stopped short of severing the link with Britain. He wove in some colourful Yiddish jokes and had the Congress in fits of laughter.

One story involved a little *shtetl*, where the Jews learned that the local magnate intended to issue a harsh decree against them. They formed a delegation which was to go to his castle and beg him to revoke the decision. But when they reached the gate of the castle, a dozen barking dogs came hurtling out and drove them off. They decided on a tactical retreat and a consultation with their rabbi. The rabbi advised that they were each to take with them a book of Psalms – and if the dogs barked at them, they were all to recite a particular Psalm. They went off confidently, but were soon back again. 'What happened?' their fellow-Jews asked anxiously. 'We read the Psalm, but the dogs kept barking.' That, said Weizmann, more or less summed up the course of his own diplomatic efforts with the British Government.

The Mapai faction seethed with disunity. Many sided with Weizmann's moderate approach and rejected what they saw as Ben-Gurion's 'extremism'. Dayan and I sided with Ben-Gurion, but we were in the minority.

On the day after the Congress officially opened, I was sitting at a session alongside Arye Bahir, a member of Kibbutz Afikim in the Jordan Valley, which was the only large kibbutz to support Ben-Gurion. Suddenly, Ben-Gurion's wife, Paula, burst into the hall and made straight for Bahir (a personal friend of the Ben-Gurions). 'Arye,' she said in Yiddish, 'he's gone mad.'

There was no doubt whom she was talking about. Bahir asked me to accompany him to the Drei Koenigen Hotel, where Ben-Gurion was staying in the same room that Herzl had stayed in for the first Zionist Congress. We went up to the room and knocked on the door. No reply. Several more knocks, and still nothing. Gingerly, we tried the handle. The door was not locked. We sidled in. Ben-Gurion stood with his back to us, a suitcase open in front of him. He was packing his clothes.

'*Shalom*, Ben-Gurion,' Bahir said. No answer. '*Shalom*,' he repeated, this time louder and more insistently.

Ben-Gurion wheeled round and stared at us. 'Are you coming with me?'

'Where are you going?' we asked.

'To form a new Zionist movement. I have no more confidence in this Congress. It's full of small-time politicians, pathetic defeatists. They won't have the courage to make the decisions that are needed at this time. Only the Jewish youth, all over the world, will provide the courage needed to face the historic challenges facing Zionism. After one-third of our nation has been wiped out – among them some of our finest young people – the survivors have no hope other than to rebuild their lives in the historic homeland, the only land that can and must open its gates wide to welcome them.'

Ben-Gurion was in a fighting mood. Bahir looked at me, and I motioned to him to tell Ben-Gurion that we would go with him. This calmed his fury somewhat, and soon we plucked up the courage to suggest that, before slamming the door on the Congress, he try one more time to win over the Mapai faction. 'If there's a majority there, we'll all stay; and if not, we won't be the only ones to leave with you; a great many more will come too.' Ben-Gurion agreed to make this last effort.

Meanwhile, word spread through the Congress corridors that a profound crisis had erupted. Mapai moderates like Sprinzak, Kaplan and Moshe Sharett, who tended towards Weizmann, nevertheless were loath to lose Ben-Gurion. As so often in the past and in the future, even those of his colleagues who differed with him and bitterly criticized his leadership retained a deep respect for his vision and for his iron will. They knew that, ultimately, there was no one like him, and no substitute for him.

At seven that evening, the crucial meeting of the Mapai faction began. As chairman the faction chose Golda Meir, who was considered a Ben-Gurionite even though she opposed partition. She was second to none in her ability to run a stormy and emotion-laden meeting.

This meeting began with a vehement attack by Ben-Gurion on 'Mr Engineer Kaplan', whom he accused of living in yesterday's world and of failing to understand that only a sovereign Jewish state, no matter how small, could provide salvation for the Holocaust refugees.

Kaplan, despite his usually calm and moderate demeanour, hit back as hard as he could. He asserted that 'Mr Advocate Ben-Gurion' was living in a dream world and was proposing fantasies instead of pragmatic policies. The meeting raged on through the night. Only at dawn was the vote called, and Ben-Gurion won by a majority – a slender majority, but a majority none the less. A wave of relief swept over us. In our hearts, we knew that at that moment the Jewish state had been born. Nothing now could deter Ben-Gurion from his goal.

The politics of the Congress made for some strange bedfellows. One such unlikely liaison evolved between the hawkish Abba Hillel Silver, the American Zionist leader, and Moshe Sneh, the head of the Haganah high command. Silver delivered a brilliant speech, and Katznelson replied with a no-less-brilliant address of his own – which did nothing to weaken the Silver–Sneh alliance. I listened very closely to Sneh's speeches on various occasions during the Congress and firmly concluded that Sneh was on a markedly different course from the rest of the Zionist fleet. He seemed to feel that the future belonged to the Soviet Union, and was determined to secure a place for himself in that brave new world. I sent an article to *Ashmoret*, in which I contended openly that Sneh had embarked on the road to communism. This article, which was immediately reproduced in several other newspapers, provoked a real storm at the Congress. Golda Meir cornered me and demanded how I dared to write such things, when it was well known that Sneh was our (ie. Mapai's) ally. But I was convinced that I was right, and sadly, time proved me right.

This was the first time – though hardly the last – that Golda directed her ire at me. Her harsh words left a bitter taste in my mouth. Ben-Gurion said nothing. He knew that the young guard – even if there were only the two of us at the Congress – supported him to the hilt. He may also have known in his heart that Sneh was ensnared in an alien ideology.

We returned to *Eretz Yisrael* via Paris – my first experience of this great city. I was entranced by its beauty, its spirit and its artistic treasures. Even the sad and weary Paris of the immediate post-war period seemed to overflow with charm and grace. I travelled home with the party Secretary, Meir Argov, later to become the long-serving Chairman of the Knesset Foreign Affairs and Defence Committee, and we became fast friends.

The contrast between the bright lights of Paris and the cold and draughty winter at Alumot was real enough. Still, I was glad to be home, with Sonia and Zviya, and I went back to my work in the cowshed and the fields with renewed vigour. Sonia worked in the clothes store during the day and in the babies' home on some nights. This was considered the most precious task of all on the kibbutz, and I would sit with her there, helping her to look after the first few babies born on Alumot. I was involved, too, in our cultural activities. We organized a Passover *Seder*★ with our own original *Haggadah*, comprising parts of the traditional service interwoven with passages that we chose from modern Hebrew literature. We also put out our own little newspaper, called *On the Mountain*. I wrote almost all of it myself, but, in order to vary the fare a little, I called one regular column 'From the Diary of a Woman-Member' and wrote it in the appropriate style. Before long, the Histadrut-owned national daily *Davar* started reproducing this column in its own pages, informing its readers that 'at last we can read authentic thoughts and feelings expressed from a woman's standpoint'.

Meanwhile, Ben-Gurion was pressing ahead with determination with his campaign to persuade people of the advantages of the 'Biltmore Programme'. In September 1947, the United Nations Special Committee on Palestine published its report, recommending partition. The Jewish state was to be created in only a small part of *Eretz Yisrael*; most of the country was to be allocated to the Arabs. Despite this disappointing partition, Ben-Gurion was in favour of the report's acceptance. He revisited the Jewish displaced persons' camps in Europe, accompanied by the Allied commander, General Dwight D. Eisenhower, and emerged deeply shaken by what he had seen. His conclusion was that time now mattered more than space: only Jewish statehood could provide salvation for the refugees. During this visit to Europe, Ben-Gurion became increasingly impressed by Eisenhower's personality and by his attitude towards the Jewish tragedy. For the rest of his life, Ben-Gurion respected Eisenhower, both before and after he became President of the United States.

Ben-Gurion knew that a UN resolution alone could not create the Jewish state and that the Arabs would attempt to choke the new-born state by force of arms. He devoted himself to building up our armed strength, so that we could defend ourselves once the British pulled out and the Arabs were finally able to drive home their assaults. When the UN General Assembly voted to adopt the partition resolution on 29 November 1947, the Jews of Palestine danced in the streets. I was standing

★ The ceremonial meal eaten on the first night of Passover.

alongside Ben-Gurion and I shall never forget his remark: 'Today they are dancing; tomorrow they will have to shed blood.'

He collected a group of close aides and confidants to work with him on defence: Levi Eshkol, Shaul Avigur, Pinhas Sapir and others. He enlisted the Jewish officers who had served in the Jewish Brigade, formed by the British army towards the end of the war. He wanted the army of the Jewish state to represent both the pioneering spirit of the Haganah and the professional traditions of the British army. He set up a small team to locate first-rate officer material for the army-in-the-making. He wanted everything to be ready in time. This team was to include Shlomo Shamir, David Shaltiel and Asaf Simhoni (all later generals in the Israel Defence Forces [IDF]), as well as Arye Bahir and myself.

In May 1947, Levi Eshkol was at the gates of Alumot again, this time with a letter from Ben-Gurion requiring that I be seconded forthwith to the Haganah high command. Obviously, our general meeting gave its assent without much ado, and I left the kibbutz for a second time – this time for a job whose definition was unclear, and for a period whose duration was uncertain.

6 FOUNDING FATHERS

Nineteen forty-seven was a hard year, but a great one. The incipient collapse of the British Mandate was almost palpable. We were conscious of living through the birth-pangs of the new Jewish state. The suffering of the refugees incarcerated in Cyprus and in the displaced persons' camps in Europe was on everyone's mind, and the profound political divisions between left and right within the *Yishuv* took on new urgency and intensity.

The right were known as 'The Secessionists', signifying the refusal of their underground groups, Etzel★ and Lehi,† to accept the authority of the *Yishuv*'s elected political leadership. The two groups ran their own arms procurement programmes, using those arms without reference to the policies of the national leadership. They vehemently rejected the principle of partition and hinted that they would continue to operate in those sections of the country that were destined to fall outside the sovereign area of the Jewish state.

Within the left, meanwhile, a separate dispute raged over Ben-Gurion's determination to dissolve the Palmach as an independent military organization and to incorporate it into the Haganah. This quarrel pitted Mapai against Ahdut Haavoda, but also caused discord within Mapai itself where not everyone was comfortable with Ben-Gurion's decision.‡

★ The Hebrew acronym for National Military Organization, commanded by Menachem Begin.
† The Hebrew acronym for Freedom Fighters of Israel, also known as the Stern Gang, commanded by a triumvirate that included Yitzhak Shamir.
‡ Ben-Gurion eventually implemented his decision in November 1948, disbanding the Palmach and incorporating its units into the IDF.

The most important tasks were to prepare the state-in-the-making and to build its army. There was much tension and confusion as the key officials and policy-makers went about their business with frenetic energy. The figure of David Ben-Gurion – fearless, totally consistent and totally determined – towered above the rest. His purpose was to expedite the departure of the British and to be ready, when that moment arrived, to put in place the framework of the sovereign Jewish state. His immediate objectives, once the state was established, were to open its gates to Jewish immigration and to assert its authority by dismantling Etzel, Lehi and, also, the Palmach. During the months before the birth of the state, he feared that a war with the Arabs would catch us before we had fully prepared our army, and that, as a result, we would be forced to create an army before we could create the state. This chronology, in Ben-Gurion's view, could endanger the democratic character of the future state. He was determined, therefore, to proceed on both fronts simultaneously and not to allow our preoccupation with defence to defer the orderly creation of the state and its democratic institutions.

When I arrived at the 'Red House', the headquarters of the Haganah on the Tel Aviv sea-front, I was directed to Josef Yizreeli, deputy head of the General Staff. He suggested that I take over the manpower department, noting that mobilization of all available manpower was now the most critical task, apart from the procurement of weapons to defend ourselves.

I soon became aware, however, that there was someone else who was also in charge of manpower for the Haganah high command. This was Moshe Zadok (he later became a general). I tried to evolve a productive working relationship with him – he was a stickler for formalities, an unbending man of principle and straight as a die in all his dealings – and both of us had sense enough to co-operate. We decided that he would be responsible for existing manpower, and I for mobilizing new strength.

The arrangement did not last long; soon, various Haganah commanders loaded me with additional assignments. Finally, Levi Eshkol, having cleared the proposal with Ben-Gurion himself, suggested that I move into arms procurement and production. I was required to work with Eshkol, who was torn between his three positions: Ben-Gurion's deputy in the Haganah, head of the settlement department at the Jewish Agency, and Secretary of the Tel Aviv Labour Council.

Eshkol also oversaw military intelligence, and he gave me a largely free hand in running his various defence assignments for him. We plunged into this new and stormy sea together. He never lost his famous, wry sense of humour. One day, for instance, bumping into me on the steps of the Red House, he asked in Yiddish: 'Young man, have you ever been to America?' I said, 'No.' 'Can you speak English?' Again, I had to say 'No.' 'In that case, you're the very man I'm looking for. I hereby appoint you, in addition to everything else, head of the American department of the Haganah.'

I had no idea what trouble I was letting myself in for. What had happened was that a day earlier, an urgent cable had arrived from Teddy Kollek,★ who was head of the Haganah's mission in the United States. He would be returning to Israel the following Sunday for a visit, and if by then they had not appointed someone who knew America well and had a fluent command of English to head the department and co-ordinate with him, he would quit his job and refuse to return to New York.

Kollek duly arrived and almost resigned on the spot when he heard whom they had decided to appoint . He knew me well enough; after all, we were sort of neighbours across the Sea of Galilee. His kibbutz, Ein Gev, sits on the eastern shore of the lake, and Alumot is on the west. But he also knew that I lacked the two obvious requirements for the job. A major storm brewed, which required Ben-Gurion's personal intervention.

Once again, I entered a new world, a world of mysterious missions and anonymous agents, a world peopled by superb professionals and also by a sprinkling of mavericks and dreamers who would file dramatic reports that reflected their fantasies rather than the complex realities. I waded in with my usual enthusiasm, aided by a character trait that was to prove useful in similar situations throughout my career – a relentless capacity to work day and night, especially with the people in the field, who gradually gave me their trust and confidence.

The situation within the high command was a matter of concern to the national leadership. The Chief of Staff, Yaacov Dori, was a sick man and effectively inactive. Nevertheless, he was not replaced. The senior officers, while highly committed, did not all share the same high level of military professionalism. Moreover, years of operating in the underground had imbued them with traits and traditions that suited the style

★ Later Mayor of Jerusalem from 1965 to 1993.

of Yisrael Galili, head of the Haganah's National Command, but were not necessarily appropriate for the sort of staff work that Ben-Gurion required of them.

Galili was, in effect, one Ben-Gurion's three deputies; the other two were Eshkol and Shaul Avigur. The three were as different from one another as the seasons of the year.

Galili was the first native-born Israeli to reach a position of central importance. He had begun his political career in Hanoar Haoved and was a founder-member of Kibbutz Naan. At first, he was a follower of Katznelson, but gradually his political views shifted and he joined forces with Yitzhak Tabenkin. He was short, like Ben-Gurion himself. He wrote in a stylish and flawless Hebrew and was a captivating public speaker. He was widely considered the future leader of Ahdut Haavoda; and Ahdut Haavoda, to its credit or discredit, was adept at cultivating a personality cult around the men whom it destined for leadership roles.

Apart from his sagacity, which was profound, Galili was brilliant at human relations. People were drawn to him, and many stayed with him even though they disagreed with his political positions. Eventually, he won the total support of the entire Ahdut Haavoda leadership, old and young alike.

Heading the Palmach, with its close affiliation to Ahdut Haavoda, were Yitzhak Sadeh and Yigal Allon. Sadeh was a legend in his own lifetime, a one-time stonemason who radiated enormous charisma and martial expertise. Allon was a handsome young officer from Kibbutz Ginossar, on the Sea of Galilee. He was regarded as a man with a great future and was appointed commander of the Palmach at the age of twenty-eight. Both Sadeh and Allon were entirely devoted to Galili and drew their inspiration from him.

Ben-Gurion admired Galili, and even liked him, but he did not trust him. He claimed that a member of Naan had once told him that Galili was not to be trusted. Beyond that, though, there was a more fundamental reason for Ben-Gurion's attitude: he felt that Galili's loyalty to his own party was so intense that it would come between him and Ben-Gurion, especially in light of Ben-Gurion's determination to mould a unified army and to do away with the independent existence of the Palmach. By the same token, Ben-Gurion felt that Galili automatically preferred Palmach officers to Haganah men who had served in the British army during the war and were now available for enlistment.

Galili was not one for paperwork. Most of the areas that he dealt with – and he dealt with most of the sensitive ones – were stored in his head. He built up an impressive structure of mutual confidence between himself and his senior subordinates. But the shadow of the inevitable split – over Ben-Gurion's decision to dismantle the Palmach – began to darken the atmosphere in the high command, even before the creation of the state. Galili's resignation became a matter of time. Eventually he left, taking with him a number of top officers in what became known as 'the generals' revolt'. His departure★ left a yawning chasm – both in the formal sense, because he was responsible for so many areas, and in a broader sense, because of his personality and the way he had run his departments. Eshkol, who was appointed to take over, told me later that he had asked his predecessor for some 'leads', at least, in the form of basic documents, but he had received nothing.

My own relations with Galili were complicated. We had once spent a month together at a Hanoar Haoved seminar in Haifa, but we knew even then that we belonged to two distinct camps. He, a Hanoar Haoved veteran, led the large Ahdut Haavoda following within our movement. I was a youngster at the beginning of my political career, but I was never part of his following. Our friendship revived only years later, when we both served as Ministers in Golda Meir's Government of National Unity. Galili was Golda's confidant, the politician closest to her. His positions, especially on settlements, were very sharply defined, and it was he who in effect determined the national settlement map in the years following the 1967 Six Day War, sometimes in collaboration with Moshe Dayan, then Minister of Defence, and sometimes alone.

Eshkol, who had immigrated to *Eretz Yisrael* from the Ukraine as a young man, was a founder of Kibbutz Degania. He was stockily built, with a finely shaped head, and his face revealed a balance of toughness and sentimentality. He was a superb organizer and administrator, always resourceful and always ready with a humorous remark to ease tensions. He was the most stable figure among the national leaders and enjoyed the widest support from his colleagues. Politically, although he was more 'activist' than the mainstream Degania membership, his activism never took on the Marxist overtones that affected that other major kibbutz, Ein Harod (and later led to a split in that kibbutz's ranks).

★ Galili's post as head of the Haganah's National Command was abolished by Ben-Gurion in early May 1948. He stayed on at the Ministry of Defence for several months without a formal title, fulfilling many of the duties of the sick Chief of Staff, Dori. Following further tensions with Ben-Gurion, Galili quit finally in September 1948.

Eshkol's abilities were not always evident on first acquaintance, but Ben-Gurion valued him and relied on him implicitly, both for his sound judgment and for his capacity for hard work. That was why Ben-Gurion insisted on having him in the Haganah high command, in addition to his other jobs. Eshkol, for his part, seemed to find time for everything. He never shied away from responsibility, yet never seemed ambitious. Like Galili, he preferred to operate almost entirely without paperwork. He wrote in a particularly large script, thus managing to produce the minimum number of pages expected from a man of his station.

When Galili went and Eshkol took over his responsibilities, in addition to his own, he was put in charge of the entire mobilization effort of the *Yishuv*. His first action was to select Pinhas Sapir as his right-hand man, conferring upon him the titular rank of colonel. Never was there a more dynamic and less swaggering colonel in the army. Sapir, who was later to serve as Minister of Finance under Eshkol and Golda, was totally uninterested in rank or pomp. All he wanted was to get the job done, and very soon he became an institution in his own right, like Galili and Eshkol.

The third of Ben-Gurion's deputies was Shaul Avigur. At the time, his name was Meirov, but later he took the name Avigur (in Hebrew, Father of Gur) after his only son, Gur, who was killed during the 1948 War of Independence. He was a stern and demanding man, closed and mysterious. A longtime leader of the Haganah, his 'military career' dated back to the defence of Tel Hai, with Joseph Trumpeldor, in 1920.*

Avigur was regarded as the conscience of the Haganah. His frugal, almost ascetic personal lifestyle, coupled with his rigid official parsimony and his economy with words, made him something of a living legend. The most extravagant refreshment he would ever offer a guest was a cup of tea and a handful of dates brought from his home at Kibbutz Kinneret. He had no sense of humour whatsoever; throughout our long acquaintance, he told only one 'joke', which he would repeat whenever he felt that the situation required some light relief. It was about someone who came to Kibbutz Kinneret and saw a combine harvester standing in the yard. 'What's that?' the visitor asked. 'A combine.' 'What does it do?' 'It provides work for the guys in the garage. It was created only to be repaired.' That was his joke.

---

* Tel Hai, a small Jewish settlement in the Upper Galilee, was attacked by Arabs. Trumpeldor and seven comrades fell in its defence.

Avigur suffered from a rare disease, which caused him to swell up periodically, and this enhanced his natural tendency to secrecy. (One story told about him was that when he wrote a cable, he would censor even the passages that he quoted from newspaper clippings.) He worked behind closed doors, mostly alone. But he was a figure of enormous personal authority, and on the rare occasions when he did speak in public, everyone turned out to hear him. He never hesitated to speak out critically when he felt the need, against both his subordinates and his superiors. His responsibilities in the pre-state period were in the two areas of greatest secrecy: arms procurement and illegal immigration. He spent much of the time in Europe, running networks.

Ben-Gurion respected him enormously, though they never developed a close personal relationship. Avigur was not always happy with Ben-Gurion's attitude towards the Haganah, while Ben-Gurion felt that Avigur was sometimes too cautious and too conditioned by past realities which had since changed.

Although I was seen as the most junior of the staffers, and as an unswerving 'Ben-Gurionist', Avigur treated me with kindness and was always ready to hear what I had to say – though not always to agree with it. I had been Gur's youth leader in Hanoar Haoved. After his death, Avigur asked me to write down everything I remembered about his son, who had been the light of his life. I wrote with tears in my eyes.

Soon after, Avigur asked to be relieved of his duties and suggested that I replace him as the head of arms procurement. I will never forget the precision with which he handed over the department. Everything had been meticulously recorded in well-ordered documents, most of them written in code. He offered his assessment of each of the key men working in the department. Finally – I didn't know whether to laugh or to gasp in admiration – he handed me his purse. This was divided into compartments, each one containing a few coins from the different European countries which he had visited in the course of his work. Avigur explained patiently how I ought to record every franc, cent or penny that I spent, and how to make sure that the coins did not get mixed up. This was a legacy that few men can leave behind them – and few are privileged to receive.

The most remarkable character of all, though, was Ben-Gurion himself. I do not believe that the state would have been created without him. That was my feeling at the time and, looking back today on his handling of the War of Independence, I am still convinced of it.

Ben-Gurion had to fight on three fronts simultaneously. The first, of course, was the military front: seven Arab states attacking Israel as soon as it came into being on 15 May 1948.* The seven Arab states had armies; Israel had an army-in-the-making. Their armies had weapons; we had limited quantities of assorted weaponry, which had been stockpiled in secret during the preparatory period.

The War of Independence lasted for a year and a half. The actual fighting was conducted in spasms, with the truce periods declared between rounds. We took advantage of these truces to build up both the state and the army. This was truly a war of the few against the many; the few, moreover, had few arms, while the many had many.

Ben-Gurion ran the war down to its smallest detail. His Chief of Staff, Dori, was still on his sickbed and effectively *hors de combat*. Moreover, Ben-Gurion was forced to contend with relentless, seething opposition both from the former high command of the Haganah – and especially from its main fighting force, the Palmach – and from among the ranks of the younger officers whom he had brought into the top echelon of the new army.

The second front was the international diplomatic arena. Even though thirty-three UN member-states had voted in favour of Israel's creation, virtually all of them proceeded to impose an arms embargo on the new state. Harry Truman was among the first world leaders to recognize Israel, along with Andrei Gromyko, who spoke for Stalin. But the United States refused to sell Israel even rifles for personal self-defence, to say nothing of heavier weapons. To the present day, I find that difficult to understand. Once, as Deputy Defence Minister in 1964, I was invited by the eminent American diplomat, Averell Harriman, to lunch at the White House. After a glass or two of vodka – 'Let's drink it for its taste', he said, 'and ignore its origin' – Harriman asked me to spell out our grievances against the American Government. I began with the War of Independence. How did he explain Truman's refusal to sell us arms? Harriman replied without hesitation that it had been 'a mistake'. For the United States, of course, it was merely a political mistake; for Israel, it could well have been fatal.

---

* 15 May was the date on which the British Mandate officially ended; but it was a Saturday, the Jewish day of rest, and so the formal declaration of independence was advanced to Friday, 14 May.

The three other countries that produced the kind of arms we needed – Russia, Britain and France – also refused to supply them. The issue of arms procurement thus became the central problem facing fledgling Israel. A large number of men and minds were mobilized to solve it by every manner of backhanded, undercover means available to us. Virtually every type or make of weapon was welcome. The essence was speed of delivery; price was all but irrelevant. The international community applauded little Israel, but left it isolated and defenceless against the significantly superior forces of its aggressors.

Ben-Gurion's third front was the domestic political battlefield. The Jewish Agency and the Histadrut had existed prior to the state, and were in many respects the nuclei of the state's political and administrative structures, but they had functioned on the basis of agreements between the various political parties rather than in strict accordance with the outcome of democratic elections. Beneath the former façade of unity within the organized *Yishuv*, deep political differences existed. And beyond the 'establishment', of course, there were the dissident underground groups, Etzel and Lehi, and the political forces that they represented.

This complex situation required unbending, unflinching determination. It is simpler sometimes to fight an external enemy than to stand up to challenges from within. Ben-Gurion never wavered in his insistence that the underground organizations should disband completely and that all fighting forces should be subordinate to the authority of the state and its civilian government. The undergrounds pledged to disband, but it was far from easy for them actually to do so.

The confrontation with Etzel came to a head in June 1948, just weeks after the creation of the state, with the arrival off the coast of Tel Aviv of the *Altalena*, a cargo vessel carrying arms purchased by the organization. Ben-Gurion insisted that all the arms be delivered to the Government. He suspected that Etzel would try to set up a state-within-a-state, or a separate army, or that it would try to establish its own state and army in the area of Palestine not incorporated into Israel. In any event, he failed to understand why Etzel, which said it was prepared to accept the sovereign authority of the new state, was not prepared to accept the Government's orders in this matter. He felt that any hesitation on his part, any misunderstanding or show of weakness in the negotiations with Etzel, would be taken by the outside world, and especially by the Arab world, as evidence that Israel was not united under an authoritative government. He issued unequivocal orders to the army to seize the ship and her cargo.

The actual negotiations with Etzel were handled by Galili, who reported back to Ben-Gurion and Eshkol several times a day. The tension at army headquarters, which were now in Ramat Gan, north of Tel Aviv, mounted hourly. It was no simple matter to give orders to shell the ship. The people on board were Jews, after all, and the arms were desperately needed. There were those who feared the outbreak of a civil war, in the midst of a bitter national war. Some of these, among them Interior Minister Yitzhak Gruenbaum, the General Zionist Party leader, pressed Ben-Gurion to relent and find a compromise. But however cruel this may sound, a compromise is sometimes the worst of all possible solutions and leads to precisely the opposite results from those intended. I am entirely convinced that if Ben-Gurion had not firmly adhered to his belief that state authority is indivisible, the danger of a civil war would have increased immeasurably. The dissenting underground groups, after all, had long been used to having their own policy and to operating outside the national political structure.

I spent those fateful hours with Ben-Gurion and Eshkol. The night before the ship was shelled, I slept alongside them, a rifle at hand, in case the army headquarters were stormed by protesters.

In the end, the Etzel commander, Menachem Begin, went aboard the *Altalena* and eventually agreed to Ben-Gurion's conditions. I watched Ben-Gurion listening to Begin's hysterical speech from the ship on the radio, after the episode ended. Begin claimed that IDF snipers had been ordered to assassinate him: 'But a great idea cannot be destroyed by killing the messenger . . .' Ben-Gurion reacted with contempt.

The episode troubled Begin for the rest of his life. He raised it with me twenty-five years later, in a private conversation which we had after the Six Day War (during the war he served as a Minister in the Government of National Unity under Eshkol). I explained to him at length what Ben-Gurion's considerations had been. He railed that he 'never had any intention of setting up an army within the army, or of refusing to accept the legal authority of the state'. I explained that the suspicion was not so much that he might challenge the state within its sovereign borders, but that he might try to establish a separate Jewish authority beyond the borders of the state, or possibly in Jerusalem, which was not to be a part of Israel under the partition plan. Begin denied this, too.

Although this conversation was supposed to have been private, Begin leaked it to a sympathetic journalist, who promptly published it, reporting, wrongly, that I had said that Ben-Gurion had 'made a mistake'. I had said nothing of the kind. Even in that conversation, so long after the event, Begin had failed to explain why he had not simply accepted the terms of the army high command and handed over the arms unconditionally.

In 1948, Lehi, a second dissident group, also challenged the new Government. One of its commanders, Natan Friedman-Yellin, was eventually prosecuted over the group's refusal to accept the state's authority. I gave evidence, based on an exchange of correspondence between the Haganah and Lehi.

The dissidents were by no means our only problem. Within the army high command itself, two groups squared off in a constant battle for influence and power. While the former Haganah commanders were loyal, devoted comrades, the ex-British army officers understood far better what a national army in a democratic society was all about. Ben-Gurion was determined to create a national army that would be unsullied by any party-political influences. He wanted an organized disciplined army, loyal to one hierarchy only – that of the high command, which was itself subordinate to the Government. Yet at the same time, for all his admiration of British democracy, he wanted our army to be different from the British army in two major respects. Firstly, he wanted it to be a pioneering army, with a social and a national role in addition to responsibility for defence. He believed that the new army should help both to absorb the immigrants and to settle the land. Soldiers would teach the newcomers Hebrew; they would also show them how to live and farm in the outlying areas. To this end, Ben-Gurion created the Nahal (the Hebrew acrostic for Pioneering Fighting Youth) as a brigade within the army. He saw it as the spiritual heir of the Palmach, whose units had also been based in kibbutzim and new settlements.

The second unique characteristic that Ben-Gurion sought to build into our army was an absence of the snobbery and pomposity that are so central to the traditions of the British army. He was against any decorations for soldiers or officers, arguing that courage and martial prowess ought to flow from inner motivation and, therefore, did not require outward signs of recognition.

The tension between the Haganah veterans and the young ex-British army officers was oppressive. Ben-Gurion was determined to make room for the second group, and not leave matters entirely to the former

Haganah commanders. The issue came to a head when Ben-Gurion ordered the disbandment of the Palmach. The ensuing storm was not confined to the Palmach itself or to the Haganah, but embraced large sections of public opinion – including opinion within Ben-Gurion's own party, Mapai. Once again, well-meaning people counselled him to compromise, but he stood as firm as a rock, defending his beliefs: one army, one hierarchy, one command structure.

He applied the same principles, too, when faced with demands by Orthodox politicians to set up separate Orthodox units in the army. They argued that Orthodox soldiers had to have kosher food and ought not to be required to desecrate the sabbath when no military emergency existed. Ben-Gurion's reply was to order the entire army to observe the religious laws of kosher food and sabbath observance. There would be no separate units, he insisted, of any kind.

Thus, Ben-Gurion was forced to fight on these various fronts sim-ultaneously throughout the War of Independence. He fought against the enemy without; he fought against the established order – in a bid to create new and healthier foundations for the state; and he fought against new challenges that arose during the course of the war. To see the war only from the Israeli–Arab perspective is to miss the full picture.

As in any political leadership, there was a formal hierarchy and a less formal structure of authority. In the running of the war itself, Ben-Gurion's authority was paramount, but beneath him the structure was flexible and changed in accordance with changing circumstances. Eshkol and Galili were effectively Ben-Gurion's deputies, even though they never bore these formal titles. When Galili left, Eshkol remained Ben-Gurion's right-hand man and, although only twenty-five years old, I was Eshkol's right-hand man, with my office in army headquarters. Gradually, I began to acquire my own areas of authority, and many of the senior officers turned to me for advice or direction, or to obtain the Government's approval for their various projects.

Formally, Dori was the Chief of Staff, but, as he was still chronically ill, his functions were discharged in practice by Yigael Yadin, who had previously served as Dori's aide-de-camp and then as chief of operations. Yadin was thirty-four years old at that time. He had been a promising archaeologist, the son of a famous professor of archaeology at the Hebrew University of Jerusalem. Ben-Gurion thought very highly of him indeed, partly because of Yadin's thorough knowledge of the Bible. Ben-Gurion had already decided that one of his goals as national leader would be to bring the People back to the Book, and the Book back to the People. Much of the military nomenclature developed at that time, including all the ranks, were taken or adapted from biblical Hebrew. Yadin saw himself as neither an ex-British officer nor an ex-Palmach commander, but as a biblical figure, a David standing against Goliath, or a Saul organizing a fighting army.

Often Ben-Gurion and Yadin would get into raging arguments, in the heat of a battle, over the interpretation of some obscure phrase in the Bible. Ben-Gurion cherished these sparring matches. Yadin was a charismatic figure who would make his points during strategy sessions with drama and force, his burning eyes surveying each participant in turn. He would prepare meticulously for every such meeting, mastering the issue down to the smallest details and compiling a cogent statement of his position.

But the quality in Yadin which won Ben-Gurion's admiration most of all was his totally impartial devotion to the state – and complete aloofness from all party-political considerations. He made a powerful impact on the entire General Staff, including Ben-Gurion himself, when he ordered the arrest of one of the top officials at the Ministry of Finance who had failed to appear for reserve duty. 'There are no special privileges in this army,' Yadin announced. 'Everyone is equal before the law.' Ben-Gurion, who fought a running battle against that common Jewish trait of 'doing people favours', which quickly grows into tendentiousness and discrimination, especially appreciated Yadin's uncompromising stand in this affair.

A feature of Yadin's personality which I myself found particularly admirable was his custom never to criticize Ben-Gurion behind his back – or to withhold criticism of the Premier to his face. There was hardly a meeting in which Yadin failed to criticize Ben-Gurion, his Government or his Ministers. He regarded the Government as an inefficient and convoluted body, wrapped up in irrelevant inter-party wrangling. The army, on the other hand, was an effective and streamlined machine, in his opinion. When someone once remarked to him that the army was basically a machine for cutting down trees, with scant knowledge of how hard it is to make trees grow, he flew into a rage, retorting that, 'If trees are planted properly, it's not hard for them to keep growing – and there's no need to cut them down.'

Despite the warm relationship between Ben-Gurion and Yadin, there were tensions between them too. Yadin believed that the key theatre in the war was the Egyptian front and that the top priority, therefore, was to liberate the Negev. For Ben-Gurion, however, the key, strategically as well as historically, was Jerusalem. He demanded that the army focus its main efforts on breaking the siege of Jerusalem. This dispute reached its high point during Operation Nahshon, which was to loosen the stranglehold on Jerusalem, and the bloody battles of Latrun in May 1948.

Interestingly, a similar dispute arose on the Jordanian side between King Abdullah and the commander of the Arab Legion, Glubb Pasha. Abdullah wanted to concentrate the main Jordanian effort on Jerusalem, while General Glubb favoured a combined thrust in the north with other Arab forces, driving from the River Jordan at Beit Shean towards Haifa in an attempt to cut Israel's spine in two.

7 NAVAL PERSON

We knew that the battle for Jerusalem would be determined in large part by our ability to keep the beleaguered city supplied with its basic needs, while supplying the units trying to break the siege with the weapons they required. Eshkol was in charge of both of these efforts, and I worked alongside him. I remember driving with him up to Latrun, where we helped to transfer sacks of flour from the trucks that had brought them from Tel Aviv on to smaller, hardier vehicles that could negotiate the famous 'Burma Road' – an alternative route to Jerusalem that the army had hacked through the hills. General Shimon Avidan, meanwhile, was massing his troops at Kibbutz Hulda nearby, ready to launch Operation Nahshon. But he did not have even enough rifles to arm all his men, let alone enough heavier weapons.

Our main hope lay in shipments of arms from Czechoslovakia, which were due to arrive at any minute. Russia and its satellites joined the international arms boycott against Israel, but Czechoslovakia was an exception. It agreed to sell us weapons of every kind – from Messerschmitt planes to Czech-made rifles – for a handsome price.

To the present day, it is hard to know for certain what prompted communist Czechoslovakia to sell us arms, to allow us to train our paratroopers on its soil, and to serve as a transit point for planes that we smuggled out of the United States. But it is clear that Czechoslovakia made a fundamental policy decision to maintain warm relations with the new Jewish state in secret, while adopting a posture of cool reserve in public. There were probably several factors at play. Shmuel Mikunis, the Israeli Communist Party leader, claimed that he was responsible for persuading the Kremlin to leave the Czech window open to us. No doubt our cash payments, in US dollars, had an effect too. Perhaps the

Czech communist leader, Rudolf Slansky, who was of Jewish descent (and was later tried and executed for treason and for an alleged 'Zionist conspiracy'), allowed personal sympathies to affect his decision-making.

One thing is certain: we had a team of the highest calibre handling our affairs in Czechoslovakia. The senior man was Ehud Avriel, one of the brightest of the bright young men whom Ben-Gurion gathered around him. A kibbutznik from the Lower Galilee, Avriel was endowed with a brilliant mind, a creative imagination, great personal charm and urbane manners. He was appointed Ambassador to Prague at the age of thirty-two, and won many Czechs to our cause – including communists. Avriel operated in Prague as though he were in Tel Aviv. All doors seemed to open before him. He issued documents, signed them, and handled himself with daring and aplomb.

The weaponry that reached us from Czechoslovakia was not uniformly reliable. The Messerschmitts, for instance, which were manufactured there under the Nazi occupation, were both expensive and hazardous. Their cannons were supposed to be synchronized with their propellers, but in several instances this system failed and the guns shot off the propeller blades, resulting in tragedy. The Czech heavy machine-guns, on the other hand, proved very effective indeed.

Above all, we were grateful for the Czech rifles, which were to be a staple in our army for years. When the Czechs, after much frustrating delay, eventually permitted the first shipment of these to be sent, we found to our horror that we had no ship available to take them. A Tel Aviv businessman, Efraim Ilin, came to our aid. He had been involved in arms procurement in Italy, and now he located an ancient tramp steamer which, he said, could be loaded with vegetables – with the rifles hidden beneath. The ship, the *Nora*, finally set out, at the maddening speed of four knots an hour. Then, to cap it all, we lost radio contact with her in the middle of the Mediterranean.

Eshkol joked that this was the first ship ever that had discovered that the sea, like the shore, comprised hills and valleys, and she was now making her way uphill as best she could. Eventually, though, she arrived off Tel Aviv and we all dashed down to the dock to greet the longed-for guns. They were taken by truck to Kibbutz Hulda, near Latrun, still wrapped in their oil-paper.

While Czechoslovakia was the main source of arms, it was not the sole source. A group of young American Jews who had served in the US air force decided to volunteer to fight in our war, in our air force, the IAF. Their leader was Al Schwimmer, one of the most courageous, most patriotic and most capable men I have ever known. He was a senior flight engineer with TWA and could certainly have pursued a brilliant career in aviation in America. But for Al, his people meant more to him than his pocket.

When he and his friends volunteered for service in the IDF, he was immediately appointed chief engineer of our air force. However, he soon learned that this was an air force with virtually no aeroplanes. He decided, therefore, that he and his friends would bring aeroplanes with them. To this end, he somehow took possession of three ex-USAF B-17 Flying Fortresses that happened to be in the Canary Islands. One bright morning, they all three suddenly took off – and landed in Czechoslovakia. There, they loaded up with weapons and took off again for Israel, bombing a column of Egyptian troops on the way for good measure.

Schwimmer was a man who knew no fear, a natural leader who inspired the men who worked under him. He was a walking encyclopedia of aviation, with an intimate, first-hand knowledge of the inner workings of virtually every plane that flew. He knew airports and flight routes too, and had friends in the aviation business in the most unlikely places. His contribution to the State of Israel was enormous, both during the War of Independence and later, when we created the Israel Aircraft Industries (IAI) and built it up into a vast and successful concern.

As a man of unshakable opinions, Schwimmer tended to clash with his superiors in the air force. The first commander of the IAF was Yisrael Amir, who had previously been commander of the Haganah intelligence service, the Shai. Amir was a decent and straightforward man, but he knew absolutely nothing about flying. He was later replaced by Aharon Remez, who had been a fighter pilot in the Royal Air Force, and thus had some knowledge and experience of aerial combat. Schwimmer had boundless faith in Ben-Gurion, and Ben-Gurion asked me to step in and try to mend the fractured relations between Schwimmer and his volunteers on the one hand, and the senior officers of the IAF on the other. Schwimmer and I struck up a close friendship, which has continued to this day, which underpinned our partnership in many different projects, and which eventually led to the creation of the IAI.

After Schwimmer arrived with the Flying Fortresses, it was decided that an 'air bridge' should be set up between Czechoslovakia and Israel, mainly using cargo planes (Dakotas and Constellations). The planes would land on dirt strips in the Negev, giving the operation its codename, Operation Dust. It was run by Munya Mardor, a key figure in the arms procurement programme who later headed the Weapons Research and Development Authority (Rafael in its Hebrew acronym). With him, too, I developed a close and productive friendship that lasted until his death.

Throughout the war, I relied on informal relations with people rather than on precise hierarchical demarcations to get things done. My authority, in practice, was wider than my formal position, but when Chief of Staff Dori suggested that he might promote me to the position of colonel, I refused. I thought the rank would hamper me.

In addition to Czechoslovakia, we had another major arms procurement centre in Italy, run by Yehuda Arazi, one of the most colourful and gifted men ever to serve the Jewish state. Arazi had a razor-sharp mind, inexhaustible resourcefulness and a flair for drama. He had been, on Haganah orders, an officer in the Mandatory police force and was thus responsible for many delicate and daring operations. He was the man who later made the world hold its breath, when, as captain of the *Exodus*, he defied the might of the Royal Navy. He led his refugee passengers in their headline-making hunger-strike while anchored off Naples, conducting a cogent and heart-rending debate with Harold Laski, the British Labour Party Chairman, who came to the Italian port to study the situation of the ship and her passengers. Arazi was not only fluent in several languages, but he could also find the right images and metaphors in each of them to illustrate and press home his point.

He also had a knack for winning exceptional men to our cause. One of these was an Italian naval officer named Capriotti who, in addition to being a brave and able seaman, was also the owner of a dockyard that specialized in speed-boats and pocket submarines. Our little navy had a soft spot for such craft. One of the most successful missions in the war in fact occurred when a speed-boat packed with dynamite was used to sink the *Farouk*, an Egyptian warship.

Arazi also put us in touch with a Polish count named Stefan Czernitsky, another remarkable individual who supplied us with arms for a 10 per cent commission. Stefan was the brother of the Polish commander whose forces were swept aside by the Nazi *blitzkrieg* in 1939. From that day on, Stefan always wore a black tie as a sign of mourning. He lived in a gorgeous palace outside Paris called Malmaison, which had originally been built by Napoleon as a gift to Josephine. He was married to a beautiful Polish actress, and the couple gave lavish dinner parties, with fine crystal and golden cutlery. The palace had a king-size swimming-pool, which various emissaries of ours would make use of during the long, hot, Parisian summers.

Czernitsky was always meticulously dressed in the height of fashion, with never a crease or a mark on his clothes. His mother-tongue was Polish, but he also spoke a passable French. He knew everyone: ministers, diplomats, businessmen and shipowners in every country in Europe. He was a good organizer and usually reliable. He worshipped Yehuda Arazi, but later, when he came under the control of Pinhas Sapir, he developed a relationship with him too, addressing him in flowing Polish.

Sadly, it fell to me eventually to sever the link between Israel and Czernitsky. When I became Director-General of the Ministry of Defence in 1952, we were buying arms through him to the value of $100 million or more, which meant that he was earning $10 million from us in commission – a very sizeable sum in those days, and one I hardly felt I could justify. I asked him why he demanded such large sums, and he replied that he needed the money to 'soften' certain key Cabinet Ministers. I asked him who they were, but he refused to give me names. I said that if he would not give the names, I would be forced to cease our relationship. Eventually – and unluckily for him – he volunteered the name of Paul Reynaud, the pre-war anti-appeasement leader, who was Deputy Prime Minister of France at this time. I asked him to arrange a meeting for me with Reynaud, assuring him that I would say nothing at all about arms sales. He said that he would do so immediately.

Months passed, and I heard nothing from him. Finally, during a visit to Paris, I called Reynaud up directly and asked to see him. He received me in his office on the same day. He was seventy-four years old by this time, but had recently married and his wife had given birth to a baby boy. Reynaud rode a motor-bike, in order to prove, as he put it, that there are people who determine their own age and deny Father Time the right to dictate it to them. I remember the powerful impact that this particular passage in Reynaud's autobiography made on Ben-Gurion.

Our meeting was cordial. He expressed warm sympathy for Israel. He plainly had no idea that Israel wished to buy arms from France – and when he heard, he immediately offered his help. He made no conditions and asked for no recompense. He simply wanted a list of the items we needed. A few days later, we received, for the first time ever, a formal French government authorization to purchase French-made artillery pieces.

Meanwhile, Czernitsky was entirely unaware of these developments and kept promising that the meeting with Reynaud would take place 'very soon'. I had no choice but to dispense with his services, though I was truly sorry that his relationship with Israel had to end in this way. Under the most unfavourable conditions he had helped Arazi obtain artillery pieces, anti-aircraft guns, machine-guns and other much-needed weaponry.

Arazi was a man who seemed to need less sleep than ordinary mortals. He could regale a group of friends with fascinating anecdotes all night and show no signs of wear in the morning. But he was also a man of sterling principles, and his burning zeal would surprise people when it suddenly flashed forth. One such occasion was during the Toubiansky Affair, the case of a Haganah commander who was accused, in 1948, of having spied for the British. He was summarily tried by court martial and sentenced to death. Arazi arrived in Israel at this time for a brief visit, and I shall never forget how he stormed into my office, straight from the airport, at the dead of night, announcing that 'Toubiansky is innocent – he never committed treason.'

I asked him how he was so certain. He said that he had investigated the affair in his own way and was completely confident 'that no Jew would betray his people at a time like this'. He demanded that I go at once to Shaul Avigur and to Ben-Gurion to convince them of Toubiansky's innocence.

I went, but it was too late. The sentence had been carried out. There was some consolation, however, in the fact that Ben-Gurion took a decision which only a leader of his stature would have been capable of taking: to set up a new inquiry and review the entire case once again. This second investigation revealed that there had been no solid basis to the accusations levelled against Toubiansky. His execution had been a miscarriage of justice. Yehuda Arazi was right.

During the War of Independence, the initial structure of the defence forces included Secretaries of the air force and the navy, in addition to the air force and navy commanders. The system was presumably modelled on the American one. The Secretary of the air force, a pleasant and personable man named Haim Isacharov, concentrated his attention on procurement. He was well liked within the force and did his utmost to provide it with the best planes available.

In the navy, however, the situation was less felicitous. The commander was Paul Shulman, who had served in the US navy and whose mother, Rivka, was a prominent figure in the women's Zionist organization. When he immigrated to Israel, Ben-Gurion invited him to head the navy, in spite of the fact that he only spoke English. Shulman had strong ideas of what his job entailed and of how he ought to be doing it.

The Secretary of the navy, Gershon Zak, was an entirely different breed. He had been Levi Eshkol's chief assistant at the Tel Aviv Labour Council and had set up a movement of 'non-party members' who supported Ben-Gurion's Mapai. Although a first-rate organizer, Zak always had a penchant for minor exhibitionism. When he was appointed Secretary of the navy, he quickly ensconced himself in a suite of offices at the naval headquarters near Haifa and set up a smaller bureau in the Defence Ministry in Tel Aviv. He worked hard to build the navy into a credible fighting force, but he also gave way to his weakness for pomp, ordering a special pennant to be designed for him and insisting that it fly at all times from his official car. His relations with the no-nonsense navy commander grew progressively worse, and soon became the talk of the force.

One day, a fire broke out at the naval stores on Mount Carmel. Fishman, the chief quartermaster, was accused of negligence, and since he was a Zak appointee, the critical broadside was aimed at Zak too. Zak was also criticized for his involvement in an unauthorized purchase, from Canada, of an aircraft carrier. Although converted to civilian use after the Second World War, its Israeli buyers hoped to return it to its original military purpose. But their ambitious plan took no account of the fact that Israel had no aeroplanes capable of landing or taking off on an aircraft carrier. To our great good fortune, the ship sank at sea, and the insurance money that we received covered the original, misguided outlay.

These various episodes eventually led to a complete rupture between Zak and Shulman, and Ben-Gurion instructed Chief of Staff Dori and Shaul Avigur to investigate the situation and to recommend a solution. Their recommendation was that my friend Munya Mardor and I replace Shulman and Zak respectively, as a temporary measure.

So there I was, a twenty-six-year-old kibbutznik from Alumot with the rank of private, running complex defence programmes and then, on top of everything else, becoming the acting Secretary of the navy. My naval experience consisted of a moderate proficiency at breast-stroke and one childhood attempt to build a raft and launch it off the coast of Tel

Aviv. I was weighed down, moreover, with all my other duties: arms procurements, arms production, intelligence, research and development.

Gershon Zak duly transferred the two bureaux and the car with the pennant. But my relations with Mardor were too close for any such formality. The two of us, working in harmony, quickly managed to put the navy back on its sea-legs. We bought motor-torpedo boats, corvettes and submarines in Canada. We even managed to furnish the officers with silver-plated insignia of rank, no mean feat in those days. Soon after, an earthquake struck Greece and all the fleets of the Mediterranean steamed towards Athens to offer assistance. We decided to send our modest corvettes, too. When the King of Greece held a reception for all the visiting officers, our men were able to turn out proudly in their dress uniforms and shining metal epaulettes. At one point, a senior British officer approached them. 'What country are you from?' he asked, looking uncertainly at their resplendent uniforms.

'Israel.'

'Where the hell's that?' asked the distinguished Englishman.

'Israel is what used to be Palestine,' our officer replied.

'Ah yes, Palestine,' the Royal Navy man replied. 'Are the Jews still making trouble there?'

After the war, I began to be troubled by the gap between the level of my responsibilities and the level of my education. I felt that the gap would grow unless I did something to narrow it, and decided that this was the time – perhaps the last time – for me to take action. I approached Ben-Gurion, and he agreed to my being sent abroad for a period of work and study.

Accordingly, in 1949, Sonia and I took up residence in New York with our little daughter Zviya for what was to be two-year stay. I was appointed deputy head of the Defence Ministry's mission in New York, and later head of the mission. Our tasks were to enlist people and to purchase equipment – all within the general purpose of building a modern and self-sufficient fighting force.

My other, private purpose I pursued through diligent attendance at night classes at the New School for Social Research, near Greenwich Village. This was a most remarkable institution. Its faculty included such luminaries as Justice Felix Frankfurter, Reinhold Niebuhr and Max Lerner (who turned out to be a distant relative of mine). Their lectures were few and far between, but every one of them was a memorable event. I shall never forget Frankfurter's eulogy of his friend Harold Laski, the British socialist ideologue. It reminded me of Berl Katznelson's eulogy of Chaim Arlosoroff:* a great man, no longer young, mourning a friend, full of promise, who died while still unfulfilled. From Reinhold Niebuhr I heard lectures on the foundations of Jewish and Greek culture, which left me spellbound. At first, though, I had to grapple with nightly depression brought on by the frustrating inadequacy of my English.

We lived in a seven-room apartment on Riverside Drive at 95th Street, from which we could gaze down and watch the Hudson River changing colours in time with the weather and the seasons of the year. Since our flat was large, we could set up a sort of kibbutz-commune for a number of bachelors working in New York or passing through. Among these was Gad Hilb, the captain of a Zim† ship; Micha Peri, a Palmach commander during the war; and Ya'acov (Shapik) Shapira, who was my deputy at the defence mission. Sonia would make breakfast for us all on those long, lazy, Sunday mornings, and we would bury ourselves in the endless sections of the *New York Times* before going out to Radio City or to a show on Broadway. A rigorous rota determined who baby-sat for Zviya.

After two years in New York, I moved to Boston for a four-month course in advanced management at Harvard University. Another Israeli in this programme was Aharon Remez, commander of our air force. All the students were senior executives, trades-union officials or army officers from various units of the US armed services. It was a concentrated learning experience, in which one could absorb knowledge and enrichment from one's fellow students as well as from the lecturers. We learned without let-up, from proper deportment at a cocktail party (this was the first time I tasted whisky) to in-depth case studies in policy and administration.

Looking back now, I see my entire stay in America as a period of constant and concentrated learning, in myriad forms. It was a formative period both in my life and in my intellectual and political development. My own desire to learn was matched by the unparalleled opportunity offered to me – both by the schools in New York and Boston and by the full and varied cultural life of these two cities. Every corner of that great country presents fascinating information and insights for the curious

---

* A prominent Labour Zionist leader in Palestine, assassinated in 1934, at the age of thirty-three.
† Israel's government-owned shipping line.

observer. I was immediately swept up by the originality, ingenuity and boundless enthusiasm of the people, especially the young. The elevator attendant at our office, in the Fisk Building on Broadway and 57th Street, came to stand, in my mind, as an example of the pride that people take in their work in America. I noted with interest and humility his starched uniform and shining buttons, and was impressed by the pride he took in knowing and greeting all of his passengers personally. He opened the doors and called out the floors as if he were a rabbi opening the Holy Ark in the synagogue and chanting the prayers.

In the process of my discovery of America, I thought a lot about Columbus. I decided that the New World did not come into being as a result of his discovery, but that the essence of the New World, of America, was the mass immigration to its shores from the Old World, an immigration that reflected rebellion against both religious intolerance and feudalism. America is not so much a continent as a constitution. It was not so much discovered as created. Men like Thomas Jefferson, Benjamin Franklin and Abraham Lincoln, the shapers of the Constitution, were the men who moulded the new reality, unprecedented in human history, that is America.

Within two centuries of its birth, America became the strongest state on earth. But it grew to this great strength along entirely new lines. The Constitution sought to strike a fine balance between the rights of the individual and his duty to society, between religious tolerance and ethnic identity, between generosity and originality. An objective survey of America's relatively brief history yields a remarkable conclusion: what has been achieved in practice is not markedly inferior or significantly different from the plans that the architects of the republic conceived in theory more than two centuries ago.

The United States of America has fought many wars. Its young men have poured out their blood on the soil of Europe, on the islands of Asia and on the shores of other lands in their own hemisphere. In almost every war, America emerged triumphant. In almost every war, it conquered territories. But in none of them did it even attempt to retain either territories or resources, or to rule over another nation. America overcame two terrible foes: it defeated Japan and gave the Japanese people democracy; and it crushed Germany and liberated Germany from Nazism – though as Jews there will always be a bitter complaint in our hearts that America did not do more to rescue the victims of the Nazi Holocaust. America's young men have gone off to battle, time after time, not when America was endangered, but when freedom and democracy were endangered.

The United States has become the richest nation on earth, but it has not become a greedy nation. The federal Government, Congress and individual American citizens have distinguished themselves by their altruism and generosity. Aid to others, whether philanthropic, material or spiritual, is a hallmark of the American ethos. Never in history has there been such a magnanimous world power.

The United States has plenty of problems of its own, yet it does not turn its back on the problems of others. True, there has always been an isolationist school active in American public life, but that school has invariably been overwhelmed by the majority's sense of idealism and of responsibility towards the fates of individuals and of free societies throughout the world. No great empire – neither the Greek nor the Roman nor the British nor the French – was endowed with these qualities. America, for its part, could easily have become an empire like the others, had it wished to do so. But it never wished to.

Americans are often described as a pragmatic people, but I am not convinced by that characterization. Despite all the materialism in American society, it is not the dollar that is the strong underpinning of that society but the Bible, both the New Testament and the Old.

By the same token, the basis of the special relationship that developed between the United States and Israel was not a common enemy, but rather common values. I was never convinced by grandiose talk of a 'strategic alliance' between the Americans and ourselves, not even at the height of the Cold War. I never believed that the United States needed us on its side in the global confrontation with the Soviet Union – nor that Washington sought a place alongside us in our conflict with the Arabs. True, the United States stood by us against the Arab threat. True, that threat resulted in conflicts in which the IDF repeatedly demonstrated the superiority of American weapons over Soviet-built armaments. But the two types of weaponry seemed to me to carry an ideological message: the American planners were concerned with the safety and comfort of the pilot or tank-crew; their Soviet counterparts were concerned above all with communist statistics – with building as many planes or tanks as they could.

8 AFFAIRS OF STATE

By the early 1950s, Ben-Gurion began to show signs of fatigue. It was hard to know what was troubling him more – philosophical concerns or biological problems.

Philosophically, he was afraid of becoming jaded by the routine of his job, by the 'more-of-the-same' syndrome. He felt that he was repeating himself: dealing with the same questions every day or every week, confronting the same issues. Ben-Gurion was essentially a revolutionary, a leader who found it hard to live at peace with the status quo.

At this time, too, he began taking an interest in biology. His daughter, Renana, worked in a biological research institute, and with her help he embarked on a thorough study of this science. To his shock and profound dismay, he learned that while the human body is based on the mutation of cells, there are two types of cells that do not regenerate: brain cells and tooth cells. Whenever he found himself forgetting a name or a place, he would sink into the deepest despondency – because some brain cells had died and would not be replaced by new ones. As he saw it, the ageing process was affecting him and eroding his intellectual faculties.

The effects of monotony and of ageing were Ben-Gurion's two major worries at that time. They led him to think about quitting, or at least cutting down his daily workload (in 1953, he was sixty-seven years old). The next question, naturally, was who would take over from him – particularly in his capacity as Defence Minister, which he regarded as equally important to, if not more important than, his role as Prime Minister. He believed that the Jewish People had no shortage of visionary leaders, but he felt that there was a definite dearth of realistic statesmen, by which he meant men endowed with both visionary leadership and the practical ability to get things done. A visionary without executive ability remains, at the end of the day, merely a theoretician, whereas the technocrat bereft of vision is in danger of succumbing to unprincipled opportunism.

I do not think it would be out of place to say that I had a role in Ben-Gurion's choice of the next Defence Minister – and thus a role in one of the greatest mistakes in the history of Israel. It was a mistake with repercussions that continued to affect politics and public life for decades. It was I who first began persuading Ben-Gurion that he should choose Pinhas Lavon for his replacement as Defence Minister. We had returned from America in 1952, and I immediately resumed working in the Ministry, as Deputy Director-General. I consulted both Moshe Dayan, who was Chief of Operations in the army General Staff and was soon to become Chief of Staff, and Haim Laskov, another top army officer, about Lavon. In fact, I took Laskov to see Lavon and to brief him on the state of the army, and Laskov came away much impressed – which strengthened my own conviction that Lavon was the right man for the job.

Lavon was Minister of Agriculture at this time. He had been Secretary of the Hever Hakvutzot kibbutz movement when I was a member of the Secretariat. I admired his analytical powers, his rhetorical skills and his ability to stand up for his opinions. I felt that the army, headed as it was by young and gifted men, and dependent on the high morale of these men for its strength and success, could benefit from Lavon's leadership. He could provide the right kind of ideological inspiration to sustain morale in the delicate situation of no-peace-no-war that we had settled into following the War of Independence. Lavon also took a keen and intelligent interest in economic and strategic issues. He did his homework and spoke with authority. My own relations with him were excellent, and I thought that he, Dayan and I could work well together at the helm of the defence establishment.

Ben-Gurion began, with the help of a highly regarded professional army officer named Shalom (Fritz) Eshet, an in-depth review of the army and the defence establishment, with a view to formulating a comprehensive plan for the years ahead. (This was later published as Ben-Gurion's 'Eighteen-Point Plan'.) After submitting this, Ben-Gurion formally resigned and took up residence with his wife, Paula, in the remote Negev kibbutz of Sde Boker. Moshe Sharett, the Foreign Minister, who had been the most prominent spokesman and diplomat of the pre-state *Yishuv* as Chairman of the Jewish Agency's Political Department, took over as Prime Minister; and Lavon was confirmed as Minister of Defence.

My relations with Sharett were poor to begin with, and they were only to get worse. He regarded me as Ben-Gurion's man, which was true, but also believed that I sought to interfere with the running of Israel's foreign affairs to satisfy my personal ambition, which was absolutely false. For him, I was one of 'Ben-Gurion's boys' and, therefore, could not be trusted. He did not understand that what I was trying to do – in the evolving 'back-channel' relationship with France, for instance – was to break the arms embargo that threatened to choke the country.

I was not one of the small group of Foreign Ministry officials whom Sharett admired. These were all native English-speakers or urbane Central Europeans, schooled in the niceties of diplomatic etiquette. Some had worked for him back in pre-state days; others were enlisted later. Sharett had welded these men into the nucleus of Israel's foreign service; I patently did not fit the bill.

As for Lavon, it quickly became clear, to me at any rate, that we had made a ghastly mistake. Lavon had been hitherto thought of as a 'dove', but no sooner had he taken over the Defence Ministry than he began to exhibit frighteningly 'hawkish' tendencies. I think that he felt the need to compete against the man who outshone everyone else at that time – Moshe Dayan. Lavon wanted to impress upon the army that it was he, rather than Dayan, who was setting the tone and making the decisions in military matters. This attitude led him to take disastrous decisions. One obvious example was an IDF reprisal action against the Jordanians in October 1953, following the murder of an Israeli family by infiltrators from across the border. Sixty-nine civilians in the village of Kibiye were killed in that action, and Israel suffered a stinging and unanimous condemnation at the United Nations. Another was his insistence that a special unit, previously jointly subordinate to the Defence Minister and the Foreign Minister, now come under his exclusive jurisdiction. In the final analysis, the fatal blunder in Egypt was also a product of Lavon's adventurist and truculent frame of mind.

Lavon developed obsessive suspicions. He suspected Dayan and me of constantly conspiring against him. One minor but telling example of the atmosphere generated by Lavon's distrust concerned a leading American watch company, Bulova, which had set up a plant in Tel Aviv, that eventually went bankrupt. I met the firm's Israeli representative, Joe

Buxenbaum, with a view to acquiring the plant for the Military Industries (which were a wholly owned subsidiary of the Ministry of Defence). Naturally, I reported back to Lavon. He said that he wanted to think it over, but the Managing Director of the Military Industries, Zvi Dar, went ahead and signed a contract with Buxenbaum without informing me while Lavon was still thinking it over. I frankly saw no great disaster in this as I thought that the deal was basically good for us. But when Lavon happened to meet Buxenbaum, who told him *en passant* that he had signed with Dar, he immediately concluded that a major act of duplicity had been perpetrated; he saw himself as the victim of a conspiracy spearheaded by me. All that had in fact happened was that there had been a bureaucratic crossed-wire, an event that occurs from time to time in any administration; no one was to blame and no sinister double-cross had been intended.

Lavon also suspected me and my colleagues of concluding arms deals with France behind his back. On one occasion in 1954, Dayan threatened to resign when Lavon tried to reverse a decision to buy French tanks. 'It's crazy to hitch ourselves to the French wagon,' Lavon railed. I replied quietly that no other wagons were lining up for us to hitch up to. In military matters, he suspected Dayan of keeping things from him and acting without his authority. He decided to run the entire defence establishment on his own – both the economic side and the military – because he could rely on neither Dayan nor myself. Meanwhile, his hawkishness was building up into a veritable allergy towards the Americans and the British. Here, too, suspicion and distrust were the main features of his policy. He believed that the Americans and the British were out to trap us.

I was frankly stunned that a man as clever as Lavon should have developed such an outlook. His paranoia is exemplified by an incident which occurred in 1953, when the US army head of intelligence visited Israel, and Binyamin Gibli, the head of our military intelligence, held a cocktail party for him. In his speech, the guest of honour said that he was enormously impressed by what he had seen here. He had not known, he said, that Jews could be such good farmers and soldiers. For Lavon, this was positive proof of the anti-Semitism which, he said, pervaded the American military. 'This is why we can never rely on them,' he solemnly warned his aides.

I cite this minor incident as an illustration of the attitude Lavon was adopting towards the Western powers. This attitude informed his policy-making: he believed that as the Americans were acting against us, we should act against them.

It was in this context that discussions opened as to whether we (Israel) could do anything to disrupt American relations with Egypt. The idea was that by causing unrest in Egypt and by provoking tension between Egypt and the Western powers, it was hoped that we would bring about the cancellation or deferment of Britain's commitment, given during negotiations with Nasser, to withdraw its forces from the Suez Canal Zone. I was present at several such discussions, which took place, *inter alia*, at the weekly Minister's Staff Meetings. The regular participants were the Minister (Lavon), the army Chief of Staff (Dayan), his deputy (General Yosef Avidar), the Director-General of the Ministry (myself) and my own deputy (when I had one). Individual officers such as Gibli would be asked to attend from time to time, when specific issues of direct concern to them were brought up. No order was ever issued in my presence actually to carry out any such action, but certainly there was discussion of what Israel could do against American interests or facilities in Egypt that would create tension and alienation between the two countries. I expressed reservations about the entire idea. But it did not surprise me, later, that some of the men who had heard Lavon at such meetings came to believe that a covert operation would accord with the Minister's new *weltanschauung*. I cannot say – and I want to make this totally clear – that I ever heard such specific order from Lavon's mouth, but the general policy-direction was there; it was present in the air at those meetings.

The 'unfortunate mishap' itself, as the event was euphemistically and mysteriously referred to – due to censorship restrictions – in the press, took place in July 1954. Two groups of young Egyptian Zionist Jews, one in Cairo and the other in Alexandria, tried to plant incendiary devices in American libraries and other public places. The amateurish devices either failed to explode or caused only minor damage. In Alexandria, one of the would-be firebombers was arrested when the bomb he was carrying caught fire in his pocket. Soon, the other members of the two groups were rounded up.

A public trial ended in January 1955 with death sentences for two of the activists – Shmuel Azar and Dr Moussa Marzuk – and long jail terms for six others. An Israeli agent operating in Egypt, Major Max Bennet, was also captured as a result of this episode and committed suicide in prison.

In Israel (which officially denied any knowledge of or involvement in the affair), a commission of inquiry was set up to determine who had ordered the operation. Lavon insisted that he had not, Dayan was out of the country at the time, and Gibli maintained that he had received the order from Lavon. This commission – it was to be the first of many – was comprised of the former IDF Chief of Staff, Yaacov Dori, and the President of the Supreme Court, Yitzhak Olshan. On 13 January 1955, it submitted the following inconclusive statement: 'We were not convinced beyond reasonable doubt that the head of military intelligence did not receive the order from the Minister of Defence. At the same time, we are not sure that the Minister of Defence did give the order attributed to him.'

Years later, it became clear that Avri (Zeidman) Elad, the Israeli agent who commanded the groups in Egypt and escaped unscathed, was a double-agent. In fact, I remember how shocked I was when I first heard that he had been enlisted and sent to Egypt on our behalf. I couldn't believe it. I had known him for years: he was a pupil at Ben-Shemen, in the class below me, and also continued to Kibbutz Alumot. Even then, he was a crook – and had actually been caught red-handed. As I have already mentioned, it was my job as kibbutz treasurer to go off one day each week to Tel Aviv, to do the rounds of the various offices and suppliers. On one of these occasions, I was about to board the bus to Tel Aviv when I found that I had no money to pay for my ticket. My wallet was empty. Later, its contents were discovered, still bearing the three-fold imprint of my wallet, in the possession of Elad. There were many other episodes that led me to doubt his integrity. Therefore, I was both surprised and dismayed to find that he had made his way into our intelligence service.

After the arrests in Egypt and the repercussions of the disaster began to send their first tremors through the defence establishment in Israel, I found myself personally involved in two ways. Firstly, the affair leaked out, in a deliberately obscure and esoteric form, in a poem published by the leading poet Nathan Alterman in his widely read and enormously influential weekly newspaper column – and Prime Minister Sharett immediately concluded that I was responsible. I demanded an inquiry, and indeed, months later, Sharett called me in and apologized, admitting that there was no evidence linking me with the leak. In fact, the source of the leak was not in the Ministry of Defence but in the army.

Secondly, and of longer-term significance, Lavon accused me of disloyalty to him, claiming that I had allegedly 'concealed' from him the evidence that I gave to the Olshan–Dori commission. I had been summoned by the commission and solemnly warned by Justice Olshan that everything that transpired there must remain secret – even the very fact that I had testified. Replying to the commission's specific and detailed questions, I told them everything I knew, describing the proceedings at the Minister's Staff Meetings which I had attended. Lavon, however, accused me of volunteering to testify before the commission, and of refusing to disclose my testimony to him, even though I was legally entitled to do so. His implication was that I had testified against him. Olshan, by the way, in his memoirs,* justified my behaviour completely.

Lavon's accusations fuelled the growing political pressure against me from within the Mapai leadership. Zalman Aran, a senior Minister, called me in, for instance, and suggested matter-of-factly that I 'take a ticket and travel around the world for six months' before coming back to resume my position. 'Ziama,' I replied, 'why should I leave and let others make me the scapegoat for this whole affair?' I felt as though they were trussing me up as the sacrifice. From Aran, I went straight to Moshe Dayan, and we agreed to stand together in this matter. Lavon was demanding that Dayan should also be dismissed as his 'condition' for staying on at the Defence Ministry. Sharett wavered for some time – this was during January–February 1955 – between his own desire to get rid of Lavon, whom he saw as ministerially responsible, if not directly to blame, for the Cairo disaster, and the old guard's reluctance to unleash a public storm before the elections that were due in that year.

Between Dayan and me everything was open and on the table. There was no scheming, no dissimulating and no 'deals'. From time to time, we would go down to Sde Boker to see Ben-Gurion, but we never involved him in all these goings-on, neither before the disaster in Egypt nor in its aftermath. The stories that Ben-Gurion somehow 'pulled the strings' in the Government or the army even after he left power are simply unfounded.

For me, these were some of the hardest months of my life. I was young and seen as dangerously ambitious. I felt that I was being 'set up' as the fall-guy for the Mapai establishment. All those who were against Ben-Gurion, but did not dare to attack him publicly, attacked me instead.

* *Din Udevarim – Memoirs* (Schocken, Tel Aviv, 1978).

They spun a web of lies and rumours to the effect that we were planning a 'revolution' in the party.

The truth was that we were a group of young people, active in public life, who shared a perspective on politics and government. The group consisted of Dayan, myself, Teddy Kollek (sometimes), Ehud Avriel, Abba Eban and others. We would meet and talk about what was going on and what ought to be done. The media – and especially one scurrilous magazine called *Haolam Hazeh* – carried fanciful and entirely groundless reports about how we were plotting some sort of coup against the party old guard; and the old guard themselves believed them. After all, this particular period has to be seen in the broader context of the old guard's basic suspicion that Ben-Gurion was grooming a 'young guard' – people like Dayan and myself – to take over the leadership and effectively marginalize them.

That, by the way, was equally fanciful and groundless. Certainly, Ben-Gurion sought out bright young men and put them in positions of responsibility, but he never meant to leap-frog them over the old guard. He regarded himself as an integral part of that old guard and never intended for us youngsters to elbow the old guard out of office.

Levi Eshkol, and to a certain extent Golda Meir too, had always been deeply ambivalent about Lavon, and in the wake of the 'mishap' the two of them led a growing body of opinion in the top echelon of the party that demanded his removal. Lavon stepped down in February 1955. Later, by way of 'compensation', he was made Secretary-General of the Histadrut.

The Mapai elders sent a delegation to Sde Boker to persuade Ben-Gurion to return to the Defence Ministry. He acceded to the call of the party and served as Defence Minister under Sharett until an election in July of that year, after which he resumed his rightful mantle as party leader and Prime Minister.

The Lavon Affair, or simply The Affair as it came to be know, burst forth upon the political community and the general public five years later. Lavon received new evidence from an army officer, which, he claimed, completely exonerated him from the suspicion of having given The Order. He demanded that Ben-Gurion take steps formally to clear his name. Ben-Gurion set up another commission of inquiry, comprising Supreme Court Justice Haim Cohn and two army officers. Meanwhile, Lavon testified before the Knesset Foreign Affairs and Defence Committee, and his evidence, in which he blamed Gibli for the 'mishap' and accused him and others of an elaborate cover-up, was leaked to the press, triggering an unprecedented furore. While the precise facts of the 'mishap' were still censored, the public learned of a profound and widening split within the ruling party. Lavon, backed by most of the Mapai old guard, claimed that he was being victimized by Ben-Gurion and his young cohorts (myself among them). Ben-Gurion, for his part, insisted that Lavon could only be exonerated – or indicted – by a judicial inquiry.

The Affair reached its crescendo towards the end of 1960, when the Cabinet overruled Ben-Gurion and set up a seven-man ministerial commission of inquiry. This panel found for Lavon. 'He did not give The Order,' the seven Ministers wrote, 'and the "mishap" took place without his knowledge.' Ben-Gurion, furious, insisted that 'Ministers cannot be judges' – and resigned.

To placate him, the party central committee fired Lavon from his post as Secretary-General of the Histadrut. Eventually, Ben-Gurion was persuaded to stay on as Prime Minister and, after elections later in 1961, we formed a new Mapai-led coalition, which held power until his final resignation in June 1963. But The Affair had irreparably corroded relations within the Mapai leadership. Ben-Gurion developed a profound animosity towards his longtime colleague and chosen successor, Eshkol, after Eshkol refused to reopen The Affair yet again, in 1964, on the basis of new evidence that had come to light at that time. Ben-Gurion demanded a judicial commission. Eshkol, with the party majority now behind him, refused. Moreover, Eshkol urged the party to rehabilitate Lavon, which it duly did in a central committee decision in May 1964. The Affair continued to tear at the heart of Mapai. Ben-Gurion and his followers set up their own ginger-group, still within the party ranks, but a fully fledged schism grew inexorably closer.

David Ben-Gurion was a leader who valued and respected the law. He had studied law before the First World War in Constantinople, and throughout the subsequent years he worked to make the principles of Anglo-Saxon democracy and jurisprudence – especially the separation of powers – the basis of Israel's political system. He was deeply influenced by Abraham Lincoln, and would often cite the Gettysburg Address, explaining that a tyrant too can claim to be 'of the people' and to rule 'for the people', but that his rule is not 'by the people'. Similarly, a government can claim to rule 'by the people' while not truly ruling 'for the people'.

Ben-Gurion also saw his role as the defender of the army's honour. He believed that unless the army retained the devotion and respect of the people, it would be hard to expect young soldiers and officers to risk their lives and sustain high morale. He did not believe that the best army officers sought personal fame and glory, but rather that they needed the confidence of the civilian leadership and the admiration of the broader public.

All of these principles came into focus in the Lavon Affair. Ben-Gurion felt uncomfortable with Lavon's attempt to cast all the blame on a senior army officer while taking none of it on his own shoulders. Instinctively, Ben-Gurion felt that a Minister of Defence is not solely someone who takes the credit for military successes, but one who also takes responsibility for the failures. Thus, on the one hand, he did not like Lavon's attitude, but on the other, he was not prepared to determine an issue that was essentially judicial, when he himself was part of the executive branch. He felt that there was room for doubt, and was prepared to leave that doubt open.

But Lavon insisted on being totally exonerated, demanding that the entire blame be laid on Gibli, all without due judicial process. For Ben-Gurion, however, this violated one of the fundamental tenets of constitutional democracy.

There was also another factor in Ben-Gurion's position, which many people at the time found it difficult to understand. Ben-Gurion deeply feared what he felt was a character trait present among the Jewish People: a tendency to acquiesce in dishonesty, to forgive and forget untruth. He believed this stemmed from the Jewish People's predisposition for mercy. Jews tend to be forgiving and understanding, but Ben-Gurion believed that this quality could easily degenerate into a flexible attitude towards the truth. He saw it as a 'galuti' or Diaspora trait, and felt that it had no place in the reborn Jewish state, where truth must be the supreme value and where the leadership must tell the truth to the nation. It was no accident that his most memorable article on the Lavon Affair was entitled, 'The Truth Above All Else'.

Ben-Gurion knew from the start that he wanted an impartial, judicial forum to investigate The Affair, but it took him time to crystallize his precise proposal. There was no Commissions of Inquiries Law on the statute book at that time; it was passed only in 1968, in the wake of the Lavon Affair. Legal experts invoked British law and Mandatory precedents. Because of this uncertainty, some of Ben-Gurion's closest party colleagues – particularly Eshkol and Golda – felt that he was hesitant. And, in a way, he was. He was drawn into The Affair despite himself. Between 1955, when he returned to the Defence Ministry after Lavon's resignation, and 1959–60, when The Affair burst out into the open, he did nothing to reopen it. On the contrary, he steered clear of it, content to leave the uncertainty of the Olshan–Dori commission's finding in place.

I, of course, was deeply involved with Ben-Gurion as The Affair unfolded and the division in the party deepened. But I believe I was able to retain a certain detached perspective. I remember being shocked anew every morning at the vast disparities between the reports in the newspapers, most of which were pro-Lavon, and what I knew to be reality in terms of Ben-Gurion's attitudes and actions. But by the same token, I recall being unpleasantly surprised, time after time, by Ben-Gurion's decisions and public pronouncements. At the time, people thought that each morning we, his close aides – Yitzhak Navon, Haim Ben-David, Haim Yisraeli and Teddy Kollek – would hold a 'council of war' with Ben-Gurion, reporting to him on the state of the battlefield and offering our tactical advice. But that was far from the case. Often he consulted no one and took decisions which all of us thought were ill-advised. As The Affair progressed, he grew more and more lonely, isolated from his longtime party comrades and solitary in his decision-making. He even began to like his loneliness and seemed, in a strange way, to enjoy it. We found it increasingly hard to present him with a realistic appraisal of the political situation surrounding The Affair.

Looking back, I believe that, had he allowed me into his heart, I could at least have prevented the isolation. He did not realize until too late that his close colleagues were drifting away from him.

We, his young aides, though we often found ourselves disagreeing with him over tactics, never lost our respect and admiration for him. We saw in him what others failed to see, or stopped seeing: his deeper motives throughout The Affair. The press and many among his own party comrades thought that his purpose was to even the score with Lavon or to crush him politically, so as to make way for 'the youngsters'.

We knew differently. We knew that for Ben-Gurion this was a battle over principles, not a political power-play. This was the position he took when Mapai, in a final rupture, set up a 'court of honour', where

Ben-Gurion and several of his followers, myself among them, were drummed out of the party. The 'prosecutor' was the Minister of Justice, Ya'acov Shimshon Shapira, who hurled the full force of his courtroom rhetoric at the 'accused'. He even resorted to the term 'neo-fascist' to describe our group.

Looking back today, I believe that Ben-Gurion was right about the principles, but wrong in his tactics. I believe that his battle proved to be enormously costly to him, but made an enormous contribution to the state. Since The Affair, and as a result of it, people in power have been careful not to mix politics with the judicial process, and have tried to maintain the distinction between the executive and judicial branches. There has never been another attempt to turn the Cabinet, in effect, into an *ad hoc* judicial organ. Moreover, I believe that Ben-Gurion's stand in The Affair resulted in a heightened regard in Israeli public life for the truth. I am not saying that the public record has been flawless since then, or even nearly flawless, but I have no doubt at all that this was one of the greatest battles fought by a great man – not against a rival camp or an opposing state, but against a trait of character in a nation's formative period.

I do not claim that Ben-Gurion was totally innocent of personal sentiments during The Affair. It is probably impossible to conduct a sustained and bitter struggle of this kind and remain completely neutral throughout it in terms of the personalities involved, but I am utterly convinced that his was a battle over principle, over values.

My own role in The Affair was miserable by definition. Looking back today, I still feel I behaved correctly. In the toughest moments, my loyalty to Ben-Gurion and to his principles was unswerving. Thus, I isolated myself to a very great extent within the party. My situation was exacerbated because I became, in practice, a lightning rod for Ben-Gurion. People levelled all manner of unfounded charges at me and attributed to me nefarious qualities that I never had. They even went so far as to suggest that I had some kind of magical influence over Ben-Gurion, which was completely untrue.

I thought at the time, and continue to think, that the eventual secession of Ben-Gurion and his supporters from the Labour Party was a bad mistake. I believe that we should have continued fighting for Ben-Gurion's principles from within the party. Ben-Gurion justified the move on the grounds that it would be temporary. The name he chose for our new group, Rafi, was itself intended to indicate this: Rafi is an acronym for Reshimat Poalei Yisrael, or Israeli Workers' List: list, not party, meaning that it was to be a short-term parliamentary faction rather than a fully fledged political movement.

Ben-Gurion was misled by wildly optimistic prognoses regarding our electoral prospects. Yosef Almogi, who was the Haifa party boss at that time, was particularly fanciful in this respect. He promised Ben-Gurion that he would bring out all of Haifa – a traditional Mapai stronghold – to vote for Rafi. But his performance, as it turned out, could not match his confidence.

The act of secession, on 29 June 1965, was a drama in itself. It began at a meeting of our caucus or ginger-group – then still within the party fold – at the offices that we had been lent by a wealthy supporter in the El Al tower in downtown Tel Aviv. The majority was solidly against secession. Only Almogi and a handful of others were in favour. Suddenly, Paula Ben-Gurion appeared and informed us that Ben-Gurion wanted to see us. We all made our way over to the Ben-Gurions' house on Keren Kayemet Boulevard, and I, as chairman of the meeting, began to report on what had taken place so far.

I had hardly begun when Ben-Gurion broke in. 'I will chair the meeting from now on,' he announced. 'I have decided to secede from the party. Who will join me in setting up a new list?' That same night, he issued an official statement announcing the name of the new list, Rafi, and outlining its manifesto.

I was bitterly hurt and went home mortified. I felt both that Ben-Gurion was wrong and that he had treated me badly. Early next morning, the phone rang. It was Ben-Gurion. He wanted to come round to my home immediately to apologize for his behaviour. I said that I would come to him. As I walked in, he embraced me and launched into a profuse and emotional apology. He said that there was no way that he could create the new list without Dayan and me. Dayan was on a trip to Ethiopia at the time. I decided on the spot that, as far as I was concerned, my loyalty to Ben-Gurion took priority over everything else – including my belief that he was making the wrong decision. I recalled another conversation with Ben-Gurion that had left an indelible imprint on my mind. 'You are one of the very few', he had said, 'who, when they walk into my room, I know they have not come to ask something for themselves, or to bad-mouth someone else: their interest is only in the issue at hand.'

I knew the secession meant that I would inevitably forfeit my job, which I loved, as Deputy Defence Minister – and, indeed, within a short time felt that I had to resign. We hoped to win fifteen seats (out of 120 in the Knesset). Some of us thought that would make us indispensable as a coalition partner. Others thought in terms of our ability to compel the creation of a judicial commission of inquiry into the Lavon Affair. My own plans were in the area of science and technology. I believed Israel's future lay in hi-tech (though, of course, that term itself was not yet in use): electronics, avionics and nuclear energy.

Rafi attracted an impressive array of young and gifted people to its ranks, among them many who would one day rise to prominence in Israeli politics. Our first cash contribution, for the then-considerable sum of 150 lirot, came from a young paratroop officer, Rafael (Raful) Eitan.* Our activists included Teddy Kollek, Vivian (Chaim) Herzog (later a Labour Party MK and subsequently President of Israel); Yitzhak Navon (another subsequent President of the state); Arye Gurel (later Mayor of Haifa); Yigal Hurwitz (later Minister of Finance in the Likud Government); S. Yizhar the author; Gad Ya'acobi (later a Labour Party Minister); Ram Caspi, a leading attorney; Rifka Guber, a writer and mother who had lost both her sons in the army; and Yael Dayan, Moshe's daughter, who later was to embark on a political career of her own. Nathan Alterman, the poet, gave me enormous moral support, and I consulted him on every step we took.

None the less, we won only ten seats, and Eshkol was able to set up a stable government without us. We drew some consolation from the fact that Teddy Kollek had won the mayoral election in Jerusalem in 1965. It had not been easy to persuade him to stand. Kollek, Navon and I had met in the gardens of the Sheraton Hotel in Tel Aviv. Summoning up all of my diplomatic skills, I gingerly suggested that Kollek was the right man to run in Jerusalem. He replied with a torrent of curses, which made heads turn all around us.

For my part, I ended up in the unaccustomed role of opposition back-bencher and Secretary-General of a small party, deep in debt and far from the centre of decision-making where I had lived for more than fifteen years. In the opening debate of the new Knesset, I delivered a spirited tirade against the Government. 'Shimon,' Eshkol commented, without rancour, 'you're worse than Begin.' Many of the party enthusi-

---

* Later Chief of Staff, Minister of Agriculture and founder of Tsomet, which won eight seats in the 1992 election.

asts soon melted away, leaving only the hard core of founder-members like myself to carry on the daily grind. I remember having to mortgage our refrigerator at home to help cover Rafi's debts. I remember, too, rejecting a gift to the party of 50,000 lirot from my friend Al Schwimmer, then Director-General of Israel Aircraft Industries. I sent it back when I discovered, upon inquiry, that it represented the proceeds of a mortgage that Schwimmer had taken out on his home. There was no way I could guarantee, if we took the money, that the Schwimmers would continue to have a roof over their heads.

Twelve years later, the exigencies of those salad days came sharply back to my mind in an unlikely setting. Menachem Begin, then Prime Minister-designate after his election triumph in May 1977, suffered a serious heart attack and I, the trounced and chastened leader of the opposition, went to visit him in hospital. He greatly appreciated this gesture, and we launched into a pleasant enough conversation. 'Menachem,' I said, 'no one knows better than I the true cause of your heart condition. The depth of pain and embarrassment that a party leader has to suffer when the coffers are empty are something that one can't understand unless one has suffered them oneself.' Begin's Herut Party, the larger but poorer component of the Herut–Liberal alignment that made up the Likud, was struggling at that time under a mountain of debt, and Begin was manfully trying to raise funds at home and abroad to stave off bankruptcy, as I had twelve years before. Begin smiled wanly: 'You are absolutely right.'

After the 1965 election, Ben-Gurion spent most of his time in Sde Boker, from whence he made ringing proclamations whenever the fancy took him. He put in an appearance at the Knesset from time to time, but took little part in running the parliamentary faction. Almogi, the ardent secessionist, quickly began negotiating behind my back with Eshkol over his return to the party fold. Moshe Dayan announced right at the start that he would make six election speeches – and no more. After the election, he invited me to lunch and said, 'Shimon, it's up to you. If you decide to return to the party, I'm with you. If you decide to stay out, I'm with you too. But you should know that you can't rely on me for anything!' Dayan basically felt that we had proved our loyalty by seceding with Ben-Gurion and by fighting the election with him on a separate ticket. He was never fully convinced about who was telling the truth about The Order, but his overall attitude towards Lavon was highly critical. He revered Ben-Gurion and agreed with his view that it was both wrong and ill-advised to victimize an individual officer – even though he suspected that the particular officer in question, Gibli, was not entirely blameless in The Affair. From the reports he had received as Chief of Staff, and from all the subsequent information, Dayan felt that there was no real difference of opinion between Lavon and Gibli regarding policy – regardless of which of them had actually issued The Order.

Dayan was very wise. As a senior officer and later as Chief of Staff, he would occasionally propose a military action only to have it turned down by the Minister of Defence. Unlike other officers, he would not see this as a cause for anger or exasperation. On the contrary, he recognized that this was the Defence Minister's role. He did not, therefore, at all enjoy his situation under Lavon, in which he found himself in a weird competition with his Minister over which of them could approve more military actions.

During our period in opposition, my lunches with Dayan became a weekly fixture. We would discuss politics, the intricacies of which he fully understood but heartily disliked. 'I would never want to be Prime Minister,' he asserted time and time again. 'I couldn't stand all the political infighting.' Yet he knew full well that without 'politics', in the less edifying sense of the term, he could not hope for influence in the areas that concerned him most – defence and foreign policy.

That truth became dramatically clear when, after two years of enforced idleness on the opposition benches, we suddenly found ourselves in the vortex of a national crisis. In 1967, the IDF General Staff, then under Chief of Staff Yitzhak Rabin, began to focus the army's and the nation's attention on what it said was a threat to Israel's existence: Syria's efforts to divert the streams feeding the River Jordan for its own use. These streams were an important component of Israel's water supply, and this diversion by Syria was described as a major and immediate danger. Rabin proposed – and the Prime Minister and Minister of Defence, Eshkol, approved – that we send 100 warplanes over Damascus to demonstrate how seriously we regarded the issue. 'You'll see,' Dayan said at our weekly lunch, 'this will end in war.'

Events quickly bore out his prediction. Egypt's President Nasser came to Syria's aid by blockading the Straits of Tiran at the southern end of the gulf of Aqaba. The drumbeat of imminent war grew louder day by day. The Egyptians moved massive reinforcements into Sinai and the Syrians bolstered their deployments on the Golan Heights. In Israel, the Government and the army considered possible responses. Eshkol hesitated and did not take a clear-cut position. The country was swept by a sense of perplexed concern. The name of Moshe Dayan seemed to be on everyone's lips; he was the man, people said, who could save the situation.

In Rafi, almost all of us believed the appropriate political solution was to set up a government of national unity. With Ben-Gurion's approval, I approached the National Religious Party (NRP) leader, Moshe Haim Shapira, and the Likud leader, Menachem Begin. Given the gravity of the hour, Ben-Gurion was prepared to set aside his aversion for Begin's hollow rhetoric. Begin asked me if I felt that Ben-Gurion was still capable of being Prime Minister, and also if that was what he wanted. 'He's certainly up to the job,' I replied, 'but I don't know if he wants it.'

Ben-Gurion's magnanimity towards Begin was not matched by any softening of his enmity towards Eshkol. He would not hear of joining Eshkol's Government. 'He has certain characteristics that make him unsuitable to be Prime Minister,' Ben-Gurion said of Eshkol, 'and he lacks the qualities that are vital for a national leader.' Ben-Gurion liked the idea that Rafi might join with the Likud (it was called Gahal at that time), the NRP and sections of Mapai to form an alternative government with the express purpose of removing Eshkol from power. Begin, for his part, went to ask Eshkol if he was prepared to set up a government jointly with Ben-Gurion – and came back discouraged. 'These two horses', Eshkol said of Ben-Gurion and himself, 'cannot pull the wagon in the same direction.'

Precious time was passing and nothing was moving. I decided, therefore, to launch an initiative of my own. The national emergency, I declared in a statement to the press, required the reunification of the labour movement. Ironically, this drew an instantly positive response from Ahdut Haavoda. Mapai, in the person of its Secretary-General, Golda Meir, replied warmly to Ahdut Haavoda's overture. But Golda's hatred of Rafi knew no bounds; she could not bring herself, even at this time of crisis, to mitigate it. Many people in Mapai favoured the idea that Dayan become Minister of Defence under Eshkol; but she set herself implacably against it, urging Eshkol not to surrender the Defence Ministry to Dayan. Ahdut Haavoda hoped that the pivotal portfolio would go to its leader, Yigal Allon, who (perhaps unluckily for him) was out of the country at the time on an official visit to the Soviet Union.

Despite Golda's resistance, my call for labour unity struck a deep chord in Mapai, where many members were never comfortable with the traumatic departure of Ben-Gurion and wanted to see Dayan and me back within the party fold. Two parallel negotiations began, one concerning the creation of a government of national unity and the other on the reunification of the labour movement. As the politicians talked, they knew that the moment was inexorably approaching when Israel would have to make its decision – whether to go to war or not. The IDF began mobilizing the reserves. As the streets emptied of men of military age, they filled with rumour and speculation. The eve-of-war atmosphere seemed steadily to sap public confidence in the Eshkol Government and to reinforce the widespread desire that Dayan be placed in command of the nation's defences.

The three opposition parties, Gahal, NRP and Rafi, co-ordinated their positions in the negotiations with the Eshkol Government. In practice, that meant close and constant contact between Begin, Shapira and myself. For me, the major problem was the relationship between Ben-Gurion and Eshkol. Ben-Gurion was immovable in his rejection of any coalition in which Eshkol remained as Prime Minister.

The policy-positions of the various potential partners in regard to the military situation were not entirely clear either. They all said that they wanted a decision, but no one said specifically what that decision should be. Here, too, Ben-Gurion took a firm stand: Israel, he insisted, must obtain the support of at least one of the Great Powers – preferably the United States, or else France – for whatever course it proposed to take. He feared that we would expend all our resources and *matériel* in the course of the war and find ourselves depleted and exhausted, with no friendly supplier to replenish our arsenals.

Dayan went to Eshkol and asked his permission to tour the southern front, where most of the army was encamped, poised for action. Eshkol willingly agreed. Wherever he went, Dayan was cheered enthusiastically by the soldiers. He returned to Eshkol and suggested that he be mobilized to serve as commander of the southern front. With the other members of the Knesset Defence and Foreign Affairs Committee, Dayan and I heard briefing after briefing as the days passed, among them a concerned briefing from Rabin. He depicted the situation darkly, which added to the general confusion and perplexity. Within Rafi, we had our own informal defence committee, comprised of former military men. We met almost nightly, careful even amongst ourselves to speak allusively for fear of disclosing state secrets.

At the tripartite political negotiations, Begin began to grow despondent. His conclusion after meeting with Eshkol, he explained, was that there was no real possibility of setting up a government under anybody else. The most, therefore, that could be hoped for was to have Dayan brought in as Minister of Defence. Dayan telephoned from the southern front. 'Shimon, forget it. Nothing will come out of it. They'll never make me Defence Minister.' But minutes later the phone rang again. It was Avraham Ofer, a key Mapai figure, who spoke for Eshkol. He was authorized, he said, to offer me a Cabinet seat as Minister without Portfolio. The same offer was being made to Begin.

My reply was an instant and angry rejection. Our purpose was not merely to have someone in the Government. Ofer tried to calm me: Dayan would be appointed O/C Southern Command, he said. Other Mapai activists telephoned me with the same urgent plea – to get Ben-Gurion, somehow, to let Rafi join the Eshkol Government. Gradually, I concluded that this was indeed the only way of responding, if only in part, to the pressing need of the hour. If Dayan were to become Minister of Defence, I told myself and my colleagues, that would be a vital contribution both to the national morale now and to the course of the war itself.

But the problem was not to convince myself or the others, but to obtain the consent of Ben-Gurion. I asked a good friend, Avraham Schweitzer, the *Ha'aretz* columnist, to accompany me on my difficult mission to Ben-Gurion's home in Tel Aviv. He received us with his usual warmth. I decided to get straight to the point. 'Ben-Gurion,' I said, 'I've done everything I could. But there are no other parties, apart from Rafi, that support the removal of Eshkol as Prime Minister. The most we can achieve is Dayan's appointment as Minister of Defence. The war is imminent. With Moshe in command we have the best chance of winning it.'

Ben-Gurion's face suddenly changed. I felt a terrible wave of anger building up within him. It erupted like a torrent of lava. 'I thought you were a friend and I thought you were a statesman. But you are neither the one nor the other. How dare you forgo the single most important change that must be made – the replacement of Levi Eshkol?'

My own face blanched. This was one of the worst moments of my life. I had tried everything I knew to fulfil Ben-Gurion's wishes. I had worked tirelessly, making new enemies, losing old friends, creating a weird coalition of disparate parties, rejecting the various temptations and blandishments that had been offered to me – and this was my reward: to hear from the man whom I so much admired that I was no longer his friend. But even in the heat of that awful moment, I knew I had to stand my ground. I took a deep breath and looked back at him. 'Ben-Gurion,' I said quietly, 'I want to ask you a question. You have often said that if the needs of the movement were placed on one side of the scales, and the country's defence interests on the other side – the defence interests must outweigh all else. My question is – does that rule apply to everyone else except Ben-Gurion, or does it apply to Ben-Gurion too?'

Ben-Gurion seemed thunderstruck. Eventually, he muttered, 'Perhaps you're right.'

Ben-Gurion's acceptance of Dayan's appointment as Minister of Defence flashed through the country. The response was electric. That same evening, all the Rafi leadership met at Ben-Gurion's home. Ben-Gurion embraced me and said: 'I know many people who are prepared to work hard and make sacrifices in order to attain their goal, but I know no one like Shimon who will do this so devotedly, without taking into account any personal interest or calculation whatsoever. This is how he has conducted these negotiations, and he has attained the most that could be attained.'

But there was still one last, thoroughly unpleasant hurdle for me to cross. At a formal session of the Rafi executive, Ben-Gurion placed a condition on his consent to our joining the Government of National Unity: I was to go to Eshkol and tell him that, even though we agreed to serve under him, we retained our view that he was unfit to be Prime Minister. Moreover, we would continue, in the future, to seek to unseat him. There was no option for me but to swallow this final indignity. It would be bitter and distasteful to me, but I knew that for Ben-Gurion the prospect of our joining a government under Eshkol was as bitter as gall, and I was not going to make it worse for him by refusing to accede to his wishes. Accordingly, on Friday, 3 June, I presented myself, together with Yitzhak Navon, at Eshkol's office. My knees felt weak. I was about to do something that made me heartily uncomfortable.

'Prime Minister,' I announced, 'we have come to inform you officially of Rafi's decision to serve in your Government, with Moshe Dayan to be appointed Minister of Defence.' Eshkol was delighted by our decision. 'But there is something I must add,' I continued, 'and that is that Rafi has not changed its mind regarding your unsuitability for the task of Prime Minister, and this will continue to be its position in the future.'

I awaited the Prime Minister's injured rejoinder, but Eshkol refused to be stirred. He replied with his customary humour: 'You have failed to surprise me! I understand precisely why you had to add that rider to your statement...'

I asked for a few minutes alone with him. 'The dispute between you and Ben-Gurion is an unbearable burden not just for the two of you, but for all of us,' I said. 'The time has come now to end it.' Eshkol knew full well that Ben-Gurion was our greatest statesman and that his prestige around the world was second to none. My proposal was that he, Eshkol, ask Ben-Gurion to undertake a special mission to the United States and France to explain our situation to the governments of, and public opinion in, those countries and to seek their aid and support after the war was over. Ben-Gurion knew nothing of this proposal, and I did not know whether he would accept it if offered, but I felt that this was a great moment in our nation's history, a moment to set aside the animosities of the past.

Eshkol replied with the Arabic expression 'stenna shwaya', 'wait a moment'. What if Ben-Gurion refuses, he asked. I said that I would go over to Ben-Gurion's home right away to find out whether he was prepared to undertake such a mission. If he was, Eshkol would suggest it to him. I could see Eshkol liked the idea, but he still did not give me an immediate answer. 'I have to consult,' he said. 'I'll let you know this afternoon.' At nightfall, he telephoned. 'I've considered it carefully', he said, 'and I fully understand your motives.' But regretfully, he could not accept it. I said that I was sorry. In my heart, I knew that the quarrel between these two men would continue to the grave.

And indeed it did. When Eshkol died in 1968, a number of us went to Ben-Gurion to persuade him to attend the funeral. 'I'm not going to his funeral,' the Old Man announced, 'and he shouldn't come to my funeral either, and that's all there is to it!' His disappointment with Eshkol – disappointment, never hatred – was implacable. Ben-Gurion believed that Eshkol had the intellectual qualities to make a fine Prime Minister, but that he had failed the test of character posed by the Lavon Affair. Ben-Gurion felt Eshkol's position throughout The Affair was grounded in expediency and compromise, instead of in principle.

Later that same evening, I called on Dayan at the Ministry of Defence. He told me that the die was cast: it was to be war. On the morning of Monday, 5 June, when the war broke out, I was with the other members of the Knesset Foreign Affairs and Defence Committee, about to emplane at the Sde Dov airfield in Tel Aviv for a tour of the southern front. Because of the hostilities, our flight was cancelled. I invited the committee members to my home nearby to await developments. It was there, two hours later, that we received first word of the virtual elimination of the Egyptian air force. Our planes, in wave after wave of attacks on all of Egypt's military airfields, destroyed most of Nasser's front-line jets on the ground. The war had just begun – and already our victory was certain. But Israel did not rush to trumpet its victory. It had taken command of the skies, but left Egypt in command of the airwaves. For the whole day, Cairo Radio proclaimed the Egyptian army's successes and described the progress of its advance on Tel Aviv.

The war was conducted superbly, by both the Government and the army. Eshkol urged King Hussein of Jordan to stay out, but to no avail. Dayan, who personally supervised all the major military moves, later described the Six Day War as three separate campaigns: a two-day war against Egypt, followed by two days of fighting to drive Jordan from the West Bank and Jerusalem, and concluded with a bloody two-day contest against Syria on the Golan Heights. The outside world, which had been much impressed by Nasser's bluster and saw Israel as weak and mortally endangered, looked on in wonderment and disbelief. All of the Sinai, the West Bank and the Golan fell into our hands. But above all, we had liberated and reunited Jerusalem. I went with Ben-Gurion for a first visit to the Old City and was present when he asked that the street-sign 'Wailing Wall Road' in Arabic and English be taken down. It was the end of an era for Israel, and for me personally, and the start of a new and very different period in the life of the nation.

Had it not been for the war, I daresay I would have been idle for a longer period. But I would not like to think that my political career would have been destroyed for ever. Firstly, 'for ever' is not really a concept that exists in politics – certainly not in Israeli politics. Secondly, leading figures in Mapai were telling me throughout this traumatic period that they regarded me as the foremost candidate in my generation eventually to become Prime Minister. Mordechai Namir, for instance, the powerful head of the Tel Aviv-based Gush, or bloc within Mapai, called me in – this was during the height of the crisis – to say that of all the younger figures on the horizon he saw me as best suited for national leadership, and that I ought not to sink my energies into the secession. Even Eshkol saw me as the future leader – as he confided to his diaries, which his widow, Miriam, kept in her archives. In fact, Ben-Gurion, when he resigned in 1963, told me that ideally he would have wanted me to succeed him as Minister of Defence, but that would have raised enormous resistance and, therefore, he had no choice but to install Eshkol both as Premier and Defence Minister.

Ben-Gurion told me several times over the years that he expected to die at the age of eighty-six. His father, he said, had died at that age. He was right in the end, though not entirely: his father had actually lived till he was eighty-seven – as, indeed, did Ben-Gurion. He devoted the last decade of his life to writing a history of Israel, 'in order to teach the younger generation the truth of our existence'. He put an enormous amount of work into this project; even at this age, he was able to spend ten or twelve hours a day reading and writing. But the creative muses refused to attend him now with the same inspiration and generosity that they had lavished on him in earlier years.

He faced the tribulations of old age philosophically. He maintained his dignity. He never complained, never quarrelled or bickered – and never ceased to look to the future. Death held no terror for him. He often expressed his hope that Sde Boker, the Negev kibbutz which he had made his home, would grow into a great spiritual and scientific centre, a kind of Oxford and Yavneh★ rolled into one. He selected a grave-site for himself and his wife, Paula, near the kibbutz, at a spot overlooking a deep wadi and waterfall, a scene of wild, majestic splendour.

In January 1968, Paula died. She had always fussed and worried over him like a Jewish mother over her only son. She insisted that he eat only the right foods and that he rest at the right times; she made sure that he took his pills and medicines (she was a nurse by training) and kept away bothersome visitors. Paula claimed that Ben-Gurion needed her help in assessing people, that he – like most men – was naïve when it came to other people.

When she died, Haim Yisraeli† telephoned me, and we drove together to the hospital in Beersheba. We found Ben-Gurion sitting hunched on a chair, wrapped up in his own thoughts. He seemed more alone than ever. The doctors had told him that her end was near, so her death was no surprise to him. He looked up at us and muttered, 'Let's go to Sde

★ The seat of Talmudic learning after the destruction of the Second Temple in 70 AD.
† See page 145.

Boker.' We got into his car and drove in silence to his hut in the desert. He said that we needed a drink, and rummaged in his study until he found some vermouth. He was never much of a drinker. Now he began to pour out his heart. 'Twice she followed me without question: once to *Eretz Yisrael*, though she knew neither the country nor the language and had a baby to look after; and once again here to the desert, to the loneliness and the isolation. Each time she had to leave her friends and her lifestyle to come with me. I will never forget that: "... the love of thine espousals, when thou wentest after me in the wilderness" [Jeremiah 2: 2]. I only ever made one mistake about Paula,' Ben-Gurion continued. 'I was sure that I would die before her, and now she has gone before me. But there is no running away from death, or any need to dread it.'

Five years later, on a Saturday morning in December 1973, Haim Yisraeli telephoned me at home. He said just one word: 'Ben-Gurion.' I rushed to the Tel Hashomer hospital outside Tel Aviv. Ben-Gurion's family were standing outside his room. I asked their consent and walked in. Ben-Gurion lay on his back, his domed forehead looking even larger and paler in death than it had in life. He resembled an ancient marble bust. For the first time ever, I remember thinking, he has attained rest. The grief of a whole nation filled the room. The true father and founder of Israel lay there, dead.

Ben-Gurion's role in Jewish history was played during a period of supreme trial for our nation. The nation lived with a sense of misfortune and tragedy; Ben-Gurion lived with a sense of mission. He stormed the stage of history with his indomitable willpower and inexhaustible funds of strength and faith. His leadership inspired and energized the nation. He gave it a new sense of security, confidence and pride. He exorcised its tendency to despair and succeeded in awakening its long and ancient traditions of heroism. He demanded from the nation hard work, steadfast courage and justice. He stood at the forefront of Israel's external battle for survival and security, while constantly battling against what he perceived as pernicious internal ills endangering the country. He spoke words of vision, words of truth. He fought relentlessly for his principles, in word and deed, but even in the heat of battle his soul remained clean and pure.

The greatness of Ben-Gurion's leadership lay in his ability to draw on the innermost spirit of the Jewish People, a spirit of unflagging determination, a restless, rebellious spirit, a spirit of renaissance and creativity. He not only exemplified this spirit, but he also personified it.

He enhanced it, guarded it, guided it and gave it direction. As the embodiment of this spirit, he rose to those rare heights where the history of a nation encounters its future and where new horizons are created. When he left the stage of Jewish history, the nation was firmly set on the new path that he had mapped out. From a dispersed and dying nation, without a land or a language of its own, the Jews had re-established their sovereignty in their land. After a 2,000-year interlude, they had rejoined history. All this took place under Ben-Gurion's leadership. I shudder to think what would have befallen our people without him.

For me personally, the death of Ben-Gurion meant the passing of the man who had moulded my life. For eighteen years I worked with him, through days of joy and days of sadness, years of lofty achievement and years of deep bitterness. My admiration for him only grew with the passage of time. In him, I saw – and from him I learned – that a human being *can* do things differently, if he wishes; that he can *be* different, if he strives to be; ultimately, it depends only on him.

9 GOLDA

Had it not been for his handling of the Lavon Affair, Ben-Gurion would probably have remained Prime Minister for longer. But had it not been for his handling of The Affair, Ben-Gurion would not have been Ben-Gurion. He preserved his character, but lost his office.

There was a profound political paradox built into The Affair: people who totally opposed and even condemned Lavon nevertheless supported him, because they sought the opportunity to hit at Ben-Gurion. Golda Meir, Sharett and Sapir were all among Lavon's harshest detractors, as was Zalman Aran, but they chose to oppose Ben-Gurion and to stand alongside Lavon for reasons that were largely unrelated to the substance of The Affair itself.

I am too experienced now – and was even then – to believe that there was some sort of preconceived plot on their part. Rather, these veteran Mapai leaders acted out of instinct, out of powerful feelings that they had buried deep within themselves. They persuaded themselves that Ben-Gurion had, as the phrase was then, 'dressed his young aides in coats of many colours' – a reference to the biblical story of Jacob, who favoured Joseph above all his other sons. By the same token, they came to believe that Ben-Gurion did not sufficiently appreciate them as political leaders and statesmen.

It is not easy, after all, to stand tall under the shadow of a great man. The grass hardly grows in the shade of a broad tree. The Affair brought to the surface deep currents of frustration, jealousy and suspicion – those powerful human emotions with which politics are so often richly imbued. Golda and her allies saw themselves as the protectors of authentic party values. The issue for them was not the Government, but rather the well-being of socialism and of the Histadrut. They accused Ben-Gurion –

who had created the Histadrut back in the early 1920s – of now disparaging his own creation. He advocated a 'national youth movement', which they saw as undermining the traditional party-based youth movements. Ben-Gurion, in their view, was betraying his own cause.

My relations with Golda Meir were always complex and ambivalent, and usually unhappy. With Golda, as I learned over the years, there was no such thing as middle ground: either you were 100 per cent for her, or she was 100 per cent against you. She could not tolerate anything less than adulation. Teddy Kollek once said of her, 'She doesn't so much conduct a foreign policy as maintain a hate-list.' On her list were Dag Hammarskjöld, the United Nations Secretary-General; Christian Herter, the American Secretary of State; Kwame Nkrumah, the Ghanaian leader; Michel Debré, the French statesman; our own Abba Eban – and myself. She regarded me as someone who failed to appreciate her sufficiently – probably, as she saw it, because of my unswerving loyalty to Ben-Gurion.

Our rocky relationship began back in the days of Young Mapai, when I wrote newspaper articles criticizing Moshe Sneh, the Haganah leader.★ Matters deteriorated when I became Director-General of the Defence Ministry in 1952, and quickly worsened when she became Foreign Minister in 1955. She accused me, in effect, of conducting a separate and secret foreign policy.

Our relations reached a crisis-point during a crucial mission to France on the eve of the 1956 Suez Campaign, when France and Britain attacked Egypt by sea and air while Israel struck at the Egyptian army in the Sinai Peninsula.† Golda was mission head, and the other members included Moshe Carmel, an Ahdut Haavoda Minister and former general, Moshe Dayan and myself. I had reported to Ben-Gurion that the French were interested in joint military action, and this mission was intended to formalize and finalize plans. We flew in a French air-force bomber, via Casablanca. When we landed near Paris, I learned to my horror from the Defence Ministry representative in Paris, Yosef Nahmias, that Prime Minister Guy Mollet, who was to head the French team at the talks with us, had chosen not to participate. The French had that day intercepted a plane carrying Algerian rebel leaders, and Mollet had to defend the action in the National Assembly.

I knew at once that I was facing a catastrophe: Golda could now

★ See page 58.
† See page 123.

confirm her suspicions that I had been over-optimistic in my reporting. I dashed from the airport straight to Mollet's office and explained to him the nature of the problem. He agreed to meet Golda alone.

Nevertheless, some damage had been done. At the plenary sessions, Foreign Minister Christian Pineau, an intellectual with a natural propensity for pensive sadness, presented a thoroughly downbeat assessment of likely reactions to a joint French–(British)–Israeli operation at this time, just before the American Presidential election and with a crisis hanging over Hungary. Golda returned to Israel and reported to Ben-Gurion that my assertions that the French wanted a joint operation were groundless, or at least wildly exaggerated.

Even after this allegation was itself proved groundless by subsequent events, Foreign Ministry diplomats continued to bad-mouth me and my actions. The Ambassador to France, Yaacov Tsur, was sometimes unhappy about the intimate relationship between our countries' two defence establishments. (Israeli officials actually worked out of the French Defence Ministry during the period of the Sinai Campaign, in addition to a liaison presence with Allied – that is, British and French – forward headquarters in Cyprus.)

Sometimes the animosity between Golda and myself became downright ridiculous. Once, for instance, the London-based *Jewish Observer and Middle East Review* published a report that Golda was sick. At six o'clock the next morning I was awakened by Giora Yosephtal, who was party Secretary-General at the time, with the news that Golda was on the verge of an apoplectic fit. She accused me of planting the story with Jon Kimche, the editor of the *Jewish Observer*. While it was true that I had helped Kimche with his weekly paper, which I believed was a worthwhile publication, it was absurd to imagine that I had planted any such story about Golda's health. Anyone who knew me would have known that I would never stoop to any such thing. But for Golda, everything was part of a plot to undermine her.

True to her hostility towards me and towards Rafi, she fought against Dayan's return to the Defence Ministry on the eve of the Six Day War – she argued that Israel would win without him – and was also against Rafi's eventual return to the Labour fold two years later.

But she failed on both occasions. In 1967, she had become party Secretary and found herself with me as her deputy, ensconced in the office opposite hers at the party headquarters on the Tel Aviv seafront. We held many long and very frank conversations, and it was only then that I began to understand her personality and her problems. One day, I volunteered that Ben-Gurion had greatly admired her. She replied that what I had said was completely groundless. I asked her why she said that. She replied with a series of stories from the past that she had obviously kept bottled up inside her. One went back to the Provisional Government of 1948.

What she told me was that Ben-Gurion had told his Ministers that it was most important to get more arms. But to buy arms we needed money, and in order to raise money he would have to go to America. 'Ben-Gurion,' Golda said. 'I, too, can go to America and raise money. But only you can run the war the way you are doing. Therefore I propose that you stay here, and I go to America instead.' The Ministers voted, and Golda 'won'. She was sure that Ben-Gurion was angry with her.

Anyway, she flew down by Piper plane from beleaguered Jerusalem to Tel Aviv, checked into the one sizeable hotel that existed in the city at that time, the Katie Dan, and prepared to leave for America the next day. In the evening, there was a knock at her door: 'Mrs Myerson, Mr Ben-Gurion is in the lobby for you.'

'I was so moved,' she told me. 'I had "defeated" him at Cabinet, yet he had made the special effort to come down to see me off. He said, "Good evening, Golda. Are you off to America?", as if he didn't know. "When are you flying out? Tomorrow?" And then he pulled out a folded piece of paper from his waistcoat pocket. "Look here, Golda, there are a number of books that I haven't been able to lay my hands on here. If you could possibly buy them for me in New York, I would be very grateful."' She was deeply hurt. She had thought that he had come to bid her Godspeed on her mission, and here he was with a list of books for her to buy for him.

I tried to explain. 'Of course he came especially to say goodbye to you,' I said. 'And I'm sure he thought long and hard about what to say – and came up with the idea of the books, which was just an excuse. If he had really been interested only in the books, he could have telephoned. He needn't have come round personally with the list.' But she still couldn't see it that way.

When she came back from the United States, Ben-Gurion referred to her publicly as 'the woman who saved the state'. But he did not offer her a job, and for a fairly long time she was out of action and felt frustrated. I know this because by chance I was once issued a desk that had previously been used by the Chief of Staff. Buried in a drawer, I found a note from Golda to Ben-Gurion, which read: 'I have been home for several weeks and am not doing anything.' It was signed, 'The woman who saved the state'.

Another incident, several years later, which Golda also recollected during our heart-to-heart talks in 1969, illustrates her suspicious and insecure nature. Golda, then Minister of Labour, was due to attend a conference of the International Labour Organization in Geneva. The weekly Cabinet meeting on Sunday gave its formal approval, but when she came to take her leave of the Prime Minister the next day, Ben-Gurion seemed to have forgotten where she was going and what she was going for. He asked what time her flight was. 'Tomorrow at ten,' she answered. 'Oh, really. Then you'll be flying with Shimon.' That, for her, added insult to injury. Ben-Gurion was obviously uninterested in her mission, though she was a fully fledged Cabinet Minister, but he remembered the logistic details of his young Director-General's trips.

Again, I tried to explain to her that it wasn't 'favouritism' on Ben-Gurion's part: he was simply preoccupied with defence matters – he was both Prime Minister and Minister of Defence – while he paid less attention to the Ministry of Labour.

But it was hopeless. She saw a hidden hand and ulterior motive in almost everything that happened. In her mind, we were for ever out to undermine her and weaken her standing. Moshe Dayan, always capable of winning a woman's heart, used to praise her for her diplomatic successes in Africa. He knew these meant a lot to her. When he served as her Defence Minister (1969–74), they built up a very close working relationship.

Our relationship changed dramatically during the 1973 Yom Kippur War. I was a junior Minister, not directly involved in national decision-making before and during the war, but I stood by her. I genuinely admired her rock-like resolve during those days of great adversity. When she came under attack, I defended her. At one point, I remember, not a single Minister was prepared to speak for the Government in a Knesset debate on the war – and I volunteered.

Our relations grew even closer after Labour's defeat in 1977. As party Chairman, I consulted her on all major issues and kept her informed of political developments. In December 1978, I proposed a formula designed to break a deadlock in negotiations between Israel and Egypt. This was after President Sadat's visit to Jerusalem and the Camp David conference. Sadat indicated his approval, but I wanted to consult Golda.

She was in the Hadassah Hospital in Jerusalem. I telephoned to ask if I could come. When I arrived, I was kept waiting outside her room for ten or fifteen minutes, which was quite unlike Golda. Then I went in, we had our consultation, which was thoroughly businesslike, and I left. On the way out, I asked her bodyguard why she had kept me waiting. He said that she had decided to put on make-up before receiving me. This was the last time we spoke. The next day, she died.

Despite the radical improvement in our relationship towards the end of her life, her antipathy towards me hung like a dark shadow over my own political career. Time after time, in the early years, she would ask Ben-Gurion to rein me in, to stop me from going on a particular mission or promoting a particular project. Each time he refused, her resentment deepened.

When Ben-Gurion resigned in 1963, he specifically asked Eshkol to keep me on as Deputy Defence Minister. 'You are both Jordan Valley men,' he said at the hand-over ceremony at the Ministry. 'I'm sure you'll work well together.' Golda probably hoped that Eshkol would dump me. But the truth was that Eshkol did not particularly like Golda, although in their case the public façade of amicability remained intact.

10 FRENCH CONNECTION

France was Israel's first powerful friend and ally. Its support helped the Jewish state grow in strength and maturity, from the difficult early years following the War of Independence until the eve of the Six Day War nearly a generation later.

At first, small-scale arms purchases were made on our behalf in Paris through private middle-men, but by 1953 it became clear – to me, at any rate – that our interest lay in developing a solid government-to-government relationship. From that time on, I worked hard to nurture that relationship. Despite my relative youth and inexperience, I began cultivating a network of personal contacts with French establishment figures, from Charles de Gaulle to Pierre Mendès-France. The first project in which I was directly involved, working with the then-Deputy Prime Minister, Paul Reynaud, in 1954, resulted in the supply of modern, long-range cannon to the IDF's artillery corps which had hitherto made do with an assortment of old field pieces. Soon, I found myself conducting negotiations with government officials and private industrialists for the purchase of tanks, jet planes (the Mystère) and military transport aircraft (the Nord Atlas).

The strategic considerations on our side were painfully clear. Of all the major arms producers in the world, France was the only one that was not hostile to us and did not boycott us. The Soviet Union fell into the first category as its support for the Arab states became more and more pronounced during the 1950s. Britain remained firmly committed to the arms embargo that it had proclaimed with the creation of the state; and despite its political support, the United States never wavered from the embargo it had imposed upon us at the height of the War of Independence, when it stolidly denied us even the most basic weapons.

As I came to know France intimately during the early 1950s, I learned how much it had changed in the short period since the Second World War. It was no longer a country divided between Catholics and Protestants, rich and poor, Parisians and provincials. There was a different and entirely new division that permeated French society: the France of the Maquis as against the France of the collaborators. Fighting France, the France that had never acquiesced in the German occupation, comprised both Catholics and Protestants, rich and poor, men of letters and of manual work, city sophisticates and simple country people. That France now evolved a new national leadership – men who had been at the forefront of the resistance movement (and who had survived). That France, a principled and indomitable France, gave its support almost instinctively to the new-born and still-struggling Jewish state. Our appeal to the new French leadership to come to our aid resounded powerfully throughout the new France.

Before long, I had been introduced to all the major figures at the pinnacle of French politics and felt that I was a welcome guest in their offices and homes. To a man, they pledged their country's help to Israel. At the end of 1955, during the election campaign which was to put the socialists under Guy Mollet in power, I ventured to Mollet that socialists had tended to support us while in opposition only to forget us when in power. 'You will see for yourself,' Mollet responded firmly, 'with us it will be different.'

Moshe Dayan, in his position as Chief of Staff after 1954, fully agreed with my analysis of our international position in relation to arms procurement, and closely followed our ripening romance with Paris. I was able to foster a warm working relationship between him and General Pierre Koenig, who served as Minister of Defence in Mendès-France's short-lived Government. Dayan was decorated with the *Légion d'Honneur*, a gesture both towards the man and his country that held out the promise of intimate military ties in the future. I worked hard at our French connection, at times actually commuting between Tel Aviv and Paris. Perhaps inevitably, these activities, which were conducted secretly, gave rise to rumours and resentful accusations. We were collaborating with the French, it was said, in their war against the FLN in Algeria. We had created 'an unclean alliance with the forces of imperialism'. Amidst the welter of whispered criticism, I knew that I could rely on Dayan to stand behind me in my efforts to broaden and deepen the relationship with France.

My efforts, of course, were conducted with the full authority of Ben-Gurion. But Ben-Gurion's attitude to the French was never entirely free of certain reservations. 'Why did they surrender to the Nazis?' he would often ask David Shaltiel, a Military Attaché in Europe, who had served in the French Foreign Legion during the 1930s. He had reservations about de Gaulle too, before he finally met him in 1960, and would pointedly quote Churchill's famous wartime quip that of all the crosses he had to bear, the Cross of Lorraine was the heaviest. When de Gaulle wrote his memoirs, I persuaded an Israeli publisher, Am Hasefer, to translate them into Hebrew. They agreed – on condition that Ben-Gurion write the introduction. I asked Ben-Gurion, arguing that the work was an even greater literary masterpiece than Churchill's auto-biographical account of the war. But Ben-Gurion disagreed and flatly refused to write the introduction. In the end, I wrote the introduction to the first Hebrew edition. Later, however, after Ben-Gurion and de Gaulle had met and struck up an immediate and mutual admiration, Ben-Gurion changed his mind and offered to write an introduction to subsequent editions.

The need to ensure a steady flow of modern weapons to the IDF took on new urgency with the conclusion, in September 1955, of a major arms deal between Egypt and Czechoslovakia. Prague, now firmly within the Eastern Bloc, was regarded as acting on behalf (or at least with the consent) of the Soviet Union, which made this development all the more ominous from Israel's viewpoint. The deal, once implemented, would enormously enhance Egypt's military strength, especially in the key areas of armour and air power. A month after the signing, Nasser announced that the Straits of Tiran, at the southern end of the Gulf of Aqaba, would be closed to Israeli shipping (as he would later do on the eve of the Six Day War). Ben-Gurion had said previously that for him blockading the Straits was a *casus belli*, and I, knowing Ben-Gurion, knew that he meant what he said. In December, after lengthy consultations with Dayan, Ben-Gurion submitted to the Cabinet a plan for the IDF to seize and reopen the Straits; but a majority of Ministers voted against it. Feeling that this was not the end of the matter, I none the less redoubled my efforts in France.

I was careful to keep Dayan fully informed of every development, for, with all his wisdom and cynicism, he was not without pride. 'I don't care about prestige,' he would say, 'particularly other people's prestige.' I sought an opportunity to involve him personally in the relationship that we were creating. In the early months of 1956, after much negotiation, we were able to conclude a comprehensive security understanding with the new socialist Government of Guy Mollet. I thought this success was the appropriate moment to initiate a formal, though secret, conference between the senior military echelons of the two countries – both to work on outstanding technical details of the deal and to signify, by their participation, the heightened level of intimacy achieved by the two defence establishments. The French Defence Minister, Maurice Bourges-Maunoury, immediately agreed, and we jointly set the time and place: 22 June at a delightful château in Vermars, outside Paris, belonging to the Levin family, the producers of Vichy and Perrier water. Dayan and I flew out secretly aboard an IAF Nord, accompanied by a small number of IDF officers and by the Defence Ministry's head of mission in Paris, Yosef Nahmias.

The first session of what was to be an intensive two-day conference began at 11 a.m. Dayan had spent much of the previous day and evening preparing his opening speech. Every word was important to him. He was a great believer in the importance of words and of the way one presented one's case. The right choice of phrase, he felt, could go a long way towards forging deeper, closer relations between individuals and countries. He spoke at length of the danger Nasser posed to the entire Middle East and beyond. Nasser's goals, Dayan said, were to eliminate all European influence from the region and to turn Egypt into a forward base for Soviet power. When he finished, he glanced at me briefly, as though to ask, 'How did I do?' I signalled back that he had done brilliantly, which indeed he had. He had plainly struck a responsive chord when he opened with a few carefully constructed sentences about France, the values it symbolized and its role in the world. He then moved on to speak 'as a soldier to soldiers'. His audience, which included France's top soldiers and intelligence chiefs, listened with respect and responded with warmth.

Subsequent sessions were devoted to detailed discussions of the proposed arms deal. By the end of the second day, all was worked out. The bill for the hardware – 72 Mystère planes, 200 AMX tanks, large quantities of ammunition – came to more than $100 million, a vast sum in those days. Without hesitation, I took out my pen and signed. Nahmias whispered darkly that I would be hanged for not having obtained prior authorization from the Finance Ministry. 'We won't let them hang him,' Dayan whispered back. All of us shared a sense of historic achievement.

The agreement, which included a detailed delivery schedule – the first French landing-craft was to offload its precious cargo of tanks at Haifa on 18 July – was clearly a decisive contribution to the IDF's capacity to deter or, if necessary, defeat the Arab side. Neither our Ambassador in Paris nor our Foreign Minister, Golda Meir, knew of the Vermars conference; the French insisted that neither Foreign Ministry be brought into the picture. The results of the conference meant that our efforts over the previous years to build a special relationship between Israel and France had proved worthwhile. But there was more to come.

One month after the secret conference at Vermars, Nasser announced the nationalization of the Suez Canal. Suddenly, the crisis that had been building up for months burst upon the Middle East. The British, whose troops had occupied the Canal Zone for decades under a treaty with Egypt, had recently, and somewhat reluctantly, withdrawn. The operations of the British- and French-owned Suez Canal Company and its international commitments were now protected only by the sovereign power, Egypt. At the same time, Nasser had been negotiating with the United States and British Governments for a substantial loan to fund construction of the Aswan Dam. The dam was to supply electricity, control Nile flooding and, by enhancing irrigation, increase considerably the area of arable land in Egypt. These negotiations failed – in part because Nasser was conducting parallel negotiations with the Soviets, and this incensed the US Secretary of State, John Foster Dulles. Dulles announced that there would be no loan, and the nationalization was Nasser's instant, infuriated response.

The move was a blatant violation of Egypt's treaty obligations. The West viewed it with grave concern, and a round of frenetic diplomatic activity began, led by the United States. To Britain and France, the nationalization was a direct blow both to their economic interests (the Suez Canal Company) and to their strategic concerns. It brought a major oil- and trade-route under alien and potentially hostile control. Moreover, the two European powers were affected by their still-recent and traumatic struggle with a totalitarian dictator; they regarded Nasser, with his pretensions to regional supremacy, as a nascent Hitler who had to be stopped. They began to prepare plans to take back the Canal Zone by force (and they hoped, in so doing, to topple Nasser's regime).

Israel was drawn into this rush of dramatic events almost immediately, as was I. On 26 July, Nasser made his nationalization speech. On 27 July, Bourges-Maunoury asked me to his office for an urgent meeting. I arrived with Nahmias and was surprised to find the Minister flanked by several of his senior generals. Bourges-Maunoury wasted little time. How long, he asked, would it take the IDF to fight its way across the Sinai and reach the Canal?

While I was unprepared at the time to be asked this particular question, the subject itself was hardly unfamiliar to me. We had been thinking about it and talking about it a good deal over the previous months. I replied that, in my assessment, we could do it in two weeks. The military men seemed stunned. How was that possible, they asked. I said that this was merely my assessment – but I stuck to it. Bourges-Maunoury then followed up with another question, which was apparently the purpose of this hastily convened consultation. Would Israel be prepared to take part in a tripartite military operation, in which Israel's specific role would be to cross the Sinai? I replied, without hesitation, that 'under certain circumstances I assume that we would be so prepared'. Thereupon, Bourges-Maunoury briefed me on the evolving plans of Operation Musketeer, a joint French and British scheme to land troops in the Canal Zone and reassert their rights by force.

The French Minister said that there were disputes between Paris and London. The French wanted to go ahead as soon as possible, 'before our Government falls and before summer turns to autumn'. The British, focusing their tactical thinking on their base in Cyprus, insisted on lengthy and meticulous planning, as though what was intended was a second invasion of Europe. 'Can we work together?' Bourges-Maunoury asked again, and I repeated that I believed we could. But there would have to be consultations on the highest level, I added. We agreed to schedule a ministerial meeting in Paris as soon as possible.

As we left, Nahmias turned to me with a breathless whisper: 'This time you deserve to be hanged! How could give those replies, on a matter of such gravity, without prior authorization?' I said that if they hanged me, there would probably be good reason for it, 'but I would rather risk my neck than risk missing a unique opportunity like this'. Anyway, I added, if the final decision in Jerusalem went against Israel's involvement, they would be able to say that I had spoken out of turn.

I cabled the contents of our meeting with Bourges-Maunoury to Ben-Gurion. I also informed Dayan, and we arranged to meet as soon as I returned home. Dayan cabled that Ben-Gurion would be flying up from Sde Boker to attend the weekly Cabinet meeting just after I was to arrive. He suggested that we all three drive up to Jerusalem together and discuss my news on the way. Dayan picked me up at Lydda Airport (now Ben-Gurion Airport) outside Tel Aviv and I filled him in on my talks in Paris as we drove to a military airfield nearby, where Ben-Gurion's Piper Cub touched down. His enthusiasm over what had been achieved matched my own.

We crowded into the back seat of Ben-Gurion's car and Dayan began with a business-as-usual report on the army's request to conduct a reprisal raid against a Jordanian army camp, following a recent terrorist infiltration across the border. Ben-Gurion listened quietly. At Bab el-Wad, halfway up to Jerusalem, he gave his consent. Dayan could submit the IDF request at the Cabinet meeting. Then he turned to me and asked, with a mischievous smile, 'Well, Shimon, what's news from your France?' I gave a full report on the meeting with Bourges-Maunoury and the French generals. 'Perhaps we ought to put off the Jordanian operation', Ben-Gurion commented laconically, 'and concentrate on the French issue.' We discussed the composition of an Israeli delegation to the proposed high-level conference in Paris. Dayan and I recommended that Eshkol head the team. He knew a little French and, no less important, he was not prejudiced against the two of us as were other Mapai Ministers. But Ben-Gurion preferred Golda Meir, whom he had recently appointed Foreign Minister in place of Moshe Sharett. Alongside Golda, he wanted Moshe Carmel of Ahdut Haavoda, a fluent French speaker, and the two of us. The Labour Ministers' caucus, and later the Cabinet, duly approved, and on 3 August we set off aboard a French Lancaster bomber sent secretly to fetch us.

Our mission nearly ended in disaster before it began. Carmel, looking for the lavatory aboard the dark and noisy plane, fell into the bomb-bay. He remained suspended there between life and death, legs flailing helplessly, until we managed to haul him back inside. He arrived in Paris bruised and battered, but gamely insisted on staying with the mission.

I have recounted elsewhere★ the second near-disaster that struck our mission at its outset when the French Prime Minister, Guy Mollet, sent word that he would be unable to attend the talks with us. For Golda, who was curt and morose throughout the trip, this was instant confirmation of her suspicion that I was leading her and the whole Government up the garden path. An unorthodox appeal to the Premier persuaded him to receive her and thereby saved the day, but she remained sceptical and dour

★ See pages 112–13.

as the talks proceeded. Dayan, by contrast, was vigorously businesslike, launching straight into a detailed discussion of armaments and supplies and of speeded-up delivery schedules that would now be necessary. He had come well prepared, and handled himself with confidence and authority. He was careful not to divulge specific details of our operational plans. The Sinai Campaign would be the IDF's alone, he insisted; our plans must remain secret.

When we returned home, our reports differed starkly. Golda told the Cabinet glumly that the French were not unequivocally resolved to take military action. Moreover, her impression was that their military preparations were not yet seriously advanced. Through the grapevine, I heard that she had gone to Ben-Gurion privately and told him in blunt terms that I had misled the Cabinet and that the talks with the French leaders had been a charade. Ben-Gurion said nothing to me about Golda's allegations. For my part, I reported to him what had happened with Mollet and spoke of Foreign Minister Christian Pineau's habitual dourness and supreme caution – which Golda had seen as evidence of French hesitancy. The single most important fact, I argued, was that this high-level conference had taken place and that the French side had approved in principle all of our practical requests. If they were not resolved to fight, I said, why would they have gone to the trouble of holding the conference? Dayan was four-square behind me. He met Ben-Gurion separately and reported essentially along the same lines as I had, as indeed did Moshe Carmel.

Preparations for the campaign now moved into the operational phase, involving ever-closer co-ordination with the French. At first, Dayan accepted this situation with a certain ambivalence. He had favoured an entirely independent Israeli military action back in December (when the Cabinet majority opposed it), and both he and Ben-Gurion still jealously guarded the separate and independent role that Israel was to play within the broader plan. Ben-Gurion quoted Churchill, who advised that in a war coalition it is best for each national army to have its own well-defined front or mission, linked as closely as possible to its own national interest. Our national interest was to break the stranglehold on our trade route to Africa and Asia, to put an end to *fedayeen* terrorist incursions into Israel from the Gaza Strip, and to destroy to the greatest possible extent Egypt's military machine, a substantial part of which was now deployed in the Sinai Peninsula.

Dayan and I worked in total harmony and trust. Our relations with the French also developed into a rare example of mutual confidence between governments. I spoke several times during this period with Prime Minister Mollet by telephone. (We used an open line, on the assumption that no one would bother eavesdropping on an unscrambled conversation.) With Bourges-Maunoury our contacts were daily, conducted through Nahmias in Paris.

Dayan, perhaps contrary to his public image, was a very thorough and meticulous planner. He spent long hours bent over his maps, going over every detail of the battle-plans and logistics, and even longer hours at his various archaeological excavations. There, while digging into the past, he would be digging into his own fertile mind, seeking simultaneously for treasures of history and for novel solutions to current problems.

Ben-Gurion gave us broad leeway on the practical plane and never disparaged our ideas or suggestions. But ultimately, the decision was his to make, and, as the deadline approached, we still did not know what his final decision would be. We were preparing a military campaign, in co-ordination with our French friends and their British allies, but we did not know if Ben-Gurion intended our plans to be realized. The hints that he let drop were contradictory, and all that those around him could do was analyse them. On 21 September, for instance, Bourges-Maunoury told me in Paris that the British were dragging their feet and wanted to postpone the operation for a couple of months. France, on the other hand, was anxious to proceed in October as planned. 'Tell him', Ben-Gurion cabled in response to my own cabled report, 'that the French timing suits ours.' Yet, during the weeks that followed, as preparations went ahead for a crucial summit conference proposed by the French, Ben-Gurion asked me innumerable times, 'Are you sure that Mollet knows we have not committed ourselves?' Ben-Gurion, we knew, was deeply troubled by the fear that Egypt might bomb our population centres. Our own air force, he felt, was not sufficiently large or adequately equipped both to provide close support for the ground forces in the field and, at the same time, to keep the skies over Israel clear and protected. To allay this concern, we negotiated with the French the stationing in Israel, for the duration of the Sinai Campaign, of two French air-force interceptor squadrons (although they were not in fact needed).

We also knew that Ben-Gurion had a second condition, which, while not expressly articulated, would not be forgone. He insisted that the British participate actively in the military operation. Information had reached him from a very well-placed source (I believe I was the only other person with whom he shared this) to the effect that Britain's assurances were not to be relied upon. Ben-Gurion feared that at the last moment Britain might yet turn its back on us, or even turn against us, invoking its treaty relationships with Jordan and Iraq. This fear-cum-suspicion was heightened by Britain's behaviour during a brief but bloody battle between the IDF and Jordan's Arab Legion at the West Bank village of Kalkilya on the night of 11 October. The action grew out of a reprisal raid by an IDF paratroop unit. The paratroopers found themselves cut off by Jordanian forces, and the IDF had to use armour, artillery and air strikes to help them fight their way out. At dawn, as the battle raged on, the British Chargé d'Affaires called on Ben-Gurion at home to deliver a most urgent message from London. Israel would do well to remember, the message advised, that Jordan had a defence treaty with Britain; if the Israeli 'aggression' continued, Britain would be forced to take action.

Given Ben-Gurion's position, I sought repeatedly to impress upon my French interlocutors that if the British were out, we were out too. Moreover, Britain's commitment would need to be completely official and unequivocal; no wink-and-nod arrangement would satisfy Ben-Gurion. The French, accordingly, redoubled their own efforts on the Paris–London line, aware that any whiff of opacity from Whitehall could jeopardize the whole operation.

In conditions of total secrecy, Ben-Gurion set out for the fateful summit, together with Dayan and me and our close aides. Ben-Gurion wore a soft fedora to conceal his give-away white mane. Dayan removed his eye-patch and put on dark glasses for the trip. As we sat in silence behind the curtained windows of an unmarked car, heading for a military airfield, Ben-Gurion turned to me yet again: 'Shimon, are you absolutely sure they know we haven't committed ourselves? Do they know we're coming to this meeting solely as an act of friendship? If not, let's turn round now ...' Again I assured him that I had made his position totally clear to the French leadership.

We flew on a French plane that had originally been presented to de Gaulle as a gift from President Roosevelt on behalf of the United States Government. Thick clouds covered Paris, and we were forced to turn around and head back southwards, landing at an air base near Marseilles to refuel and then continuing on, as the pilots searched for a break in the clouds. All in all, the journey lasted seventeen hours, but Ben-Gurion seemed fine and was quickly whisked off by limousine to a villa at Sèvres, where the talks were to take place, while the rest of us were taken to a quiet hotel in Paris.

The first session began in the late afternoon of 22 October. It was intended as an opportunity for the French leadership – Prime Minister Mollet, Foreign Minister Pineau and Defence Minister Bourges-Maunoury – to get to know Ben-Gurion, and for him to meet them. After initial pleasantries, he launched into a lengthy exposition of a futuristic – he termed it 'fantastic' – scheme for a new and peaceful Middle East. He also delved into various philological and philosophical issues even farther removed from the issues at hand. The nitty-gritty negotiating, he was signalling, would be handled at this stage by his subordinates.

Ben-Gurion also spoke to the French of his deep dissatisfaction with a British proposal that Israel provide the pretext, in the form of a unilateral attack on Egypt, for subsequent Franco–British intervention. This dissatisfaction took on a much sharper edge later that same evening, when the British Foreign Secretary, Selwyn Lloyd, joined the talks and reiterated Britain's proposal. 'My reply is categorically negative,' Ben-Gurion told the suave British statesman. There was little left now of the warm ambience that had characterized the earlier, bilateral session between the French and ourselves. 'Israel has no desire to be branded as an aggressor', Ben-Gurion continued, 'and to be handed an ultimatum to withdraw from the Canal Zone.' Israel was not prepared to launch the war against Egypt on its own. If it were attacked, however, it would defend itself and was confident of eventual victory.

The atmosphere was grim, but now Ben-Gurion, handling himself with consummate diplomatic skill, deftly steered the conference away from deadlock. Israeli forces, he suggested, could carry out a reprisal action against Egypt on the agreed D-day in an area close to the Canal Zone. On that same night, he continued (and not two days later, as the British were proposing), Britain and France would issue an ultimatum to Egypt to withdraw its forces from the Canal Zone since the Canal was in danger, and to Israel not to approach the Zone. Egypt would reject the demand – and the two Western allies would then decide together what action to take.

For Lloyd, both the scope of the proposed Israeli operation and the time-span between Israel's action and that of the allies were inadequate. But Ben-Gurion's intervention meant the talks were not doomed. Lloyd flew back to London, and Pineau was due to follow him the next afternoon to hear the British position personally from the Prime Minister, Sir Anthony Eden. Meanwhile, the French leaders tried to win further flexibility from Ben-Gurion, arguing that to miss the present opportunity to attack Nasser might well mean having to give up the project for ever. We knew, however, that for Ben-Gurion the negotiations were still tentative: he had not yet taken the decision to go to war. He spent long hours alone at Sèvres, wrestling with his own thoughts and the weight of his responsibility.

Lunch next day saw another near-crisis – and another facet of Ben-Gurion's statesmanship. The French Deputy Chief of Staff, General Challe, suggested that Israel might 'stage' an Egyptian bombing raid on Beersheba as a pretext to declare war on Egypt, thereby triggering the desired Franco–British intervention against Egypt. As the General explained his idea, Ben-Gurion's face visibly darkened. Eventually, he spoke, instructing that his words be translated into French 'sentence by sentence'. 'I know that my reply to General Challe's proposal may seem irrational or perhaps naïve,' he said, 'but there are some things that I cannot do, and that I cannot advise my Government and my country to do. One of them is to lie to the world . . . to lie to the world in order to make things more convenient for England!

'. . . The Jewish People has many bitter grievances against the world, especially over what happened barely a decade ago, when almost all of European Jewry was slaughtered and the world remained silent. But there is one thing that protected us throughout the ages: our faith in the justice of our cause. Now, too, we believe in the justice of our cause and in our right to do what we are planning to do. But if I am required to do something that I cannot justify, something that is deceitful – that I will not do.'

A long moment of silence ensured. Challe tried sheepishly to explain away his abortive idea. Pineau and Bourges-Maunoury quickly stepped in to clear the air, offering Ben-Gurion a formal guarantee from France to Israel that Britain would live up to whatever was finally agreed between the three countries. The two delegations adjourned for private consultations. It was now that Dayan submitted to Ben-Gurion his operational plan in its final form: an IDF paratroop drop, at the outset of the campaign, on the strategic Mitla Pass, deep in Sinai and fairly close to the Canal.

This was Dayan at his best. In addition to its military advantages, the plan would provide the British and French with the 'pretext' they needed – and which Ben-Gurion could live with. In terms of Israel's own limited military goals in the campaign, the proposal was a stroke of strategic genius. We would start our war from the end. The Egyptian high command would be confused and outmanoeuvred. Our paratroopers would fight their way back, towards home, to link up with ground forces racing towards them. Dayan's plan called for two other armoured columns to strike simultaneously deep into enemy territory: one to take Sharm el-Sheikh, where Egyptian guns commanded the Straits of Tiran, the other to sweep into the Gaza Strip, from where the Palestinian *fedayeen* launched their murderous raids into Israel. But these elements of our military thinking Israel need not share with the French, and certainly not with the British. Ben-Gurion instructed Dayan to present the Mitla scheme to the French in vague terms as an informal idea which Pineau could take with him to London.

Two external events had converged, meanwhile, on the secret conference to make a favourable outcome more likely. In Jordan, parliamentary elections produced a decisive victory for the pro-Egyptian forces. The new Prime Minister, Suleiman Nabulsi, immediately proclaimed his intention of scrapping the treaty with Britain and leading Jordan into an alliance with Egypt and Syria. And in France itself, anti-Nasser feeling reached a new high with the arrest by the French navy off the cost of Algeria of an Egyptian vessel ferrying arms to the FLN. Press and public demanded a vigorous and unequivocal reaction from the Government. We knew, however, that whatever the decision of the French Government, the British had yet to say their final word – as had Ben-Gurion.

Next morning, Ben-Gurion telephoned Dayan and me in Paris and asked us to come to Sèvres at once. We found him in the garden, sitting under a tree with Nehemia Argov, looking grey and haggard. Plainly he had spent a sleepless night. Had he reached a decision? We still did not know? 'What,' he said, looking up at us, 'you're here so soon?' He asked Dayan to go over the plan once more, to show him the intended moves on a map. We had no map with us. I tore open a packet of cigarettes and Dayan drew the outline of Sinai on it, showing with bold arrows the proposed lines of advance. Ben-Gurion pulled out a piece of paper with a long list of detailed questions on it. As he read them out, a wave of relief washed over us. He had not said expressly what his decision was, but from the questions we understood that it was positive. These were not questions as to whether or not to undertake the operation, but as to how, when and where. Not all of them were answerable. Some were political, some were military and some dealt with the minutiae of the campaign. But by the very act of posing them, Ben-Gurion was telling us that his mind was made up.

He was also telling us that he had no territorial ambitions in this campaign, except, perhaps, for a strip of land along the Sinai coast to Sharm el-Sheikh. In the Cabinet the next day, when he sought his colleagues' approval for what had been agreed, he made the same point. The IDF would sweep across the whole of Sinai and Gaza, but it would not stay there. Our war aims were not to conquer territory, but to assert our right of passage through an international waterway and to put a stop to terrorist incursions across our border.

Pineau returned to Sèvres from London with Eden's agreement-in-principle to Dayan's proposal. A final tripartite session was held later that evening; two British officials, Sir Patrick Dean and Donald Logan, haggled with us and the French over the wording of a seven-point agreement – the 'Sèvres Protocol'.

Before the final signing, I asked Ben-Gurion for a brief adjournment, during which I met Mollet and Bourges-Maunoury alone. It was here that I finalized with these two leaders an agreement for the building of a nuclear reactor at Dimona, in southern Israel (which is discussed in greater detail in the next chapter), and the supply of natural uranium to fuel it. I put forward a series of detailed proposals and, after discussion, they accepted them.

Eventually, the Protocol was signed. Ben-Gurion carefully folded his copy and thrust it deep into his waistcoat pocket. Dayan cabled his deputy, General Meir Amit: 'Prospects for early execution of campaign. Mobilize all armoured units immediately . . . Leaving tonight.'

The Sinai–Suez war, which began five days later with the IDF paratroop drop at the Mitla Pass, was a huge military success for Israel, which swept through the Sinai Peninsula in a week, devastating the Egyptian army there. Not so, however, for Britain and France. Their forces reached their theatre, the Suez Canal Zone, belatedly and in disarray, ran up against Egyptian resistance, and were quickly brought to a halt by pressure from the two superpowers.★ That pressure was directed at Israel too, and

---

★ President Eisenhower's vigorous opposition to the British, French and Israeli actions came as something of a shock, at least to the British. The US Secretary of State, John Foster Dulles, had heard hints of the British plan from Prime Minister Eden and had reacted non-committally.

couched in the most brutal terms. A message from Soviet Prime Minister Nikolai Bulganin to Ben-Gurion on 6 November contained barely veiled threats against the very existence of Israel unless it ceased its fire immediately and withdrew. Ben-Gurion sent Golda Meir and me to Paris on 8 November to see if the French could do anything to help us. We met Pineau and Bourges-Maunoury. Pineau, more dour than ever, said that they were ready to share with us everything they had, but they had nothing that could shoot down Soviet missiles. As we were collecting our bags at the hotel, however, Bourges-Maunoury telephoned me to say that the French had intelligence information to the effect that Russia – despite its sabre-rattling – would not in fact take military action against Israel. In any event, he declared, France stood shoulder-to-shoulder with the Jewish state.

That night, Ben-Gurion received a tough, though polite, letter from President Eisenhower, and within hours he announced Israel's readiness to withdraw. Sustained international pressure eventually forced Israel to withdraw from all of the Sinai, including Sharm el-Sheikh, and, the following March, the Gaza Strip.

In immediate terms, however, the IDF achieved all of its goals in 100 hours of fast-moving desert warfare that both dazzled the world and established Moshe Dayan's reputation as a brilliant military commander and strategist. His instructions from the outset were to avoid killing Egyptian troops when possible. Our purpose was to destroy or capture their Soviet-supplied weaponry. This was achieved in vast quantities, and thousands of Egyptian soldiers were taken prisoner. Sharm el-Sheikh was taken and the Straits were reopened. They were to stay open for the next decade, a decade of growth for Israel, during which we expanded our economic and political ties with the emerging countries of Africa and Asia. The IDF conquered the Gaza Strip and purged the Palestinian terror bases there. That border, too, was to remain quiet during the decade of consolidation and development between 1956 and 1967.

11 NUCLEAR POWER

That brief 'time-out' in Sèvres between Mollet, Bourges-Maunoury and myself marked the culmination of years of effort by a tiny handful of Israelis. It marked, too, the start of the next, even more exciting and fateful phase, the phase of implementation. From the inception of the state, the issue of nuclear power had both fascinated and frightened Israel. A subject such as this, so vast yet so unknown, was bound to intrigue a leader of Ben-Gurion's intellectual curiosity – and, sure enough, he was both deeply intrigued and intensely curious.

Ben-Gurion believed that Science could compensate us for what Nature had denied us, in terms of resources and raw materials. Nature, indeed, has been niggardly with us. Israel is the only state in the region, other than Jordan and Lebanon, that has no oil. It has precious little water as well, and no minerals to speak of, apart from potash and phosphates. Half of the country, the Negev, is desert. In terms of conventional defence, too, Israel's geography has been unkind. The state is shaped in an elongated strip, without strategic breath along most of its length. Its extremities – the Galilee panhandle and the area around Eilat in the far south – are relatively isolated and difficult to defend. Its central heartland is threatened and overshadowed by the hill-country of the West Bank.

Nuclear power, therefore, was seen as a necessary option for a country bereft of natural resources and beset by danger. Ben-Gurion believed that through an intelligent use of nuclear power, we could produce electricity without resorting to oil or coal and enhance our water resources by desalinating sea-water.

In the early years of the state, there was some optimism in scientific circles regarding our ability to produce 'home-grown' uranium from our reserves of phosphate. Ben-Gurion was particularly enthusiastic. He had discussed the subject with a visiting American scientist and was convinced that the proven healing properties of the thermal hot-springs in Tiberias – which he himself frequented for medical purposes – demonstrated their radioactive potential. But over the years, we concluded that our uranium production process was too costly, and preferred to acquire the uranium we needed from foreign sources instead.

Ben-Gurion maintained a close relationship with the scientific community. The scientists, for their part, were mostly ambivalent. They admired him, but they feared an overly stifling embrace by the Government and were especially wary of an intimate link between science and defence, which, they felt, could compromise their standing in the international scientific community. Most of the leading physicists, moreover, while they supported the idea of young Israeli scientists studying nuclear physics both at home and abroad, believed that it was idle for a small country like Israel to dream of applying this discipline in a practical form. Their common wisdom was that nuclear energy was an option for Great Powers, not for small countries. A man of international repute like Professor Yoel (Giulio) Racah was totally opposed to any effort on Israel's part to enter upon the nuclear age. A younger man, the brilliant and charismatic Amos de Shalit, head of nuclear physics at the Weizmann Institute in Rehovot, also thought it irresponsible to lead Israel along 'this dangerous path'. Ben-Gurion, however, was not deterred and never ceased wooing the best scientific minds and encouraging them to 'think big'.

Among those whom he succeeded in wooing – or had no need to woo – were professors Yisrael Dostrovsky and Ernst David Bergman, both of the Weizmann Institute. Dostrovsky invented a process for manufacturing heavy water, which was later acquired by the French atomic energy authority.

But without doubt, it was Bergman who was the most impressive and the most consistently enthusiastic of the leading scientists involved in the Government's top-secret nuclear programme. Bergman was one of the most impressive people it was ever my good fortune to know. When Professor Chaim Weizmann decided to set up the Weizmann Institute in 1934 (then, it was named the Sieff Institute), he asked Albert Einstein to recommend a distinguished scientist to head it. Without hesitation, Einstein suggested Bergman, then a young and relatively unknown chemist.

Politically, Bergman moved steadily away from Weizmann's 'dove-ishness' and towards the defence-oriented approach of Ben-Gurion. In time, he became Ben-Gurion's chief scientific aide. When I became Director-General of the Ministry of Defence, Bergman moved into the Ministry – and the two of us struck out on an intimate partnership that continued for the rest of his life. Throughout that time, I never ceased to admire the man, despite the flaws in his personality that made him difficult to work with.

One of these flaws was an over-abundance of zeal. Professor Bergman was convinced that there was no problem that science could not solve. Moreover, as the chief scientist of the Defence Ministry, he regarded it as his job to provide solutions to every problem – and we often found ourselves having to cool his ardour for the sake of saving his own credibility. It was not that Bergman was out to delude anyone, but simply that he was so full of optimism and goodwill that he tended on occasion to advocate 'solutions' that looked good on paper but that had not been empirically tested, let alone proven.

Another weakness was his periodic lapses of discretion. He was so courteous and friendly to everyone that he sometimes forgot himself, or allowed himself to be carried away by his own exuberance. It was no wonder that he often found himself severely criticized by those within the closed coterie of scientists and officials who developed and shared the state's most valuable secrets.

I was as intrigued as Ben-Gurion and as enthusiastic as Bergman. But, as the projects developed, it became my responsibility to decide what could be done and what could not. On the face of it, that appears almost absurd. How could I have been given the responsibility for screening ideas, and vetoing those that seemed impractical, when my basic devotion to Israel's nuclear pretensions seemed, in the eyes of most of my colleagues at the time, a reflection of irresponsible adventurism? Throughout the many years during which the nuclear programme was the highest priority in my life, a good deal of my time was taken up with delicate inter-personal and inter-departmental diplomacy, all designed to keep the best people 'on the job' with the minimum of friction between them.

From the outset, I resolved to keep my role entirely out of the public limelight. However little was known in general about our nuclear programme, I wanted even less to be known about my own involvement. I felt that if I were exposed, the press could quickly destroy both me and the programme. After all, I was politically controversial, known as a reckless fantasizer, and the programme itself seemed so fantastic.

For this reason, my name was never included in any formal committee created in the area of atomic energy. That did not, however, prevent me from effectively running the entire programme on behalf of Ben-Gurion, nor did it in any way impair my authority. Ben-Gurion trusted me. Professor Bergman worked with me with no reservations. In time, I was able to win the trust and confidence of the other scientists, engineers and senior personnel engaged on the project.

Another resolution that I took at the outset was to insist that we need not invent things that had already been invented by others elsewhere. Originality was necessary, of course, but it was not an end in itself. This outlook brought me into headlong collision with Bergman. He believed that Israel had the potential and the ability to build its own nuclear reactor; I maintained that, if it were at all possible, we would do better to buy one abroad.

My third guiding principle was that, of all the countries engaged in nuclear research and development, only France might be prepared to help us. I believed, therefore, that all our diplomatic efforts should be focused on France – on the French Government and on the French scientific and industrial community.

Finally, I concluded early on that Israel's own nuclear physics 'establishment', in the main, would not be a source of support. Most of the top men simply did not believe that Israel had the ability to build its own nuclear option, and they gave frank voice to their opinion. My decision, therefore, was to approach the younger generation, men just recently graduated from the Technion in Haifa, who had an initial grounding in the discipline and had not yet been infected by the doubts and reservations of their more senior colleagues. In any event, most of the Israeli scientists who worked on building and operating our nuclear reactor were drawn from the ranks of these younger graduates.

I realized that much would depend on the character and ability of the project manager. I looked for a 'pedant', a man who would not compromise over detail, whether vital or ostensibly marginal. I knew that in the nuclear realm the most minor relaxation of standards could lead to national disaster. At the same time, the candidate had to be a man with an 'open mind', that is, a capacity to learn on the job; after all, he would not have had any prior experience in building nuclear reactors. My choice fell on Manes Pratt, whom I had come to know and respect during the War of Independence, when he had served as head of the Ordnance Corps.

Pratt had three university degrees and a finely developed aesthetic sense, which stood in incongruous contrast to his tough, no-nonsense approach to work. One of his strengths was his ability to familiarize himself with the details of an abstruse subject and then to present his conclusions and recommendations with remarkable clarity and cogency. I knew, when I appointed him, that he would give me a hard time, and indeed he did: he was never prepared to accept any product of our own Military Industries unless it met the most stringent international standards.

Earlier, I had arranged for his appointment as Military Attaché to Burma, where we were helping to build a national defence force, and it was thus from Burma that I summoned him home, to his amazement, to take control of the nuclear project. He asked for some time to learn the subject. Within a few months, he had become Israel's foremost expert in nuclear engineering. I use the term 'engineering' advisedly: there is a difference between the scientist and the engineer, akin perhaps to the difference between a lover and a husband. While Pratt became a real expert, I too developed into something of an authority in engin-eering, in physics and even in architecture. Whenever there were doubts or problems – and rarely a day went by without one – I was expected to decide and to sign.

Moreover, throughout this period, we were hamstrung by a profound lack of enthusiasm on the part of most of the Cabinet-level policy-makers other than Ben-Gurion. Golda Meir instinctively opposed anything to do with me; Pinhas Sapir tended to support her; and Levi Eshkol, the Minister of Finance, naturally recoiled at the high cost of building the reactor. Abba Eban, who returned to Israel in 1959, after a decade as Ambassador in the United States and became a Cabinet Minister, described the reactor as 'an enormous alligator stranded on dry land'. Even David Hacohen, a leading figure in Mapai and one of my few consistent supporters, said that he was afraid the nuclear programme would turn out to be 'so expensive that we shall be left without bread and even without rice'.

The bottom line for me, therefore, was that I would have to raise money 'on the side' to help pay for the reactor. We set up a discreet fund-raising operation, which raised contributions totalling more than $40 million – half the cost of the reactor, and a very considerable sum in those days. Most of this money came from direct personal appeals, by Ben-Gurion and myself, to friends of Israel around the world.

The problem of where to locate the reactor quickly brought together all its opponents – those who were against it for political reasons, those who feared the economic implications, and the scientists who opposed it on technical grounds. The choice was either a sea-shore location, where water, needed for cooling, would be easily available, or a site in the Negev desert. In the end, considerations of safety carried the day. Most of Israel's coastline is fairly heavily populated, whereas in the Negev we could find a relatively large and empty area, so that the nightmare scenario of a radioactive spillage would be less catastrophic.

The next question that came up was where to house the hundreds of French scientists and technicians who were to work on the project. Our solution was to build a separate suburb in Beersheba, the only sizeable town in the Negev. Our own young scientists and their families were reluctant to leave the centre of the country and set up home in this remote and sandy 'outback'. I remember meeting a group of their wives and promising them that there would be a modern hospital in Beersheba (now the Soroka Medical Centre, which the Ministry of Defence helped to build) and even a beauty salon as good as anything in Tel Aviv.

Beauty salon aside, our plans called for building roads and laying miles of power lines and water pipes. Manes Pratt and I decided between ourselves that the Dimona reactor would be an industrial park of the highest and most aesthetically pleasing standards. We commissioned the country's top architects, and indeed the office blocks, residential buildings and scientific facilities that they planned and erected still comprise the most attractive industrial complex in the country, graced by tall, swaying palms, planted to relieve the starkness of the desert skyline.

The first stage of construction was a vast excavation. A bird's-eye view would have revealed great gashes dug into the desert. A spy-plane or satellite would have had the same view, which was enough to send twinges of trepidation through the minds of my Cabinet opponents.

I was in Senegal at the time, representing Israel at the installation of President Leopold Senghor, when an urgent cable reached me ordering my immediate return. This was awkward, to say the least. I was on close terms with the Senegalese Defence Minister and was his personal guest at the celebrations. I had flown in, on a Moroccan government plane, together with the Aga Khan, and was in the process of forming an important friendship with him. He was the highest-ranking personage at the event, as he enjoyed international fame due to his status as a religious leader, while the rest of us merely represented governments. Everyone wanted to be introduced to him, and I, as his intimate companion, was expected to make the introductions. Lady Bird Johnson, the then Vice-President-designate's wife, prevailed on me to arrange a lunch à trois. Now, suddenly, I was forced to leave.

However, the cable brooked no delay. I made my apologies as well as I could and arrived in Israel on Passover eve. I flew straight from the airport – together with a sour-faced Golda and the head of the Mossad, Isser Harel – to Ben-Gurion at Sde Boker. Before that, I had had to field reporters' questions about my trip to Senegal, without disclosing either my own nervousness or the fact that Golda was sitting in a helicopter nearby, even more nervous, waiting grimly to take off for the south. When I finally climbed aboard, she and Harel barely replied to my 'Shalom'. Instinctively, I knew there was little point in questioning them about what had happened and why I had been recalled. We reached Sde Boker and filed into Ben-Gurion's hut. 'Well,' he said, turning to Harel, 'explain the situation.'

Harel began by reporting that he had reliable information to the effect that Andrei Gromyko, the Soviet Foreign Minister, had flown unexpectedly to Washington to see Secretary of State John Foster Dulles. He also had information that a Soviet satellite had recently overflown and photographed Dimona. Putting two and two together was relatively simple, Harel went on. The Russians had obviously found out what we were up to, and they had decided to make a dramatic protest to the United States over the dangers inherent in our activity. Gromyko would be demanding that Dulles exercise the most vigorous American pressure on Israel to get it to stop building the reactor.

Israel, therefore, said Harel, faced a most grave situation, with the two superpowers likely to confront it jointly and to demand acquiescence. He proposed that Ben-Gurion, or at the very least Golda Meir, fly forthwith to Washington and assure the Americans that we had no intention of doing what they obviously suspected us of intending to do.

Ben-Gurion asked Golda if she had anything to add. She said that the facts spoke for themselves and that their gravity could hardly be exaggerated. She agreed with Harel that Israel must act with the utmost dispatch to prevent Gromyko from persuading the Americans to take action against us.

There was a sense both of certainty and of hopelessness in the air when Ben-Gurion asked for my reaction. I replied that everything that had been said so far seemed frankly weird to me. So what if a Soviet satellite had overflown the Negev? What had it photographed? Just holes in the ground. What could be proved from holes in the ground? After all, every building needs foundations. What was to say that those emplacements were not intended for the foundations for a perfectly ordinary building? As for Gromyko, I continued, there could be a thousand valid reasons why he had gone on an unannounced trip to America.

In the worst-case scenario, if Harel was right and the two superpower statesmen concluded that our construction was intended for nuclear purposes, we could offer *then* whatever explanations and assurances Harel and Golda proposed we give now. Why jump the gun? Moreover, it would be quite wrong for Ben-Gurion to fly to Washington without first co-ordinating with France. This matter was, after all, of no little concern to the French. One thing I could promise: if we were looking for a way to destroy our relations with France, this was the way. In fact, I concluded, there was really no need to go to Paris: the French would be only too pleased to drop out of the entire project at the slightest hint from Israel that it, too, had cold feet.

My performance put Ben-Gurion in a difficult position. Once again, he had to choose between taking a decision which would look as if he were taking sides with me against Golda and the others, or agreeing with them even though in his heart he agreed with me. He tried to make a concluding statement that was vague enough to reconcile the opposing positions. Yes, he said, the matter was indeed grave and might well become graver still. But I seemed to be right, he went on, in that we had time before making our move, and that whatever we did must be co-ordinated with the French.

Golda could not conceal her disappointment. The Mossad chief was fuming. I swallowed hard and kept quiet. Frankly, I did not understand why Ben-Gurion had cut short my mission to West Africa and ordered me home. We trooped back to the helicopter. Soon the sun would set and Passover would begin. It was *Seder* night − the family time *par excellence* of the Jewish year. We were supposed to drop off Golda in Jerusalem, where she was to celebrate the *Seder* with her family and friends, but the city was covered in a blanket of cloud. Nothing was said, but I felt that Golda blamed me for that too. Eventually, we landed at Lydda Airport, where my car was waiting for me. (Golda's car and driver were up in Jerusalem.) I offered her a ride to the capital, and this seemed to placate her a little. After taking her, I returned home for my own family *Seder*. Sonia looked at me and seemed to understand everything, without a word being said.

This was not the only time that our nuclear project was in danger of premature termination. Maurice Bourges-Maunoury became Prime Minister of France after the fall of Guy Mollet's Government in June 1957. I was very close friends with both of them. Bourges-Maunoury had a wonderfully sardonic sense of humour, which sometimes misled people as to the thoughtful character that lay beneath it. (I remember once asking him to define the ideology of the Radical Party, whose President he was. 'To represent the changes that have occurred in the situation' was his wry reply.) Mollet, on the other hand, was a schoolmaster both by vocation and by disposition. He liked to launch into long and complicated explanations about everything, and he thoroughly disliked Bourges-Maunoury's brief and pithy one-liners. I urged Mollet to look beneath Bourges-Maunoury's superficial jocularity and see the man's true gifts. When the crisis broke out, I tried to persuade Mollet to support Bourges-Maunoury as his successor – and eventually he agreed. When I told Bourges-Maunoury, he could scarcely believe his ears.

The Bourges-Maunoury Government was weak and fragile from the outset – so much so, in fact, that Bourges-Maunoury said that he would 'count the Ministers at the beginning and end of each Cabinet meeting. If they're all still there,' he explained, 'I feel like I've won a major victory!' Soon enough, it crumbled, but just as its final Cabinet meeting was taking place, we realized, to our horror, that the Foreign Minister had not yet signed, in the name of France, the nuclear agreement between our two countries. I knew that if the Bourges-Maunoury Government did not sign, the document might never be signed. The Government was expected to fall that same day.

This was a moment for unorthodox diplomacy. Together with Yosef Nahmias, I rushed to the Hôtel Matignon, where the Cabinet was in session. I asked an aide to Bourges-Maunoury, who was also a good friend of ours, to slip a note to his boss: we had to speak to him, just for a couple of minutes, before the end of the meeting. Bourges-Maunoury took an unorthodox step, too: he stopped the Cabinet meeting for a few minutes and came out to talk to me. I briefly explained to him what had happened, and he promised to put matters right before relinquishing office. And sure enough, before the Cabinet meeting ended, the outgoing

Prime Minister pushed through a decision requiring the Foreign Minister to sign the agreement with Israel at once.

A third occasion when our nuclear programme came close to extinction – and was saved in a dramatic meeting in Paris – was in 1959. At this time, General de Gaulle was in power, and he had appointed Maurice Couve de Murville as his Foreign Minister, a professional diplomat who had formerly served as Ambassador to Egypt. It seemed – to us at any rate – that while France's Ambassador to Israel during the 1950s, Pierre Gilbert, had developed a warm respect for Zionism, his colleague in Cairo had embraced some of Egypt's hostile approach to the Jewish state. The personal relationship between these two diplomats was certainly cold, and de Murville wasted little time, once he had become Minister, before recalling Gilbert from Tel Aviv.

Without mincing words, de Murville told his Israeli counterpart, Golda Meir, that France had decided to abrogate its nuclear agreement with Israel. He demanded that Israel halt the building of the Dimona facility and offered to reimburse Israel for the expenditures on French goods in connection with the project. Golda's cable left no room for doubt, or for hope: the French decision was final.

Ben-Gurion asked me what I thought we could do, and, to be frank, I had no answer for him. But I felt that we could not just throw up our hands without a fight, and I asked him therefore to send me to Paris to speak to de Murville. Ben-Gurion said that he could not do that without Golda's consent, and, to her lasting credit, she readily agreed. Her condition was that the Israeli Ambassador to France accompany me to the meeting.

I flew to Paris, thoroughly depressed. I knew that without the French Dimona was doomed: there was no realistic alternative. And I knew de Murville: he was a serious man with a fine, calculating mind; a devout Protestant, who knew long passages of the Bible by heart. As I pondered the conversation that awaited me, it struck me that, to a man like de Murville, diplomacy was like a game of chess. You planned your moves and tried to read your opponent's mind. But if he caught you unawares with a deft move of his own, you had no option but to recognize the consequences and graciously accept defeat.

As I waited in the ante-room, I still did not know how the pieces on our chessboard would be moved. The clock struck twelve noon. I knew that the double doors would open precisely at that moment, and that we would be ushered in. De Murville was as punctual as a Swiss watch. He smiled at me courteously, as if to say, 'We both know what you're here for, and you know that it's hopeless, but because our countries have a long friendship, which we share, I have agreed to meet you.'

He then proceeded to repeat all the arguments he had presented to Golda and the conclusions he had reached. I replied that what he was proposing meant both reneging on previous French government decisions and robbing Israel of its eventual reactor and of five years of Herculean effort. No amount of money could compensate us for the wasted work.

Furthermore, I added quietly, he was proposing to violate unilaterally a bilateral undertaking not to reveal the details of the agreement between us to the Arab world, and most especially to the officials who ran the Arab boycott and who would be eager to punish foreign (meaning French) firms that had co-operated with us. De Murville broke in at this point, saying that he had no intention of violating the undertaking not to publish our agreement. France would divulge nothing, he said, neither the broad outline of the agreement nor its specific details. To this I replied that if he were unilaterally abrogating the essence of the agreement, we would be unable to maintain those aspects of it that he wished to be maintained, viz. the non-publication provision. He asked me what I was proposing. I said that he could abrogate the agreement, if he so insisted, from this moment on. But as for what had been done in the past, he had no right to abrogate any of these decisions retroactively.

De Murville thought for a moment and then said, 'You have a point.' The chess game had ended.

12 MOSHE DAYAN

For many years, Moshe Dayan was the most admired Israeli in the world, and he was much respected in Israel too. His sharp photogenic features, with the black eye-patch covering his war wound, were familiar to every child. His heroic exploits, real or imaginary, and his quick wit, acquired that international renown that is the hallmark of a living legend.

I have come across his name in some of the most unexpected places. Once, when I was on a visit to a certain African country, my car pulled in to a gas station to fill up. The pumps carried the then universal advertising slogan, 'Put a Tiger in your Tank'. Only in this particular out-of-the-way garage, the attendant had deleted 'Tiger' and painted 'Dayan' in its place, sticking a photo of Moshe over the original picture of the tiger. On another occasion, I was walking on one of the main streets of San Francisco when I saw three huge photographs in a shop window: of Mao Tse-tung, Che Guevara and Moshe Dayan. When I came home, I told Dayan, and the two of us laughed heartily as we tried to find a common denominator uniting these three disparate world figures.

My own acquaintance with Dayan began in the early 1940s. Even before I met him, I had heard of him. At a regional Haganah meeting in Kibbutz Geva, where I and my friends were on *hachshara* (preparing to found our own kibbutz), a Haganah commander read to us a report, written by Dayan's friend Zalman Mart, on how he had lost his eye in an engagement in Lebanon. The report was written in terse and factual military language, but it still sounded like an epic of bravery. Dayan, who was scouting for an Australian unit in Allied operations against the Vichy French, was hit by a sniper whose bullet struck his binoculars. His face drenched in blood, he gave no outward sign of pain. Quickly assessing his condition, he merely observed that, henceforth, he would be limited to a single vision in his view of the world.

I first met Dayan face to face at his family home in the moshav of Nahalal. I was a close friend of his brother Zorik, who was to fall in the War of Independence in a battle against Druze forces at Ramat Yohanan. While Zorik was tall and broad, Moshe was short and stocky. But already the power of his personality radiated from his tough and muscular frame. Moshe made no effort to impress; rather, his brief, businesslike questions were framed to elicit the information about me that he wanted to know. That was his style: he preferred the dry facts, succinctly delivered, stripped of any overlay or padding. In all our long years of close acquaintance, I never once heard him boast, or sentimentalize, or say anything silly. His regard was for the bare, elemental truth; wintertime truth, unadorned by spring's flowers or foliage. When his colleagues tried to have him take a political course which he had set his mind against, he would say, 'If I took your advice – I would be like you. And then you wouldn't have to advise me.' But in fact, he was never like us.

Through my political work, I came to know Dayan's parents, Shmuel and Dvora. His mother was the woman whom he most admired throughout his life. She was short and wore her black hair in two plaits, wrapped around her head. (Her hair stayed black into her later years, a genetic trait that Moshe inherited.) Her face, delicately featured, projected a sense of sadness mixed with steely determination. She spoke quietly, almost whispered, and her articles, which appeared regularly in *Dvar Hapoalot*, *Davar*'s supplement for women, were always beautifully written. Moshe must have inherited his own notable talent for writing, and his love of poetry and prose, from his mother.

His father, a Mapai Member of the Knesset in the early years of the state, was altogether different. He was a hard and stubborn man, industrious and conscientious, but narrow-minded. He represented the moshav movement within the party, a role that gave him both power and importance.

Our casual acquaintanceship began to grow into a closer relationship when Dayan and I were chosen to represent the younger generation of the party at the Zionist Congress in Basel in 1946.*

During the War of Independence, Dayan fought as a rising young general while I worked under Ben-Gurion and Eshkol at the army

* See page 54.

high command. His name often came up in conversation, triggering remarkably varied reactions (often from the same person). Eshkol once called him 'Abu Jilda', after an Arab gang leader. Moshe Sharett, the always cautious, politically moderate Foreign Minister, had deep reservations about him, which he readily shared with others. And Yigael Yadin, the Deputy Chief of Staff, clearly preferred Yigal Allon over Dayan. Allon was also a young wartime general, the commander of the elite Palmach corps until Ben-Gurion disbanded it. The rivalry between these two went back to pre-war days and was to continue until their deaths, more than thirty years later.

Dayan himself was entirely taken up with the fighting and had little time for the corridor gossip of the high command. He commanded an armoured brigade and cut a dashing figure in his jeep, at the head of a column of armoured vehicles, charging through small Arab towns.

When controversies erupted around him, as they often did then and later, he could always count on my support, and also on that of two close aides to Ben-Gurion: his military aide-de-camp, Nehemiah Argov, and his *chef de cabinet*, Haim Yisraeli. In 1957, Argov was to take his own life. I felt such a close bond to him that I decided, with Sonia, to name our second son (born soon after) Nehemiah in his memory.* Haim Yisraeli continued to work into the 1990s as the discreet and trusted aide of every successive Minister of Defence. He is one of the wisest and most loyal men I have known.

All three of us – Argov, Yisraeli and myself – believed in Dayan. We saw personified in him the unique traits of our evolving nation, with its greatnesses and its foibles. I felt that his leadership potential – both military and political – was still largely untapped. He would sometimes offer me his strategic or diplomatic assessments of situations, always tinged with pessimism, yet always crafted so as to hold out the prospect of an original but workable solution. I would duly convey Dayan's thoughts and ideas to Ben-Gurion and Eshkol. In the most important strategic dispute of the war, over whether to concentrate all our available power on smashing the siege of Jerusalem, or to focus on the Egyptian invasion of the Negev, Dayan sided firmly with Ben-Gurion and in favour of the Jerusalem option. Yadin took the other view, which

---

* Sonia and I have three children: Zviya (Zikki), who teaches psycho-linguistics and the computerization of education; Yonatan (Yoni), who is a veterinarian; and Nehemiah (Hemi), who was a pilot in the air force and is now an industrialist.

further contributed to his less-than-enthusiastic attitude towards Dayan.

Yadin was a great stickler for military form and discipline, which, in his view, meant primarily a soldierly appearance by both officers and men. In Dayan, who had not served, as Yadin had, for any length of time in the British army, and who was by nature and predilection hardly a spit-and-polish soldier, Yadin saw the image of the partisan or irregular fighter, which he so wanted to eliminate from the new state's army.

I shall never forget a session of the General Staff, when Dayan was already a full general and head of Southern Command. Yadin prepared himself meticulously for these meetings. Calling the officers to order, his eyes would move quickly down the table, ensuring that all were present and correct. This time he stopped at Dayan. 'How', he asked dryly, 'can senior officers expect their subordinates to obey the rules laid down by the high command if they themselves neglect to obey them?'

A heavy silence descended on the room. Dayan plainly had no idea what the Chief of Staff was driving at. But Yadin's stony gaze never wavered from him. Slowly, he began examining himself. At last, he alighted upon his shirt pocket. The button was undone. Sheepishly, sweating in embarrassment, he did it up. I think that was the only time I saw Dayan completely nonplussed.

When, at the age of twenty-eight and with the nominal title of Deputy Director-General of the Ministry of Defence, I began attending the weekly meetings of 'the Defence Minister's Forum' – the Minister, his top aide, the Chief of Staff, his deputy and the head of military intelligence – Yadin hardly hid his disapproval. Not that he himself was that much older than me (he was thirty-four at the time), but he felt that I was too inexperienced for such weighty deliberations. Yet, in effect, I was running the Ministry: the Director-General, Ze'ev Schind, doubled as Director-General of the Ministry of Transport and spent more of his energies there than at Defence, as he sensed his lack of 'chemistry' with Ben-Gurion. Indeed, within a year, in October 1952, I was formally appointed Director-General.

I had great respect for Yadin. Apart from his great promise as an archaeologist, his talents as a moving and powerful speaker, and his profound and consistent devotion to the tenets of *mamlachtiut* – the doctrine of state interest taking precedence over all party or sectoral interests, as preached by Ben-Gurion – he ran the army brilliantly. He handled the General Staff with aplomb, and his personal relationship with Ben-Gurion was a model that, sadly perhaps, only few others in the senior echelons of political and military life were high-minded enough to follow: he would praise the Old Man behind his back – and criticize him to his face. Ben-Gurion valued Yadin enormously. In his heart, he saw him as his eventual successor.

My own relationship with Yadin was to improve in later years, as our careers went their separate ways, following his departure from the army. (Yadin retired from the army in 1952 and returned to academic life. He declined various attempts over the years to draw him back into national affairs. But, in 1977, he took the plunge, creating the Democratic Movement for Change, which ran in the election that year and joined Menachem Begin's Government. Yadin became Deputy Prime Minister.*)

In those early years, however, we were sharply at odds over the role of the Cabinet and of civilian officials in overseeing the military. Yadin maintained that the army should report solely and directly to the Minister of Defence, and to no one else. There was friction over more mundane matters, too. He claimed that the soldiers were not getting enough to eat. He also said that their housing and uniforms were inadequate, and that there wasn't enough money for training programmes. I insisted that every spare penny should go to arms purchases abroad and to military research and development at home. We had won the War of Independence by a miracle and were left with our meagre arsenals totally depleted. Arms embargoes imposed on us during the war continued after the armistice, while the Arabs managed with relative ease to replenish their stocks. To the present day, as I have already mentioned, I find it hard to comprehend why the United States, having recognized Israel as a state, refused to sell us even rifles to defend ourselves from the Arab onslaught that followed independence.

I was so singled-minded in the matter of defence spending and priorities that I even proposed reducing the size of the standing army – if that could free funds for buying the hardware we needed. By the same token, I insisted – indeed demanded – that the army slim down by ridding itself of a whole number of essentially non-military units: the army laundry, the army bakery, the army hospital at Tel Hashomer whose staff numbered more than a thousand. All these should be turned over to civilian management, I argued, and the army would contract for the services it needed.

I had two rock-solid supporters in this conflict with Yadin: Generals Moshe Dayan and Mordechai (Motke) Makleff. Dayan had never been

* See pages 174, 274–5.

overly impressed with Yadin's administrative side. He felt that Yadin was for ever setting up staffs and needlessly complicating the bureaucracy. For Dayan, the be-all and end-all was the fighting man and the front-line units. He thought that Yadin devoted too much of the army's slender resources to the various rear echelons.

The real surprise, though, was General Makleff, who was Yadin's Deputy Chief of Staff. He was regarded very much as Yadin's man. Nevertheless, it was Makleff who came to me, on his own initiative, to say how much he thought that I was in the right, and that Yadin was mistaken, in this argument between us. We would meet alone before each session of the Minister's Forum, to go over the agenda, and in these meetings Makleff was even more extreme than I in urging a redefinition of the army's order of priorities. He approached Yadin a number of times, but the Chief of Staff remained unmoved. He would only give ground, Yadin declared, if ordered to do so by Ben-Gurion. I therefore pressed my own views on Ben-Gurion, stressing that Makleff fully endorsed them.

In the end, Ben-Gurion issued explicit orders to reduce the pro-fessional army by some 5,000 men and to transfer several military services and installations to civilian control. Yadin, a man of great dignity, resigned immediately. Makleff was appointed his successor. I looked forward to a new period of close and harmonious relations between the Ministry and the army.

I was to be quickly disappointed, however. For no sooner had Makleff become Chief of Staff than he became as doggedly 'territorial' as Yadin. He was ready to forgo the laundry and the bakery, but he wanted the professional army expanded again. More significantly, his position on the issue of civilian control verged on the absurd. He wanted the Ministry of Defence to be made formally subordinate to the army General Staff. I shall never know what brought about this rapid and radical metamorphosis; perhaps Makleff wanted to prove, after the fact, that he had remained loyal to Yadin after all.

In any event, Makleff overreached himself when he presented Ben-Gurion with a list of thirty senior officers whom he wanted fired. My name also appeared on his list. Everyone felt at the time that something strange and unfathomable was happening to this excellent soldier and administrator, who had previously got on so well with the people he had worked with. Ben-Gurion decided that he would have to go, even though he had been in office for less than a year. The high command

and the political establishment were plunged into a whirl of rumours, pressures and speculation regarding his successor. The leading candidates were Generals Dayan, Haim Laskov and Shlomo Shamir.

Ben-Gurion was very fond of Laskov. He called him 'Israel's Number One soldier' (which led Ariel [Arik] Sharon, then a rising young officer, to comment acerbically that what was needed at the head of the IDF was not a soldier but a general). I was also close to Laskov. He used to come round to our home on Friday afternoons to play with our children. He was childless himself and adored children. Whenever he came, he would bring an armful of books that he wanted me to read in preparation for the position that he believed I would soon hold: Minister of Defence.

Nevertheless, I backed Dayan for Chief of Staff. I believed that Dayan alone could breathe a new and much-needed fighting spirit into the army. I lobbied actively for Dayan with Ben-Gurion, and sought, too, to win over Nehemiah Argov, whose views weighed heavily with Ben-Gurion. Ben-Gurion, of course, had heard all the unfavourable stories and rumours about Dayan: that he was disorganized, undisciplined, irresponsible and so forth. I argued that much of this was false or tendentious and that, despite his off-beat image, Dayan was in fact a rigorous administrator, a stickler for detail, and a tactician who never lost sight of his military objective. I maintained enthusiastically that, as Chief of Staff, Dayan would give Ben-Gurion the practical support which his political strategy required. Ben-Gurion adored Dayan, and my arguments fell on fertile soil.

In the end, Dayan won the appointment. He was thirty-eight years old – not the youngest of Israel's Chiefs of Staff, but certainly the most outspoken, and in many ways the most remarkable.

Indeed, these qualities in Dayan nearly caused me a heart attack. I was in my office at the Defence Ministry when I suddenly received a telephone call from Ben-Gurion from the floor above. This in itself was somewhat rare: Ben-Gurion seldom used the phone. When he did so, he was terse, like a telegram. He would dispense with 'Shalom' at the beginning and end of the conversation, restricting himself to the substance of what he wanted to convey. This time, that substance was conveyed in three words: 'Shimon, come immediately.'

I ran up the stairs and into Ben-Gurion's room. 'That Moshe of yours', he spat at me as I entered, 'is standing on the balcony of the IDF headquarters with a rifle and shooting indiscriminately.'

I mumbled something to the effect that this was impossible, that there must be a mistake, and rushed over to the two-storey General Staff building next door. Sure enough, Dayan was there, on the balcony, with a shotgun. I flew up the stairs and burst in. 'Have you gone mad?' I began. He turned round calmly. 'Have you received an invitation to dinner at my house tonight?' he asked. I confirmed that I had. 'Do you know what the occasion is?' I admitted that I did not. 'It's my thirty-ninth birthday,' he explained sweetly. 'I've decided to invite forty guests. The main course will be roast pigeon – and now I'm bagging the pigeons.'

Dayan's appointment as Chief of Staff created an immediate and momentous change of atmosphere throughout the army. He coined the slogan 'After Me', which was to become the watchword of the new generation of IDF officers, who were expected to lead their men into the attack. 'Better guns than socks' was another Dayan motto. He used it to persuade his staff of the new order of priorities that he proposed to introduce. He created new paratroop units that were to carry out most of the reprisal actions that preceded the 1956 Sinai Campaign. He spoke to the nation, in public appearances and through the media, in clear, straightforward language (and wonderful Hebrew), explaining the situation as he saw it. The army veritably worshipped him – as did many 'ordinary' Israelis.

Working relations between Dayan and myself were superb. At our first business meeting after his appointment, Dayan proposed a simple but sophisticated rule-of-thumb. 'In matters dealt with primarily by the army high command, you will help the high command; in areas mainly dealt with by the Ministry, I will help the Ministry.' He suggested that we jointly appoint a financial adviser, who would supervise the budgets of both organizations. He advocated what he called an 'open-book policy': everything that went on in his office would be open to me, and everything that I was involved with would be similarly accessible to him. He insisted that I take part not only in full sessions of the General Staff, but also in smaller, informal meetings and consultations with officers of various ranks, and willingly enabled me to communicate directly with all sections of the armed forces. Ben-Gurion was enormously gratified by the extent and intensity of our co-operation, upon which many of the key structures of our defence policy were built: the relationship with France, the development of the Israel Aircraft Industries, the creation of the Weapons Research and Development Authority, the establishment of our earliest electronics industries and, above all, the nuclear reactor at Dimona.

The downside, of course, was that this close co-operation between Dayan and myself, and Ben-Gurion's attitude towards the two of us and towards our closeness, provoked jealous rumours throughout the political community. We began to be referred to, not always with warmth, as 'the Old Man's youngsters', and steadily a feeling grew within the top echelons of Mapai that he intended to leap-frog us to national power over the heads of the expectant but impatient 'next generation', the Old Man's longtime followers.

Over the years, my friendship with Dayan developed beyond strictly political and professional lines. We also had common intellectual interests. Both of us valued Nathan Alterman and S. Yizhar among our closest friends. These two men of letters differed greatly. Alterman's friendship was warm and intimate, and he loved to hold long, rambling conversations with a single interlocutor. Yizhar was more reserved and introverted; every sentence he spoke was like a carefully crafted work of literature.

Alterman's friendship was a central pillar, firm and unshakable, in my life. Like Albert Camus, Alterman grappled constantly with the issue of suicide, which he viewed as the greatest existential problem in his philosophy. I remember seeing him in our home, in 1970, just two days before he entered the hospital with the stomach ailment that eventually took his life. Both Sonia and I felt that he had lost the will to live. But sceptical as he was about himself, Alterman was filled with unremitting enthusiasm for his country and his people. For him, national security was always the first priority. He was a believer in Greater Israel, but in private conversation he stressed that if Israel were to come under a Soviet or an American threat, and its survival as a sovereign state were to be put in jeopardy, then ensuring national security must take priority over Greater Israel. Alterman was a true believer, but not a fanatic. Poetry stirred him; reality made him smile, wryly.

Yizhar, for his part, would raise our spirits through his speeches and articles, with his matchless Hebrew prose and his unequalled ability to go straight to the heart of a matter. We would drink in his words, in speech or in print, with a thirst that was almost physical.

Dayan, in addition to his love of literature, had an artistic streak of his own. Apart from his famous diligence in delicately reconstructing ancient artefacts from shards he had unearthed at archaeological sites, he sometimes found time to paint and often tried his hand at verse. Whatever he wrote – his autobiographical *Avnei Derech*★ is one of the best political biographies published in Israel – involved painstaking, unflagging care to find precisely the right words or phrases to express his finely nuanced thoughts. He loved words – as he hated verbosity. He could recite whole tracts of Avraham Shlonsky's poetry by heart.

The press, disparagingly, would call us 'doers' – meaning that we were essentially pragmatists, good at getting things done, but shallow when it came to thinking things through. (Later in life, I would often be deprecated as a 'visionary'. I never seemed to enjoy measured, balanced appreciation and criticism.) I always knew in my heart, though, that there was another side to life, not 'pragmatic' or to do with 'doing', that gave our pragmatism meaning and imbued our mundane work with vision and purpose. I felt that this band of 'doers' – Ben-Gurion, Dayan, Alterman, Yizhar and myself – had a shared, secret world. It was unspoken, but it meant everything. Somewhere in the depths of the soul, there was a magnetic pull – towards the poem, the story, the line of prose, the historical intuition, the exotic land and eccentric life of the Jewish People. This pull, moreover, was no less real than the plane, the tank and the gun which we spent our days and nights working to procure.

One of the differences between Dayan and myself was his profound attraction to the ancient past and my no less intense curiosity about the future. Dayan identified as wholly with our forebears, in their flowing robes and sandals, as he did with our contemporaries in the cockpits of jet fighters. Every ancient discovery was to him of immediate and urgent significance. My own mind was fixed on the future: on what was likely to happen, or, more importantly, what could be done now to influence what would happen later. He inclined to pessimism; I was given to unwarranted optimism.

In 1958, we were invited to Burma, as the guests of General Ne Win, the army Chief of Staff and effectively the country's strongman. We were entertained lavishly and graciously. A splendid government guest-house, set amid lakes and woodlands, was at our disposal in Rangoon; in the countryside, we visited temples and pagodas, and made our stately way through Mandalay by river, rowed by oarsmen whose oars were tied to their feet. The scenes seemed so different from the descriptions in Kipling. Wherever we went, we were warmly greeted by ordinary folk

★ Edanim, Tel Aviv, 1976.

The Peres family, 1945. Left to right, standing: Peres's wife Sonia, brother Gershon and his wife, Carmella. Seated: Shimon Peres, his mother and father.

With Ben-Gurion during the Sèvres Conference, 1956.

With Sonia after receiving the Légion d'Honneur, *1957.*

The family in 1955. Left to right, son Hemi, father Yitzhak, mother Sara, son Yoni, Sonia, niece Ruthi, daughter Zikki, Shimon Peres, Gershon and Carmella.

*With two political comrades in
Rafi, 1969; Moshe Dayan
(left) and Teddy Kollek.*

*On an Israeli navy missile boat
when he was Minister of
Defence, 1976.*

A press conference after the Entebbe rescue, with Brigadier General Dan Shomron who headed the commando seated left, July 1976.

With President Sadat and former Prime Minister Golda Meir at the Knesset during Sadat's historic visit to Jerusalem, November 1977.

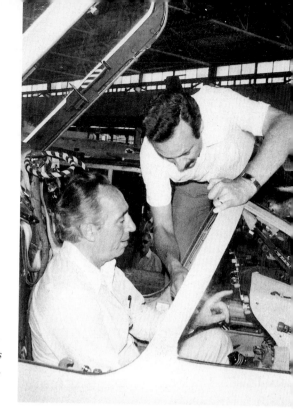

In the cockpit of an Israeli-made Kfir jet fighter, 1980.

Election night, June 1981. Early euphoria gave way to disappointment as the returns showed Peres's Labour Party and its rival, the Likud, almost tied. Likud formed the new Government.

A handshake between Peres and Yitzhak Shamir, leader of the Likud bloc, after a meeting to 'consider the possibility' of forming a government of national unity, August 1984.

As Prime Minister in 1985, meeting President Reagan to discuss beginning peace negotiations with Jordan.

Meeting Ethiopian Jews, recently arrived in Israel, in Eilat, 1985.

With King Hassan II of Morocco, 1986.

The secret signing ceremony in Oslo, August 1993. Johan Holst sits in front of Shimon Peres with Abu Ala'a (on his right) and Uri Savir.

A more relaxed moment in Oslo. Left to right, Terje Larsen, Shimon Peres, Johan Holst and Abu Ala'a.

and fussed over by officials. Each evening colourful pageants and dances were laid on in our honour. When these were finished, storytellers would take over, terrifying the company – ourselves among them – with tales of tigers and poisonous snakes.

Ne Win himself, a military man to his fingertips, accompanied us throughout our two-week stay. He was an extreme nationalist, determined not just to shore up his country's hard-won independence, but in effect to sever Burma – which he increasingly and brutally did in later years – from much of the rest of the world. He said that the only country he believed in was Israel. At that time, he seemed to us incorruptible in a country riddled with corruption. Despite his single-mindedness, not to say fanaticism, we built a close personal relationship. Later, Israel helped Burma develop its agriculture. The Burmese sent hundreds of youngsters for courses in Israel; some of them had never seen mechanized farming until their experiences on our kibbutzim and in our agricultural schools. Some had never seen a wristwatch before they were flown to Israel.

Dayan was clearly enjoying this exotic break, but I could tell he wasn't completely at ease. 'What's wrong?' I asked. 'Archaeology and history,' he replied. 'There's something missing here.' In fact, the Burmese have hardly any written history, and their Buddhism evolved more as an oral tradition than as a written one.

Nevertheless, the East wrought its magic on Dayan; later, he was to return to observe the Vietnam War at close quarters. We flew back via India, and here Dayan showed his gruff side. Landing at New Delhi, we were met by the Israeli Honorary Consul, a local Jewish doctor who made his rounds on an ancient bicycle. With evident pride and gratification, he informed us that he had arranged a lunch in our honour at the Rotary Club. 'Have you arranged a meeting with the Minister of Defence?' Dayan asked curtly. 'No, only with the Deputy Minister.' 'Then no meeting,' was Dayan's instant verdict. The Honorary Consul almost fainted. 'What about the lunch at the Rotary Club?' he murmured weakly. 'You've got a bicycle,' Dayan retorted. 'Get on it and pedal around from guest to guest cancelling the invitation.'

I tried to intervene, but to no avail. The Honorary Consul went off, pained and embarrassed. 'What do you want to do then?' I asked Dayan. He suggested that we spend our time looking for antiquities. Upon this remark, I chased after the Consul and, with much effort, managed to smooth things over. The three of us set out for an antiques market, where, to Dayan's great joy, we alighted on some dried palm-leaves delicately inscribed with poems in honour of Buddha. But his joy turned to disappointment when he learned that these 'ancient' leaves were only a couple of hundred years old. To him, steeped as he was in his own country's history and surrounded by finds from past millennia, that was hardly old at all.

To others, it seemed that Dayan was the man who had everything. Fame, glory and wealth (he always had a profound respect for money). Men obeyed him; women fell into his arms ('What do people want from me?' he once asked me during an intimate conversation. 'Have I ever drowned a girl in a river?'). Nor was he unaffected by adulation; in fact, he positively revelled in it. Nevertheless, I don't think I would be mistaken in saying that in all the years I was close to him, I hardly ever saw him truly happy. Perhaps success came too easily to him. Or perhaps his successes – some at least – proved too transient, their taste fading before he had the chance fully to enjoy them. It is possible that his terrible headaches, the result of his eye injury, sapped his enjoyment of life. Or that a sense of dissatisfaction was an innate part of his personality. Or perhaps it was a certain inconstancy in his character that caused him to seek stormy seas, even when he could have anchored securely in safe havens.

In policy and party matters too, Dayan seemed to seek stormy and unsettled seas. Every event of national importance triggered an immediate reaction from him, but almost every reaction later became the subject of regret. Often though, his initial, spontaneous, instinctive reactions bore within them more of his special genius than the subsequent, more thought-out responses. He was constantly shifting his political positions. It wasn't that his views lacked backbone; rather, they lacked permanence. The best exposition of his political thinking could be found in a collection of articles that he published, in which he argued that relations between peoples were ultimately more important than the borders dividing them. Perhaps he was right, at least in theory. In any event, this theory said a great deal about him, both as a person and a statesman. In both capacities, he was wise and original.

While Dayan was never entirely happy, he often found amusement in youthful exuberances, which he would pursue with the same originality and purposefulness that he devoted to matters of state. Like the games children choose to play, some of these episodes afforded fleeting insights into the depths of his complex personality.

Once, for instance, we were returning from Tiberias, where Ben-Gurion was vacationing. There were three of us in the back seat of the official car: Yadin, Dayan and myself. 'We can't drive back to Tel Aviv'. Dayan asserted, 'without passing Nahalal, which, as you know, is where I live. In my house, furthermore, you can taste the finest sour cream in the entire country, sour cream like they don't make any more . . . . And with it, the kind of freshly baked bread that is hard to come by these days.' Yadin and I were both hungry and curious, and so we agreed at once to stop at Dayan's home.

As we entered, our nostrils were assailed not by the aroma of freshly baked bread, but by a much heavier and less pleasant smell. Dayan gave his half-smile, the one with which he melted the hardest of hearts. 'I know you're offended by the smell. But if you hear the whole story, I'm sure you'll change your minds.' We gave him the chance to explain, and he launched into his tale.

He had read in an American magazine of a millionaire who was 'so crazily in love with his wife' that he vowed to give her 'the most unique set of necklaces in the world'. He organized a safari to Africa, bagged a number of lions and tigers, and had a necklace made from their claws. He hunted eagles and peacocks, and had a necklace made of their beaks. 'I'm not sure if I'm known as the world's greatest husband, but the idea caught my fancy. What could I do? We don't have lions and tigers in Israel, and precious few eagles and peacocks. But then I remembered: we've got sharks.'

To cut his long story short, some time later Dayan decided to visit Eilat. Making a bee-line for the fishermen in the then tiny Red Sea port, he got chatting with them. 'How's the fishing?' 'Not bad,' they replied, 'but dangerous.' 'Why's that?' Dayan asked disingenuously. 'Sharks.' 'What, real sharks?' 'Yes, sir,' they chorused. 'Well I never. Could you show me one? I'm leaving this evening.'

With that he went off to visit the army bases in the area, returning to the airstrip at sunset to find the fishermen – but no shark. Disappointed, he ordered the crew to take off for Tel Aviv. Just then, he saw one fisherman running after the plane and waving. 'Stop,' Dayan ordered and jumped down. 'We got him, sir,' the fisherman cried triumphantly. In his van was a sizeable shark, two or three metres long. 'No one in Tel Aviv will believe this,' Dayan remarked – with the immediate (and intended) effect of persuading the fisherman to cut off the shark's head and present it to the General. Dayan ordered his aide-de-camp to empty his kitbag of all the files and equipment in it, and to stuff their newly acquired trophy in their place.

From Tel Aviv, the shark's head made its way to Nahalal, but then problems arose. Try as he would, with pliers and hammer, Dayan could not extract the teeth. It was his wife, Ruth, who suggested boiling the head, in order to soften the gums. They boiled it for a whole day, with no results. They boiled it for a second day, still with no success. Only after a third whole day of boiling did the shark finally give up. 'Hence,' Dayan brought us back to humdrum reality, 'the smell in the house. I told you that when you'd heard the story, you would feel differently.'

We ate our bread and sour cream with relish. When we left, Dayan took the shark's teeth with him. Later, I heard that he had put the army dental corps to work drilling holes through them in order to thread them on the silver chain which he had bought to complete his gift.

After the Yom Kippur War disaster, some of those who had been among his most slavish admirers were among his first critics. He was spat at in a military graveyard, cursed at public meetings and execrated in the press. To him, it seemed the world had turned against him. My own friendship with him remained firm throughout these tribulations. After Golda Meir resigned, Dayan feared that Pinhas Sapir would be installed in her place – a prospect that he regarded as a potential calamity for the country. He began persuading his ex-Rafi comrades to secede once again from the Labour Party if that should happen. At this point, I stepped in – I was dead against another split – and said that I was ready to run against Sapir, or against any other candidate of Golda's. But I made my move on one condition: that all our group, including Dayan, commit themselves to accept the outcome of the party vote – whatever it was.

Dayan and the others agreed. In the end, the party establishment decided to put up Yitzhak Rabin as their candidate. The entire weight of the Labour machine was thrown into the fray on Rabin's behalf, and his victory in the central committee vote was seen as a foregone conclusion. I had a team of volunteers under Micha Harish. Dayan gave me all his support.

Rabin did indeed win, but the result came as a surprise to some, and a shock to others: barely 2 per cent separated us.

Dayan was never the same after the Yom Kippur War. In 1977, when I was unanimously elected party leader in preparation for that year's election, I had a hard time placing him in a high-ranking position on the Labour list. I insisted, though, and in the end he was put in at Number 7. I already knew that he was building up a great wall of bitterness against his party in his heart, especially against certain ostensible comrades. And sure enough, when the election results came through and the Likud won, Menachem Begin invited Dayan to join his Government as Foreign Minister – and Dayan immediately accepted. He called me that evening at home to tell me, adding a typically Dayanesque comment: 'You're probably mad at me, Shimon, for not consulting you first. It wasn't that I forgot. I didn't consult you for the simple reason that you would have urged me not to do it. And I wouldn't have listened to you. So what for? Better like this.'

I had no doubt that Dayan would become the key figure in Begin's Government's quest to reach peace with Egypt. This would be his atonement for Yom Kippur – even though he never regarded himself as solely or mainly to blame for Israel's having been taken by surprise. Earlier that year (1973), he had addressed a stern and solemn warning to the IDF high command to 'prepare for war', and in the week before Yom Kippur, in response to worrying signs on the Golan Heights, he ordered some reinforcement of Israeli armour there.

On that fateful Yom Kippur morning, 6 October, he had called me up and invited me over to his office. There would be war at dusk, he said; but he was against mobilizing the entire army at once* for fear that Israel would be accused of aggression. In any case, it was impossible to call up all the reserves and to deploy them effectively in a single day. He believed that we could contain the expected attack by a skilful deployment of the forces available to us. I agreed. We had worked together for many years and I saw the logic in his argument.

I myself had worked in the Ministry of Defence, as Director-General and then as Deputy Minister, for fifteen years. For two more years, from 1969 to 1971, as a Minister without Portfolio in Golda Meir's Government, I had been in charge of economic development in the administered territories, working closely with Dayan out of the Defence Ministry. Together, we had set up the first 'Build your own Home' programme for Palestinian refugees, and had laid the foundations for joint Israeli–Palestinian industries at Erez, on the border of the Gaza

---

* Dayan approved the full mobilization of the air force, the navy, and two out of our four reserve army corps. The argument with the Chief of Staff, therefore, narrowed down to the other two corps.

Strip. I would go out to sea with the Gaza fishermen and visit the run-down refugee camps, where the lovely, frightened eyes of the young girls followed my every move. Little did I dream, on that Yom Kippur morning, that just a few months later Dayan would be standing there, in that same office, handing the Ministry over to me for safekeeping, and generously praising my ability to shoulder the heavy burden of responsibility.

During his years as Foreign Minister (1977–9), we kept up our friendship and made sure that we met regularly. But our political polarization had an effect: there wasn't the same intimacy in our relationship.

Whenever I met President Sadat of Egypt, I would call on Dayan first. Once, to my great embarrassment, he asked me to try to find out why Sadat was so negative about him. I asked Sadat straight out and received a surprising answer. 'Shimon,' he said, 'have you ever seen Moshe take hold of a problem – and hand it back less complicated than it was before he dealt with it?' I didn't have the heart to relay this reply to Dayan. But, in the final analysis, it was without doubt Dayan, more than any other protagonist, who devised the creative ideas and compromises necessary to push the Israeli–Egyptian negotiations to a successful conclusion. This was true at the Camp David peace conference in September 1978,* and it continued to be true throughout the subsequent negotiations that led to the eventual conclusion of the Israeli–Egyptian peace treaty in March 1979.

I watched as Dayan steadily declined. Age, work, wars, illness, and his sudden swings from great heights to black depths – all these took their toll of him. He tried to shake off the effects of these various adversities, but to no avail. Once, many years before, Dayan and I were caught in a crossfire as we drove in a jeep north of Jerusalem. Miraculously, we escaped without injury. 'Don't you know fear?' I asked him afterwards. 'When I find myself under fire or facing death,' Dayan replied, 'I feel as though I am in a sort of fog. And I'm not afraid of fog.'

But soon the fog closed in around him, and at last he succumbed. In 1981, I followed his bier in sorrow and in homage. He was buried on a hilltop near Nahalal, under the shade of cypress trees. The Valley of Jezreel unfolded beneath, in all its beauty and grandeur. Moshe Dayan was at peace.

He left a grand and noble heritage: the man who, more than any

* See pages 293–5.

other, imbued the IDF with its fighting spirit and traditions; the victorious general, whose battles are still studied as models of military tactics; the deft negotiator, who won more from the Jordanians in 1948 at the negotiating table than could be wrested from them on the battlefield. Dayan was also the key figure in reaching peace with Egypt. He ignited the imaginations of thousands of young people in Israel and millions around the world. He walked his own path, the path that he had blazed from boyhood on, true only to himself, but always true to himself. Yes, he sinned sometimes, against both man and God. But he was constant in his determination never to compromise with the humdrum and the predictable, but always to originate, to invent, to seek novel ideas and approaches. He went on and on, until his energies gave out. But his legend continues to light up our lives, as we continue to yearn for heroes who become legends in their lifetimes.

13 DEFENCE

When Yitzhak Rabin formed his first government in June 1974, I was appointed Minister of Defence, which in Israel is seen as the second most important Cabinet portfolio after that of Prime Minister. I was given the post chiefly because I had come so close to beating Rabin in the party central committee, in spite of the fact that he had the full weight of the party 'machine' on his side. In addition, my appointment was the express desire of the outgoing Minister, Moshe Dayan, and it thus enabled the handover to be made smoothly and efficiently. And lastly, there was my long experience in the Defence Ministry and my achievements there, which even my political foes could not deny.

I plunged straight into the task of rebuilding and strengthening the army. After the Yom Kippur War surprise attack, it was no longer possible for 'the political echelon' – in my case, the Minister of Defence – to permit itself to rely on assessments submitted by the Intelligence Corps. The policy-makers had to go over key elements of the 'raw material' themselves. I had to read literally hundreds of documents each day in order to be able to go to sleep each night with the sense that I hadn't missed anything.

I also made frequent, unannounced spot-checks at emergency stores to ensure that the kind of neglect and inadequacies that had been exposed, to our grievous cost, at the outbreak of the Yom Kippur War would never recur.

Unfortunately, I had to spend much of my time putting out – or at least controlling – the fires that were being ignited by the various 'wars of the generals', which kept breaking out as senior officers published their conflicting versions of the Yom Kippur battles. The questions regarding who was to blame for the disaster, and who among the generals had saved the situation, became the burning issues of the day. They threatened to paralyse the work of the army General Staff. When the Agranat commission on the outbreak of the war published its findings and recommendations, we had no choice but to accept the resignations of a number of senior officers – not a pleasant task, even at the best of times. (The wartime Chief of Staff, Lieutenant-General David Elazar, had been required to step down by the commission in its interim findings, issued in April 1974. Dayan – in consultation with me – nominated Major-General Mordechai Gur for the post. He was a fighting officer with a fine record – he had commanded the paratroop brigade that liberated the Old City of Jerusalem in 1967 – and had been serving as our Military Attaché in Washington during the Yom Kippur War.) Gur and I spent long hours meeting in private with individual generals and attending sessions of the General Staff, where the traumas of the recent war still permeated the air.

I had known Gur since the 1950s and had always been impressed with him as a straight talker with a firm grasp of strategy. He seemed to have the personality of a natural educator. I remember him as a young battalion commander at one exercise in the north explaining to Ben-Gurion and other senior officers the tactical essence of the exercise. Ben-Gurion asked me, 'Who is that young man?' I said, 'He'll be Chief of Staff one day.'

We worked well together. Often, we worked eighteen or even twenty hours a day: the general mood of aftershock and depression that pervaded the nation made us doubly aware of the responsibilities at the helm of the nation's defences. I had full confidence in him and gave him my total political support. We confronted a situation in which our arsenals needed not merely replenishing, but replenishing with new generations of hardware that would deter the Arabs from trying again. We thus devoted much time and energy to detailed questions of military purchases abroad, while promoting expansion in many areas of our own military industries and encouraging a wide range of defence research projects. We acquired new anti-tank weapons, more advanced radar systems and new attack helicopters. We also groomed a new generation of promising officers, among them Dan Shomron and Ehud Barak. They laid the groundwork for what came to be called the 'long-arm option' – a capacity to strike hard and fast at ranges far beyond our immediate frontiers. This manoeuvre, of course, was crowned with success in the Entebbe rescue operation of 1976.*

* See chapter 14.

This was the backdrop, from my perspective, to the negotiations with Egypt which we conducted, through the good offices of Henry Kissinger, during much of 1975. Rabin led the Israeli side, which included, besides Rabin, Foreign Minister Yigal Allon and me; and a back-up team made up of senior officials from our three departments and of army officers.

Each time we were informed that Kissinger was due, we prepared for another sleepless night. Eventually, we learned his technique. His plane would always land on time, but he would always arrive late for our scheduled meetings. He deliberately kept us waiting for an hour or two, during which time reports would come in over the news-agency wires on what the 'senior official aboard the Secretary's plane' had had to say. The 'senior official' would usually pepper his remarks in these airborne briefings alternately with compliments and criticisms of the various figures in the region with whom he was negotiating. On touchdown, however, the suave Secretary would have only praise and warm smiles for whoever was greeting him. His remarks to the microphones were unfailingly laudatory. And we, his hosts at his various shuttle-stops, always smiled back and never rejected his accolades.

Our negotiating sessions were held in the large room adjoining the Prime Minister's bureau. At the appointed hour, the long table would stand ready, laden with fruit, nuts and biscuits. Often, though, we found ourselves nervously nibbling away while we waited, and by the time Kissinger arrived there was not much left.

We also came to learn, and indeed appreciate, his negotiating style. He would invariably begin the first round of discussions by reviewing the state of the world since his last visit, describing, in dire terms, how the situation had deteriorated and the dangers multiplied. Anti-Semitism was on the rise everywhere, he warned. The Arab world was restless and resentful; he had barely managed to retain their interest in the peace process. If we failed now, disaster would follow.

Kissinger laid on these grim scenarios with enormous skill, lacing them, as though for light relief, with marvellous anecdotes which he recounted with much panache. I shall never forget how he described his first visit to Saudi Arabia. Many of the accompanying journalists, Kissinger recalled, were Jewish, and he was uncertain until the last moment whether the Saudis would actually allow them to land. At the hotel, every member of the Secretary's party received a personal gift: an embossed leather folder containing *The Protocols of the Elders of Zion.*★

At sunset, Kissinger was ushered into the royal presence, led through the long throne-room by two chamberlains with drawn swords. 'I receive you', King Faisal declared, 'not as a Jew but as a human being who is us Secretary of State.' According to Kissinger, his reply to this was, 'Some of my best friends are human beings.' The King went on to explain to his guest, at great length, how the Jews were taking over the world, buying up all the banks and newspapers and even governments. He recited a list of ministers in various Western governments who were of Jewish origin. The Jews, Faisal assured his guest, were going ahead with their long-laid plan for world domination. It was they who had sent Lenin and Trotsky to take over Russia and draw it away from Christian control and into the Jewish sphere of influence. Now that same danger faced the United States, where Jewish influence was growing ever stronger.

Kissinger, as he told the tale, decided not to be drawn into this historical-philosophical discussion. Instead, he resolved to try to shift the conversation to a neutral subject – a large painting behind the King's throne. Try as he did though, he could not make out what the picture was about. He decided that it must be a work of the modern school and began praising the King on his artistic taste. Faisal coldly enlightened him: the painting was of the Ka'aba, the holy stone at Mecca, upon which Mohammed had laid his head.

Kissinger's graphic story-telling had us weeping with laughter. The hours would pass in this way until, amidst his predictions of imminent regional or global catastrophe and his whimsical accounts of his own virtuoso diplomacy, the shape would slowly but unmistakably emerge of the concession that the Secretary had actually come to squeeze out of us.

The main issue of dispute – over which the negotiations fell apart in March 1975, only to be resumed after much us–Israeli acrimony later that year – was where the disengagement line was to run in the Sinai. We were determined not to cede to the Egyptians, in what was, after all, an interim accord that fell far short of full peace, strategic control of the key passes – the Mitla and the Gidi – which guarded the way from the Suez Canal to the heart of the peninsula, and on towards Israel.

This sort of challenge often brings out a degree of political resourcefulness on my part. On this occasion, I came up with the idea of policing

★ A notorious, anti-Semitic forgery published at the turn of the century, purporting to disclose a Jewish scheme for world domination.

a small part of the Mitla–Gidi area with an international force. Rabin doubted that the United States would agree. I proposed that we send our Ambassador to Washington, Simcha Dinitz, to see Kissinger secretly in the Virgin Islands, where he was vacationing. Kissinger voiced his fear that the idea might be seen by public opinion as an attempt to drag American ground forces into the Middle East arena, but he agreed to try it on a number of leading senators and congressmen – and found a generally favourable reaction to what was, after all, a strictly defined, limited operation. Eventually, the Sinai Field Mission, which was deployed in the passes and monitored observance of the disengagement agreement, was manned by American civilians rather than uniformed officers, in order further to allay domestic qualms in America.*

As for the Palestinian question and the prospects of peace with Jordan, my position during the 1974–7 Government was that Israel and Jordan should jointly run the West Bank and Gaza as an interim solution, pending a final settlement. King Hussein of Jordan did not reject this approach outright, but nor did he ever explicitly endorse it, or tacitly support it by acting so as to help bring it about.

Historians and other writers have tended to ascribe to the King at that time a rigid position, demanding the same kind of disengagement between Israel and Jordan as we had negotiated with the Egyptians and the Syrians. In fact, he was much more imaginative. But he was inhibited by his difficult position within the Arab world. Jordan had ruled the West Bank and East Jerusalem for nearly two decades (1948–67), and King Hussein continued to feel responsible for the present condition and future disposition of these territories and their Palestinian inhabitants. In this capacity, he received political and financial support from other Arab states. But at the same time, his own position in the Arab world was difficult and dangerous. Some of his Arab neighbours harboured hostile designs towards his kingdom. He could never fully trust any of them. With Israel, he was formally in a state of war. With the PLO, he was in a state of deep mutual distrust in the wake of 'Black September' – September 1970, when the PLO tried to destabilize the kingdom, and Hussein acted with firmness and severity to quell the uprising. The PLO leadership had transferred to Beirut following that violent episode, but since then Hussein could not be entirely certain of the loyalty of all of his Palestinian citizens, who comprised a very substantial part of Jordan's population.

* See pages 167–8.

Jordan has neither oil reserves nor other natural resources, except for the potash and chemicals of the Dead Sea region. The country's economic situation, therefore, was an additional headache for the King, as indeed it continues to be to the present day. Shakespeare's famous line, 'Uneasy lies the head that wears a crown', was never more apposite.

I was depicted in the press at that time as the 'hardliner' among the top policy-makers, but there was a great deal of deliberate misinformation in that image. I never wavered from Labour Zionism's fundamental acceptance of partition as the solution to the conflict in Palestine. I had always supported Ben-Gurion's view that partition was the solution.

Thus, after 1967 I never favoured annexation of the West Bank and Gaza. During the 1970s, I favoured the idea of 'functional compromise' – that is, a sharing of power – as an alternative to territorial partition. At that time, the advocates of territorial partition within the Government and the Labour movement proposed the Allon Plan. This called for Israel to retain the Jordan Valley, which is relatively sparsely populated, under its own sovereignty and control, as well as the area around Jerusalem. However, Dayan and I felt that it was more important for us to hold on to the hill range running down the centre of Judea and Samaria (the Jerusalem hills are part of that range).

Basically, I suggested that the West Bank, which was to be demilitarized, could be administered by the Palestinians themselves, under the joint control of Israel and Jordan – at least for an interim period. Israeli control would ensure freedom of movement for Israelis throughout the territories and freedom of worship at the Holy Places. Israel and Jordan, together with this Palestinian entity, would comprise a regional unit of close economic co-operation. I certainly did not envisage – and do not envisage today either – a physical or economic separation between Israel and the West Bank–Gaza.

The 1974–7 Government was adversely affected for much of its duration by an undercurrent of tension between Yitzhak Rabin and myself. Rabin, in his notoriously tendentious autobiography *Service Notebook*, published in 1979, purports to trace the animosity between us back to the early 1960s. He describes a meeting between us in Paris, in March 1963, at which I allegedly 'paled' when he informed me that Ben-Gurion had promised to appoint him the next Chief of Staff.

In fact, Ben-Gurion had told me of his intention to appoint Rabin long before, so the news came as neither a surprise nor a shock to me. I didn't tell Rabin that I knew. As a rule, when people tell me things I have learned in confidence from other sources, I am careful not to react or divulge in any way my prior information. I never opposed Rabin's appointment. His description of my ostensible reaction to it, written sixteen years later, is the product of unfounded assumptions.

Rabin is a man of solid intellectual gifts, but some of us feel that he tends to be over-suspicious. Obviously, he was a good military man – otherwise he would not have risen so high and so fast in the army. Dayan though, as I recall, was reluctant to acknowledge this. I remember before the Sinai Campaign, Dayan appointed him O/C Northern Command, 'where he won't get in our way'. We planned to fight in the south and expected possible action in the east, too, but we assumed that the northern front against Syria and Lebanon would stay quiet.

At any rate, as far as I am concerned, my relationship with Rabin was wholesome and proper – he as a general and later a diplomat, I as Director of the Defence Ministry and then as a politician – until we ran against each other for the Prime Ministership and Labour Party leadership in 1974.

Our paths had crossed frequently over the years; I never felt any animosity from him, nor did I harbour any towards him. When he ended his term as Ambassador to Washington, before the Yom Kippur War of 1973, and was at a loose end for some time, I remember taking him around with me on my official business as Minister of Transport, and otherwise spending time with him pleasantly enough. Granted, I had come out of Mapai and Rafi, while he had come up through the Palmach and was always considered close to Ahdut Haavoda. There was not, therefore, a special comradeship between us. But my private diaries contain a number of warm and laudatory references to Rabin during the 1950s and 1960s. After one engagement against the Syrians, I wrote of the 'quiet and efficient way in which Yitzhak ran the forward headquarters'. And when he was under consideration for Chief of Staff, I commented on his 'brilliance in both political and military analysis', though I added that he seemed 'hesitant ... too cautious, and his personal relationships are too bound up with memories of the past'.

I was aghast, therefore, to read in Rabin's book that I allegedly went around during the tense waiting-period before the Six Day War spreading gloom, telling people that we couldn't win and that we mustn't fight. My contribution during that dramatic period was something that I still cannot write about openly, for reasons of state security. After Dayan was appointed Defence Minister, I submitted to him a certain proposal which, in my opinion then – and in my opinion today, nearly three decades later – would have deterred the Arabs and prevented the war. My proposal, which, by the way, Yigael Yadin knew about and supported, was considered – and rejected.

Both Rabin and I have devoted much of our lives to the defence of our country. Rabin wore the uniform of an IDF officer. I, too, was inducted into the IDF in 1948 and donned a uniform, but declined to take a military rank. I think, in all modesty, that my contribution to our national defence, from 1948 on, is recognized even by my traducers. It was Ben-Gurion who appointed me Director-General of the Defence Ministry and later his Deputy Minister. His judgment, both of merit and of moral qualities, was certainly not inferior to anybody else's.

In another passage, Rabin writes that during the Kissinger shuttles of 1976, when we were negotiating the Interim Agreement with Egypt, I proposed 'deploying an American–Soviet military force' in the disputed mountain passes in the Sinai, the Mitla and the Gidi. He continues:

I was astounded. The Defence Minister's 'strategic thinking' had soared this time to unimaginable heights. Had I not heard with my own ears that a senior Israeli minister was proposing the insertion of Soviet troops between Israel and Egypt, I would have thought that Peres' enemies had made the story up.

The true story is that Israel, through a fresh idea that I advanced, managed to break the log-jam that had snarled up the negotiations with Egypt and had led an angry and frustrated United States administration to announce a 'reassessment' of its policy towards the Middle East. Certainly, I proposed an American, or an American–Soviet, presence in the passes. It wasn't to be a military presence. A small number of Americans, with or without Russians, were to man key intelligence sites in the area, monitoring and conveying information to the two sides, thereby ensuring that the military restrictions undertaken in the Interim Agreement were being adhered to.

I suggested that I fly to Kissinger, who was vacationing in the Virgin Islands, and lay out the idea to him personally and discreetly. Rabin objected. As I have already mentioned, this is when I proposed that Simcha Dinitz make the presentation – to which Rabin agreed.

And that, in effect, marked the turning-point in the talks with Egypt. Kissinger didn't want the Soviets, and in the event the Sinai Field Mission was manned solely by American civilian personnel. But neither I nor anyone else was suggesting a military deployment of Soviet – or, indeed, American – ground forces. The entire field mission was conceived from the outset as a small, technical team. Soviet military officers were present on the ground in Sinai anyway – as they were on all of Israel's borders – as part of the United Nations Truce Supervisory Organization (UNTSO), which had been created in 1948 and has never been dismantled, down to the present day, despite all the changes in the region. The Soviets and all their satellites except Romania had severed their diplomatic ties with us in 1967, but their participation in UNTSO continued unaffected. So it wasn't as though we could prevent the Soviets – as well as UNTSO officers from Soviet satellite countries – from travelling around and observing. Nominally they reported to UN headquarters, but we had no doubt that they were reporting to their own governments too.

Rabin's charge that I was involved in the leakage of stenographic records of the conversations with Kissinger is another unfounded allegation. I resented and regretted it deeply.

His depiction in the book of another important episode during his first Premiership questions my loyalty. The period following the trauma of the Yom Kippur War saw the rise of a neo-Messianic settlement movement, Gush Emunim (Block of the Faithful). These young men and women were the products of Zionist Orthodox schools and yeshivot (Talmudic colleges) and of the National Religious Party youth movement, Bnei Akiva. The NRP had traditionally been allied to Labour from pre-state days, and its leaders had served in almost every government since 1948. Labour and the NRP spoke of an 'historic alliance' between them. The foremost figures in the NRP, Rabbi Yehuda Leib Maimon (1875–1962) and Moshe Haim Shapira (1902–70), were moderate men, concerned to meld their movement into the mainstream of state-building without losing or compromising its special religious and ideological character.

But the younger generation, especially the intellectual and spiritual elite who attended the small but influential Merkaz Harav Kook Yeshiva in Jerusalem during the 1960s, approached the teachings and dogmas of Zionist Orthodoxy with little of the moderation and pragmatism that characterized the older leaders. Disciples of the Yeshiva dean, Rabbi Zvi Yehuda Kook, they developed a radical theology which saw the reborn State of Israel not only as 'the beginning of the growth of our Redemption',* but also as the tangible and immediate embodiment of the Divine process.

The Six Day War, with its near-miraculous victories, and especially the liberation of Arab-held Jerusalem, inspired these young men into a veritable explosion of religious fervour. This, in turn, was channelled into pioneering and political activism: settlement-building in the newly restored areas of the biblical homeland, and the steady conquest of the NRP from within as the springboard for a sustained campaign to influence the political spirit of the nation.

By 1974, the NRP was deeply split, but it was still in alliance with us, and its twelve Knesset seats were an invaluable component of the Labour-led coalition. At the same time, the Emunim activists, who mounted their settlement efforts with the planning and precision of military exercises, were clashing frequently with the army, which was under government orders to prevent Jewish settlement in the thickly populated heartlands of the West Bank.

One memorable such showdown took place in December 1974 near the village of Sebastia in the hills of Samaria. The situation between the Ministry of Defence and the Prime Minister's Office had already become complicated by this time, due to Rabin's appointment of Arik Sharon, the IDF general-become-Likud politician, as his personal defence adviser. Rabin claimed, when this move was criticized, that Sharon was not to be a 'defence adviser' but rather a 'general adviser'. However, the appointment was seen to threaten my own position as well as that of the Chief of Staff. In his book, Rabin finds fault with me for appointing Professor Yuval Neeman, who was later to lead the far-right Tehiya Party, as my scientific adviser in the Ministry of Defence, while defending his own appointment of Sharon. In fact, Neeman, a physicist of international repute, functioned mainly in his professional capacity, while Sharon, with all his proven capacity for working outside the boundaries of accepted norms, threatened the stability of an already tenuous Government.

During the Sebastia stand-off, when IDF soldiers sought to block the would-be settlers without resorting to outright force, someone set up a pseudo-military headquarters in Tel Aviv, from where he transmitted

---

* This deliberately vague formula is used in the Prayer for the State compiled by the then-Chief Rabbi, Isaac Herzog.

advice and guidance to the settlers on how to dodge the army patrols and reach their designated settlement site in the face of the army's efforts – and orders – to prevent them. Clearly, the man who did this was in possession of first-hand and fully updated information.

In the end, I went out to the site to try to implement the Government's decision to block the proposed settlement while avoiding violence and possible bloodshed. This was not the first time this group had pitched camp at Sebastia; on several previous occasions, they had been removed without undue trouble. This time, however, by significant coincidence, world Jewish leaders were assembled that same day in Jerusalem, in a show of solidarity with Israel in the wake of a UN General Assembly resolution equating Zionism with racism. Obviously, we wanted to enhance that solidarity – not point up divisions within our own ranks. Rabin and I had gone up in a helicopter earlier, with Chief of Staff Mordechai Gur, to assess the situation at first hand from the air. We saw thousands of youngsters milling about, some hardly more than children.

The settlers greeted us with singing and dancing, but when I read out my mandate, they changed their tune. One of their leaders, Rabbi Moshe Levinger of Hebron, tore his jacket – the traditional Jewish act of mourning. We adjourned to a tent, ostensibly to discuss the arrangements for their evacuation. But then I found the poet Haim Guri involved in the negotiations – and clearly looking for a compromise acceptable to the settlers. In the end, they were allowed to pitch camp at a site nearby, purportedly for one month. Later, under the Begin Government, they finally built their settlement, Elon Moreh, at a third spot, also in the area.

The deal was widely criticized as a surrender by the Government. It is seen today as the start of Emunim's settlement drive in the heartland of Judea and Samaria – the heavily populated Palestinian areas which our Government had sought to keep free of Jewish settlements. The compromise, to the extent that we did compromise, was due largely to the efforts of Yisrael Galili, Minister without Portfolio, veteran leader of Ahdut Haavoda and a Cabinet member with much influence on Rabin. Guri was in constant contact from Sebastia with Galili in Jerusalem, and Galili was in and out of Rabin's room throughout the negotiations. The section of Ahdut Haavoda that always espoused the doctrine of Greater Israel – Galili among them – harboured a certain sympathy for the Gush Emunim settlers, even though they hailed from a very different ideological background. I did not object to the compromise.

DEFENCE

I, too, had a feeling for some of the Emunim youngsters, especially the soldier-students of the hesder* yeshivas who formed the backbone of the movement. I will never forget an experience I had at the hesder yeshivas of Ramat Magshimim, on the Golan Heights, on the night of 20 November 1975, when three students there were killed by infiltrators from Syria.

I flew up there with the Chief of Staff after midnight. It was a bitterly cold night. The settlement of Ramat Magshimim itself was in a state of shock, men and women plainly reeling from the sudden and unexpected onslaught (the first – and, as it has turned out, the last – since the signing of the Disengagement Agreement with Syria the previous year). The study hall of the yeshiva was still unfinished and unheated, but it was full, and the boys were all learning, vigorously, fervently studying the Talmud. To a visitor, it seemed as though nothing had happened. This was their way of mourning and of redoubling their commitment to their ideals. Outside, hardly thirty yards away, were rows of tanks, ready for immediate action.

'These boys are all tank crewmen,' their commanding officer explained. 'They are prepared instantly to lay aside their books and climb into their turrets.'

In Hebrew, we have an expression, 'safra vesayfa' – scribe and swordsman. Never, I think, has it been more fully embodied than in the lives of these young men. It was then that I came to appreciate the strength of the Emunim movement, and I have never since disparaged the depth of their commitment or the vibrancy of their pioneering spirit. But I have always feared that they elevate the Holy Land to a level that supersedes the holiness of Man. And in that, in my view, they have perverted the true scale of values of authentic Judaism.

Rabin writes that I tried to 'undermine' him during the 1974–7 Government, that I never accepted the close result in the party central committee vote in 1974, but immediately resolved to fight him again for the leadership. I have accusations of my own, and detailed rebuttals to his, but now it is either too early or too late to go into all the old quarrels. I give just one example: he writes in his book that my battles in the 1974–7 Cabinet for a higher defence budget were 'the apogee of Peres'

* Lit. arrangement. Hesder yeshivas are Talmudical colleges where the students combine religious studies with army service.

171

subversion' of his Premiership. He accuses me of conducting these battles, for the first time in the history of the state, in the public arena rather than in the closed and secret discussions of the Cabinet. But this surely is tendentious. Every Defence Minister fights for higher budgets. Indeed, the second Chief of Staff, Yigael Yadin, resigned back in 1952 amid a blaze of public controversy surrounding his demand for greater defence spending. Neither I nor Chief of Staff Mordechai Gur meant to 'undermine' or 'subvert' Rabin's standing as Prime Minister when we warned the Cabinet of the dangers that could result from scrimping on defence.

I served the 1974–7 Government, and the man who led it, loyally, fully shouldering the collective responsibility of a Cabinet member. I worked day and night to rebuild and replenish the army – both its arsenals and its morale. In part, no doubt, the personal problems between Rabin and myself during this time reflected certain underlying tensions in the recent reunification of Mapai, Ahdut Haavoda and Rafi to form the Labour Party. Nominally, we were all in the same party, but in many ways we carried on as though we still belonged to different and rival groups.

In the end, the Rabin Government fell – and with it the Labour movement's hegemony in Israeli politics – not because of the strained relations between the Premier and myself, nor even because the peace process had ground to a halt, but because a series of scandals eroded public confidence.

Nothing in politics undermines a government's popular support more than a sense of corruption in high places. Indeed, the healthy position for any electorate to take towards its government in a democratic society is best summed up by the ancient Hebrew adage, 'Honour him – but suspect him.' Once corruption takes hold – and begins to be exposed – the honour steadily wanes as the suspicion rises.

The honour of our Government, and of our party, took a mighty blow with the arrest, in 1976, of Asher Yadlin, our nominee for the august post of Governor of the Bank of Israel, on charges of bribery and embezzlement. A one-time kibbutznik, Yadlin had risen through the managerial ranks of the Histadrut's holding company, Hevrat Ovdim, to become Director-General of the mammoth Kupat Holim sick fund. He was sentenced to five years' imprisonment, amid a welter of accusations and assertions – some from Yadlin himself, all unproven – that he had taken the bribe-money on behalf of the party.

Another luminary in Israel's financial firmament jailed that year was Michael Tsur, head of the Israel Corporation, a major finance and investment concern. Although not an active Labour Party member, Tsur had also risen to prominence, and power, as a protégé of Pinhas Sapir, the Minister of Finance under Eshkol and Golda Meir. Tsur had been Director-General of the Ministry of Trade and Industry during part of that period.

The Government was also rocked by a personal disaster: the suicide, in January 1977, of Housing Minister Avraham Ofer, who was under police investigation. Ofer, a former kibbutz member, was another gifted economist whom Sapir had taken under his tutelage and groomed for high office. The allegations against him – never proved – concerned his time as head of a vast Histadrut-owned contracting company.

Three months later, the Prime Minister himself resigned. While the affair that triggered his resignation had been discussed in the newspapers for several days, his decision took me by surprise. I learned of it together with the rest of the country – from his statement on television, late in the evening of 7 April 1977 – after I returned home from a meeting at Abba Eban's house. I was equally surprised to learn from the television that Rabin had proposed me as his replacement.

The affair involved a dollar account held in a bank in Washington from the time of Rabin's Ambassadorship. It was published in *Ha'aretz* by the newspaper's Washington correspondent, Dan Margalit. This was an offence against Israeli currency regulations, and Rabin's wife Leah, who formally owned the account, was to be prosecuted (she was eventually fined). Rabin therefore felt that he had to quit. Three days later, the Labour Party central committee unanimously endorsed me as leader and Prime Ministerial candidate.

From my own perspective, as reprehensible as the legal infraction itself was the attempt by various people to insinuate a link between the story in *Ha'aretz* and circles connected to me. Margalit himself refuted that baseless allegation.

The result of these various affairs, and the recriminations they triggered, was the undermining of the Labour Party's credibility, which contributed in no small measure to the party's massive defeat at the polls five weeks later, on 17 May.

Plainly, though, the deeper cause of Labour's loss was the Yom Kippur War and the 'wars of the generals' that came in its aftermath. Confidence in the Labour leadership's ability to run the country – confidence that had always been present to a greater or lesser degree in the public mind – was suddenly and irreparably ruptured. I never doubted that the day would come when we would pay a heavy political price for Yom Kippur.

Nevertheless, the extent of the defeat came as a shock to everyone, myself included. The Labour Alignment (the electoral bloc comprising Labour and Mapam), which went into the election with fifty-one Knesset seats (out of 120), emerged with only thirty-three seats. Most of its lost votes went to Yigael Yadin's newly founded, short-lived Democratic Movement for Change, which was billed as a force for 'clean politics' and which won fifteen seats; it joined Menachem Begin's coalition of the Likud (forty-five seats) and the two Orthodox parties (sixteen).

Our three years in office had ended badly. Our party was in the depths of depression; the corridors of its headquarters in Tel Aviv echoed emptily as I settled into the Chairman's office, and into the daunting task of rebuilding morale and confidence. But the outgoing Government's record, seen in more dispassionate historical perspective, was by no means negative. We had made major progress on the road to peace with Egypt, the strongest of the Arab nations. We had restored and greatly expanded Israel's war-battered military might. The economy had been carefully husbanded back to health after the trauma of war. But the single most memorable feat that history would record to our credit was, without a doubt, Operation Yoni – the IDF's daring rescue mission to Entebbe.

14 ENTEBBE

The Entebbe hijack drama lasted one week, in the summer of 1976. But it was a week that, like the Six Day War, will live on in Israel's history as a source of pride and inspiration. At the time, the rescue provided a burst of light during a grey and difficult period. The IDF's daring and success were a beacon for the free world, engaged at that time in a desperate struggle against international terrorism in its various forms. I kept a diary during the days and nights of that memorable week. This chapter is based on extracts from it.

Sunday, 27 June 1976
The first report of the hijack reached Jerusalem during the weekly Cabinet meeting. We were deep into a discussion of cuts in the defence budget when my military aide, Colonel Ilan Tehilla, handed me a hastily handwritten note: 'Air France flight 139 from Ben-Gurion Airport to Paris Orly has been hijacked after a stopover in Athens. The plane is now in the air, its destination unknown.' I quietly informed Rabin. He decided to convene an urgent meeting of the relevant Ministers – Foreign, Defence, Transport – as soon as the full Cabinet adjourned.

As we began the consultation, one thing seemed clear: since this was a plane belonging to the French national carrier, and bearing the French national flag, France ought to take the prime responsibility for dealing with the situation. On our side, Foreign Minister Yigal Allon would take the lead in handling what would obviously be an intense and constant dialogue with Paris.

We decided to issue an official statement outlining the facts as we knew them, without, at this stage, publishing a list of names of the hijacked passengers. (We did not yet possess an accurate list.) The statement was to affirm that Israel would not submit to blackmail on the part of the hijackers.

After the ministerial meeting I hurried down to Tel Aviv, where I met Chief of Staff Mordechai Gur and his key aides. We resolved that if the hijackers tried to land at Ben-Gurion, we would enable them to do so and then try to storm the plane using a crack paratroop unit, the way we had when a Belgian Sabena aeroplane had been hijacked and re-routed to Ben-Gurion in May 1972. (In that incident, our soldiers, dressed as airport maintenance men, were able to approach the aircraft while negotiations proceeded with the control tower. They suddenly swarmed aboard, shot and killed the two male hijackers and overpowered the two female ones. Only two of the 100-odd passengers were injured. As Minister of Transport at the time, I was at the airport, working alongside Moshe Dayan, the Defence Minister, during a long night of negotiation and preparation.)

At 21.00 a report came through that the Air France plane had been refuelled at Benghazi, Libya, and had taken off. Its course was unknown. At 23.00 Gur told me that the hijackers appeared intent on landing in Israel. I briefed Rabin by phone and then headed for Ben-Gurion. At 01.00 the plane was over Khartoum, Sudan, where permission to land was refused. I calculated that even if it were now to head for Israel, it would take between two and three hours to reach us, and decided to use the time visiting the special unit that was preparing to storm the plane. I set out by jeep with Major-General Yekutiel (Kuti) Adam, the O/C Operations Branch at the General Staff, and soon we were at the unit's assembly point.

This is one of the finest units in the IDF, composed entirely of volunteers, whose 'speciality' is taking on the toughest assignments and seeing them through. They have a special way about them too, an unmistakable look – defiantly unkempt hair, sun-tanned faces, even in the winter, and tight-pressed, silent lips.

We were ushered into a darkened hut. Several of the soldiers were inside, looking serious and businesslike. They showed no signs of tension. In the front, at a table, stood Yoni Netanyahu, the unit's recently appointed commander, strikingly handsome, his brow knitted in con-centration. I had heard of him long before his appointment to this elite command. He was widely spoken of in the army as a man with a promising future. He had a reputation both as a courageous battlefield commander and as a serious young intellectual: he had earned a decoration for bravery in combat and a degree in philosophy from Harvard.

Kuti Adam and I stayed to hear Netanyahu brief the troops; we then met separately with him and the other officers. I asked them if all was ready, and they assured me that it was.

We returned to the airport at 04.00, to be told that the hijacked plane had flown south from Khartoum and had just landed at Entebbe, Uganda, on the shores of Lake Victoria. Plainly, it was not coming to Israel – at least not that night. I headed wearily for home, arriving with the first rays of dawn.

Monday, 28 June

I phoned Rabin early to report on the night's events. I told him that I had seen no point in waking him, and he replied that he had indeed slept well and without interruption. I showered, made myself some coffee and headed back to the Defence Ministry, where a ceaseless flow of reports was being monitored. Some appeared fanciful, others just plain contradictory. It was hard to sift fact from fiction. According to one report, the hijacked passengers included a group of senior IDF officers. But by this time we had obtained a complete and accurate list from Air France and were in a position to know that this report, at least, was unfounded.

In the afternoon, I drove up to Jerusalem for a meeting of all the coalition Knesset Members with the Minister of Finance, Yehoshua Rabinowitz, who was to expound on his proposals for cutting the defence budget. I was determined to fight back hard. It was a strange thing, I observed bitterly when Rabinowitz had finished speaking, that in Washington US senators were demanding higher allocations for military aid to Israel in the wake of the Yom Kippur War, while here in Jerusalem Government ministers and coalition MKs were ready to vote for lower defence spending.

This debate, tense though it was, served somehow as a respite in the relentless tension through which we had been living since the day before. Back in the office in Tel Aviv, there was still no shaft of clarity through the pall of uncertainty and speculation that surrounded the hijack saga. The plane was on the tarmac in Entebbe, and no one seemed to know what the hijackers' intentions were. Experience had taught me that, at the end of the day, we would have to rescue the hostages ourselves. But it was far too early – indeed, it was impossible – to translate this principled position into an operational plan.

Tuesday, 29 June

I was due in Jerusalem very early. Before leaving, I stopped off at the Ministry to see if the night's reports had brought any new information. Basically – nothing. Just a lot of 'colour stories': the mood at the airport, visits by various dignitaries, a string of bombastic but essentially meaningless declarations by the Ugandan President, Idi Amin.

At the Knesset, there was a session of the Defence and Foreign Affairs Committee with the Prime Minister, myself and the Chief of Staff. Even though nearly three years had passed since the Yom Kippur War, its impact lay heavily on all our deliberations. The Committee devoted much of its session to the ongoing process within the IDF of applying the lessons of the war. Rabin reported briefly on the hijack, but there was not much new information he could add. At midday, the Committee adjourned, and in the early afternoon Rabin convened the *ad hoc* ministerial committee to analyse the situation and consider our policy.

Our most serious problem, it seemed to me, was the grave lack of credible and reliable intelligence information. Rabin opened the discussion, saying that in the absence of any other options we would have to negotiate (in other words, accede to the hijackers' demands to release imprisoned terrorists). Outwardly though, he continued, we would maintain our position that 'France is responsible; Israel will not capitulate.'

I felt differently. Our lack of authoritative information regarding the hijackers' conditions and the hostages' situation ought not, it seemed to me, to dictate any preference at this stage for any particular option. Why rush into a decision favouring one option (freeing the hostages through negotiations), when its feasibility was unclear, at the expense of an alternative option (freeing the hostages by force), when there was no definite evidence to show that this was not feasible?

I said nothing. Gur, however, observed that the IDF was looking into the feasibility of a military option. Gur had flown by helicopter to Jerusalem straight from an army exercise in Sinai, and we had been unable to confer together before the meeting. I wrote him a note asking what he had in mind. He wrote back saying that he had instructed the General Staff by phone from Sinai to work on the possibility of parachuting troops near Entebbe Airport, either on land or on Lake Victoria. These troops would storm the airport, kill the hijackers and stay on to guard the hostages until they were freed. 'I know these guys,' he added, referring to the Ministers. 'That's why I've prepared something that leaves the options open.' I understood how he felt: he was determined that no one should say, then or later, that the IDF had no military plan for rescuing the hostages.

But, as Minister of Defence, I had to remain cautious and reserved. I said that there was no operational proposal, as yet, that had been thoroughly checked out. We would be able to submit such a proposal only after meticulous examination. After this ministerial meeting, Gur formally instructed Kuti Adam to start work at once on planning several alternative military operations.

The meeting resolved that the Ministry of Transport was to set up a liaison office at Ben-Gurion Airport to co-ordinate with the hostages' families. These people were going through a terrible time, their desperate worry exacerbated by our frustrating ignorance.

That afternoon, a list arrived of the names of the prisoners whom the hijackers wanted released. It was woefully confused and full of spelling mistakes. Back in Tel Aviv, I called together the General Staff for a further consultation with Gur and myself. Most of the generals seemed to feel that a military rescue operation was not possible. Nevertheless, they all kept coming up with ideas of how to overcome the myriad difficulties. No country or army had ever had to contemplate a challenge of this dimension. My instructions to the General Staff were to continue raising new ideas and checking them out – no matter how weird or crazy they sounded.

By the end of that evening, three practical proposals seemed to have evolved, though all of them were still in their embryonic stages. The first was devised by the Chief of Staff himself and relied heavily on the element of surprise. Our troops were to make a seaborne attack on the airport from Lake Victoria, having either set out by boat from Kenya, across the lake, or parachuted, with their boats, on to the lake. They would take the hijackers completely unawares and, once they had killed them, would remain with the hostages until they were all freed.

An alternative scheme, put forward by Kuti Adam, involved inducing the hijackers to transact a prisoners-for-hostages exchange here in Israel – and jumping them before they could leave. This would require the co-operation of the French, who would have to approve of the Air France plane taking off from Entebbe and flying to Ben-Gurion.

A third proposal, sweeping in scope, breathtaking in audacity, came from the commander of the air force, Major-General Benny Peled. His idea was that Israel should take over Uganda itself, albeit for a short time – or at least conquer Entebbe. The air force, he said, was capable of parachuting sufficient troops to occupy the city, the harbour and the airport. Once all these objectives were secured, the hijackers would be attacked and killed, and the hostages rescued and flown home aboard the huge Hercules military transport planes that we had recently purchased from the United States.

At first, Peled's plan seemed totally far-fetched, as it probably had to him, too. But the more I thought about it, the more realistic it seemed to become. The others did not agree. The Chief of Staff dismissed the plan as fantastic and suggested that we would all do well to forget about it. Within days, he and the others were to change their tune.

Late that night, the ministerial committee reassembled to discuss the hijackers' demands. These included the release of forty terrorists in prison in Israel, six in Kenya, five in Germany (among them, members of the Baader-Meinhof organization), and one each in Switzerland and France. The Kenyans denied ever holding the six (they had, in fact, been caught trying to shoot down an Israeli jetliner at Nairobi Airport). The Germans made no clear statement; I doubted if they would be prepared to hand over convicted terrorists. Nevertheless, Rabin urged that Israel announce its readiness to release its prisoners.

The atmosphere in the ministerial committee grew steadily more tense. Rabin was impatient, perhaps understandably, cutting short other speakers while explaining at length and repeatedly why he favoured negotiating with the hijackers. There was no other option, he kept saying, glancing at me each time. There were precedents for such an exchange. I argued quietly that we had never agreed in the past to free prisoners who had killed innocent civilian victims. But the hijackers' list, I said, included such terrorist murderers. Rabin countered that the relatives of the hostages were saying that Israel had freed terrorists after the 1973 war in exchange for the bodies of dead soldiers – so how could it now refuse to free terrorists in return for living people, whose lives were in terrible danger?

Wednesday, 30 June
One of my bodyguards, O., often had insightful comments to make. He had served in the past as an aide and adviser to Idi Amin and knew the 'field-marshal' well. When the hijacked plane landed in Uganda, O. said to me, 'Idi Amin won't rush to kill white people. He will try to drag this thing out for as long as he can.' His remark persuaded me to call

together a number of IDF officers who had served in Uganda and knew Amin. We met at my office in Tel Aviv at 8.30. One of the officers, Colonel Baruch (Borka) Bar-Lev, had headed the IDF's mission to Uganda before Amin severed relations in 1973. He had grown close to Amin and had built up ties of trust and friendship. Another was Lieutenant-Colonel Yosef Salan, who had commanded an IAF team in Uganda which had tried to help it set up its own air force. Salan was intimately familiar with the air installations in the country, including those in Entebbe. A third officer was Major B., also an IAF officer. He had served for a time as Amin's personal pilot and, in that capacity, had had the opportunity to observe him closely.

I asked them to describe the Ugandan army, to give their assessments of Amin, his motives and his methods, and to put forward any proposals they might have for future action. Bar-Lev was the first to reply. He spoke at machine-gun pace. Idi Amin, he said, obtained most of his information from talking to other people. He was greatly influenced by those close to him and tended to rely heavily on their judgment and their personal loyalty to him. He did not believe that Amin would massacre the hostages, but he would not get into a fire-fight with the hijackers either. These two presumptions would remain valid so long as Amin 'doesn't dream something during the night'. If he did, that could change everything. Salan broadly agreed and warned that if we tried to use force, 'that could short-circuit all Amin's fuses'. If this were to happen, he might go wild and there was no knowing how it might end. Major B., however, added that in the case of a battle between IDF troops and the hijackers, he believed that the Ugandans would not intervene. They generally preferred to steer clear of other people's wars.

When I asked whether Amin was a brave man, they all three replied, unhesitatingly, that he was a coward. O. added that he was also cruel. He recalled that once, when Amin was given a rifle as a present, he immediately began spraying bullets across the courtyard of his villa, hitting innocent and unarmed people.

This had been a fascinating and revealing discussion. I summed it up, in my own mind, in the following way: Idi Amin would be interested in dragging out the hijack drama for as long as he could, since it provided him with an unparalleled opportunity for getting world attention. He would not, on his own initiative, kill the hostages. He played fast and loose with the lives of his own people, but was wary of harming 'white' people. To him, all the hostages – Jews, Arabs and Europeans – were, in that sense, 'white'. If we used force, therefore, the Ugandans would not intervene, even if some Ugandans were hurt or killed during the operation. But if the hostages remained in the Ugandans' hands *after* such an operation, they might well be killed in revenge. I thus concluded that the Ugandan army need not be regarded as a serious obstacle in the way of a military operation. Moreover, the way to address Amin was not through diplomatic protocol or sweet reason, but through his ego – appealing to his pride and honour, suggesting that there could be a Nobel Peace Prize in this for him, referring to his international standing and appealing to the mystique surrounding his role as national leader.

I concluded that we must try to set up a telephone link with Amin as soon as possible. This could provide us with the detailed information we lacked about the hijackers and the hostages – and enable us to form a more accurate assessment of the situation on the ground at Entebbe. I asked Bar-Lev to make the connection, presenting himself to Amin as speaking for people 'close to the top policy-making echelon in Israel'.

Following this meeting with our 'Ugandans', I again met key officers of the General Staff: the Chief of Staff, the O/C Operations Branch, the air-force commander, the head of intelligence and other senior officers. Chief of Staff Gur now laid out his plan in detail. The troops were to approach Entebbe by boat from Lake Victoria, attack the hijackers and kill them, and then withdraw. One problem with this scheme was that having withdrawn the soldiers would no longer be in a position to protect the hostages. The Ugandans might take out their anger and frustration on the defenceless hostages. The hijackers, moreover, had set an ultimatum for the next day at 11.00 a.m., whereas Gur's scheme could only be executed in thirty-six hours, at the earliest. It seemed too drawn-out and too cumbersome.

We went on to analyse the other possibilities and their obstacles. A solitary report from Entebbe claimed that an entire battalion of Ugandan troops had now been deployed at the airport to guard the hostages. But we did not know if the hostages were still in the plane or whether they had been moved to the terminal. If they were still aboard, the plane might have been booby-trapped with high-explosives. We simply did not know enough to mount a military operation – especially an operation whose success would depend, above all, on surprise.

Thus, I summed up my own position at this stage: 'If we give in to the hijackers' demands and release terrorists, everyone will understand us, but no one will respect us. If, on the other hand, we conduct a military operation to free the hostages, it is possible that no one will understand us, but everyone will respect us – depending, of course, on the outcome of the operation.'

Bar-Lev succeeded in getting through by phone to Idi Amin. The 'field-marshal' seemed pleased to hear from his old and trusted friend. He told Bar-Lev that the plane was indeed booby-trapped, as was the entire airport. There were at least seven hijackers, he continued, and perhaps as many as twenty. He had personally visited the airport and spoken to the hostages, and could report that they were in good health. He said that the hostages had asked him to transmit to Israel their urgent pleas that we accede to the hijackers' demands. Bar-Lev explained to Amin the supreme importance of ensuring the continued well-being of the hostages. He said that Amin would be inscribed in the annals of history as a great prince of peace, and that he might even receive the Nobel Prize for Peace, if he took it upon himself to protect the hostages.

Later that evening, a second telephone conversation took place between Bar-Lev and Amin. This time, the Ugandan leader said that he had received 'the Number One man of the freedom fighters'. We assumed this was a reference to Wadia Haddad, the head of the Black September Palestinian terrorist group that was behind the hijack. Amin said that this man had asked him to tell 'Colonel Bar-Lev' that Israel must release the forty prisoners forthwith. From this, we concluded that Wadia Haddad was actually standing alongside Amin, helping him to conduct the conversation.

Thursday, 1 July

Time was beginning to run out. The hijackers ultimatum was due to lapse at 11.00 a.m. Greenwich Meantime. I brought the O/C Operations, Major-General Adam, and the O/C Intelligence, Major-General Shlomo Gazit, to that morning's meeting of the ministerial committee. The hijackers had released forty-eight of the passengers – all those who were not Jewish. Some of them had already reached Paris and were able to provide detailed information of the situation in Entebbe. I proposed that we look into the possibility of co-operating with France in a joint military operation, but Rabin dismissed this peremptorily. 'If anyone wants to propose an operation of this kind, let him submit it to the vote of the full Cabinet.' Neither Rabin nor Foreign Minister Allon believed that enough time was left for a military operation of our own. Allon said, 'Let's concentrate on what is possible,' and Rabin forthrightly added, 'And not on pie-in-the-sky dreams'. The meeting proceeded as sparks openly flew between the Prime Minister and myself. I warned that an Israeli surrender to the hijackers would create a potentially disastrous precedent. 'It isn't that I lack concern for the lives and safety of the hostages. On the contrary, I am concerned for the lives and safety of passengers in the future.'

I asked Bar-Lev to phone Amin once again, and to tell him that he (Bar-Lev) was ready to fly to Uganda at once to bring with him an important message from the Government of Israel regarding the possibility of conducting negotiations. But this time, Amin was cold and distant. He said angrily that their previous conversations had been recorded without his consent, and complained that the recordings had made their way to the 'Voice of America'. 'Suddenly, I hear myself speaking on the "Voice of America",' he thundered. 'I never agreed to that.' He told Bar-Lev to tell the Government of Israel that it would do well to keep an ear open for a statement by the Popular Front for the Liberation of Palestine to be issued at 11.00 a.m.

The statement was duly broadcast: it announced a postponement of the ultimatum until 11.00 on Sunday morning. Suddenly, we had been granted three to four days' grace – just the time we needed to perfect and execute a military rescue plan. The immediate priorities were first, as throughout the hijack, more and better intelligence information, and second, a safe stopover in case a rescue operation ran into difficulties.

At 15.00, I convened a meeting of key officers on the General Staff. Gur called it 'the fantasy council' – a reference to the scepticism that had been voiced at Cabinet and, indeed, to Gur's own doubts that any realistic proposal could be drawn up. To Gur's great credit, he invited to this 'fantasy council' precisely those officers who could turn fantasy into reality, and who, moreover, were fired by a burning desire to do so. These included Kuti Adam, the air-force commander Benny Peled, his head of operations Rafi Har-Lev, Brigadier Dan Shomron, the chief infantry and paratroop officer, Brigadier Avigdor (Yanosh) Ben-Gal, and the brilliant young Ehud Barak, who had commanded the Sabena rescue in 1972 and was as confident now as he had been then that a rescue operation would succeed. Gur, Adam and Peled were as shocked as I was at the possibility that we might negotiate with the hijackers for the release of convicted terrorists imprisoned in Israel.

It was at this Thursday afternoon meeting that the outline for a workable rescue plan finally began to emerge. Though all of those present wanted to go ahead with this plan, there were still sombre differences of opinion regarding its chances of success. Gur was the most reserved, preferring to give his final approval only when further intelligence information became available.

In the interests of secrecy, we decided that the training facility where preparations would be made must immediately be hermetically sealed from the outside world. We appointed Shomron overall commander of the operation, and Colonel A. commander of the airborne unit that was to carry it out.

It was late evening by the time I could get away from the ongoing consultations to call Moshe Dayan. I wanted to fill him in. He was out for the evening with guests from Australia, at a sea-front restaurant in Tel Aviv. There wasn't time to wait for him to end his social engagement, so I drove over to the restaurant with my military aide, Arye Braun, who had been Dayan's aide, too, when he had been Defence Minister. At first, Dayan had no idea why I was so insistent on disturbing his dinner party just as they were embarking on their soup. His guests must have thought me very rude. I apologized to them and to Dayan's wife, Rahel, and pulled him over to a corner table. The waiters brought over glasses of red wine – the first nourishment I had had for hours. Braun pulled out a little map of the world, and I began explaining. As I talked, Dayan's unpatched eye began to sparkle. I diligently recounted the objections that had been raised and the obstacles that were anticipated, but Dayan brushed them aside. 'This is a plan that I support not one hundred per cent, but one hundred and fifty per cent!' he declared. His encouragement was enormously important to me. After all, he was a man whose opinions, especially on such matters, I profoundly respected.

Now the time had come to win over the Cabinet to the military option, starting with the members of the *ad hoc* ministerial committee. I rang Transport Minister Gad Ya'acobi and asked him over. Briefly, I outlined to him the main elements of the plan and asked for his support. Soon after, word came through from the Prime Minister's Office that another meeting of the ministerial committee had been set for 23.00.

This session was particularly tense. From the outset, the Prime Minister was impatient, to the consternation of several of the participants. Foreign Minister Allon kept cool, reiterating that France was to be seen as directly responsible for the plane and its passengers. But Rabin responded dismissively, which led to a bitter exchange between them. When this was over, Rabin asked Major-General (Res.) Rehavam Ze'evi to present to the Ministers how he proposed to conduct the negotiations with the hijackers. Rabin had appointed Ze'evi (nicknamed 'Gandhi') to organize the negotiations, and while I remained opposed in principle to acceding to the hijackers' demands, I did not object to this assignment. Ze'evi had made a reputation for himself for thoroughness during his long army service.★ Now he presented his report in a businesslike and efficient manner. Israel, he said, should announce from the start that it was negotiating only on its own behalf – not on behalf of the other countries that were required to release prisoners under the hijackers' demands. Furthermore, Israel should announce the number of prisoners it was prepared to release – forty – and not waver from that number. The list of men to be freed would be compiled by Israel. Gandhi proposed that the negotiations be conducted in France, with France or another third party providing good offices to facilitate communications between the parties. The handover of hostages for prisoners should take place at a French military airfield. Alternatively, a plane carrying the prisoners and another carrying the hostages would take off simultaneously from Tel Aviv and Entebbe, under a mutually agreeable third-party supervision.

Israel's plans to concede to the hijackers had been worked out to their minutest detail. Yet the unease among the Ministers remained. Rabin said that there was no need to go into details at this stage. He doubted that France would provide logistic help beyond carrying messages between the two sides. 'They won't fight Uganda,' Allon observed sarcastically, but this only triggered another brusque response from Rabin. The two of them argued vehemently over whether and under what mandate Ze'evi was to be sent to Paris to conduct the negotiations. As the meeting drew to an end, Allon shot at Rabin, 'If I'm getting in your way, appoint someone else to serve as acting Foreign Minister.'

At any rate, the decision was to get a negotiation going, which, from my perspective, was welcome, because it meant there would be much diplomatic activity to span the two-and-a-half days until the hijackers' latest ultimatum ran out – and to create a convenient cover beneath which we could go ahead with our preparations for a military rescue.

Before calling it a night, I met again, this time alone, with Gur, who still could not allay his reservations over the military plan. I told him that our decision to act or to refrain from acting would have major consequences for the fate of the Jewish state and the Jewish People.

★ Ze'evi is now leader of the ultra-rightist Moledet Party.

Friday, 2 July

After a snatched sleep, I awoke to find myself confronting a new source of resistance from an unexpected quarter – I had a raging toothache. It had been coming on all week, but I had tried to ignore it, simply because I could not find the time to go to a dentist. Now there was no choice but to succumb. I fixed an appointment with Dr Langer for later in the morning and headed to my office. There, a welcome piece of news awaited me: Kenya had consented that our planes could land on its soil in the event of difficulties during the flight. I went round to Gur to deliver this good news in person. His eyes visibly brightened. We agreed between us that Kenya's position enabled us to advance the date of the operation – from Sunday night to Saturday night. This was much to be preferred, since the ultimatum would not have elapsed by then and the negotiations would still be in progress. We were not worried that the Kenyans might leak our plans. Their policy, plainly, was to continue denying that they held any of the terrorists demanded by the hijackers; their interest was in a successful rescue operation by Israel.

Until this moment, I had not told Rabin about the plan for a military rescue operation. So long as there was no full agreement between myself and the Chief of Staff, I felt that it would be wrong to present it. I was concerned, moreover, that if I presented it too soon, it might be shot down, as was Gur's earlier plan for a seaborne assault from Lake Victoria. (Rabin had compared that idea to the ill-starred Bay of Pigs operation.) Now, however, with the plan rapidly becoming operational, I decided the time was right to report its existence to the Prime Minister, and to recount the doubts that still surrounded it and the differences of opinion that it had aroused among the General Staff. I told him that 'at this moment, speaking personally rather than officially, I am convinced that we have available a real military option'.

I reiterated my view that releasing prisoners in response to the hijackers' demand would gravely demoralize the public at home and would seriously weaken Israel's standing and prestige abroad, among friend and foe alike. I then described the plan in broad terms. Rabin reacted coolly. If the plan failed, he said, the blow to the IDF and to Israel itself would be very great. Moreover, the plan was flawed right at its outset: the first plane to land at Entebbe might be identified and attacked before the rest of the force had time to land and deploy. 'Anyway,' Rabin added, 'I am bound by the Cabinet's decision.'

I observed that Peled was confident the first plane could land without arousing any suspicions on the ground. But I saw that Rabin had not yet decided. I felt that I would have to campaign for the plan among the other senior Ministers.

But first – to Dr Langer. As he told me some time later, Dr Langer's son was one of the soldiers soon to take part in the Entebbe rescue. But the only question the deft-handed doctor ventured at the time was whether I knew why his son had had his weekend leave cancelled.

From there, I went over to Minister of Justice Haim Zadok, whom I chose as the first target of my canvassing. An important figure in the Cabinet, both by virtue of his position and of his personality, Zadok heard me out quietly. But I felt his support and commitment steadily growing. When I left him, I knew that I had a firm ally.

Another session with the key General Staff officers was called, this time together with the head of the Mossad. Gur asked what the troops were to do if they encountered resistance from Ugandan forces at Entebbe Airport, and I replied, without hesitation, that they could shoot to kill. That, said Gur, would make the detailed planning of the operation much easier. We discussed the news that Idi Amin had flown to a meeting of the Organization of African States in Mauritius and would not be back in Uganda until late Saturday night or Sunday. Somebody suggested that we appoint a 'stand-in' for the absent President: one of our soldiers, of appropriate height and girth, his face suitably darkened, would dress up as Amin and arrive at the airport aboard the Presidential limousine (to roll off one of our Hercules planes).

The Hercules planes would take off from Sharm el-Sheikh, at the southern tip of Sinai, late Saturday afternoon. They would fly high over Ethiopia, which we knew did not possess radar capable of spotting high-flying aircraft. They would approach Entebbe from over Lake Victoria – the route regularly used by commercial airliners coming in to land there. Gur listed the stages of the operation on the ground: two minutes from the moment the first plane switched on its landing lights until it taxied to a halt; two minutes for the troops aboard to disembark; the other planes would come in in quick succession; five minutes to reach the terminal building; five more minutes to complete the rescue operation.

I telephoned Rabin and asked for an immediate consultation to go over the plan in greater detail. Apart from the two of us and our military aides, this meeting was attended by the Chief of Staff and the head of the Mossad. The Prime Minister spoke first of the ongoing efforts in Paris to conduct negotiations with the hijackers via the French. Then,

Gur made his presentation, with Rabin interjecting questions about conditions on the ground at Entebbe. At noon, this meeting was broadened to include all the members of the ministerial committee, and Gur expounded the proposal anew. Plainly, the final decision had to be taken by the full Cabinet. Gur kept stressing the supreme importance of maintaining total secrecy. I suggested that the Ministers be informed of a possible session of the Cabinet, sitting as the secret ministerial defence committee, the following day. This would enable the Orthodox Ministers, who do not drive on the sabbath, to stay within walking distance of the government offices in Tel Aviv.

Rabin closed the meeting on a cautious and still undecided note. 'There are ninety-eight Israelis trapped in that terminal,' he observed. 'Yet the intelligence information we have at our disposal is far from adequate . . . . I am in favour of all the preparations going ahead,' he said, 'but I propose that we still see this thing as subsidiary to the ongoing negotiations. If only I could get them to release the women and children . . . that would change the whole picture.'

In the evening, Sonia and I entertained Professor Zbigniew Brzezinski at our home for sabbath dinner. He was said to be a likely candidate for National Security Adviser if the Democratic candidate, Jimmy Carter, should win the American election in November, and the Foreign Ministry had asked me some weeks ago to have him over during his visit to Israel. We could hardly put it off now without triggering just the sort of speculation that we so wanted to avoid.

Sonia and I had invited Gur and his wife, Rita. But Rita's father had died that day, and Gur wanted to join the Hercules transports on a trial flight; he wanted to get to know the pilots personally and review their flight performance as part of his preparations for the mission. Kuti Adam filled in for the absent Chief of Staff and turned in a sterling performance, never allowing a nerve in his face to show the tension he felt. Also on the guest list were O/C Intelligence, Shlomo Gazit, another consummate poker-face, brimful of fascinating knowledge, and Gershom Schocken, editor and publisher of the leading liberal newspaper, *Ha'aretz*, who knew nothing of the plan and thus could appreciate only in retrospect the great performances of his fellow diners.

Brzezinski pressed me as to why Israel was not launching a military rescue operation, and I, unwilling to lie yet unable to tell the truth, lamely listed the many obstacles – distance, lack of reliable intelligence, presence of Ugandan troops – that could thwart such an operation. I glanced at Schocken – a noted 'dove' – for support, but he remained silent. Later, after our eminent American guest had gone, I asked Schocken what he thought of Brzezinski's idea. To my surprise, he said that he was violently opposed to the Government's decision to make a deal with the hijackers and vigorously supported the military option. Brzezinski later wrote me a gracious note, praising not only the rescue operation itself, but also Israel's success in keeping it secret.

Saturday, 3 July
After midnight, the Chief of Staff telephoned to say that the airborne exercise had been successful, and he now wanted to set a firm time for the operation on Saturday evening. Specifically, he wanted my authorization for his sending the planes and men down to Sharm el-Sheikh, which was to be their jump-off point, in time to take off from there on Saturday afternoon. I agreed.

In the morning, I met once again with the generals and senior officers involved in the planning and control of the operation. I asked Gur to go over it slowly, stage by stage. There would be four Hercules, he said. They would take off two-and-a-half hours before nightfall and be over Entebbe at 23.00. The first plane would come to a halt at the end of the runway and would disgorge several jeeps and the 'presidential' Mercedes, all with soldiers aboard, guns at the ready. These vehicles would head immediately for the old terminal building, where, as we knew from the released passengers, the Israeli hostages were being held. They would then neutralize the hijackers and take over the building. Five to seven minutes later, the other three planes would land in close succession, protected on the ground by a detail from the fighting force aboard the first plane. They would unload armoured cars, which would be used (if necessary) to fight the Ugandan troops. They would also bring the medical team, and a unit whose job would be to take care of the hostages and to help them emplane. The first plane would now draw up alongside the terminal building, board the hostages and take off. The other three planes would taxi to the new terminal building and board the troops and the vehicles, before they took off. Any medical treatment necessary would be performed aboard the planes.

Gur said that at a full 'dress rehearsal' conducted the day before the whole operation on the ground had taken fifty-five minutes. If all went well, therefore, we should be in and out within an hour. If a fire-fight developed with the Ugandan forces, however, or if there were many casualties, it could take much longer. In any event, the operation on the ground would end before 02.00. The latest intelligence information from Entebbe was encouraging: the Air France plane seemed to be empty, and there was no reason to believe that the hijackers had mined or booby-trapped the approaches to the old terminal building.

The major challenge now was to ensure that a majority of the Cabinet approved the plan. Much depended on Rabin. I phoned him and suggested that the pre-Cabinet consultation between the two of us, scheduled for 12.00, be brought forward to 11.00. The timetable was beginning to look tight. The planes were to leave Ben-Gurion for Sharm el-Sheikh at 11.30. It was within my authority to authorize that flight – since the planes would not be leaving Israeli air space – and I had done so. But by 16.00 they would have to be in the air again, and this time their flight path would be taking them far from Israel. That was the deadline, then, for the Cabinet decision.

At the meeting, I explained that the prospects for a successful rescue operation were better now than they had ever been. The Chief of Staff was now totally in favour of the operation. Foreign Minister Allon had said earlier that he supported it, and I had no reason to think that he had changed his mind. My own position was well known to everyone in the room. Now it was up to Rabin to take a final position.

Rabin spoke of the chance of failure, and of what such a failure would mean for the IDF's prestige and strength as a deterrent force. He noted that the intelligence information we had was from Friday; things on the ground might have changed over the past twenty-four hours. He spoke of possible alternatives. Clearly, he was still undecided.

I spoke again. We had lectured the world against giving in to terrorism. If we gave in now, our prestige would suffer greatly. I reminded them of the fact that the hijackers had conducted a 'selection' – that dread word, fraught with Holocaust associations – separating the Jews from the others aboard the plane. If the proposed operation succeeded, I said, the mood of the entire country would improve suddenly and dramatically.

Certainly, the operation would put our finest soldiers at risk. But we had always been ready to risk lives to save a larger number of lives by using our own forces, without recourse to outside assistance.

Rabin broke into my short but impassioned speech. 'When does the take-off order have to be given?' he asked. This was the first indication that he was coming round.

The Cabinet, sitting as the ministerial defence committee, convened at 14.00. The meeting proceeded in a formal and businesslike fashion, with no echoes of the earlier differences of opinion. Rabin opened with a brief presentation of the proposed plan. I followed with reasoned arguments in favour of approving it. Gur laid out the operational details. As the discussion developed, I slipped out with Gur and we drove over to the military airfield, where the troops were preparing to embark. The soldiers were in their full webbing and obviously in high spirits. The officers asked us if the Cabinet was going to give the final okay. 'Don't worry, Shimon,' said Dan Shomron. 'Everything will work perfectly.' Yoni Netanyahu came up to shake my hand and he, too, assured me that the plan was 'one hundred per cent'. We embraced them and watched them climb up into the bellies of the vast planes, smiling as if they were off on holiday.

Back at the Cabinet, the decision was formally drafted and approved at 14.30: 'It has been decided that we shall endorse a rescue operation by the IDF according to the operational plan submitted by the Minister of Defence and the Chief of Staff.' Rabin left the room to brief the Likud opposition leaders, Menachem Begin and Elimelech Rimalt, and the Chairman of the Knesset Foreign Affairs and Defence Committee, Yitzhak Navon.

With the planes in the air, an expectant lull descended over us. The orders were to maintain complete radio silence unless any problems arose. Benny Peled and Kuti Adam flew separately aboard a converted Boeing 707, which was to serve as the command and control vehicle, keeping at a distance of about 100 kilometres from the Hercules transports in the air, and circling overhead while they were on the ground. In my office, the communications equipment was tuned to the operation's wave-band, and, to our growing satisfaction, as the hours passed we heard nothing. I decided to go to the bar-mitzvah party of the grandson of Dr Herzl Rosenblum, the editor of the mass-circulation newspaper *Yediot Aharonot* (lit. Latest News). I thought that my attendance would help keep up the façade of discretion that was working so well in protecting the secrecy of the operation.

All the big names in Israeli journalism were there, and not one of them had any inkling of what was afoot. Some remarked how well I looked; others said that I looked tired. Both observations were intended, presumably, to elicit hints of what I was doing, if anything, in connection with the ongoing hijack saga. To those who asked about the hostages, I replied that they would be back home very soon, perhaps within twenty-four hours. The intended – and achieved – effect of that remark was to heighten speculation as to the state of behind-the-scenes negotiations between Israel and the hijackers.

As the scheduled landing time approached, I returned to my office with my aides and the Transport Minister, Gad Ya'acobi. Rabin and his aides and the head of the Mossad joined us there. At 11.03, the first sounds came crackling over the radio receivers: the lead plane had landed safely.

11.10 Dan Shomron's cool, clipped voice: 'Everything is all right. Will report later.' This was followed by staccato sounds. Gunfire? Or the plane engines?

11.18 The code-word 'Shefel', meaning that the other planes had landed.

11.20 Shomron again: 'Everything is going well. You will soon receive a full report.' And then the codeword 'Falastin', which meant that the attack on the terminal had begun.

11.32 'Jefferson'. This meant that the evacuation of the hostages was under way.

11.33 'Move everything to "Galila".' From this we deduced that they were taking the hostages to the plane for boarding.

It all sounded perfect. But then, at 11.50, we suddenly heard a call for first aid for 'Mateh Shkedim' – Netanyahu's unit. There were 'two Ekaterina', meaning two casualties. Who were they? Obviously, we could not ask.

A minute later, at 11.51, the word 'Carmel' came over the airwaves, signifying wheels up and away for all the planes. Our hearts leapt with joy. We decided that the planes should stop in Kenya to refuel. We would make no official statement until the morning. Rabin went back to his office. I joined Gur at army headquarters. All the members of the General Staff had been called in. Not all of them knew in advance of the operation; their shouts of enthusiasm mingled with the jubilation and relief of those who had known and had shared the anxiety and anticipation.

I sent for Bar-Lev and asked him to call up Idi Amin. I wanted to know if the President had learned yet of the nocturnal visit to his country. He had not.

Amin: 'President Amin speaking.'

Bar-Lev: 'Thank you, sir. I want to thank you for the co-operation. Thank you very much, sir.'

Amin: 'You know you did not succeed...'

Bar-Lev: 'Thank you for the co-operation, sir. The co-operation did not succeed? Why?'

Amin asked if we had done anything, and Bar-Lev replied that we had done exactly what he, Amin, had wanted. By now the President began to realize that something had happened, something that he did not know about.

Amin: 'What has happened? Can you tell me?'

Bar-Lev: 'No, I don't know. I was asked just to thank you for your co-operation. My friends, who have close connections with the Government, asked me to say that to you.'

In Gur's office, the champagne began to flow. Gur made a little speech, in which he said that apart from Netanyahu – whom we now knew had been hit – and another paratrooper, the force had apparently suffered no other injuries. All the hostages had been rescued unharmed, save for one woman, Mrs Dora Bloch, who had been taken to a hospital in Entebbe. (We later established that she had been killed.) The hijackers, who were Arabs and Germans, had all been shot dead. The operation was certainly one of the most successful that the IDF had ever undertaken. Gur added that he could not conclude even this preliminary summation 'without singling out the one man whose determination made it happen – the Minister of Defence. I don't know if it's possible to apportion credit among those responsible for the decision to undertake this operation, but if it is, the biggest share of the credit goes to the Defence Minister....'

At 01.15, I called up Rabin and told him of Bar-Lev's conversation with Idi Amin. He burst out laughing and invited me to his office, where Begin, Rimalt and Navon had joined him. He telephoned the President of the State, the Speaker of the Knesset and Golda Meir. I telephoned Sonia; she was thunderstruck. We drafted a laconic statement to be issued by the army spokesman: 'IDF forces have tonight rescued the hostages and air-crew from Entebbe Airport.' When the first word of 'an Israeli attack on Entebbe' was published, by Agence France Presse, I instructed our spokesman to issue the statement.

At three o'clock, I lay down at last on a couch in my office and tried to sleep, but without success. I kept thinking of the hostages, what they must be feeling now, in the belly of the Hercules. I felt Gur's presence in the room before I saw him. 'Shimon,' he said quietly, 'Yoni's gone. The bullet hit him in the back and went through his heart. He was shot from the control tower.'

I turned to the wall. For the first time that week, I gave vent to my feelings. The tears flowed freely. I remembered Yoni at Ben-Gurion Airport on Sunday night, when we had thought that the Air France plane would land here. His eyes had been sad.

As morning came and the news spread, the whole world seemed to join with Israel in a moment of wonderment and rejoicing. But in Israel, the joy was tinged with sadness because of Yoni's death. When the planes touched down, at a military airfield, I felt myself torn between the hugs and happiness and the stretcher that bore Yoni's body. At the funeral the next day, I spoke the immortal words of David in his lament for Jonathan (2 Samuel 1:19–26): 'The beauty of Israel is slain upon thy high places: how are the mighty fallen ... I am distressed for thee, my brother Jonathan: very pleasant hast thou been unto me: thy love to me was wonderful.' We called the rescue Operation Yoni. Its glory has not dimmed with the passing years.

15 COMRADES AND FRIENDS

The Socialist International is probably the most important non-governmental political organization in Europe, if not in the world. It has a long and proud tradition and has played an influential international role between wars. Of course, when wars actually break out, the long and proud tradition of socialist solidarity often gives way to more immediate interests of wartime coalitions.

The Socialist International has undergone many transitions in its history. First, there was the split between the original Socialist International, which stood for social democracy, and the Comintern, which supported dictatorship – albeit ostensibly for the lofty purpose of attaining social justice. Then, after the Second World War, it underwent a further change, from an international organization to a global organization – that is, an organization that looks at the world as a whole, at the zones of relative prosperity and also at the vast areas where poverty still prevails, focusing on relations between North and South at least as much as on East–West confrontations. François Mitterrand, in one of our many conversations over the years, defined his own political philosophy thus: 'In the East–West conflict, I am with the West; in the North–South conflict, I am with the South.'

For many years, I served as one of the Socialist International's Vice-Presidents, but my relations with the organization were always complicated. On the one hand, as it was a largely European body, the International harboured a sense of guilt towards the Jewish People. Socialist leaders also felt a strong sense of admiration for the original and vibrant socialist movement that had developed in Israel. On the other hand, however, the Socialist International's strong Third World sympathies meant that many of its members were intensely exercised by the plight of the Palestinians.

The Israeli labour movement always sought a close dialogue with the International. The old guard remembered that in the days of the Mandate, the British Labour Party had stood firmly behind us (until it came to power in 1945, when Ernest Bevin, then Foreign Secretary, conducted a policy of outright hostility towards us). Our close ties with British labour were considered a political and ideological asset of prime importance. The Zionist-socialist movement in Britain, Poalei Zion, led by Dr S. S. Levenberg and supported by the prominent left-wing MP, Ian Mikardo, was an important part of the labour movement there.

Ben-Gurion was less enthusiastic than some of his longtime comrades about the Socialist International and our ties with it. He would have preferred an affiliation with an Afro-Asian organization, with a socialist tilt of course, rather than with the European-based International, with its faintly patronizing attitudes to both Africa and Asia.

Moreover, Ben-Gurion had an abiding dislike of certain foreign words. At a speech he once delivered at my kibbutz, Alumot, he launched a blistering attack on the word 'colonization', then widely used to denote the building of new kibbutzim and moshavim. The Hebrew word 'hityashvut', meaning settlement, was much to be preferred, he insisted. Similarly, he thought that 'socialism' should be discarded, in favour of the biblical Hebrew noun 'tzedek' and the modern adjective 'hevrati' – together meaning 'social justice', which was socialism by another name.

I knew what he was getting at. He had never considered that the founders of modern-day socialism – Marx and Engels, Lenin and Trotsky, Ferdinand Lassalle, Rosa Luxemburg, Jean Jaurès and Léon Blum – had, in fact, given birth to the socialist ideal. Rather, he saw in the biblical prophets the true source of man's historic struggle for social justice.

The concept of universal peace and brotherhood, in Ben-Gurion's view, was also first articulated in the Bible, by the prophet Isaiah in his famous vision, 'They shall beat their swords into plowshares' (2:4). It was never more nobly or more movingly expressed. Why, therefore, Ben-Gurion was asking, should we look for foreign-language translations of these lofty ideas, translations which were anyway only pale copies of the original?

At the same time, of course, Ben-Gurion fully appreciated the importance of our international ties and supported our relationship with the Socialist International.

I came to appreciate the significance of the International at a conference that took place in 1977. Many of the top leaders were present,
among them François Mitterrand and the Spanish leader, Felipe González. At the time, our own party was in disarray, as I have already
recounted. All of my colleagues at the International came up to me to
shake my hand and offer me a word of encouragement.

During that period, the International was run, in effect, by an informal
troika: Willy Brandt, the German statesman who served as President of
the International; Bruno Kreisky, the Chancellor of Austria and the
International's uncrowned ideologue; and Olaf Palme of Sweden, who
was considered the coming man in European socialism.

Brandt had been Mayor of Berlin and Foreign Minister in the Federal
Government before he became Chancellor. He was a man of enormous
personal magnetism. Tall and imposing, handsome well into his later
years, he radiated an air of spring-like vigour and freshness. He had a
winning way with people, and was forgiven if not everything then almost
everything. There was little of the pristine socialist ascetic about Brandt.
He enjoyed a good bottle of wine, a fine cigar, a scintillating conversation,
a racy joke and the company of attractive women. Women were
entranced by him, and it was not hard to see why. He never believed that
being a socialist meant being sad or sombre. But despite his wholehearted
hedonism, Brandt was not a corrupt or a wanton man; on the contrary,
he was a man of strong principles, for which he was prepared to fight.
Thus, as a young man in Hitler's Germany, he not only resisted Nazi
blandishments, but actually fought against the Nazi authorities, so that
he was eventually forced into exile in Norway.

While Konrad Adenauer was the Chancellor who rebuilt post-war
Germany's relations with the West, Brandt was the leader who first
opened the way to the East. He was the first European statesman who
developed the *Ostpolitik*, that is, a policy of controlled thaw in East–
West relations. That policy earned him the Nobel Prize for Peace and
eventually brought about the reunification of Germany. It was a policy
that required a great deal of personal and political courage. It entailed
Germany's renunciation of its claims to large tracts of territory beyond
the Oder–Neisse line. It entailed, too, persuading the world that Germany
was no longer the ominous, threatening force in Europe that it had been
for much of the past century.

Brandt also had a profound, almost spiritual, relationship with the
Jewish People and the State of Israel. His gesture of kneeling at the

Warsaw Ghetto became the single most famous action of his life. He consistently sought to bring the Palestine Liberation Organization (PLO) into the Socialist International, and to broker an understanding between it and Israel. But he was extremely careful never to do anything that might have led to our secession from the International. I had made it clear to him that if the PLO were in, we would be out. And indeed, the Socialist International remained one of the few major international organizations to which the PLO was not admitted.

Our personal relations grew very close. Brandt would often consult me over the affairs of the International. He even appointed me chairman of a conciliation committee that attempted to end the conflict between Morocco and the Polisario rebels – which I thought something of an historic irony. He would speak to me with total frankness about the inner workings of the German SDP, and I would tell him about our problems in the Israeli Labour Party.

One of my biggest problems was trying to explain to Brandt and other leaders of the Socialist International why we decided to enter a government of national unity with the Likud in 1984 and again in 1988. Each time, our decision followed an inconclusive election, which left both major parties, Labour and Likud, unable to form a more homo-geneous coalition. Brandt supported me. He was enormously amused when I reported to the International the conversation I had had with Rabbi Ovadia Yosef, an eminent Talmudic sage and the spiritual leader of Shas, the Sephardic ultra-Orthodox party.

'Don't be sad,' Yosef consoled me, 'there is an historical precedent.'

'Where?' I asked.

'In the Garden of Eden,' he replied, smiling.

'How's that?' I asked.

'Simple,' the Rabbi said. 'When Adam realized that there was no woman available other than Eve, and Eve understood that she had no alternative either, other than Adam, they decided to set up home together and named it Paradise.'

I explained to my socialist colleagues that the long-hoped-for result of our union with the right was a peace process with the Arabs – and that was the principal reason for our decision to join the Government of National Unity.

Brandt visited us in Israel, and we planted a grove of trees in his honour. I flew to Germany twice to attend events in his honour. One was his seventy-fifth birthday party, given by the Federal President,

Richard von Weizsäcker. In my brief remarks, I cited the Psalmist's blessing: 'The righteous shall flourish like the palm tree.... They shall still bring forth fruit in old age' (Psalm 92, 12–14). The second occasion was a less joyful one: it the huge funeral in October 1992 with which the German people honoured Willy Brandt. There was hardly a dry eye among the thousands who paid this last tribute to one of the great statesmen of the twentieth-century.

Only a few months earlier, we had spent a glorious evening together in one of the grand palaces of Istanbul, at a lavish entertainment in honour of the Socialist International that included a sound-and-light pageant of Turkey's history and a fashion show. Brandt waltzed through the evening, dancing like a young man. I knew, though, that his lively legs did not convey the true condition of his heart. He had asked me earlier, in a private conversation, who I thought ought to replace him as President of the International, because, as he said with an impish smile, 'There is an understanding between myself and Nature that the time has come for me to go.' I did not know then that this would be Willy Brandt's last dance.

The second central figure in the Socialist International during this period was Bruno Kreisky. He was considered both an outstanding Chancellor and an outstanding intellectual. Under his leadership, Austria maintained excellent relations with both East and West, and North and South. Inflation and unemployment were kept to a minimum, and the Government was run, under Kreisky's impregnable authority, in such a way as to incur the envy of other statesmen and politicians. Behind his back, he was dubbed 'Kaiser Bruno I', not without affection, by his loyal subjects. He always maintained direct and constant personal contact with the public. Every morning, between 8 and 9, his home telephone line was open so that anyone could call and speak to the Chancellor. Many of the calls, he once told me, were a waste of his time – such as the two young boys who bet a schilling on whether the Chancellor would lift the receiver in person. One celebrated call concerned a dog who insisted on relieving itself on the neighbour's lawn. The Chancellor invested much effort in securing an amicable accord between the two angry neighbours.

Kreisky also wrote a weekly column in the socialist party newspaper, where he would answer readers' questions on political matters. I think he felt that Vienna was too small a stage for an actor of his talents and ambitions. There were persistent rumours that he saw himself as a suitable candidate for Secretary-General of the United Nations.

That was one side of his public persona. The other side was his complex relationship with his Jewishness. Kreisky ceaselessly wrestled with himself for having been born a Jew. On the one hand, he never sought to deny it; on the other, he was never able to reconcile himself to it. Whenever he spoke of his life story, he would dwell on the Austrian aspects and play down the Jewish dimension.

Kreisky had a brother in Tel Aviv, who worked for a number of years for my father. I never mentioned this to the Chancellor, though he himself once broached the subject of his brother, saying, in an injured tone, that he had heard it said that he did not help his brother. 'An outright lie,' he asserted. He had always helped him, he assured me, 'in a steady and regular way'.

He would regale me with Austrian stories and then admit, on an intimate note, that there was anti-Semitism in Austria and that he himself had encountered it from time to time. Once, he said, he had been left literally speechless at a party meeting when, in the course of a long an vigorous reply to his critics, someone in the audience had shouted: 'What do you think this is, a kibbutz?'

Brandt once said to me of Kreisky, 'He is a wonderfully gifted man. But there is something so very Jewish about him: that streak of self-destructiveness.'

Kreisky's 'Jewish complex' came into play in his relations with the Jewish state. He was full of admiration for Israel – and full of criticism. He identified with the PLO standpoint and regarded its Chairman, Yasser Arafat, as a close personal friend – a sentiment that was apparently reciprocated with equal ardour by Arafat. Kreisky would wax poetic in praise of Arafat. The PLO Chairman could have been an outstanding engineer, Kreisky once assured me, but he had chosen to sacrifice his life for his people. That was why he had never married (eventually he did, but that was after Kreisky's death), because he had dedicated his life to his cause. He was married to the Palestinian people and truly desired peace.

Kreisky tried his hardest to persuade us to recognize the PLO and to negotiate with it. But the more he praised Arafat, the more I voiced my profound reservations about him. I stressed his involvement in terrorism, his notorious inability to be decisive, his penchant for endless and ultimately self-defeating tactical manoeuvres. Arafat, I asserted to Kreisky time after time, was not prepared to pay the price for peace.

In this context, I once told Kreisky the story of my first personal encounter with Ben-Gurion. He had taken me in his car from Tel Aviv to Haifa – I the young unknown, he already a legend. I had prepared for this opportunity with breathless anticipation. But Ben-Gurion sank into his heavy overcoat and said nothing for most of the journey. As we passed Zichron Yaacov, some three-quarters of the way to Haifa, he suddenly looked at me and said, 'You know, Trotsky was no statesman.' To this day I don't know how Trotsky had entered his mind at that particular moment, but, anxious to prolong the conversation, I immediately asked him, 'Why was that?'

'Because of his concept of no-peace-no-war. That's not statesmanship. That's some sort of Jewish invention. A statesman has to decide one way or the other: to go for peace – and pay the price; or to make war, knowing what the risks and dangers are. Lenin was Trotsky's inferior in terms of intellect, but he became the leader of Russia because he was decisive. He decided on peace and paid the heavy price that peace required.'

Kreisky was vehemently opposed to Israel's military occupation and to the Jewish settlements in the administered areas. He urged us to withdraw to the pre-1967 borders. His most virulent criticism was reserved for the Israeli right. But he voiced his bitter disappointment with the Labour Party, and with me personally, for failing to adopt the positions that he so vigorously recommended.

He kept close contacts with various left-wing politicians in Israel, from whom he gleaned his information about the political situation in our country. A good deal of this information, I might add, was coloured by the views of its purveyors as much as by those of its recipient.

Israel as a whole distinctly disliked Kreisky. Every Israeli knew how he had not offered Golda Meir 'even a glass of water', as she later reported, when she had visited him at his home in early October 1973. Kreisky himself was deeply hurt by this account. He maintained that he had offered the visiting Israeli Premier a full breakfast, but she had declined any refreshment. For years thereafter, whenever I came to visit him, the proceedings always began with a glass of water.

To me, Kreisky always remained a riddle. Judged by his political pronouncements, he was Israel's most implacable adversary among European leaders. And yet, when judged by actions rather than words, he was one of our staunchest friends. I am referring, particularly, to the Jewish exodus from the Soviet Union during the 1970s. We needed a transit-point, a halfway house where we could welcome the Jews as they came through the Iron Curtain, and organize the second leg of their voyage to Israel. (There were no diplomatic ties at that time, nor any direct air-links, between Israel and the USSR or any of its satellite states except Romania.)

No European country was prepared to offer us the transit facilities we needed. They all had their reasons and explanations, but the plain fact was that they all refused. The only one to agree was Austria, where the Chancellor made the decision on his personal authority and responsibility. Whenever we needed pressure or persuasion on behalf of a 'Prisoner of Zion' – a Jewish activist incarcerated in the Soviet gulag – we turned to Kreisky, who always responded. Whenever we needed diplomatic help in retrieving prisoners of war or in searching for men missing in action, Kreisky always rendered active assistance.

To complete this portrait of a complex relationship, I should mention Kreisky's genuinely important role, on both the political and the personal levels, during the key early phase of the Egyptian–Israeli peace process. Hassan Tohamey, the man President Sadat first sent to meet secretly with Israel's Moshe Dayan in Morocco, in the summer of 1977, had served previously as Egyptian Ambassador to Austria. A deeply religious man, indeed something of a mystic, Tohamey was one of Sadat's oldest friends and closest confidants, and Kreisky invested much effort in trying to persuade him that the time was ripe for a bold thrust towards peace. That initial Dayan–Tohamey meeting, held under the auspices of King Hassan II of Morocco, proved to be the first step on the path that led to the Camp David agreements in 1978 and to the Israeli–Egyptian peace treaty in the following year.

Actually, Kreisky tried to bring about a meeting between myself and Tohamey earlier in 1977, when Labour was still in power (the Likud election victory was in May of that year). Many things in Israel's history might have turned out differently had that proposed meeting gone ahead, and had Labour thus embarked on the peace process with Egypt instead of the Likud. But apparently Prime Minister Rabin was not convinced of the seriousness of the proposal.

In mid-1978, with the Israeli–Egyptian negotiations in crisis, Willy Brandt and Bruno Kreisky decided upon a salvaging initiative to be undertaken by the Socialist International: they invited Sadat and me to meet the two of them in Vienna.

As leader of the opposition, I sought Foreign Minister Dayan's approval. Of course, he could hardly object. I also informed Prime Minister Begin of the invitation, and I sent an unequivocal message to Sadat explaining that if he expected me to take issue publicly with the Government's positions, he would be disappointed. I was ready and willing to put forward my own position, and to listen carefully to what he had to say, but I would not use the occasion to criticize Begin. Dayan asked me to focus on the Israeli settlements in northern Sinai, which the Government was hoping to retain under a peace agreement, but which Sadat was determined to recover along with the rest of the Peninsula.

Kreisky decided to accord Sadat and myself the same protocol courtesies. When the Egyptian President flew into Vienna, a guard of honour was lined up to welcome him. Motor-cycle outriders flanked his limousine and a fleet of official cars followed behind. A helicopter circled overhead as a further security measure. When I touched down several hours later, the same pomp and circumstance awaited me. Only I had no limousine. The Israeli Embassy in Vienna had apparently decided, or been instructed, not to provide a car for me. The commander of the guard of honour almost fainted when he heard that I had no suitable vehicle at my disposal. What, then, did I propose to do, he asked, in palpable shock. I told him calmly that I proposed to take a taxi. His trauma worsened. Motor-cycle outriders and a helicopter escorting a taxi! He excused himself for a moment and rushed off to telephone the Chancellor's office. Upon his return, his relief was evident: the Chancellor had put his own limousine at my disposal.

When we arrived at the hotel, having glided through Vienna past bemused citizens, Kreisky was waiting. He fairly swept me into his embrace – and scarcely let me out of it throughout my stay.

The meeting with Sadat took place at the historic Hofburg Palace, site of Metternich's triumph at the Congress of Vienna. It lasted more than five hours. Brandt and Kreisky sat in during most of it, watching and listening. I began by explaining to Sadat that the Jewish People had never ruled over other nations, while those nations that had ruled over the Jews, at various periods in their history, had all long ceased to exist. We had no desire now to follow in their footsteps. I stressed that we, in the Labour Party, were deeply committed to peace. We were in opposition to the Government, but not in opposition to peace; if Menachem Begin moved towards peace with Egypt, we would support him unreservedly.

In fact, I initially put Kreisky's back up – as he himself told me later – by saying to Sadat, early in the conversation, that I would report back to Begin everything that transpired between us. 'Anwar,' I said – he insisted that we call each other by our first names – 'I have to warn you that every word you say to me, and every word I say to you, will go straight back to Begin. I'm not here to make political capital, but to help the cause of peace, if I can.' Kreisky was shocked, but Sadat told him later that it was this bald assertion that had particularly inspired his confidence in me.

As for the Palestinian problem, I said that we in Labour believed in a solution based on territorial compromise. I spoke at length of Ben-Gurion, stressing his historic decision to accept the concept of partition. 'Ben-Gurion believed that it was better to accept a Jewish state in part of Palestine than to insist on all of Palestine, and thereby forfeit the chance of achieving sovereignty over any of it.'

Sadat reiterated his own profound commitment to peace. He said that he was prepared to sacrifice Egypt's standing in the Arab world in order to achieve peace; however, it would be a short-term sacrifice, because the Arabs would return to Egypt sooner or later. But he was not prepared to forgo any particle of Egyptian land. Land was a matter of honour, and therefore Israel would have to restore all of it – to the last grain of sand.

'Shimon, Shimon, be a little more generous in your public statements. Make a little gesture, and then you will see that I respond with tenfold grander gestures of my own,' he said. Dayan's proposal that the settlements in northern Sinai be left in Israeli hands until the year 2010 was unacceptable. 'This is our land. We are a nation of farmers. I myself am a village boy . . .'

I quickly saw that there was not much chance of progress on the question of the settlements and switched, therefore, to the issue of the military airfields that we had built in the Sinai. I suggested that Egypt agree to leave these sites under Israeli control for a period of fifty years. Sadat asked why we needed the airfields so much. I replied that once we had signed a peace treaty with Egypt, the threat from Syria would be exacerbated. We wanted to remove our warplanes from the north and centre of the country, where the Syrians would be tempted to attack them. To my great surprise, Sadat replied that these were serious considerations and he was prepared to accede to this request. When I returned home, I conveyed this good news to Begin and Dayan, but neither of them seemed particularly overjoyed. In their minds, the battle of the future of the settlements in northern Sinai was the main issue.

Sadat and I devoted a significant part of our long conversation to discussing the possibility of a Middle East common market, once peace came. He suggested that Israel might receive water from the Nile for its agricultural needs, and spoke enthusiastically about Israeli agriculture. 'Send me some of your kibbutzniks to help save the Aswan region,' he said. 'They could teach our fishermen how to increase their catches and our farmers how to use new methods.' He questioned me searchingly about the kibbutz movement and about the role of Ben-Gurion in building first the socialist movement and later the state. Brandt and Kreisky listened transfixed. Later, Brandt told me, exaggeratedly no doubt, but not without sincerity, that this had been the most gripping and fascinating exchange he had ever witnessed.

I must add a small but significant story apropos this meeting in Vienna. In the evening, Kreisky gave a dinner at his home in honour of the Egyptian Deputy Prime Minister, Fuad Mohi ed-Din, and me. One of my security guards spent the evening sitting in the kitchen with Mrs Kreisky. At the end of the meal, the Chancellor walked into the kitchen and asked the caterer for the bill. He took it, carefully scrutinized every item, then pulled out his wallet and paid in cash. The waiter asked if he wanted a receipt. 'No' Kreisky replied, 'this dinner was on me.' I was deeply impressed by this man's great morality.

Kreisky was also active at this time in trying to set up meetings between me and Jordanian leaders. He made a point of attacking Israel vehemently at each session of the Socialist International, while behind the scenes he was busy trying to forge links between us and the Arabs. At one session, in Stockholm, I fought back with a bitter speech, in which I argued that not only was he blind and deaf, but he demanded that all the rest of us should be blind and deaf too. How could he propose to admit the PLO into the Socialist International, a social-democratic organization, when the PLO was neither socialist nor democratic, and practised terrorism to boot? I then surveyed the tragic perversity of Palestinian policies over the years, which had brought disaster to us and to them, and frustration to all who supported them.

My remarks produced a storm of applause. Kreisky looked angry and forlorn. I walked over to him and asked him frankly how it was that, on the one hand, he did so much to help us, while, on the other, he attacked us so relentlessly. For the first time, I thought I saw a strange twinkle in his eye as he replied: 'If I didn't attack you, how could I help you?'

If Willy Brandt was the charismatic elder statesman of the Socialist International at this time, and Bruno Kreisky was its ideologue, Olaf

Palme, the young Swedish socialist leader, was its rising star. He seemed a cold man, but clearly had a brilliant analytical mind, as sharp as the winter air, as deep and yet as threatening as an iceberg.

Palme's Sweden strongly favoured the PLO. Its neutrality in the Middle Eastern context was pro-Arab, rather than pro-Israeli.

Palme was a difficult man to get close to. But over the years, and with the help of Brandt, I felt the ice thaw a little. Just a few weeks before his assassination in 1986, we had a heart-to-heart conversation over a lengthy breakfast. I felt that he was trying to demonstrate some warmth and sympathy towards the Israeli cause, in his own measured and cautious way.

His murder has never been solved. I remember thinking at the time that his life, too, remained something of a mystery to me. I walked for miles at his funeral – it took place on a Saturday – in order to place a single red flower on his grave, alongside those of other socialist leaders. I knew that in front of me lay a hard man, but a young and gifted leader who had been brutally prevented from reaching his full potential.

Brandt and Kreisky had spent the war years in Scandinavia, and when with Palme they always spoke Swedish. They represented socialism of a particular kind: socialism with a Scandinavian temperament. They saw it as their historic duty to work towards ending the Cold War, and towards finding a solution to the shameful world situation which allowed belts of famine to encircle the globe, encompassing especially those whose skin God had not coloured white.

Brandt could always rely on the German SDP to support him in his leadership role in the Socialist International. In Germany, all political parties receive state funds for their educational activities at home and abroad, and the SDP used its funds generously to assist sister socialist parties in Europe, Latin America and Africa. This assistance was especially important for the Spanish and Portuguese socialist parties, who were to bring democracy to their countries after long years of dictatorship. The Spanish and Portuguese socialist leaders, Felipe González and Mario Suárez, quickly rose to prominence within our ranks. Together with Italy's Bettino Craxi, they comprised a sort of 'Latin caucus' in the International. They used to converse together in French and drew the veteran Senegalese leader, Leopold Senghor, into their circle.

González developed a warm relationship with Israel during his years in office. His Cabinet was comprised, in large part, of his close friends from student days. Together, they championed a socialist movement that had been decimated by Franco. Many of the old guard had died in the civil war; some were exiled later; others simply gave up the long and seemingly hopeless struggle.

González was blessed with all the attributes of charisma: youth, good looks, the power of persuasion and passionate sincerity. He was clever, too, and astute enough to handle the church, the monarchy, the army and the Falange – a daunting set of challenges for any politician. He avoided any head-on clash with the church, yet managed to remove it from positions of influence over the affairs of state. He honoured the officer corps, ensuring higher salaries and better conditions for all ranks in the army, while insisting, at the same time, on the army's subordination to civilian authority. He developed a solid working relationship with the King and kept the Falange off the streets.

González played a central role in the gradual rapprochement between Spain and Israel after the death of Franco, which eventually led to the establishment of full diplomatic relations between our two countries in January 1986.

This was a historic moment for both nations. Since the cruel and traumatic expulsion of Spain's Jews in 1492, the Jewish People had shunned Spain. Israel as a state cold-shouldered Franco, considering him a classical fascist and collaborator with Hitler – even though Spain gave refuge during the war to Jewish refugees fleeing the Holocaust.

González and I began a series of contacts through our respective party channels, which continued and intensified when we both became Prime Ministers. We agreed to meet in Holland, under the aegis of Dutch Prime Minister Rod Lubbers, to put the formal seal on our decision to normalize relations. This choice of venue was especially appropriate: Holland, already a bastion of religious tolerance, had provided a safe haven to many of the Jews expelled from Spain.

It was an emotional event laden with history and symbolism, signifying the end of half a millennium of alienation and shame. We both referred in our remarks to the Jewish medieval history's 'Golden Age', when, for centuries, Jewish culture, learning and science flourished on Spanish soil, contributing so much to the lifeblood of the country. 'With the renewal of relations between our two countries,' I observed, 'the Mediterranean Sea can once again come to represent what it was at the dawn of history: a cradle of culture, a pathway of life and a horizon of hope.'

16 MITTERRAND

My own ties to the Socialist International date back to the 1950s, when Guy Mollet, the French socialist Prime Minister, was a great ally of Israel. François Mitterrand, the head of the Union Démocratique et Socialiste de la Résistance, was Mollet's ally. He was not regarded as precisely a socialist. Indeed, Mitterrand has never been easy to define or classify; he is ultimately an individualist. He strives above all else to be himself, and only bends to fit into a broader framework when he has no other choice. I first met him at the home of another Frenchman I admired deeply, Pierre Mendès-France. The three of us ate dinner together. Mendès-France said, 'This man Mitterrand is the best pianist in the French parliament. He knows every note on the score, and every key on the keyboard. He is a man you can rely on.' To me, Mitterrand's pale, chiselled features seemed to express someone slow to take a stand, but immovable once he has taken it. He seemed – as he was later to prove – a man capable of absorbing harsh blows without flinching, and equally capable of enjoying heady success without losing his iron self-discipline. I particularly liked his writing style; in my opinion, Mitterrand is the most eloquent of all French socialists since Léon Blum.

The profound friendship that evolved between us has never faltered over the years. He rarely refused a request I made of him; nor have I refused anything he asked, if it was in my power to help him.

On the eve of his election as leader of the socialist party, the members of the party Secretariat resolved, without asking or informing Mitterrand, to invite the PLO to send a representative to their party congress. Mitterrand knew that to make a fight of it would cause turmoil. He sent his close friend, Georges Dayan, to Israel to try to smooth things over. I believed Dayan's message that the invitation had been issued without

Mitterrand's consent. I therefore asked our Ambassador to France, Asher Ben-Natan, not to attack Mitterrand over the decision. None the less, on Israel's thirtieth anniversary, Mitterrand and I marched side by side through the streets of Paris, as thousands of French Jews cheered.

Mitterrand always spoke openly with me about his political strategies and his relations with various political personalities, and I consulted him with the same frankness. Years before he was elected President, he explained to me at length that the French socialist party had no chance of returning to power unless it 'stops being a party of teachers and clerks, and goes back to being the party of the workers'. By 'workers', he meant both manual workers and those who work with their minds – the intelligentsia. But he was convinced that the only way to win back the French worker was to form a close political alliance with the communist party, which held the allegiance of many of the working people. He acted on this belief and, in the end, he proved successful. Mitterrand is a brilliant political strategist, certainly one of the most outstanding socialist strategists in the second half of the twentieth century.

In 1980, on the eve of his election as President, and shortly before our own elections in Israel, we met for a long talk in Madrid, during a session of the Socialist International. I explained to him that a gnawing concern troubling the Israeli electorate was the Iraqi nuclear option. France had built a nuclear reactor in Iraq and had undertaken to supply twenty-four kilograms of enriched uranium – a sufficient quantity to produce an atomic bomb. Delivery was to take place in two stages, and the first stage had already occurred. Mitterrand interrupted me. 'If I become President,' he said firmly, 'France will not make the second delivery.' I reported his promise to Prime Minister Begin.

Not long after, Begin called me in and informed me that he had decided to bomb the Iraqi reactor, the 'Tammuz' as it was called. He did not tell me the precise date he had in mind, but I learned from my own sources that it was to be the very day on which Mitterrand was to be sworn in as President. I was among the foreign guests invited to the celebrations.

The bombing of the Iraqi reactor was destined to win the sweeping approval of the Israeli public. But at the time, and indeed thereafter, there was intense opposition to it among the select circle of people familiar with all the considerations. Many of these – military men, intelligence officers, members of the Israel Atomic Energy Commission, among them dyed-in-the-wool Likud supporters – sent me desperate signals urging that I try to prevent the bombing.

Their reasons were the following:

1 The reactor was not capable, at that time, of producing plutonium or weapons-grade uranium.
2 The danger lay in the enriched uranium which Iraq hoped to get its hands on. If France did not make the second delivery, Iraq would not have a nuclear option in the immediate future.
3 It made more sense to hit the reactor after it became 'hot', when we would know what its capacity was.
4 There were other ways of hitting it, ways that would leave no tell-tale clues as to who was responsible. A bombing raid, however, would create the justification for a reprisal raid by Iraq on Israel.
5 A bombing raid would further isolate Israel in the international community.

I myself was convinced by the first reason. I knew that the reactor was not capable of producing a nuclear weapon. For that, an entire complex of ancillary facilities was required, which was harder to build than the reactor itself. I thought it was better that Saddam Hussein continue on the wrong course that he had chosen than be driven on to an alternative path, both more practical and more accessible, towards his nuclear goal.

That, indeed, was precisely what happened. In the wake of the Israeli bombing, Saddam Hussein set out on this alternative path. The evidence now available shows that he might well have reached his destination – despite the bombing – had he not pre-empted himself by invading Kuwait in 1990, thereby bringing on his eventual defeat at the hands of the UN coalition.

But there was an additional and immediate reason why the bombing should not go ahead as planned: to bomb the French-supplied reactor on the day that Mitterrand took over as President of France would rightly be seen as a deliberate provocation. I appealed to Begin, orally and in writing, at least to postpone the operation. He promised that he would. I knew that there was not much time: Begin wanted to bomb the reactor before the Israeli elections, which were only a few weeks away. He assessed, quite rightly, that the bombing raid, if successful, would be vastly popular with the Israeli public. I decided not to attend Mitterrand's inauguration, preferring to stay at home to ensure that Israel did not make its move just as he was entering the Elysée Palace. In the end, the bombing was postponed – for one week.

I had sent Begin a handwritten note, intended to remain completely confidential, explaining my reasons for opposing the bombing and stressing the need to avoid the date of Mitterrand's inauguration. Contrary to practice and precedent – and flagrantly violating the political code of honour (in Hebrew, *hadar*) by which his movement purported to operate – Begin leaked my letter immediately after the bombing. He sought thereby to double his electoral gains from the raid: not only had he had the courage to order it, but I, his challenger for the Premiership, had opposed it and tried to dissuade him from going ahead with it. I refused to be browbeaten into changing my opinion and to join the chorus of praise and approval. To the present day, I believe that Mitterrand would have kept his promise – and Saddam Hussein would have been left squandering more and more to no practical purpose.

Mitterrand always invited me to the Elysée when I was in Paris, and I enjoyed many pleasant meals there, alone with him or, less frequently, together with other Socialist International leaders. I have to grant that the palatial socialism of Mitterrand's Elysée is perhaps more impressive than other, less lavish manifestations of our movement enjoying the trappings of power. Nevertheless, the two most memorable and enjoyable days I spent with Mitterrand were not at his official residence, but at his private country home, Latché, in the Pyrenees.

The first time I was invited there I flew in from Switzerland. A helicopter was waiting at Biarritz Airport to take me to the President's home, in the heart of a thickly forested area on the Atlantic coast. The house itself is a nineteenth-century farmhouse, adapted for modern living. In the grounds, the Mitterrands have built a separate house for their son, and another little cottage which serves as the President's study. The grounds were also shared on this occasion with a number of goats, a donkey and a dog. The only neighbour within walking distance was a local farmer, whose home was pretty much as it had been when it was built, a century or more ago.

We lunched on the veranda, with Mitterrand, his wife Danielle, Danielle's sister and her husband, Roger, a well-known actor who had once worked on a kibbutz in Israel. The Mitterrands' son, Jean-Christophe, had also spent a month on a kibbutz in the north of Israel, picking fruit with other volunteers.

The cottage in which Mitterrand worked and slept reminded me of David Ben-Gurion's hut in Sde Boker: the same Spartan simplicity; the same isolation. But whereas Ben-Gurion had made his house amid the desert sands, untouched and unspoiled by human hand, Mitterrand had made his amid the trees he loved. The cottage was essentially one large room, perhaps of 100 square metres. The walls were lined with books. Even Mitterrand's bed, which stood in one corner, was surrounded by books. Alongside it stood his desk, large, simple and uncluttered. It, too, was covered with books, some of them open. I stole a glance. Some were books on forestry; others works of history and biographies. One that I noticed was a historical album, based on the writings of Fernand Braudel, the great historian whom I particularly admire.

On the shelves, too, many of the books were works on nature – treatises on birds, flowers and trees. Another section was devoted to the French and Russian classics. This was not the library of a collector, but of a reader. Most of the books were paperbacks. On the bedside table was an open Bible, also a paperback edition. Clearly this was no mere talisman, but the Bible of a Bible-reader. Along the opposite wall were six or seven pairs of solid-looking walking shoes. Mitterrand himself was dressed like Moshe Dayan – in a shirt, trousers and jacket the likes of which would hardly be available in the better Paris fashion houses. Like Dayan, he seemed to believe that clothes should somehow adjust themselves to him, rather than he to them.

We went out walking together, accompanied by a large dog. Mitterrand stopped at each tree and explained to me at length its particular characteristics. Some of them, he said with evident pride, he had planted with his own hands. He seemed to love them almost like children.

He told me then that he had grown up reading the Bible and had never stopped studying it. He had always been fascinated by the Jewish People and had never uttered a word of criticism against the Jews. Once, when I asked him why he travelled so much, he replied, smiling, 'There must be some Jewish blood in my veins.'

We went back for tea, and the whole family interrogated me about how the Soviet Jews were being absorbed into Israeli society. I observed that one of the most telling lessons to be learned from this immigration was the incredible contrast between the intelligence of the Soviet people and the stupidity of the system under which they had been living. I took the opportunity to thank Danielle Mitterrand for the courageous stand she had taken when Mikhail Gorbachev and his wife visited Paris, demanding publicly that the Soviet leader open the gates of his country to Jews seeking to leave for Israel.

Suddenly, Mitterrand asked me why I had not attended his inaugural celebrations in 1981. I told him the whole story. His reply was that we had had 'nothing to worry about: the second delivery of uranium would never have been made to Iraq'. Later, I heard from mutual friends to whom Mitterrand had recounted our conversation that he ended his account with the comment: 'How many people are there in the world like Shimon, who would stay at home just so as not to embarrass his friend?'

Mitterrand is a unique figure on the world stage. Fiercely independent and constantly creative, he seldom allows his views or positions he takes to be influenced by others. He was among the first world leaders to stress the dangers of ecological disaster, among the first to focus determinedly on women's rights, and the first socialist leader to explain socialism as a cultural, as well as a political and economic, doctrine. For Mitterrand, socialism means, among other things, bringing the treasures of art and literature to the people. During his Presidency, culture, art and architecture have flourished in France as rarely before. He has become one of the great builders of Paris. His most ambitious project – on a recent visit, he showed me a photograph of its model – is a vast library, to be housed in four towers designed to resemble an open book. He wants it to become the largest and most modern library in the world. Mitterrand explained to me that it would house, on computer, every book ever published. His own love of books knows no bounds, and he wants to share it with his entire country.

Once, we had lunch together at the Elysée. Media reports suggested that he had postponed a scheduled prostate operation in order to receive me. He took me by the arm and led me into the exquisite gardens. He described how he had changed the landscaping during his years at the Elysée. As we walked back, he remarked, deliberately within hearing of the reporters, 'Whatever Shimon wishes, he shall have.' He was deeply offended by an accusation made by a Likud parliamentarian, Eliahu Ben-Elissar, that France had helped the Iraqis to extend the range of their SCUD ground-to-ground missiles, which they had fired at Israel during the 1991 Gulf War. How could anyone think that? he asked. That France, that he, would do anything that might endanger Israel?

Often when I meet him, Mitterrand asks me how old I am, which leads me to believe that he is concerned about his own age. And indeed, the advancing years have begun to show on this great man, although his mind remains as clear, as curious and as young as it ever was.

The second time he invited me to Latche was during the heady days of late summer 1993, soon after the news was published of our historic agreement with the PLO in Oslo.* Winding up talks in Brussels on the future role of the European Community in supporting the peace process, I decided to stop in Paris and brief the French Government personally on what had been achieved and what now lay ahead. France, I reckoned, would be even more important than before in shaping the new relationship between Europe and the new Middle East which I hoped would emerge, now that the core-conflict between Israel and the Arabs was moving towards a peaceful solution. Paris, and the Paris–Bonn axis, is the heart of European policy-making, though that policy-making is a far cry from the coherence and resoluteness to which the builders of – and believers in – a united Europe still aspire.

Paris – political Paris, that is – had changed dramatically since my last visit. The elections to the National Assembly had hurt the socialists; they lost roughly two-thirds of their seats. The government ministries were now run by rightist and centrist politicians. The socialist party was a pale shadow of its former self, sapped of its confidence and pride, though Mitterrand himself still had another two years at the Elysée.

In the morning, I saw the Foreign Minister, Alain Juppé, and then boarded a Presidential plane to Biarritz, where an armoured limousine was waiting to take me to Latché. French politics can change, I remember thinking to myself, but not the bewitching spell of the French countryside. Last time, when I had been flown by helicopter from Biarritz, I had looked down on to the tree-tops, interspersed with the red roofs of holiday villas and local farm-houses. Rivers glistened like silver snakes. This time, I took in the view from another angle and admired the perfect composition of the different glades of trees, the brilliant repertoire of French architecture, the ornate bridges crossing rivers and streams. France is blessed with magnificent natural beauty. Fortunately, it is blessed, too, with a people of fine aesthetic sense, for only such a people would devote the effort and resources needed to achieve such delicate and harmonious integration of nature with the products of human creativity.

Frankly, I was worried about this meeting with Mitterrand. I thought that I would find him disconsolate: his party had been savaged at the

* See pages 325–49.

ballot box, and he himself had recently learned from his doctors that he had cancer. However, I was pleasantly surprised. He was in a vivacious mood and, even though his parchment-like skin seemed paler than usual, he read without glasses and seemed in good health. His family was with him again, as well as one other guest, the former Prime Minister, Laurent Fabius. Fabius had been groomed by Mitterrand for years, perhaps with the view to being his eventual successor. He became Prime Minister in 1984, at the very young age of thirty-seven. In 1993, he was one of the lucky socialists who retained his parliamentary seat, but the stricken party elected Michel Rocard as its leader. Fabius was fighting for his political life because he was held responsible for the tragic injection of dozens of people with the AIDS virus through infected blood transfusions.

Mitterrand's welcome was not just warm and hospitable; it was positively effervescent. He wanted to hear all about the Oslo talks: how they were conducted and when the key decisions were taken. I launched into the tale, and he listened with rapt attention. When I recounted how I had awoken one morning to a call from my good friend Amos Oz, who voiced his sudden sense that the PLO was in danger of breaking up and disappearing, and urged that I must therefore make an all-out effort to save it, an impish twinkle appeared in Mitterrand's eyes.

He asked my consent to invite Fabius to join us, and we all three sat in deep armchairs, sipping the President's superb port and mulling over the Israel–PLO agreement in an ambience of profound gratification. Mitterrand even succeeded in making me blush. 'What intellectual depth!' he said. 'What political courage!' In his view, the agreement rated among the three or four most significant events of the present century. 'Granted, the disputed land is small in size, but the dispute is vast in its complexity and its potential consequences. It has shaken the very foundations of the world order in the past.'

Notwithstanding my embarrassment, Mitterrand later repeated his comments, about the agreement and about me personally, in a television interview. He was so exhilarated that he even waived his own rules of privacy and seclusion, inviting a group of journalists who were waiting patiently outside to enter his off-limits holiday home. He knew each of them by name, and the two of us, sitting together on a rustic-style bench, held a lively and informal press conference. When one of the newsmen ventured to ask whether France had been in the picture regarding the Oslo talks, Mitterrand shot back, 'Nor was America.'

We covered many topics during that long, golden afternoon. I brought Mitterrand several Hebrew books that had recently been translated into French – a collection of poems by Yehuda Amichai, a biography of the Israeli actress Gila Almagor, and the novel *Esau* by Meir Shalev. We went on to discuss Jacques Attali, Mitterrand's brilliant former aide who had recently been forced to resign as the chief executive of the European Bank for Reconstruction and Development and whose book, *Verbatim*, had also triggered a major storm. Among its detractors was the Nobel prizewinner Eli Wiesel, who claimed that Attali had plagiarized material from a book of dialogues between Mitterrand and Wiesel that Wiesel himself was preparing for publication.

I praised both Attali and his book, which I had found fascinating, though a little long. I suggested to Mitterrand that some conversations recorded in the book had lost some of their interest with the passage of time, however, such as the lengthy dialogues between Mitterrand and German Chancellor Helmut Kohl. Others were as gripping and significant today as when they took place – for instance, a conversation between Mitterrand and Syria's President Hafez Assad, in which Assad refers to Israel as 'an American aircraft carrier'.

In that conversation, Mitterrand observes that recent excavations in Ebla, Syria, unearthed tablets written 1,500 years before Moses which carry the same message of monotheism that appears in the Ten Commandments. To this, Assad responds that the Ebla tablets pose a problem for the Old Testament, the New Testament and, indeed, the Koran in that they preceded them by so long. He goes on to note that the name Israel, according to the Old Testament, was used for the first time in reference to the Jewish people by Jacob – hinting, apparently, that Jacob was something of a latecomer to the Palestine scene. 'And you', Assad concludes triumphantly, 'speak of the role that the Bible can play in finding a solution to the Middle East conflict.' The account of this frank and freewheeling conversation is more valuable, in my view, than reams of intelligence reports in helping one to fathom the mind of the Syrian leader.

I added that I found the reference in Attali's book to Mitterrand's own interpretations of the Bible no less fascinating. He asked for examples, and I quoted his characterization of Jeremiah as an unpleasant man who had created an 'apocalyptic tone' that Mitterrand found as intolerable in prophecy as in politics. Mitterrand adds in the book: 'Joshua conquered the country and settled down to live on the land, but he died a lonely man, and no one came to his funeral.' I said that I had been surprised by the intensity of his criticism of Jeremiah's bitterness and by his insight into Joshua's loneliness. Neither of these perspectives had ever suggested themselves to me in my own reading of the texts. Mitterrand confirmed that his view of Jeremiah remains thoroughly negative. He sees this prophet as radiating his own resentments all around him. He did not reply regarding Joshua, but stressed, instead, his profound admiration for Moses – the leader who formulated the moral tenets of the nation is the true hero for Mitterrand, and not the leader who actually brought victory and peace.

'Nothing compares to the Bible,' Mitterrand closed this part of our long conversation. 'It contains both great men and great contradictions – like life itself.'

In discussing our peace breakthrough with the PLO, Mitterrand promised the steady support of his own country and its European partners in our efforts to turn our entire area into a flourishing common market, modelled on the European Community.

Like many others, I was surprised by journalist Pierre Pean's book, *Un Jeunesse Française – François Mitterrand 1934–47*,[*] which appeared in 1994 and told the story of Mitterrand's relations with the Vichy régime during the war years and of his long, subsequent friendship with René Bousquet, the man in charge of France's police during that dark period. While there is no evidence that Mitterrand was ever anti-Semitic, this chapter is a cloud that will always hang over his biography.

The issue of Israel's relations with the PLO frequently held centre-stage at sessions of the Socialist International from the mid-1970s. I remember one meeting in particular that took place in Dakar – the capital of Senegal – in April 1979. Even though Israel had no diplomatic relations with Senegal at that time – most Black African states severed their relations with us during the 1973 war – President Leopold Senghor pressed me to come, adding specifically that I should arrive on my Israeli passport.

I agreed and, as was my practice as head of a none-too-wealthy opposition party, flew into Dakar by tourist class. This proved to be something of an embarrassment: the entire Senegalese Cabinet was lined up to welcome me at the first-class gangway, while I walked down the

[*] Fayard, Paris.

other gangway and made my way to the arrivals hall to collect my bag. Once this mix-up was sorted out, Senghor asked me to drive into the city with him in his official limousine.

We had hardly started out when Senghor informed me in hushed tones, half-humorously but half-seriously, that 'There is a villa near here, where Yasser Arafat is staying. Perhaps you would care to stop off there on our way into the city and meet him? Perhaps the two of you could settle all your problems.'

'Mr President,' I replied, 'it was pretty hard for me to come here. Now do you want to make it even harder for me to get back home?'

I was thankful, as it turned out, that I had not been tempted by Senghor's offer. Just days later, terrorists sent by the PLO perpetrated a particularly brutal attack in Nahariya, northern Israel, killing a father and his two daughters. The terrorists smashed one child's skull with a rock.

On another occasion, in 1983, the Socialist International's desire to bring about a breakthrough – prematurely, as I can now assert – between the Israeli Labour Party and the PLO led directly to tragedy. We convened in Albufeira, a picturesque resort town on the Portuguese coast. On 9 April, the eve of the first session, Willy Brandt told me that they had decided to invite – unofficially, as a private person – the PLO representative in Europe, Dr Issam Sartawi. Brandt said that Sartawi was a well-known moderate and a respected intellectual, who wanted to meet me. I said that I did not know him personally, but everything I had heard about him confirmed Brandt's description. Nevertheless, I believed the invitation was a mistake. It would only highlight his moderation relative to the mainstream of the PLO – and thus confirm his isolation. It could even endanger him physically. Anyway, I added, as far as I was concerned, no good could come out of my meeting Sartawi; it would only harm both him and me.

Next morning, during a plenary session, shots suddenly rang out in the hotel. Amid the ensuing pandemonium, it emerged that someone had been shot in the hotel lobby, just a few yards from our conference room. Police and security men raced towards me. Apparently, the initial rumours were that I was the victim. But soon it became clear that Dr Sartawi had been made to pay a terrible price for his moderation.

Brandt cut the rest of the meeting short. He decided to dedicate the closing session to the memory of Sartawi and suggested two speakers:

myself and Walid Jumblatt, leader of the Lebanese socialist party (and of the Druze community in Lebanon). 'You should say in his memory everything that you could not say about him while he lived,' Brandt suggested. I spoke first, eulogizing Sartawi as an honourable opponent, who had sought to end the Israeli–Palestinian conflict through understanding, rather than through bloodshed. His own blood shed here attested both to his great courage and to the great danger that threatened a man like him who resolved to represent moderation in the Palestinian cause.

Jumblatt made a wild and disjointed speech, holding Israel indirectly responsible for Sartawi's death and urging the continuation of the Palestinian struggle. I was frankly not surprised. Jumblatt's outbursts were nothing new. I knew him to be a wily political operator. And yet, when a situation arose in which I could help him, I did so willingly. Such a situation occurred soon after the outbreak of the Lebanon War in 1982. Brandt and Mitterrand approached me on Jumblatt's behalf, reporting that he was effectively a prisoner in his fortress-home at Mukhtara, in south-eastern Lebanon, which had been overrun by the advancing Israeli forces. They had heard nothing from him and wanted to make sure that he was safe and well.

The next day, the army took the members of the Knesset Foreign Affairs and Defence Committee on a tour of the battlefields. In Sidon, on the coast, we were shown the offices of the Lebanese socialist party, which looked more like a fortified castle than a political headquarters. Two Druze soldiers had been posted at the entrance. Inside, the rooms were piled high with weapons. I had never seen socialism quite so well equipped to fight a good fight. I told the Chief of Staff, Lieutenant-General Raful Eitan, of Brandt's and Mitterrand's concern, and he kindly put a military helicopter at my disposal so that I could fly to Mukhtara and see the situation for myself.

We flew across the cedar-clad mountains until Jumblatt's castle appeared, cannons and heavy machine-guns staring ominously from the battlements. A convoy of cars with diplomatic licence plates emerged from the gates; later, I learned that the American Ambassador had been visiting, on a similar mission to my own. We landed near the heavy iron gates, and I walked through them to find Jumblatt awaiting me in the courtyard. Tall and reedy, his big eyes darting to and fro, he looked somewhat nonplussed to see me, but none the less invited me into his reception-room on the ground floor. This was a large hall, lined with chairs and low tables. On the wall behind Jumblatt hung a portrait of his father, Kemal, who had been assassinated by the Syrians in 1977. The message radiating from the canvas seemed almost audible: familial pride on the one hand, and an ever-present warning on the other.

A servant brought beer and pistachio nuts. I told Jumblatt the purpose of my visit. He said that he had been informed that he was free to come and go as he chose, but the Israeli army wanted him to turn in his weapons. I said that Israel was ready to let him keep what he needed for self-defence, but wanted him to turn over the rest. He seemed to accept this. We reviewed the situation, and he hinted that the positions he was taking publicly did not necessarily reflect his true sentiments. He would be as relieved as anyone, he appeared to be signalling, if a peaceful solution could be worked out. As for his support of the PLO against Israel, it was not as one-sided as he made it seem in public. He believed a deal with Arafat was possible, and he hoped it would occur.

We parted as friends. But the next time our paths crossed, at a Socialist International meeting, he avoided my glance; he never, thereafter, returned my greetings.

I daresay some would argue that co-opting the Druze socialists of Lebanon to the Socialist International contributed uniquely to the International's composition and deliberations. But I could never quite square their membership with the principles that were supposed to govern our movement. I believe that the original idea was Mitterrand's, who somehow saw it as a way in which France could fulfil its historic responsibility towards Lebanon.

17 NORTHERN BLIGHT

In 1976, at the height of the civil war in Lebanon, I was touring the northern border with Major-General Raful Eitan, when we were hailed by a large group of villagers from the other side of the electronic fence. 'Mr Peres,' they shouted, 'help us. We've got no hospitals, no jobs, no government to apply to for aid. Israel is our friend: you have to help us.' I turned to Eitan. Why, I asked him, shouldn't we set up crossing-points and clinics on the border, so that people in south Lebanon who needed medical help could get it, and those who wanted work could come over each day to our side? He immediately saw the humanitarian and political benefits of the idea, and began planning the logistics. Always the frustrated poet, I began casting about for a poetic name for the idea. I have often admired the Chinese for their ability to adorn prosaic political realities with pithy and poetic names – like 'The Heavenly Gate' or 'The Forbidden City'. I looked for something that would reflect the cruel complexities of the political situation in which we proposed to establish this novel project, and alighted on 'The Good Fence'. Fences usually separate people, but this one was going to bring them together. I thought that the name expressed something of the contradictions that underlay our relations with the people of war-torn Lebanon.

Eitan later became army Chief of Staff during the 1982 war in Lebanon.* He has always been a controversial figure in Israel. Whatever his critics may say about him, all admit that he is a rare individual – both in terms of his personal courage and his originality. He goes through life steadfastly ignoring many of the norms that the rest of us accept without question. Eitan is the only man I know who lives in the firm conviction

* He is presently a right-wing political leader.

that history is subordinate to him – not he to it. It is this outlook that gives him his special charm, which is recognized even by those who find his political bigotry difficult to stomach.

One day in 1974, as Minister of Defence, I took the Cabinet up to the Golan Heights for a guided tour, and Eitan, then O/C Northern Command, was their guide. Moshe Kol, the Minister of Tourism and veteran leader of the tiny Independent Liberal Party, was always one for asking Big Questions. 'What', he asked Eitan, 'has been the impact of the Yom Kippur War on Northern Command?' Unblinkingly and laconically, Eitan replied: 'From Beit Shean to Metulla [the entire north of the country] – no impact whatsoever!'

But, of course, there had been a very real and profound impact. Indeed, Eitan himself would frequently descend on the Defence Ministry in Tel Aviv to deliver baleful warnings of imminent Syrian attacks. 'They're cutting the grass on their side,' he would say ominously. 'That means they're preparing staging-areas for an assault.' I would try to reassure him that the sum of the evidence did not point to an attack, despite the grass cutting. But scarred by the Yom Kippur War, he refused to be dismissed and returned repeatedly with new warnings.

Eitan's originality came into its own in the close relations he developed with the population of southern Lebanon. He played a key role in our decision, in 1975, to create the South Lebanese Army (SLA) under Major Sa'ad Hadad, whose officers and soldiers were trained in Israel.

Lebanon, as such, never presented a military or strategic problem for Israel; our problem was Lebanon's internal situation. Lebanon's sovereignty has never rested on its inherent strength as a state, but on a delicate and shifting equilibrium among the various contending groups that comprise the state: the Maronite Christians, the Druze, the Shi'ites and the Sunni Moslems. During the 1970s, we knew that unless these four elements could find a way to reconstruct a viable balance, Lebanon would fall prey to a Syrian takeover. President Assad of Syria knew that too. He knew it better than anyone else. In an exchange of letters with Cuba's Fidel Castro which came our way, the Syrian leader explained why he insisted on intervening so vigorously in Lebanon's affairs. The Arab world, Assad wrote, had made an historic mistake in failing to stop Jewish settlement in Palestine at an early stage, thereby facilitating the eventual creation of the Jewish state. If the Arabs now failed to restrain Christian influence in Lebanon, Lebanon would become a Christian state.

For Assad, a Middle East containing both a Jewish state and a Christian state was thoroughly undesirable. The Syrians invested a great deal of their political energy in the 1970s in Lebanon, buying newspapers and trying to influence Lebanese politics through them, stirring up trouble between the rival communities. The Syrian dream is that the whole of the Fertile Crescent shall be dominated by Syria. The Crescent starts in Lebanon.

The Christians rightly prided themselves on their commercial prowess, their agricultural skills and their martial tradition. But they were plagued by internecine strife that seriously weakened them. The original sin that permanently debilitated the Christians was committed, ostensibly in their interest, by their French benefactors. In the Sykes–Picot Agreement of 1916, the French, determined to achieve as large a Lebanon as possible, engineered the annexation of relatively large tracts of Moslem-populated Syrian territory to the Christian heartland. The result was that over the years this geographical extension eroded the Christian majority that had originally dominated Lebanon.

By the 1960s, the feuding among the Christian clans, coupled with this constant demographic pressure, destabilized Lebanese politics. Then, to make matters infinitely worse, the Palestinian organizations set up shop in Lebanon in 1970, having been driven out of Jordan by King Hussein. They became a new element in the internal Lebanese equation, allying themselves with the Moslem and Druze forces against the Christians. They also sought to turn the south of the country into their main launching-pad for raids into Israel. For us, this meant that a hitherto peaceful border had become a major security headache. The majority of the population in the south were Shi'ites and Christians, but the area increasingly became a 'state within a state' controlled by the PLO.

During the 1970s, we strengthened our ties with the Lebanese Christians, with whom we had maintained cordial contacts over the years. They contended that the evolving political and military situation in their country threatened their community with a holocaust – an argument that no Israeli leader could dismiss lightly.

We tried to forge links with all the major Christian families. I was particularly impressed by two young men: Bashir Gemayel and Danny Chamoun. Their fathers, Pierre Gemayel and Camille Chamoun, then both elderly, were the heads of their respective clans and had been central figures in Lebanese politics for decades. Chamoun had served as President of Lebanon from 1952 to 1958. Their sons, handsome, urbane and

energetic, seemed to hold out the promise of strong leadership for the
Christians in the years ahead. They visited me secretly in my home in
Tel Aviv. Bashir made no secret of his ambition to be President. We also
had confidence in him.* Both Bashir and Chamoun assured me that
they had learned a lesson from their fathers' incessant feuding. They
were determined to work harmoniously with the other Christian leaders
of the younger generation. They fully understood, they said, that only
through Christian unity could they hope to secure the Christian community's constitutional status and rights.

But age-old rivalries proved stronger than they had anticipated, and
the feuding continued. This gravely weakened the Christian position, as
it enabled the Syrians to play off one clan against another in the Christian
community – just as they played the Christians off against other communities.

Israel in the mid-1970s faced a daunting dilemma. The scourge of
cross-border terrorism was growing and had to be confronted. Farther
north, the Christians were fighting the Palestinians and their Lebanese
allies, and crying out for Israeli support. We wanted to help them and
build a close and friendly relationship with them, but we were determined not to be sucked into the quagmire of internal Lebanese strife.

Our dilemma was further complicated by the entry of Syrian forces
into Lebanon, in June 1976, to support the embattled Christians. President Assad was against Lebanon becoming a wholly Christian-dominated
state, but he was just as opposed to a wholesale destabilization of the
country by the Palestinians, and his armed intervention was designed to
prevent this. The Syrian presence was later endorsed and formalized by
the Arab world, through the Riyadh Accord of October 1976. This was
a mini-Potsdam Agreement of sorts between Syria and Egypt: Egypt
undertook not to interfere in Lebanon, while Syria pledged to keep out
of areas of Egyptian interest – principally Yemen. Our response to Syria's
ensconcement in Lebanon was to lay down 'red lines' in south Lebanon
beyond which we would not countenance any Syrian military presence.
These lines were endorsed by the United States, which conveyed them
in unequivocal terms to the Syrians.

* Bashir Gemayel was indeed to fulfil his political ambition. In a tragic Lebanese blood
feud, he was elected President on 27 August 1982 – with Israeli troops surrounding Beirut –
only to be assassinated on 14 September. The next day, in an act of revenge, Christian forces
massacred several hundred Palestinians at the Sabra and Shatilla refugee camps in south
Beirut.

Even those of us who regarded Syria's semi-annexation of Lebanon as potentially dangerous for Israel (some policy-makers saw possible strategic advantages for Israel in Syria's Lebanese embroilment) did not advocate a military response. We could hardly go to war over every regional development that was not to our liking. Granted, in 1970, at the express instigation of the Nixon administration, Israel demonstratively flexed its military muscles as a way of deterring a Syrian invasion of Jordan. But in that episode – at the time of the 'Black September' battles between the Amman regime and the PLO* – we were fully coordinated with the Jordanians, while now the Christians were divided among themselves. At that time, moreover, Syria's entry into Jordan would clearly have comprised a hostile invasion; now, the Syrians were 'invited' in by Lebanon's President.

Israel's responses to the changing condition of its northern neighbour starkly reflected the differences of perception between the two major political camps in Israel. I believed that Lebanon had ultimately to decide between two realistic options: either to divide up the country so that the Christians would have a small state of their own; or to divide up political power in such a way as to re-establish a stable system of government. In practice, neither option was realized. Geography made a territorial division difficult, and demography – accompanied by steady emigration of Christians – constantly militated against a stable constitutional arrangement. I repeatedly warned the Christian leaders: don't make war unless you are sure that you have the resources to see it through. And if you do resort to force, define your aims precisely and realistically.

In the Likud Government after 1977, key policy-makers believed that Israel could forge a military alliance with the Lebanese Christians against all the forces in Lebanon that were challenging Christian hegemony. The Likud leaders – principally Menachem Begin – were taken in by the Christians' boastfulness. At the same time, they led the Christians astray with promises that they did not – or could not – keep.

This misguided approach lay at the root of the Government's decision to strike deep into Lebanon, with massive military force, in June 1982. And it also lay at the heart of the shattering disappointment that Begin suffered at the hands of the Christians, replete with betrayal and double-dealing and culminating in the massacre at Sabra and Shatilla in Sep-

* See page 164.

tember of that year. Israel's Lebanon War, which dragged on with a
bloody and pointless occupation for nearly three years, gravely weakened
the discipline and moral cohesion of Israeli society, because our soldiers
did not know why they were fighting and or what they were dying for.
In the final analysis, the Christians were also weakened by their failed
alliance with Israel.

The invasion of Lebanon was triggered by the attempted assassination
by Palestinian terrorists of Shlomo Argov, the Israeli Ambassador to
London. He was shot and gravely wounded on 3 June 1982. Israeli
armoured columns poured across the border on 6 June. Israel cited the
shooting as a clear violation of the agreement it had reached with the
PLO, through American mediator Philip Habib, a year before, following
heavy exchanges of fire across the Israeli–Lebanese border.

In fact, however, the Government had been contemplating a military
action in Lebanon for many months. There were two schools of thought
in the Cabinet at the time. One advocated an advance across south
Lebanon, to a depth of some forty kilometres, to flush out the PLO
presence in the entire area. Intelligence reports revealed that worrisome
quantities of heavy weaponry, especially Katyusha rocket-launchers, were
being amassed by Palestinian groups, posing a constant threat to our
border settlements. Even when they were not actually shooting, their
deployment within range of the border caused the residents of these
villages and kibbutzim to spend their nights in air-raid shelters, and their
days in fear.

A second school within the Cabinet proposed a much more ambitious
invasion of Lebanon, which was to start with landings at Junieh, north
of Beirut, and sweep southwards. Their plan was similar to the 1956
Sinai Campaign, which had begun with a parachute drop at the Mitla
Pass, deep inside the Sinai Peninsula. Other forces would drive up from
the south, and they would eventually all join with Christian units in the
Beirut area. The architect and advocate of the 'Big Plan' (and a veteran
of the 1956 drop) was Ariel Sharon, then Minister of Defence. Prime
Minister Begin, backed by the National Religious Party leader, Dr Yosef
Burg, preferred the more limited operation.

We were in the opposition, but our party leadership contained a
formidable phalanx of experienced military leaders, including Yitzhak
Rabin and Haim Bar-Lev, both former Chiefs of Staff. I convened
our political committee meeting one Saturday night and presented the
information at my disposal. All present were unanimous in opposing the

'Big Plan'. We knew that Sharon's 'strategic thinking' went beyond Lebanon itself. He argued that defeating the PLO in Lebanon could drive the Palestinian fighters back into Jordan, where they might succeed this time in toppling the Hashemite house. Sharon has consistently argued that Israel's interests – and the prospect of a peace settlement – would best be served by a Palestinian takeover in Amman.

Begin was so captivated by the aura of battle-hardened generals like Sharon that he effectively lost or abdicated all responsibility for political decision-making. Although the Cabinet ostensibly endorsed the more modest incursion, it was in fact the more ambitious invasion plan that unfolded. I have no complaints against the military; their duty is to carry out their mission as vigorously as they can. It is the political echelon that is supposed to define the aims and parameters of a military action, and here Begin failed badly. On the second day of the war, he was taken to the Beaufort, a Crusader castle near the border which the PLO had turned into one of its main strongholds and which the IDF had overrun. He understood, mistakenly, that there had been no casualties in this battle. He veritably bubbled over with enthusiasm.

That the Prime Minister was not 'in the picture' became a key feature of the Government's decision-making as the war continued. During one of the heaviest bombings of Beirut, for instance, I telephoned him to urge restraint – and found that he simply did not know that the bombing had been ordered, or that it was in progress. Begin was not in control of the army's actions during the Lebanon War. He did not master the flow of material, written and oral, that streamed across his desk. I do not attribute this to any problem of health or advancing age. He would not, in my opinion, have functioned any differently had he been ten years younger. Begin was too often more dramatic than realistic, influenced more by the resonance of events than by their substance.

The Cabinet thought that it had approved the forty-kilometre plan, but it constantly found itself approving – often retroactively – a broadening and deepening of the campaign. Each time, Sharon explained to his bemused colleagues why this ostensibly unplanned extension of the war was necessary.

Sharon is an excellent military tactician, as he has demonstrated time and again in Israel's wars. But with him, strategy is the handmaiden of tactics, instead of the reverse. His 'strategic vision' on the eve of the Lebanon War extended to Pakistan in the north and to Uganda in the south. He would come to briefings armed with coloured maps of the entire region and would lecture expansively on Israel's strategic role as a prime player against Soviet global designs. His 'strategy' for the war itself, starting from the landings in the north which were based on the 1956 analogy, showed up all his flaws. It was like drawing an analogy between a snake and a sausage on the grounds that both are long and round. In 1956, what stood between our paratroopers at Mitla and the main body of our army was the Egyptian army and large expanses of otherwise empty desert. Now, Sharon's seaborne forces had to traverse or swing around the sprawling city of Beirut, teeming with innocent civilians, in order to link up with the rest of the Israeli force to the south.

But the difference between the two campaigns went deeper than that. In 1956, Moshe Dayan translated Ben-Gurion's political policies into the language of a military campaign against Egypt. In 1982, Sharon, in effect, demanded that Begin do the opposite: that he translate Sharon's own military designs into a political doctrine.

At the time of the Syrian intervention in Lebanon, in 1976, some Israelis believed that Syria's action would turn out to be strategically advantageous to Israel. The Syrian army facing Israel was now strung out across two fronts: the Golan Heights and Lebanon. Its lines of communication were extended – perhaps over-extended. This deployment made it vulnerable and also reduced its offensive capacity – or, at any rate, its capacity to launch a sudden attack. Politically, this school contended, Syria would 'sink into the Lebanese quagmire'.

I never fully subscribed to this theory. In any event, today, nearly two decades later, with the Cold War over and Soviet power extinguished, I believe that it is high time for us to take a fresh look at our strategic thinking. I think we may in the past have exaggerated Syria's strength; certainly, it is unwise to do so in the present. Henry Kissinger used to warn that, 'without Egypt, there can be no war in the Middle East, and without Syria, there can be no peace'. I am not certain that either or both of these axioms was ever true. There can be peace without Syria – at any rate the beginnings of peace – as demonstrated by the agreement we concluded with the Palestinians. And there can be war without Egypt.

But whatever the validity of Kissinger's aphorism when coined, the situation is now much changed. Today, the Syrian threat – to Israel and to peace – is greatly reduced. The Syrians have suffered a string of setbacks. Their army is dug into line after line of fortifications, stretching back sixty kilometres from the Golan Heights to Damascus. But today, more than ever, the measure of a country's strength is not just how many troops it has, but how many tourists. And such questions are beginning to be asked, even in Damascus. There are conflicting trends discernible in Syrian society, just as in so many other countries grappling with the new global realities.

The Syrians have an understandable grievance regarding Lebanon, flowing from the ill-advised Sykes–Picot Agreement. They still dream dreams of the Fertile Crescent and regional domination. But the 'hunting season' is over in human history. People now are more interested in counting their calories than in totting up stags' heads or tiger-skin rugs.

Not everyone has assimilated the full import of current events. History is moving faster than our understanding of it. It will be some time before everyone catches up with what has been happening. But everywhere, people are beginning to catch on. They are starting to see that the new art of statecraft hinges on how to live with your neighbour, not how to make war with him. Ultimately, I am confident that this powerful tide in history will sweep up these three uneasy neighbours – Syria, Lebanon and Israel – into its hopeful current.

18 PRIME MINISTER

Israel's embroilment in the Lebanese quagmire, and a rapidly worsening economic crisis, furnished the backdrop for a parliamentary election in 1984. Menachem Begin had abruptly retired from office – and from public life – a year earlier, and the Likud Government was now led by the lacklustre Yitzhak Shamir. Shamir, one of the three commanders of the pre-state Lehi, or Stern Gang, underground, had spent part of the intervening period working in the Mossad, and even now as a political leader he remained taciturn and secretive.

I hoped that the objective situation in which the country found itself would persuade a sufficient number of voters to shift the balance of power from Likud to Labour. But I was to be sharply disappointed. The Likud did indeed lose support, dropping from forty-eight seats to forty-one, but Labour lost ground too – from forty-seven seats in the 1981 election to forty-four now. Although it emerged from the election as the largest party (and thus could fairly be said to have 'won'), Labour's prospects of forming a coalition government were slim, given the Orthodox parties' preference for the Likud.

But the Likud's prospects were no better. The choice facing Shamir and myself, therefore, was to call a new election – which would take months to arrange and might well reproduce the same deadlock – or to try to form a grand coalition, or, as it became known, a government of national unity. We decided to attempt the second alternative. Our point of departure was hardly auspicious. Our two parties were separated by a yawning ideological chasm, with the Likud still firmly wedded to the notion of Greater Israel and Labour pledged to seek a territorial compromise in the administered territories. Moreover, I had undertaken during the election campaign to end the Likud Government's misguided occupation of a large area of Lebanon and to bring the army home within nine months.

My good friend Ezer Weizman (now President of Israel) had an important part in making the Government of National Unity happen. He had joined the Likud in the early 1970s after retiring from the armed forces, and ran the Likud's successful election campaign in 1977. He was appointed Defence Minister and was widely regarded as Begin's chosen successor. He played a major role in the Camp David negotiations in 1978, but resigned from the Likud Government three years later in protest at what he felt was Begin's deliberate foot-dragging over implementing the Palestinian autonomy, as agreed at Camp David. Weizman ran in the 1984 election at the head of his own party and won three seats. I worked day and night to convince him to join our camp and, finally, he agreed. But even with his support, we lacked a majority.

Shamir and I began a series of meetings in a luxurious suite at the King David Hotel in Jerusalem. We would negotiate without let-up, we gamely told the press, until we reached agreement. I did not realize how difficult that pledge was to prove. Yitzhak Shamir is blessed with inexhaustible reserves of patience and equally rich stocks of stubbornness. He is capable of sitting for hours, saying little and committing himself to nothing. On the first and second days, the conversation plodded slowly around the territorial issue and the war in Lebanon. I spoke at length; Shamir's salient contributions were long silences.

At the end of each day's talks, I naturally reported back to my senior party colleagues on my experiences and impressions. Shamir, however, felt no need to do likewise. Accordingly, we witnessed the strange spectacle of top Likud men, anxious for the negotiations to succeed, seeking out their Labour counterparts to ascertain what had gone on between the two leaders. In fact, not much had gone on. On the third day, I decided to make a move. I had no mandate from my party, I said, to make any concrete proposal, but, speaking purely hypothetically, it might be worth imagining what a great architect of political compromises like the late Levi Eshkol would have come up with. Eshkol, were he to descend from heaven, might suggest a national unity government, with Labour and Likud each co-opting their respective allies. Eshkol might suggest, too, a 'rotation' of the Prime Ministership between the two of us.

'I don't believe Eshkol would have made such a suggestion,' Shamir retorted. We adjourned, with me feeling more frustrated than ever.

The eventual breakthrough came via the agency of Tel Aviv business-man Azriel Einav, a friend of mine – and of many other Israeli politicians. He telephoned me at home and indicated that Ariel Sharon was interested in a discreet meeting with me. I agreed. The next day, Sharon and I met at Einav's home and worked on the shape of a unity government, precisely along the lines of 'Levi Eshkol's suggestion'. It was here that I introduced the idea of an 'inner Cabinet', which would be comprised of only Labour and Likud Ministers, in equal numbers, with none of the smaller coalition parties represented. This forum would take all the major decisions, thus, I hoped, relieving the prospective unity govern-ment of at least some of its inevitable unwieldiness. The rotating Prime Ministership, I proposed, should be in Labour's hands first, since we were the largest party.

In fact, this question of who should be Prime Minister for the first twenty-five months of the projected government's fifty-month term – Shamir or I – was hotly debated within our Labour Party councils. I argued in favour of our being first. I could not see Shamir, if he were now to continue as Prime Minister, carrying out any of the main planks of our platform: withdrawing from Lebanon; beating inflation; reaching agreement with Egypt over Taba;* or launching negotiations with Jordan and the Palestinians. In twenty-five months' time, I said, we might well find the country in even deeper trouble – with Labour, at least in the mind of the public, sharing the blame. Indeed, I doubted if, in this scenario, a government of national unity would last its full term.

The unity government scheme, as I outlined it, greatly appealed to Sharon's pragmatism. He was convinced that new elections would lead nowhere. 'Leave it to me,' he said. 'I'll go to see Shamir, and close the deal with him.' He drove off to Jerusalem, and, two hours later, telephoned me from there: 'Everything's all right; Shamir agrees.' I could hardly believe my ears. But I realized that while Shamir could while away hours arguing with me about 'the integrity of *Eretz Ysrael*', Sharon's overriding concern was the integrity of the Likud.

Sharon, who had been forced to resign as Minister of Defence by a commission of inquiry that investigated the Sabra and Shatilla massacre, now became Minister of Commerce in the new Government.

Four months after taking office, we were ready to begin the process of disengagement from Lebanon. Defence Minister Yitzhak Rabin sub-

---

* See pages 302–3.

mitted a detailed plan to the inner Cabinet, which provided for a two-phase withdrawal that would leave the IDF patrolling a narrow security zone along the border, held by the SLA. The Likud Ministers, led by Shamir, opposed the scheme, but their ranks broke when Minister of Housing David Levy★ moved across to support the withdrawal plan. The first phase went into effect in April. By the summer, the IDF had completed its redeployment from Lebanon. The vast bulk of the troops were back in their bases inside Israel. Small forces remained on the border. This deployment is still in place at the time of writing. From the security zone, the IDF and SLA defend the civilian settlements of northern Israel against the terrorist threat, which today stems largely from the Hizbollah (Party of God) fundamentalists. This vicious and violent organization, spawned in south Lebanon with Iranian support, also sends out its tentacles of terror against Israeli and Jewish targets around the world.

Second only to the Lebanese morass on my agenda as Prime Minister was the state of the economy. When our new Government took over in September 1984, inflation – or, more accurately, hyperinflation – was running at 400 per cent a year and threatening to smash through the four-digit barrier. Our balance of payments was in crisis, and the whole economy was in a condition of chronic instability, still floored by the massive collapse of the Tel Aviv stock exchange one year earlier. Some of my friends had urged me to decline the Prime Ministership because of the state of inflation. They said that there was no way I could tackle it effectively without losing every shred of popularity. I resisted this advice – perhaps because I did not fully understand all the insidious and destructive properties of inflation. Inflation is like drugs: it destroys the internal organs while giving its victim a wonderful, floating feeling in the head. It gives rise to two new classes in society: those who wax suddenly fat on inflationary speculation, and ordinary people and pensioners who find themselves suddenly poor as their real income is eroded. Inflation is paradise for the foxes and purgatory for the ants. The sight of shop assistants marking new, higher prices of basic foodstuffs every day filled me with trepidation.

My economic advisers recommended immediate and drastic action: a devaluation of 30 per cent, which would have resulted in widespread

★ Levy was to become Foreign Minister in the 1990–2 Likud-led Government.

unemployment; a reduction of up to 50 per cent in defence spending, which would have seriously weakened Israel and exposed it to grave military dangers; sweeping budgetary cuts in all government departments; a price freeze; across-the-board wage cuts, and so forth. Even if these ideas made economic sense, I knew that politically, and indeed socially, they were non-starters. If I tried to introduce them, they would lack the minimal support needed to make them work.

This is a situation in which any government needs to look beyond its immediate political hinterland for added support and credibility. Inflation implies, above all, a nation's loss of confidence in its economy, its currency and its capacity for growth. I resolved that, alongside our broad-based political coalition, we needed a coalition of all the major economic interests in the country: the Government, the unions, the industrialists and the academic community. I created an 'Economic Council', comprised of the Secretary-General of the Histadrut Trades Union Confederation, Yisrael Kessar, and his deputy, Haim Haberfeld; the leaders of the Employers' Association, Eli Hurwitz, Dov Lautman and Dan Gillerman; the Minister of Finance, Yitzhak Modai of the Likud, and myself, representing the Government; and senior professors of economics. The trade unionists naturally contended that the real value of wages must be protected. They did not believe that the Government would genuinely prune its spending, or that the industrialists would cut their profits, and they were determined that the burden would not fall solely, or mainly, on the wage-earner. The three leading industrialists, in their initial presentations, were equally orthodox: they insisted that exports not be depressed, nor domestic prices lowered. Otherwise, they warned, manufacturers would go bankrupt in droves. My ministerial colleagues, for their part, had become used to bemoaning inflation, while resisting any cutbacks in their own particular departments.

My first remedial action took the form of a social contract – or 'package deal', as it was called – between the Government, the Histadrut and the Employers' Association, in an effort to peg prices and wages for a limited period of three months. This was subsequently extended, by agreement, for a further three months. But by mid-May 1985, it was clear that this temporary remedy had run its course. Inflation for the month of April alone was more than 15 per cent; we were back on the road to economic ruin.

One night, early in June, I convened at my home in Jerusalem a meeting of the country's leading academic economists, together with the

Finance Minister, Yitzhak Modai, his top aides, and my own economic adviser, Amnon Neubach. Among the non-government men present were Professors Michael Bruno, Eitan Berglass and Yoram Ben-Porat.

The meeting started after ten. I asked Modai to begin with a general overview of the problems we faced. Modai, bright but totally unpredictable, looked at me strangely and said, 'You called this meeting. I don't have anything to say.'

This was hardly an auspicious beginning, but I was determined not to let Modai's moodiness cloud the proceedings. 'Gentlemen,' I said, 'inflation is breaking out again and threatening to swamp us. We are here tonight to consult as to how to fight back – and beat it.' That was enough to launch an intensive discussion that went on long past midnight. Several of the participants spoke of the need for a sweeping stabilization programme and put forward their ideas on what components such a programme should include. The general direction was fairly clear, but obviously these were just initial ideas. Bringing the meeting to a close, I proposed that we set up a small working group that would prepare detailed papers on the various aspects of the programme, assisted by members of the broader panel.

The working group included Neubach, Berglass, Bruno and Emanuel Sharon, the Director-General of the Finance Ministry. They sat daily for three weeks – and not a word of their deliberations leaked out, which in itself was a considerable achievement. Every second evening, Neubach would come round to my house and brief me on their progress, and once a week I met the full group. Finance Minister Modai was passive. He was aware, obviously, of what was going on, but he seemed remote from it. He was embroiled at this time in one of his Liberal Party's* frequent internal battles and that appeared to take up most of his energies. At some of our nocturnal meetings, he had difficulty staying awake. To his credit, he did nothing to discourage or disrupt the urgent work going on all around him.

Steadily, the Economic Stabilization Plan, or ESP, took its final shape. The main elements were:

1 A major devaluation of the shekel, coupled with an announcement by the Government that the new rate would remain in force indefinitely. The system of almost daily devaluations was to be ended.

* The Liberal Party was the second-largest party, after Menachem Begin's Herut, in the Likud, which began as a bloc of several separate parties.

2 Steep rises in prices, coupled with a government announcement that prices would henceforth be frozen, until further notice. Existing price control mechanisms were to be toughened to ensure that the freeze was rigorously enforced.

3 Government subsidies for basic commodities were to be slashed by a total of $750 million. The government deficit was to be further reduced through spending cuts in individual ministries.

4 The mechanism for calculating incremental rises in monthly cost of living, which was responsible for linking wages with prices, was to be temporarily suspended, so that wage-earners would not be compensated for the effect of the price rises and the subsidy cuts. A severe erosion in the real value of wages was anticipated.

5 A restrictive monetary policy would be introduced.

On Friday, 28 June, the full working group convened in my Tel Aviv office to submit the plan. I asked the Governor of the Bank of Israel, Moshe Mandelbaum, and the Attorney-General, Yitzhak Zamir, to attend the meeting, together with Economics Minister Gad Yaacobi and Deputy Finance Minister Adi Amorai, both Labour Party men. Sharon presented the plan in great detail for final discussions and finishing touches.

By this time, word was out that new economic measures were in the making, and a large crowd of journalists had assembled outside. The meeting ended at four o'clock, and the last item on the agenda had been how to present our deliberations to the media and the public at this interim stage. The Cabinet was to meet on Sunday, as usual,* and until it had approved the plan nothing substantive could be announced. I decided, therefore, that the official line should be that three separate plans had been submitted for consideration, and all would be presented to the Cabinet on Sunday. I asked Modai to brief the press accordingly.

My aides said later that this was a major mistake on my part, since Modai immediately seized the opportunity to 'steal my thunder'. He went on television that night and told the nation that his Ministry had drafted a new economic plan designed to deal with the worsening economic situation. This plan, he announced, would be placed before the Cabinet for its endorsement on Sunday.

In the Cabinet on Sunday, it quickly became clear that, in spite of his

---

* In Israel, weekly Cabinet meetings are held on Sunday morning.

own enthusiastic claim of paternity for the ESP, Modai had failed to persuade his Likud colleagues to support it. Apart from Yitzhak Shamir and Modai himself, only one or two other Likud Ministers favoured it. The rest had plainly resolved in advance to speak and vote against it; and to kill it, if they could. Among them was Moshe Nissim, who was later to become Finance Minister and who, in that capacity, was responsible for applying the ESP.

I was prepared, however, for a tough fight and was in no way fazed by the Likud recalcitrants. I had concluded by this stage that it was up to the Government to prove its own *bona fides*, by actually deciding on drastic cuts in its own budgets, if it was to win the confidence of its two partners in the economic recovery programme, the unions and the industrialists. I personally brandished the 'knife', meticulously reviewing item after item, slashing remorselessly. Every expenditure of more than $100,000 was a legitimate subject of discussion in this extraordinary Cabinet session. I let everyone speak, no matter how long-winded they were. The meeting went on and on, but I refused to adjourn it, I even warned that I would go to the President and hand in my resignation if this plan were not approved. Morning turned to afternoon, and then to night, but still I sat there while the speech-making continued. I knew that, when it came to hanging in, I was as strong as any of them – indeed, as all of them together. Monday dawned, and still the Likud Ministers kept up their barrage of critical rhetoric. By now, though, it was clear that a solid majority of the Ministers would vote in favour of the ESP, and that I would not end the meeting until that vote had taken place. Gradually, the Likud filibuster petered out, and, twenty-four hours after it began, this fateful Cabinet meeting came to an end. The vote was fifteen to seven, with three abstentions. One abstainee was Yitzhak Rabin, the Minister of Defence. We had argued long and hard over the defence budget and, in the end, to his abiding credit, he went along with my unswerving demand that we reduce defence spending by $0.5 billion.

The next stage was to win over the Histadrut. This was not easy. Having been persuaded myself, I now had to persuade them that a plan designed to stabilize prices required, as its very first step, a massive rise in prices and a large-scale devaluation. In the end, we devalued by 33 per cent and allowed prices to rise by up to 28 per cent. Wages went up by around 15 per cent – and at that point everything was frozen. In practice, this meant a very substantial drop in the real purchasing power of the ordinary Israeli. But I knew that without this drop, effective for a period of months, the ESP would stand no chance. To compensate wage-earners to the full extent of the price rises would merely mean another vicious twist of the inflationary spiral. The cuts in government subsidies for basic commodities hit especially hard at the weakest sectors of society. I knew this full well and was braced to face the waves of angry criticism that these decisions engendered. We had been subsidizing such items as bread, milk, eggs and sugar, as well as public transport – major items in the budgets of many ordinary families.

In two weeks of intensive negotiations, I was able to convince the leaders of the Histadrut that this was the only possible solution. We agreed that wages would be allowed to rise again by the end of the year and that during 1986 living standards would gradually return to what they had been before the ESP went into effect. People hardly believed that I had taken all these draconian steps. I had not previously been thought of as wicked or unfeeling. But I was convinced that these harsh measures were the only way to win back the nation's confidence. And frequent visits to shops and factories in the months after the ESP went into effect strengthened my conviction and gave me, too, the confidence to continue.

In August, the month after the plan was implemented, inflation plummeted to 2.5 per cent, from 28 per cent in July and 20 per cent in June. By the year's end, the monthly figure was averaging 1.5 per cent. The academic economists who had helped draw up the plan now closely followed its execution. According to one of them, Professor Haim Ben-Shahar of Tel Aviv University, it fulfilled all the expectations. It is now cited in courses on economic policy in major universities around the world. The Israeli ESP was not revolutionary: it was built on classical economic foundations. Its success lay in the fact that it tackled the key issues simultaneously, across a broad front: exchange-rate policy, wages, government spending and monetary policy. But ultimately, the ESP worked because it won the trust of the Israeli public. People recovered their confidence in the economy because they believed the Government knew what it was doing. They were prepared to accept the need to sacrifice not just because the Government decreed it, but because the Government, not least in its dialogue with the unions and the employers, demonstrated a new determination and a new capacity for bold but rational thinking.

I knew that the economic mess was not my fault. But I also knew that the public – rightly – would blame me for it if my measures for solving it went awry. For months, I had tried to battle inflation through various agreements with the unions and the employers, but these 'package deals' quickly ran out of steam and inflation threatened to grow much worse. I was beset by advisers, some appointed, others welcome, and still others uninvited but nevertheless free and forceful with their advice. I tried to think things through carefully, despite the dissonant cacophony of strident voices.

When I finally moved, I did so decisively. I both personally supervised the implementation of the ESP and ran the negotiations with the Histadrut. The American administration, which had been closely following our efforts, expressed its satisfaction. Secretary of State George Shultz had insisted on sweeping economic reforms as a precondition for the emergency economic aid that we had requested. The ESP fitted the bill. Washington approved a $1.5 billion aid package, spread over two years (on top of the annual $3 billion in military and civilian aid and credits that we had been receiving and would continue to receive).

Modai's behaviour grew steadily more provocative and less tolerable. He insulted me publicly, on one occasion dubbing me 'the flying Prime Minister', as though my many brief trips abroad on government business were jet-setting luxury jaunts. When eventually I felt that the stability of the Government itself was threatened by his conduct, I fired him. But even after he left the Finance Ministry, Modai continued to vie with me for the political credit accruing to the 'father' of the ESP. Indeed, many Israelis at the time came to believe that the Finance Minister had put together the ESP while I, as Prime Minister, had merely given it moral and political support. But my hands-on diligence, coupled with the Likud's opposition, and Modai's own peculiar oscillations, eventually helped set the record straight. My ratings in the opinion polls climbed steadily, to reach levels above 80 per cent. I am not a great believer in polls, but this remarkably high showing did seem to reflect widespread appreciation of what I was trying to do.

Our Government of National Unity, born after much travail, was to become a subject of study for politicians and political scientists around the world. It was something of a precedent in democratic countries – a coalition of the two main political forces in time of peace. Looking back, I would say that the basic lesson from our experience is that it can work – but only if there is no alternative. I would not recommend a unity government as anything other than a last resort. Decision-making is desperately hard in a cabinet evenly balanced between ministers from opposing parties who know that they will be fighting each other in the next election campaign. On the other hand, once a decision is taken, it is more easily implemented than in a regular government, because it immediately enjoys the support and confidence of the great bulk of public opinion.

Indeed, to my pleasant surprise, the Government of National Unity was able to reach and implement important decisions, at least during the first half of its term. (The second half was less productive; Shamir apparently felt that the decisions taken during the first half were sufficient for the entire term.) It was hard work, but it was worth it. The Government's list of achievements during those first twenty-five months compares favourably with what most regular Governments manage to achieve in a full term.

19 BEHIND 'IRANGATE'

Iran is a country in which outsiders – and, indeed, most insiders – never know what is really happening beneath the surface of events. As Defence Minister in the 1970s, I visited Tehran as the guest of the Shah. I had dutifully read up on the 'White Revolution' that he had initiated, with its agrarian and industrial reforms designed to haul Iran into the twentieth century. But however white the revolution, it was clearly no match for the black corruption in which the entire country was wallowing. Every area of government seemed to be infected. Corruption had become almost the official way of life – both civilian and military.

The Shah invited me to visit a large airfield outside Tehran, where I was stunned to see close to a thousand modern American helicopters parked in rows on the tarmac. I knew the price of such helicopters and quickly worked out the cost of the hardware before my eyes. Meeting the pilots, I found that most of them were village youngsters who had barely completed secondary school. These boys, I remember thinking, are expected to cross a technological gap of centuries virtually overnight.

When I returned to Tehran, I asked the Shah why he needed so many helicopters. I added that I admired the idea of bringing these country lads up to the level of helicopter pilots, but frankly I doubted whether all of them could truly make the grade. He replied that his thinking was 'strategic'. If the Russians tried to attack Iran from the mountains with their tanks, he said, 'we'll stop them with our helicopters, which can fly higher than the mountains'.

I felt that this offered a genuine insight into his thinking. It revealed the one-dimensional nature of his perception of the very real communist threat to his country. To me, it seemed obvious that the way to defeat that threat was to provide better schooling, better social services, more rural development and higher living standards in the cities. The danger stemming from ignorance was greater than the menace of Russian intervention. But the Shah didn't see it that way. 'There are only two countries in this region that can stand up to communism,' he said, 'Iran and Israel. For Iran, though, the danger is closer at hand.' He then launched into a virulent attack on the American media, which, he maintained, distorted the true situation in his country.

I saw in the figure of Shah Mohammed Reza Pahlavi the personification of the contradiction that was eroding Iranian society. On the one hand, he wanted a twentieth-century economic revolution, purportedly for the benefit of his subjects; but on the other, he remained an absolute monarch, as though still living in the seventeenth century. I did not know then, of course, how long the monarchy would last, but I found myself wondering how long it could be before he succumbed to the problems and pressures that threatened to topple him.

When Ayatollah Khomeini eventually took power in Tehran in 1979, the riddle of Iran became an even more impenetrable enigma. Suddenly, with the collapse of the monarchy, the whole veneer of modernism seemed to melt away. For us, the revolution meant the end of a long and close – though unofficial – relationship. We had had strong ties with the Shah's Iran in a number of important areas.

Khomeini spoke with the rhetoric of a martyr. His language transcended both logic and political pragmatism. There seemed to be no way to talk to him, or even to argue with him. He struck fear not only in the hearts of his own people, but also in American hearts. In effect, it was Khomeini who brought about the fall of President Jimmy Carter.

I shall never forget my experience at the White House on 24 April 1980, the day that President Carter launched his abortive helicopter-borne attempt to rescue the American hostages in Tehran. At the time, of course, I knew nothing of what was going on. I was visiting Washington as leader of the opposition in Israel, and had asked to meet the President and other officials and Congressional leaders. The President's office scheduled the meeting for very early in the morning. Contrary to the normal practice, I was to see Carter before I had called on the Secretary of State. Secretary Cyrus Vance and Vice-President Walter Mondale accompanied me to the Oval Office, but Carter asked them to stay outside and ushered me into the Oval Office alone. He asked me two questions: what would I do, in his position, regarding the American Embassy hostages? And what were our considerations when we made our decisions regarding Entebbe? I told him that if there was any realistic possibility of a military option, I would take it. As for Entebbe, our greatest problem, I said, was the scarcity of information. Not everything that we needed to know to make our decision was available to us. To a certain extent, we were working in the dark. But in the end, we told ourselves that every military operation involves a gamble – and we decided to risk it. Carter said that my words had helped him. I did not know then that the helicopters were already on their ill-fated way.

Later that afternoon, I was to fly from Washington to New York. By then, the world knew that the mission had ended in abysmal failure. As I entered Washington Airport, the PA system boomed, 'Mr Peres, a call for you.' I went to a phone and was put through to the broadcaster, Barbara Walters. Would I do a live interview? I agreed without question. I said that, in my view, the President had taken the right decision. Every such decision entailed risks, I continued. There could be human errors and accidents, but the failure in no way overshadowed the President's courage in doing what he did. Moments later, the White House was on the line with a word of thanks. I was just about the only public figure who had gone on air to approve of the President's action. I knew that Carter would have to pay a price for his failure, though I did not know then that it would be the ultimate political price.

I record this incident here in order to illustrate the pall of ignorance, frustration and fear that blinded the West in its attempts to deal with Khomeini's Iran and with the new and ghastly phenomenon of hostage-taking that took root in the Middle East in the wake of the Iranian revolution. Iran's fingerprints could be found on almost every case of kidnapping in the region in the years that followed. The Iranians themselves, without batting an eyelid, would weave an elaborate tissue of lies, denying any connection with, or even knowledge of, the various hostage-taking episodes. Neither we nor the Americans were deceived.

For our part, we maintained our keen interest in Iran and continued to monitor, as best we could, the salient political and military developments there. Iran's geostrategic importance, especially in the eyes of the United States, had not altered because of the change of regime in Tehran. The new factor, regionally and internationally, was the spectre of the aggressive expansionistic Islamic fundamentalism which the mullahs who now ruled Iran appeared determined to export. The Arab states seemed to be watching warily as two regional heavyweights – fundamentalist

Iran and largely secularist Turkey – squared off for what could be an historic confrontation.

We had a number of experts on Iran, and I valued their work, though I felt that Iran was one of the subjects where expertise did not necessarily provide accurate insights into a radically changing situation. This was the backdrop to the developments that became known as 'Irangate'.

The key figure in the affair on our side, Amiram Nir, came to my notice one Friday night, early in 1981, when I was struck, while watching the weekly news, by an item on the army. It was sharply critical, but full of accurate information presented in a clear and insightful way. The man behind it, I was told, was Israel TV's defence correspondent, Amiram Nir.

The Knesset elections were scheduled for June of that year, and I was busy most nights with public gatherings and parlour meetings. At one of these, a young man was introduced to me. He had a glass eye (he had lost an eye in a military training accident), but his other eye gleamed with wisdom and vitality. He was Amiram Nir.

He asked to speak to me privately after the meeting. He told me that he was 'a longtime admirer' of mine and that he wanted to work alongside me. He was fed up with life in the media, and was considering a political career. He made a powerful impression, and not long after I suggested that he head my personal campaign staff – an offer which he accepted with alacrity. Nir was efficient and well organized in his work, and highly articulate as a speaker and a writer. In human relations, though, he was less adept, and this was his chief weakness.

Labour failed to form a government after that election,* but Nir continued to work with me. He would prepare in-depth reports and assessments on current political developments – always well founded and cogently argued. It was he who first acquainted me with the ongoing debate in the Government and the army regarding a proposed military intervention in Lebanon.† Nir had been a major in the Armoured Corps, where he was regarded as a competent and promising officer.

When the Government of National Unity was set up in September 1984, Nir asked for a position suitable to his interests and abilities. After

* The result was a virtual tie – Labour won forty-seven seats to the Likud's forty-eight – but the Orthodox parties rejected Labour's overtures, preferring to continue their coalition with the Likud.
† See page 227.

consulting Defence Minister Rabin, I proposed that he co-ordinate our fight against terrorism. He would work out of the Defence Ministry, but be in close co-ordination with the Prime Minister's Office. He accepted at once.

In May 1985, I was asked to receive Michael Ledeen, a former American official whom I had come to know some years earlier in his capacity as the administration's contact-man with the European social-democratic parties. I knew that he was also linked to the CIA. In my conversations with him, I had found him to be engaging and broad-minded, a man who always had interesting ideas to talk about. This time, he asked that we meet alone. Naturally, I agreed.

Ledeen said that he had come on a mission from Robert McFarlane, President Reagan's National Security Adviser. It was a top-secret mission, he stressed, and must remain so. Everything he would say, and any actions that might ensue, had to stay outside the normal operating channels. In other words, he was signalling that the CIA was not involved and that he did not want the Mossad involved either.

His purpose, he explained, was to see whether Israel could be of any help to the United States in seeking ways to obtain the release of the American hostages held in Lebanon by Iranian-backed groups. Israel, he said, was known to have had many and varied contacts with Iran, possibly better contacts and better information than any other Western country.

At the time, we, too, had 'missing in actions' in Lebanon, who we thought were being held by pro-Iranian groups. We also had Shi'ite prisoners, captured in Lebanon, who I thought might be factors in a hostage exchange. I had learned over the previous months, moreover, that despite Khomeini's absolute grip on the country, there were three distinct trends discernible within revolutionary Iran's policy-making circles. The first, and most hardline, was a group of religious and political leaders bent on exporting the Islamic revolution to other countries and on imposing a broad policy of nationalization inside Iran. Leaders of this group included Prime Minister Hussein Mussavi and Ayatollah Ali Akbar Meshkini. A second, more moderate group followed the Speaker of the Majlis, Hashemi Rafsanjani, and several ayatollahs allied to him. The third group, though also comprising Shi'ite clerics and revolutionary figures, was basically pro-Western and anti-Soviet. They favoured a free economy at home and had no sympathy for the export of revolutionary Islam abroad.

It goes almost without saying that my immediate decision was to respond favourably to the American request for our co-operation. The Americans had helped us, many times in the past, to get prisoners of war back and to facilitate the exodus of Jews from totalitarian countries for Israel. Ledeen's mission offered us an opportunity to repay part of the debt. What could be better? We had a deep interest in demonstrating to the United States that we stood ready, whenever they called on us, to be of help to them if we could. Foreign Minister Yitzhak Shamir and Defence Minister Rabin, both of whom I briefed fully, agreed. We knew, too, from a reliable source that Yasser Arafat had offered to help the Americans get their hostages back, and that the Syrians were also looking for ways to be helpful, in order to score political points in Washington. Obviously, we did not want to hold back while our Arab enemies were seen to be forthcoming.

In addition, we, like the Americans, were interested in forming a reliable longer-term assessment of likely developments in Iran. Was Khomeinism as widespread and firmly entrenched as the ruling mullahs claimed, or would more moderate or even secularist forces come to the fore again?

Shamir said that his Director-General, David Kimche, a former senior Mossad man, was going to Washington shortly and could, therefore, check out Ledeen's request. Kimche reported in July that the request had indeed come from McFarlane – in other words, on the authority of President Reagan. In August, Kimche visited Washington again, and this time, on our specific instructions, he mentioned to McFarlane that we wanted to be sure that Secretary Shultz was in the picture. McFarlane was reluctant at first, saying that he feared leaks, but Kimche pressed and McFarlane eventually said that he would ask the President and that Kimche should call back the next day. Kimche did so, and McFarlane told him that the President had agreed to bring Shultz in and that he (McFarlane) had accordingly already spoken to Shultz.

Since Ledeen had stipulated that any operation should not be handled through the normal channels, I cast around for a suitable alternative. My old friend Al Schwimmer was still 'on the books', as a dollar-a-year consultant to the Government, and so I asked him to co-ordinate this particular matter. I thought that his American origins, his aviation expertise and his veritable loathing of publicity in any form all equipped him admirably for the assignment. Schwimmer brought in Yaacov Nimrodi, a private businessman at that time, but previously a long-serving Israeli Military Attaché in Tehran. This was a natural choice:

Nimrodi, who spoke Farsee, knew Iran intimately; he still had many friends and contacts living there, and had accumulated much experience doing business with Iranians.

Nimrodi's assessments matched those we had already heard from other sources: there were three distinct groups within the Tehran 'establishment', distinguished by the varying degrees of extremism in their attitudes to the outside world. We called them 'Line A', 'Line B' and 'Line C'. Soon enough, envoys representing Line A that is, the most moderate of the three – made contact with us and gave us to understand that they could bring about the release of American hostages. They said that they had to prove (to Lines B and C?) that they could obtain a substantial *quid pro quo* – in the form of advanced American weaponry. For such hardware, they stressed, they were prepared to pay the full market price. They particularly wanted Hawk anti-aircraft missiles and TOW anti-tank missiles.

Their shopping-list was transmitted to Washington and quickly elicited a positive response. To expedite the release of the hostages, the Iranians were prepared to make a cash down-payment immediately, and the Americans asked us to send the missiles from our own arsenals, with the assurance that they would be replaced forthwith. I consulted Rabin, knowing that he shared my desire to help the Americans, and he released as much hardware as he could. Meanwhile, Schwimmer chartered out-of-the-way aeroplanes and crews to fly the *matériel* to Tehran. Before long, the first hostage, Reverend Benjamin Weir, was released. We rejoiced for him and his family.★

At this point, the Americans apparently decided that they wanted to get to the root of the problem and to learn more about the various groups of kidnappers, as well as their connections with Shi'ite organizations in Lebanon and their links with Iran. We were equally interested in broadening our knowledge of this relatively new and unknown enemy. This was the backdrop to my decision to bring Amiram Nir into the operation.

Nir very quickly worked himself into a central role. McFarlane and Lieutenant-Colonel Oliver North, his key aide in this operation, quickly developed an intimate and trusting relationship with Nir. He began to participate in secret meetings with Iranian emissaries, mostly in European

---

★ Weir was freed on 14 September 1985. Other releases that were linked to arms sales were those of Reverend Lawrence Jenco on 26 July 1986 and David Jacobsen on 2 November 1986.

capitals. Some of these meetings were arranged by us, others by the Americans. On one now-famous occasion Nir joined McFarlane (who had meanwhile retired, but was brought back for this assignment) and a senior CIA official, George Cave, on a secret visit to Iran itself, where they hoped to negotiate directly with senior policy-makers. That visit was not a success. Overall, though, we believed that we were doing our bit to help the American Government, while, at the same time, acquiring knowledge and experience that would be used to fight the terrorists and kidnappers in the future. As for the alleged secret and illegal diversion of funds received from Iran to the Contra rebels in Nicaragua, that was entirely unconnected to Israel's involvement in 'Irangate'.

I was encouraged by the release of Reverend Weir, which seemed to show that there was a solid foundation to the scheme. I had no way of making a judgment other than by the results – and here was a tangible one. Weir's release was received with enormous enthusiasm by the American Government and the public.

My confidence that we were sensibly serving both America's interests and our own was reinforced when I visited Washington in September 1986. After the official working session, President Reagan asked me to stay on alone. Now, without officials and briefing cards, he poured out his gratitude to me for the help we were giving the United States in trying to free its hostages.

This was an especially memorable moment in my relationship with Reagan. But the warmth of that moment was not out of character for him – nor atypical of the relationship. I genuinely liked and respected Ronald Reagan as a man. I appreciated his natural modesty and his refreshingly innocent reactions when the going got complicated. I had met him for the first time in Los Angeles in April 1980, together with Nancy Reagan and Ed Meese, then his campaign manager. I was accompanied by our Consul-General in Los Angeles, Benny Navon. Reagan welcomed me warmly and said that he had been the host of a neighbour of ours the week before, a Lebanese visitor who had spoken firmly in favour of peace with Israel. I asked Reagan if his guest had been a Lebanese Christian or a Lebanese Moslem – and a wonderful expression of innocence spread over his frank and open countenance, like a little boy who hasn't done his homework. He did not attempt to dissimulate, but turned to Meese for help. Thereafter, in meetings with me at any rate, he never pretended to 'know it all, and nothing more', in the words of Marshal Pétain. I sincerely admired him, for he was the

'Great Communicator' – a leader who may not have known the intricacies of every foreign policy issue, but who knew where he stood and what he stood for, and knew how to get his message across. As for his modesty, even two terms in the White House failed to spoil it. When an official visitor arrived, the President would stand in the receiving line alongside his senior officials to welcome the guest. He never put on airs.

After the formal meetings, he would often regale his visitor with the anti-communist jokes he so loved to tell. Thus, before this particularly memorable private meeting in September 1986, he told me the following story. At Yalta, Roosevelt went to bed early one evening, leaving Stalin and Churchill alone. They ate, drank and talked deep into the night. The next morning, Churchill said, 'Joe, we drank too much last night, and we talked too much.' 'I thought so, too,' Stalin replied, 'but don't worry. There were only the three of us there – you, me and the interpreter, and the interpreter's been shot already.'

What I didn't know, as Ronald Reagan's words of thanks and praise fell on my grateful ears, was that there had already been too much talk about this Iranian operation – too much talk and too many interpreters.

What I also did not know – indeed, could not have conceived – was the extent of the disunity in the top echelons of the Reagan administration. I believed – again perhaps naïvely – that the American Government worked like a Swiss clock, with all the wheels-within-wheels co-ordinated with each other and working together for a single purpose. It never crossed my mind that North could have been working on his own, or that Shultz was not in the picture, or that Caspar Weinberger, the Secretary of Defence, had his own very strongly conflicting position. Above all, I could not know that the authorizations that McFarlane said he had were by no means as authoritative and representative as he claimed.

When Shultz found out what had been going on, he was furious – not least with me. He imparted to me his deep feeling of unease at my having concealed the whole affair from him. I explained to him that it had never occurred to me that he might not be fully in the picture. I had been absolutely certain, I said, that the NSC Adviser had been keeping him informed, along with other top officials who needed to know what was happening. Moreover, this was the explicit impression that McFarlane had given David Kimche. It was inconceivable to me that I should have received a letter of appreciation from the President of the United States, full of praise for Amiram Nir, and that the Secretary of State would not have known about it. (This letter was the only time in our relations with the United States that a President singled out an appointed Israeli official for such special praise.)

Now, with the wisdom of hindsight and in light of Secretary Shultz's memoirs[*] and of the Senate investigation, I am, if anything, even more baffled by the relations between the key administration figures: McFarlane, Shultz, Admiral Poindexter and Weinberger. I could not have conceived of such a situation in my worst nightmares. My admiration for the United States was such that I was naturally convinced that they could always rely on the most thorough and co-ordinated staff work in reaching policy decisions.

But, on our side, it was not all a bed of roses. I had complete confidence in Schwimmer and in Nir, but I gradually began to understand that Nir wanted Schwimmer out. His reporting about Schwimmer began to look tendentious. I called him in, and he earnestly promised to co-operate fully with Schwimmer.

One day, Nir told me that the Americans now wanted to take a more hands-on role. They would no longer stay behind the scenes, as they had done until then, letting us handle the actual operations. I was naturally pleased to hear this and gave my immediate consent. Schwimmer's response was less enthusiastic; he seemed sceptical about the authenticity of Nir's information. Nir, at any rate, was in constant contact with the Americans, and he effectively took over the Israeli side of the affair.

But on the policy-making level – and this was the vast difference between us and the Americans – everything on our side was completely co-ordinated among the senior Ministers, and our decisions were taken harmoniously, after a proper process of discussion. This is all the more notable given the fact that we were a 'troika' – Rabin, Shamir and myself – representing two opposing political parties that had gone into government together only because neither of them had any other option. The rivalry between our two parties, Labour and Likud, had only been put aside for the duration, so to speak. There was never any real reconciliation. Nevertheless, it would not occur to me to make decisions in a matter like this without involving both the Defence Minister and the Foreign Minister.

Moreover, we were all three Prime Ministers, past or present. We

---

[*] *Turmoil and Triumph* (Charles Scribner's Sons, New York, 1993).

knew how to work with the Mossad, the Shin Bet,★ or, in this case, less structured secret channels. I told the Mossad, of course, of the existence of this operation and explained why it was best that they were not involved, since the Americans wanted to avoid involving any official government agency on their side. This was a decision which, albeit exceptional, Rabin and Shamir, as past Prime Ministers, could readily understand. Throughout the episode, any information reaching any one of us was immediately brought to the knowledge of the other two. There was no question of keeping anyone out of the picture: we were in it together. And even after it came unstuck, we stayed together. Our decisions had been taken unanimously, and we remained unanimous. None of us, after the event, tried to make political capital out of Irangate at the expense of the others – despite our rivalries on most other issues.

The same is true of another episode that provoked intense controversy during my Premiership, the Shin Bet Affair, as it came to be called. The story began in April 1984, before I became Prime Minister, when two young Palestinians hijacked a bus travelling from Tel Aviv to Ashkelon and tried to take it into the Gaza Strip. A shoot-out at an army roadblock resulted in the death of one passenger and the surrender of the two hijackers. They were photographed by newsmen being led away, but later the army announced that they had been killed during the shoot-out. Efforts by the military censor to prevent publication of the photographs failed; the ban was defied by newspapers in Israel and abroad.

Subsequently, two committees of inquiry were set up to investigate the killings, one under a former army major-general, Meir Zorea, and another under the State Attorney, Yonah Blatman. A senior army officer, Brigadier-General Yitzhak Mordechai, was brought to trial but eventually acquitted.

A good deal of controversy – both in the form of public debate and private whisperings – surrounded the affair by the time I took office as Prime Minister in September. But I felt that, as two properly appointed judicial boards had given their verdict, there was no need for me to reopen the case. The head of the Shin Bet, Avraham Shalom, spoke about the bus hijacking in his briefing at the outset of my term, outlining the facts and stating that he had acted 'according to the instructions' of the then Prime Minister, Yitzhak Shamir. He did not go into detail, nor

★ The Shin Bet, or Shin Bet Kaf, is the Hebrew acronym for Israel's internal security service.

did I ask him to. This was an episode from the past which was now over, or so I believed. I already had my plate full with problems of the present. Shalom did not say precisely what instructions of Shamir he was referring to, and I did not press him.

Some time later, during the course of our regular weekly meeting,* Shalom mentioned that several senior agents, among them his deputy, Reuven Hazak, were trying to undermine his authority and seeking to replace him, but he had managed to overcome their challenge. Anyway, he did not suggest, or even hint, that he wanted them removed from the service.

At the time, I did not know that the background to this internal 'uprising' was the bus hijack. But a few weeks later, when Shalom was abroad on leave and Hazak was standing in for him at the weekly briefing session, the connection emerged. Hazak alleged that there had been a massive cover-up, that both judicial inquiries had been deliberately misled by false evidence from Shin Bet operatives, that Mordechai had in effect been framed, and that Shalom was directly involved. Hazak said that he spoke also for two other senior agents, Peleg Radai and Rafi Malka.

This seemed strange to me. Why, I asked Hazak, had he waited a whole year before exposing the alleged cover-up? Why had he himself not asked to testify before Zorea or Blatman? Moreover, why had he chosen to speak out just when Shalom was out of the country?

I said that, as Prime Minister, I could not and would not function as a judicial or quasi-judicial official; I was a member of the executive branch. Judicial processes had taken their due course – and it was not for the executive to countermand them. As I spoke, I felt I could hear the voice of Ben-Gurion, in different but not altogether unsimilar circumstances. For he had fought – and sacrificed – for the principle of separation of powers, for the fundamental democratic tenet that government ministers cannot double as judges.†

As Hazak made his case, I recalled Shalom's telling me that his subordinates were conspiring against him. As I saw it, my first duty was to support the beleaguered head of a key national security agency and to stifle any insurrection in the ranks. I told Hazak that he had the option

---

* The Prime Minister is briefed once a week (at least) by the heads of the Mossad and the Shin Bet.
† See pages 94–7.

of making his accusations to Shalom's face, or of taking legal action. I, for my part, would not act against the head of the Shin Bet, in whom I retained complete confidence.

Hazak chose the second course. He and his two colleagues lodged an official complaint with the Attorney-General, Yitzhak Zamir. Zamir, a Hebrew University law professor who had held the important post of Attorney-General for more than seven years, plainly gave greater credence to Hazak and his colleagues than I had. He was prepared to initiate a criminal investigation against Shalom with a view to pressing charges. Shalom, backed by Yossi Ginossar, a senior Shin Bet official, indicated that if there were a trial he would not passively take the rap. He would hire lawyers, and they would tear open the veil of secrecy that protected the Shin Bet's operating procedures.

I saw this scenario as a grave threat to state security. I knew that a courtroom review of Shin Bet operations would not consist merely of an academic or historical survey, but that it would disclose current methods and would rob the Shin Bet, to a dangerous extent, of its effectiveness as the principal agency fighting Palestinian terrorism. In addition, Shalom claimed that he had acted with the authorization of Shamir. Therefore, I would have no option but to insist that Shamir be interrogated. This would automatically be seen as a political rather than a legal confrontation, and I would be accused of exploiting the legal powers of the Premiership for political ends.

That was never my intention. I regarded the matter as a judicial issue and I was determined to keep it clear of politics. Throughout the Shin Bet Affair, I avoided any accusations or insinuations against Shamir or any other Likud Minister. Our 'Prime Ministers' Forum', comprised of myself, Shamir and Rabin, held firm during this difficult time. We convened and consulted in the most dignified and efficient manner, took our decisions unanimously and defended them collectively.

In a series of discussions with Zamir, my basic position was that we, as Ministers, must have security considerations foremost in mind, while the Attorney-General, as the senior legal official in the government hierarchy, should represent the legal and judicial aspects of government decision-making. I acknowledged that, at the end of the day, the law must be paramount in a society governed by the rule of law. I made it clear to Zamir that he would have the last word. But I also tried to make him see my point of view. Shin Bet men, I argued, were to all intents and purposes frontline soldiers; they ought, therefore, to be judged by the criteria of military justice. Military justice takes account of battle conditions and operational considerations. The bus hijack was tantamount to a military operation. The fact that Shalom and his men did not wear military uniforms ought not to diminish their right to be treated as soldiers.

Zamir was unconvinced. Shalom felt that he was prejudiced against him. The two men had crossed swords frequently in the past in the course of their professional duties. There is almost a built-in conflict in their two roles: one represents the law, due process and the public's right to know; the other state security, secrecy and operational needs. Confrontations are inevitable across the grey areas that lie between them.

Zamir informed me that he would refuse to represent Shalom in the High Court of Justice, to which one of the three dismissed Shin Bet agents, Rafi Malka, had appealed for redress. Zamir also filed a formal complaint against Shalom with the Inspector-General of Police, requiring the police to launch a formal investigation. I decided to ask Ram Caspi, a longtime friend and leading Tel Aviv attorney, to act for Shalom and his colleagues. Caspi agreed to represent him on a voluntary basis.

I was widely accused, both at the time and later, of peremptorily firing Zamir and of appointing a new Attorney-General, so as to settle the Shin Bet Affair to my satisfaction. But the fact is that Zamir had told me long before that he wanted to resign. I actually urged him to stay on, despite our differences – indeed, because of them. I never doubted his integrity. I argued that since he decided to take legal action against Shalom, he should stay in his post to see it through. It would be awkward to change Attorneys-General midway through the judicial process, especially if the new Attorney-General's attitude to the case were different from Zamir's.

Zamir resigned in any event, and the Cabinet appointed a Tel Aviv district court judge, Yosef Harish, in his place. By this time, Shalom and his principal colleagues had agreed to resign too, as a way of ending the affair. The climax took place in my home at a meeting with Rabin and two other Ministers, at which Shalom broke down and wept. I knew, indeed we all knew, that under this man the Shin Bet had been a rarefied preserve of modesty, integrity and commitment. He himself had a record of outstanding courage and had done many selfless deeds for the country. It was a hard and unforgettable moment.

But the resignations were no longer sufficient: the police investigation had been set in motion and, according to Harish, could not now be stopped. Shalom and his men faced the prospect of criminal charges. At this point, Ram Caspi broached the idea of a collective pardon from the President of the State. I knew that this would mean further criticism and controversy, but I supported it fully, and almost the entire Cabinet concurred. That unprecedented step – altogether eleven Shin Bet men were pardoned by President Chaim Herzog – did, indeed, provoke a wave of blistering criticism, directed both at the Government and at the President.

Looking back, though, I do not regret my actions and decisions in this affair. Perhaps I did not have all the facts at my disposal, but as Prime Minister I could not have had them, because I was neither judge nor jury but the head of the executive branch of government. Perhaps my judgment of the persons involved was wrong, but I was certainly not wrong in refusing to set myself up as a judge. I believed then – and still believe now – that the principles applying to soldiers in battle should have applied to the Shin Bet men. They were entitled to be judged by the military code of justice, which takes greater account than civil courts of operational considerations.

One covert operation during my Premiership that gave us all enormous satisfaction was Operation Moses, the airlifting of thousands of Ethiopian Jews to Israel. This *aliya* began discreetly before the change of Government, but reached dramatic proportions in late 1984 and early 1985, when the American administration responded magnificently to my appeal to help us get the Jews out.

Ethiopia's Jews had lived in that land for thousands of years; their legends date back to the days of King Solomon and the Queen of Sheba. Indeed, the last negus or emperor, Haile Selassie, shared this tradition, styling himself 'Lion of Judah'. He was well disposed towards Israel, but the revolutionary Government that succeeded him in the mid-1970s, under Colonel Mengistu Haile Mariam, took a rigid and hostile Marxist stance. Many Ethiopian Jews felt threatened, and thousands of them began to flee, mostly on foot, to neighbouring Sudan. There, with the help of the Joint Distribution Committee, an old-established American Jewish aid agency, they lived in ramshackle camps, waiting for salvation.

With the utmost discretion, we began to ferry out small groups of these refugees aboard our own planes and boats. But by late 1984, our logistic capacities had become inadequate for the size and urgency of the task, and I approached the then Vice President, George Bush, with a direct appeal for help. The response of the Reagan–Bush administration was to send in a squadron of giant USAF transport planes. These landed on a makeshift strip not far from the refugee camps. An Israeli organization transported the refugees from the camps to the planes, which flew them straight to an air-force base in southern Israel.

I will never forget the night they arrived. I stood there with other officials, speechless with emotion, as the doors of these huge planes opened and the elders of the community, gaunt but stately in their robes, came down the steps and kneeled to kiss the soil of the Holy Land. After them came mothers with wide-eyed, handsome children, and then the rest of the families. Six planes landed, one after the other, and soon the terminal was full of these new arrivals. Yet not a sound of distress or complaint was to be heard. All of them, old and young alike, maintained this dignified, emotion-laden silence. Israeli stewardesses gave out candies to the children, but even these were received with grave dignity.

The American air-force pilots seemed as moved as we were as they shook hands with the elders and prepared to leave. I felt as though history had awarded me a precious ringside seat at a unique presentation. I tried to convey to George Bush and the administration the depth of my gratitude.

Over the years, I have been able to watch ten Presidents of the United States in action, some of them from close up and in circumstances of frank friendship and even intimacy.

President Truman, of course, I observed only from afar. As a young diplomat I was deeply impressed by his consistent and uncompromising insistence on being just exactly who he was, Harry S. Truman, no more and no less. He put real meaning into the famous principle of 'government of the people, by the people, for the people'.

I had the opportunity to meet Eisenhower personally, and experienced the feeling shared by so many others when he turned his smiling blue eyes on me: that he really had nothing more important on his mind at that moment than talking to me. Ben-Gurion retained an abiding respect for Eisenhower, even after relations between them soured during the Suez crisis in 1956–7. Ben-Gurion had formed his opinion of Ike when, as Allied commander, Ike escorted him through the displaced-persons camps after the Second World War. He never forgot Eisenhower's overflowing sympathy for the survivors of the Holocaust.

John Kennedy summoned me to the Oval Office, quite unexpectedly, during a visit to Washington in 1963 as Deputy Defence Minister. He was sitting in his famous rocking-chair, and I remember my initial reaction being one of surprise at the relatively large proportion of grey in his hair. During a half-hour conversation, he fired some thirty questions at me. He had no need of briefing cards; he knew it all. He knew that the head of the Mossad had quit, and why; he knew we had bought torpedo boats, and from whom. Suddenly, amid the stream of questions, he threw in, matter-of-factly: 'Are you building a nuclear option?'

I had to think fast. My spontaneous reply was, 'We will not be the first ones to introduce nuclear weapons into the Middle East.' With time, that formula became Israel's policy-position on this sensitive issue.

I tried to steer the conversation with Kennedy towards Hawk anti-aircraft missiles. These were obviously defensive weapons, which Israel badly wanted to buy from the United States; nothing like them was available from any other source. The President sent me to his brother, Bobby, the Attorney-General. 'Take your jacket off, roll up your sleeves and let's talk,' Bobby said as I walked in. He was also in shirt sleeves. I went over the Hawks issue, and he asked why I didn't submit a direct request to the Pentagon. I replied that the River Potomac separated the White House from the Pentagon, to which his rejoinder was, 'You're a young man, swim across.'

As I had entered the Oval Office for my meeting with the President, I met an old friend who was just leaving – Harold Wilson, the British Labour Party leader, then in opposition to Harold Macmillan's Government. 'Shimon,' Wilson said, 'I told you the whole thing would blow up in their faces!' The President, who had walked him to the door, immediately asked, 'What whole thing?' This was obviously what Wilson had wanted, for he immediately launched into a long and salacious account of the Profumo Affair, which was then building to a crescendo that would eventually bring down the Tory Government. Kennedy listened with rapt attention to Wilson's detailed review of the War Minister's dalliance with Christine Keeler, a sarcastic smile on his lips. He looked so youthful and mischievous at that moment. I remember thinking to myself that if America's strategy were to conquer all the women of the world, it could not have chosen a better general than Kennedy.

Ben-Gurion once told me of a meeting he had had with Kennedy in November 1960, after his election and before his inauguration as President. They met in the Waldorf Astoria in New York. As Kennedy escorted Ben-Gurion to the elevator, he said quietly, 'I was elected President of the United States with the help of your people. What can I do in return?' Ben-Gurion did not like this question at all. He replied concisely, 'Try to be a great President of the United States.'

Lyndon Johnson received Prime Minister and Defence Minister Levi Eshkol at the White House in May 1964, with me in attendance as Deputy Defence Minister. My first impression was the sheer size of him; Johnson was a mountain of a man. The furniture in the Oval Office seemed to have shrunk. He sat with a little table beside him, which had two necessary aids on it: a glass of milk and the Red Telephone. Eshkol, Ambassador Avraham Harman and I sat down on a couch opposite the President, and Johnson proceeded to read out a very warm and supportive statement. The United States, he assured us, stood 'four square behind Israel'. Eshkol winked at me and whispered, 'You hear, young man, four squares. Not three squares, but four.' As soon as he finished reading, he put aside the paper and his expression lost its stiff formality. He began questioning Eshkol about his background as a kibbutz farmer in the Galilee and very soon the conversation flowed in relaxed conviviality.

In the evening, the President and Mrs Johnson hosted an official dinner for their Israeli guests. I sat next to Lady Bird, whom I had met in Senegal. Soon the band struck up a waltz, and Johnson scooped up Miriam Eshkol and was off, whirling her round the floor. Ambassador Harman, an anxious look on his face, nudged Eshkol and whispered that he was now expected to dance with Lady Bird. But the Prime Minister was unfazed. '*Ich tanz nisht*,' he proclaimed; and then, pointing at me, he said, 'Young man, you dance.' In the interests of US–Israeli relations, I did the best I could. Johnson danced the whole evening, obviously enjoying himself, as though he had not a care in the world. He reminded us of his home state, Texas – vast and full of *joie de vivre*. In the years to come, he built up a genuinely friendly rapport with Eshkol, and, priding himself on being a political disciple of Truman, displayed a consistently favourable attitude towards Israel.

It is hardly possible to describe a modern President's foreign policy without taking into account his Secretary of State. Eisenhower and Dulles, Carter and Vance, Bush and Shultz – all these were examples of Presidents and Secretaries who worked closely together. In no case in recent American history was this truer than in that of Richard Nixon and Henry Kissinger. Nor was there ever a more unlikely team, the one a scion of small-town America, the other a European Jewish refugee: Nixon with his razor-sharp political instincts, constantly on the defensive against his myriad foes, real or imaginary; and Kissinger with his brilliant abilities, bursting through all the barriers of American prejudices. Neither man was short on ego. Yet they found their common ground, and co-operated to produce a period of creativity and dynamism in American foreign policy that remains breathtaking in its breadth and drama to the present day.

I met Nixon a number of times and was able to observe him closely when he visited Israel in June 1974, in the dying months of his Presidency. His outward appearance and bearing were never particularly attractive, and there was something harsh and forbidding in his way of talking. As the President addressed us at a working session – this was early in the 1974–7 Labour-led Government – Kissinger's body language hardly intimated admiration or even respect for his boss. The Secretary of State ostentatiously chewed a pencil, the purpose of which, it seemed, was to stifle his yawns. But in the evening, in his speech at a state dinner in his honour, a different and brilliantly impressive Nixon emerged. The dinner was held in the 'Chagall Hall' of the Knesset building in Jerusalem. The beleaguered leader of the Western world stood facing the leaders of Israel's political, intellectual, legal and business communities, with the artist's breathtaking tapestries behind him depicting the high points of Jewish history. He spoke without a note, and his words were full of wisdom and sensitivity. Many people present in that hall must have been thinking, as I was, that any man who makes it to the Presidency of the United States must have great reserves of strength and ability, which in some cases become evident only in response to great distress and adversity. It was little wonder, in my view, that Richard Nixon underwent a remarkable political renaissance after his resignation, becoming, despite his critics, a widely respected elder statesman.

While in office, he was overshadowed in statesmanship, to a great extent, by the flamboyant Kissinger. But that, too, is a mark of Nixon's calibre: there were few, if any, Presidents who would have appointed a man like Kissinger as NSC Adviser and Secretary of State knowing full well, as Nixon must have known, that the appointee would vie with his boss both in making the policy and in taking the kudos for it. In that respect, Nixon's successor, Gerald Ford, deserves the same credit for keeping Kissinger as his Secretary of State when he took over in 1974.

President Jimmy Carter always impressed me with the wealth and detail of his knowledge of whatever issue was on the agenda. One of his Cabinet Ministers once described him privately to me as 'more of a preacher than a strategist', but I found his strategic awareness no less honed than his moralism. Moreover, looking back on his contribution to international affairs with the perspective of time, I am tempted to suggest that 'preaching' can itself be a legitimate and effective strategy. I have no doubt that Carter's decision to place human rights at the very top of his foreign-policy agenda had the effect of exposing one of the gravest flaws of communism for all the world to see. The USSR was unable to defend itself in the face of Carter's human rights' demands, which gathered strength through the Helsinki conference.

I first made his acquaintance when he was still Governor of Georgia. Our Consul-General in Atlanta, Moshe Gilboa, insisted that I meet this capable young politician, who, in Gilboa's view, would be the next President of the United States. I was in Atlanta only on a Sunday, but the Governor and his wife, Rosalyn, made time for me on their day of rest, receiving me cordially in their official residence. Carter urged me to visit the local factory which produced the C-130 Hercules military transport plane that Israel was buying from the US. When I presented him with a copy of my book, *David's Sling*, which traces the growth of the IDF and of Israel's defence industries, Carter observed that nowadays Israel didn't need a sling but a plane: 'against the Arab Goliath, you need the American Hercules'.

Fortune did not smile on Jimmy Carter's Presidency,★ but from Israel's viewpoint it was the greatest good fortune that he served as President. Had it not been for him, in my opinion, there would not have been a Camp David agreement or the subsequent peace treaty with Egypt. He threw himself into the negotiations, enticing the parties to Camp David, locking them in there and isolating them from the outside world until they reached an accord. He gave each of the leaders his unlimited time and personal attention; he was directly involved in compiling draft after draft of the disputed clauses, in the indefatigable search for solutions.

I have described in the previous chapter one facet of my relationship, as Prime Minister, with President Ronald Reagan and his administration. Overall, that relationship was grounded in Reagan's extremely positive

★ See pages 243–40.

attitude towards Israel. In his pre-political days in the film world, he had made long-lasting friendships with a number of Jewish movie-men. The Jewish state, as he saw it, had a place of honour among the 'good guys' – because it was democratic, it fought to defend itself, it won, and it did not require American mothers to send their sons to fight for it.

Briefed frequently and enthusiastically by Secretary of State George Shultz, Reagan was aware and supportive of my efforts to curb inflation and introduce economic reforms, of my policy to bring the army out of Lebanon, of my attempts to resolve the Taba dispute with Egypt* and of my persistent efforts to move ahead in peace negotiations with Jordan.†

Another member of the Reagan administration with whom I formed a personal friendship was Vice-President George Bush. During a three-day visit to Israel in July 1986, I took him to see Ben-Gurion's kibbutz, Sde Boker, and the hut where Ben-Gurion and Paula had lived. It is now a national memorial. Before going in, Bush and his wife, Barbara, sat on the grass and chatted with the kibbutz children. Inside, surveying Ben-Gurion's simple possessions – a Bible open on his desk, a sculpture of Socrates, another of Gandhi, a picture of Berl Katznelson, and rows of books on world history and Jewish history crowding the plain wooden shelves – Bush asked me to describe the real Ben-Gurion. My reply took almost two hours. Bush sat riveted, stopping me only to ask incisive and thoughtful questions. Later, he described that conversation as a high-point of his visit – a meeting with the essential personality of Ben-Gurion as portrayed by a close eye-witness.

As Vice-President, and later as President, Bush was very much an internationalist. The range and variety of his previous posts in government gave him a remarkably broad knowledge of world politics as well as a deep understanding of many key areas and issues.

In my opinion, George Bush was a true friend of Israel. He stood up to Yitzhak Shamir's stonewalling with an enormous amount of patience. Despite the impression in Washington that whenever Bush's Secretary of State, James Baker, came to our region Shamir's Government would present him with another new Jewish settlement in the West Bank, neither Bush nor Baker allowed their anger and frustration to show through.

* See pages 302–3.
† However, Shultz's failure to follow through on the London agreement with King Hussein of Jordan, in April 1987, was a missed opportunity that was to prove irretrievable (see chapter 24).

In the end, their patience paid off. Baker and Bush succeeded in organizing the famous Madrid conference in November 1991, with Shamir present for Israel and the Palestinians represented by Dr Haider abdel Shafi of Gaza, a founding-member of the PLO. In agreeing to go to Madrid, Shamir violated all the principles that he had ostensibly been fighting for. He attended an international conference, though for years he had rejected that framework; he sat opposite Palestinian delegates, who were, to all intents and purposes, representatives of the PLO, though he had always refused to recognize the PLO; he succumbed to an American-orchestrated peace process, which he had always tried to avoid.

As for me, whenever I passed through Washington during this period (I was Minister of Finance from 1988 to 1990 in the Government of National Unity led by Shamir, and leader of the opposition from 1990 to 1992), President Bush would invite me to the White House. General Brent Scowcroft, Bush's wise and intimate adviser, would meet me separately and informally for further, longer chats. With both men, the conversations were open and friendly. I never withheld my opinions, but I never directly attacked Shamir.

Bush's crowning achievement in international affairs was Operation Desert Storm in 1991. This impressive use of military power against Saddam Hussein's Iraq established a number of important precedents: it was the first ever Moslem–Christian (or Arab–Western) alliance against a Moslem Arab enemy; it was the first military campaign of such size and complexity that set out clearly defined goals and timetables – and achieved them; and it was the first time in history that America's allies were required to share the vast financial cost of such an operation. Saddam Hussein was severely mauled as a result of his aggression against Kuwait, and the entire Middle East was saved from the machinations of one of its most dangerous lunatics, who was close to building a nuclear capacity.

In his lunacy, he hurled ballistic missiles at Israel, which took no part in the campaign, and against Saudi Arabia. Israel bit back its anger and stayed out, responding to President Bush's request not to upset the delicate balance of the anti-Iraq coalition. Although Saddam Hussein was not overthrown, his regime's aggressive strength was smashed and has, in effect, collapsed.

20 NEW SOCIETY

The Likud election victory in 1977 marked the end of forty-four years of Labour hegemony, beginning in the pre-state years and continuing after Israel's independence. That length of time is itself impressive, but more impressive by far was the record of achievements that Labour could rightfully point to. To gather in a people that had long been spread throughout the world, to revitalize a long-barren homeland, and to revive a long-dormant language – these were three historic undertakings that no other nation had ever attempted. In addition, under Labour's leadership, Israel successfully moulded new forms of social and economic co-operation: the kibbutzim and moshavim, and the Histadrut. The last of these was much more than just a trades-union organization. In fact, it was a blueprint for the state-in-the-making. Moreover, this list of achievements was built up under the constant pressure of actual or imminent war.

The Zionist movement was so entirely preoccupied with the question of how to restore the Jewish People to a condition of political and national normalcy that it almost ignored the significance of its historic encounter with Arab life and Arab national aspirations in the Middle East. We 'normalized' our nation, but we created a state that has had to exist in essentially abnormal conditions.

Throughout history, individuals and movements have often launched out on a particular path only to find themselves diverted, by obstacles and unexpected developments, on to a very different course. The Zionist movement set out to restore the Jewish People to its land, but the clash with the Arabs, a factor which had not been taken into account in the Zionist blueprint, placed defence and security issues at the centre of national concern. There was no escaping the mortal dangers that arose.

They had to be faced head on. In fact, the war broke out even before the state was declared. Had we lost the war, we would have lost the state. But we won the war and saved the state, only to find that the danger of war continued to overshadow our national existence.

The fact that the army – the IDF – continued to occupy the centre of our national life had far-reaching consequences, some positive, others problematic. The people loved the IDF. The IDF gave them a sense of unity, of security and of pride. It had a biblical aura about it: the few against the many, like David against Goliath. Its victories brought a sense of glory to the fledgling state. The War of Independence in 1948 was a veritable miracle, given the relative strengths of the two sides. The Sinai Campaign in 1956 was literally one of the most brilliant military operations in history. In 100 hours, the IDF swept across the whole of the Sinai and destroyed the Egyptian army. The 1967 Six Day War was an even more breathtaking victory.

Indeed, to the present day it is difficult to understand what happened to us in 1973, when the Egyptians and the Syrians launched their attack on Yom Kippur. How could our people have failed to read the writing on the wall, which was so clear and bold?

Many political observers believe that Yom Kippur 1973 was, in effect, the beginning of the end of Labour hegemony, and that our election defeat of May 1977 can be traced directly to the military catastrophe four years earlier. Personally, I am not sure that this is the reason, or at least not the whole reason. As in science, the 'Chaos Principle' must be taken into account in any analysis of political cause and effect. The flutter of butterflies' wings in China can bring about a tornado in California, as they say. In my opinion, there was an accumulation of events and processes that together brought about Labour's downfall. In general, movements of social reform reach peaks – and then slowly sink into sloth and fatigue. Power provides comfort and security, but it also steadily erodes and corrupts. People in power begin to enjoy the trappings and benefits of power, often falling into self-pity and self-justification. They harp on how hard they work and on how heavy a responsibility they must shoulder. They become insensitive to one of the infallible principles of politics in a democracy: the more one enjoys wielding power, the likelier one is to lose it.

Moreover, the public – the electorate – eventually grows tired of the same public faces, the same voices. Party machines and party hierarchies, created originally to serve the noblest goals, become bloated and parasitical in the eyes of the people. This happened to the Histadrut, to the Jewish Agency and, eventually, to the Government itself.

The kibbutzim and moshavim, central pillars of the labour movement, succumbed to the same fate. The fire that burned in the bones of the founding fathers abated with time. Even these great social experiments began to pall, radiating elitism, selfishness and apathy, rather than concern for and involvement in the problems of society.

The corruption in high places exposed during the Labour Government of 1974–7* greatly eroded our movement's standing in the public mind. In the election campaign of 1977, I heard the unmistakable thunder that heralds an impending storm. At our mass rallies, we were howled down with cries of 'Thieves, give back the money you've stolen!'

However, beneath these cries, and beneath the complex political developments, there was also a profound social upheaval taking place, which we failed adequately to discern or understand. Cracks were widening along the ethnic fault-lines formed by the various waves of immigration. A rupture was evolving in communication between the scions of the original, pioneering *aliyot*, which were largely Ashkenazi,† and the quasi-Messianic North African *aliya* of the 1950s and early 1960s. The Sephardi Jews of Morocco, Algeria and Tunisia came to Israel to find the Messiah. What they found instead were bureaucrats, who totally failed to understand them. This communication gap, instead of narrowing, grew wider as time went on until a great wave of protest welled up, sweeping along hundreds of thousands of disgruntled people.

Rarely has there been so sad a love story as that between the State of Israel and these North African Jews. For me, as for many of us, the North African *aliya* was both a great dream and a great hope. We knew that these Jewish communities were very different from those we ourselves hailed from in Eastern Europe. On the one hand, they were more traditional in matters of religion and custom; on the other, they were less riven by disputes, ideological and political, than Ashkenazi Jews. They managed, somehow, to let religious Orthodoxy and secularism coexist peacefully. The secularists wore *yarmulkas* (skull caps) without self-consciousness, when the occasion required, and the Ortho-

---

* See pages 172–3.

† Ashkenazi, lit. German, denotes Western Jewry, while Sephardi, lit. Spanish, is used to describe the Oriental Jewish communities of North Africa and the Middle East.

dox played a full role in commercial and communal life, and did not isolate themselves from the rest of the community. This atmosphere of tolerance probably owed a great deal to the French influence that pervaded their society. Many spoke French as a second language.

The strong underpinning of these communities was the family unit, in which loyalty and solidarity flowed in both directions: from children to parents no less than from parents to children.

Their *aliya* to Israel was regarded by many of us young Israelis as nothing short of miraculous. Here were Jewish communities that had lived relatively stable and untroubled lives for generations, preserving their cultural and religious character, producing their great rabbis, scholars, poets and grammarians. And suddenly, as though summoned by the clarion call of an unseen Messiah, they rose up as one man and turned their backs on their comfortable diaspora, preferring the hardships of the Holy Land. At any rate, that was how we imagined them, for we had no real knowledge or understanding of them. To the extent to which we did attempt to understand them, we naturally assumed that the political and social influences that had moulded our own outlook had shaped them, too: Zionism, socialism, pioneering values and so forth.

They were to find an Israel far different from their expectations. They assumed that they were going to a holy land, in the literal sense of the term. Instead, they encountered a largely secular society (in some sectors aggressively secular). While European Jews had made *aliya* out of distress – economic, social or political – North African Jews came in response to a Messianic call.

I remember accompanying Ben-Gurion on a visit to Ashdod, one of the first immigrant villages, which today is a bustling port city, but was then a forlorn coastal encampment. There was sand everywhere, and a handful of tiny huts under the sweltering sun. The newcomers could hardly make themselves understood with their few words of rudimentary Hebrew. They cried bitter tears, no longer certain why they had come. We cried, too, inwardly, assailed by doubts as to the wisdom of having brought them. Ben-Gurion had captivated them and held, in their eyes, the stature of a new Messiah. They were inordinately proud of him. But pride aside, both they and we had begun wondering whether the process of their absorption into Israel could be successfully undertaken and completed.

Not all North African Jews ended up in Israel. As Levi Eshkol remarked with his humour, 'They all heard the *shofar*,* but some stopped off in Paris and decided to await the Messiah there.' Among those who did remain in Paris, New York or Montreal were many of the wealthier, better educated members of their communities.

Those who chose Israel settled in places like Ashdod, Migdal Haemek, Kiryat Shmona, Dimona and the Lachish farm belt around Ashkelon. Many arrived and stayed in these places without any real preparation for their new life – whether it was agricultural or urban. Few really seemed to know where they were and what was in store for them. Nor did the more 'veteran' Israelis know – or in many cases care – about the pace or the pain of the process of absorption. Indeed, as had happened before – and was to happen again – the old-timers quickly developed an attitude of mocking, contemptuous disdain towards the newcomers. In fact, and despite all our grand talk about absorption, each wave of immigrants has had to take care of its own absorption, especially socially and culturally.

I remember as a youngster, still relatively new to Israel, adopting the arrogant, scornful attitude then prevalent towards the immigrant refugees from Germany, the *Yekkes*. Many of them were academics or professionals, but they had to take whatever work they could find. Straitlaced, distinguished-looking *Yekkes* with funny white hats would sell sausages in Mograbi Square, then the centre of downtown Tel Aviv.

At Ben-Shemen, I now recall with shame, we positively persecuted our *Yekke* room-mate. We mocked him for his knickerbocker trousers and his clipped, quaint pronunciation. We teased him about his fastidiousness and perfect punctuality. We made him wash the road with soap and water and brush the cows' teeth with toothpaste.

Yet now I recognize, as many of us do, that without the salutary influence of the *Yekke aliya*, our society would have been much the poorer. Without that *aliya*, I doubt if the Israel Philharmonic would ever have been founded or the Hebrew University of Jerusalem have become an eminent seat of learning. And without them, no Israeli would ever get anywhere on time.

The same cruel scorn was heaped upon the Yemenites – another wave of immigrants who were to make a significant contribution to Israeli society. They tended to group together in specific neighbourhoods and villages – the *Kerem Hateymanim*, or Yemenite Vineyard, in Tel Aviv, or certain districts of Rishon Lezion, Petah Tikva and Rehovot. They too

---

* The ram's horn, by tradition the harbinger of the Messiah.

found it hard, at first, to get jobs requiring the skills they had brought with them. Many had to work as porters. We youngsters mocked their curly *peyot*, or sidelocks. We imitated their strongly guttural pronunciation and tried to force them to speak Yiddish. Yet without the Yemenites' input into its evolving culture, Israel would have lacked a musical rhythm of its own. Their ancient songs and hymns have played a formative role in the ongoing development of 'Israeli music', just as the rich Yemenite liturgy and poetic heritage have been an important influence on the development of modern Hebrew. The Yemenite immigrants, more so perhaps than any other group, related to Hebrew not merely as a language, but also as an authentic echo of the voice of the Bible itself.

When the North African immigration began, in the early 1950s, all the old mistakes were repeated. The same patronizing arrogance, the same insulting sobriquets. Looking back, I would say that this initial encounter, planned in ignorance and insensitivity, and managed in incompetence, left a lasting scar on the collective psyche of the Moroccan community in Israel. The resentment and the desire to cry out in protest can probably be traced back to those early years.

However, the resentment was not entirely justified. The North Africans complain to the present day, for instance, of their parents' and grandparents' trauma at being sprayed on arrival with DDT. But this – a carry-over from British Mandate practices – was done to all immigrants no matter where they came from. They were angered by being forced to live in tents at first; but at that time virtually every Israeli had had to live in a tent at some point in his or her life, just as every Israeli, regardless of his qualifications or expertise, had spent at least some time doing physical labour. There was no discrimination here. But to many North African newcomers, the requirement that they work in farms and factories appeared to be a deliberate attempt to humiliate them.

By the time the North African immigrants began arriving in large numbers, most senior positions in the various key institutions – the civil service, the army, the local authorities – were filled, and no one was offering to step aside. Nor were the bureaucrats bending over backwards to help these immigrants. To the newcomers, it seemed – not entirely without justice – that if your name was Rabinovitch you would receive faster, more efficient and more courteous service in most government departments than if it was Buzaglo. If you spoke Hebrew with an

Ashkenazi accent rather than a North African lilt, the face of officialdom was more likely to smile upon you.

Among the Moroccans, there were many large families who needed the aid of the welfare agencies to get by. Many brought sicknesses and other infirmities with them from their home countries. Many were the times when political figures, myself included, would be confronted, while appearing on public platforms, by immigrant families with sick and elderly in tow, demanding instant solutions to their particular problem.

I believe that I was among the first to understand the evolving tragedy. I invested a large part of my political energies in the North African community. I set up groups and social clubs designed to draw them into public life. I found work for many qualified or promising immigrants in the Defence Ministry. I established particularly close relationships with a number of mayors of development towns, who in turn always looked to me as their political ally. In 1959, when I was appointed Deputy Minister of Defence, the workers of Ashdod threw a party for me. Their leader, Yehoshua Peretz, a colourful figure who was later to rise to national prominence as an outspoken labour union leader, declared that 'If your name wasn't Peretz [a common Moroccan name], you'd be Minister of Defence already!'

But I was not the only politician to discern the signs of deep social unrest and upheaval: Menachem Begin discerned them too. Begin gave voice to the suspicion among the North Africans that their problems, both objective and subjective, had not grown out of an unfortunate or mismanaged social situation, but rather out of deliberate discrimination. No amount of explaining seemed to help counter this hardening resentment, which Begin cynically reinforced and exploited.

The truth was that Ben-Gurion had devoted his life not just to the 'ingathering of the exiles' in the Jewish sovereign state, but also to what he called the 'melding of the exiles' – in other words, the full integration of the different immigrant communities into the evolving new society. He reacted to the attacks on him in this context with utter disbelief – as though he were being charged with a completely false accusation. Sometimes it is harder for a politician to defend himself convincingly against a false accusation than against one with some truth to it.

Begin, a gifted speaker (some would call him a demagogic speaker), rode the wave of protest to his rhetorical and political advantage. It is so much easier, after all, to articulate pain and anger than to give voice to feelings of well-being and contentment. Begin became the voice of the disaffected sectors of Israel's (Jewish) society. He played the role brilliantly.

Begin would criss-cross the land, especially during election time, punching home his points in simple – and tendentious – slogans. He would declare, for instance, that the United States was giving Israel $3 billion a year, which came approximately to $1,000 per man, woman and child. 'Well, have you received your money yet?' he would ask rhetorically. In the 1981 campaign, he seized on a thoughtless phrase thrown out by a television comedian at a Labour Party rally* and used it to turn ethnic tensions into a key issue in the election. He excited his crowds with bombastic tales of Israel's military prowess and potential – and then stirred their wrath by harping on and exaggerating problems of ethnic discrimination. Some people actually believed that Begin himself had been born in Morocco. The 1981 election campaign was the ugliest and most violent ever fought in Israel. I was the target of slurs and insults – and rotten fruit at many public rallies.

Begin's rhetorical power lay not in his origins, but rather in his intended goal, which was the complete discrediting of the labour movement and everything it stood for. Kibbutzniks, for instance, were depicted, in his speeches, as millionaires who spent all their time lolling beside their swimming-pools. He cleverly took advantage of the strains that existed within the Labour leadership. In the 1981 election campaign, he made frequent use of Rabin's book, and in particular of its references to me. In 1977, he exploited the weaknesses and corruptions that had been exposed during the 1974–7 government, and played upon the disappointment that was widely felt.

However, a number of North African immigrants did rise to prominence in the 1960s, but their difficulties with absorption into Israeli society did not always match their eminence. One such figure was Professor André Chouraqui, a towering intellectual who won respect and acclaim, both in Europe and in his native Morocco, for his many books and learned articles. He translated several sections of the Bible into majestic French prose. A sincere effort was made to find a suitable role for Chouraqui in Israeli public life. He was elected Deputy Mayor of Jerusalem and seemed to be launched on a promising public career, but that promise was never realized.

* Comedian Dudu Topaz commented that there were 'no *chachachim* here'; the word is low slang denoting North African immigrants.

Chouraqui's inability fully to express his great talents in the public arena was probably due to a certain underlying contradiction between the intellectual in him and the politician he was expected to become. At the end of the day, the pull of his study, in the beautiful home he built on the border between East and West Jerusalem, triumphed over the hurly-burly of city politics. Unwittingly, I had helped advise him on the plot of land which he bought to build his home on. 'Don't you think it's dangerous?' he asked me. This was in the early 1960s. I answered, almost instinctively, that I was sure Jerusalem would be reunified and that his home would then be in the very centre of the city – as, indeed, it was within a few years.

Another notable Sephardi figure in Israeli public life has been Aharon Uzan, a practical-minded Tunisian immigrant who made his career in the moshav movement. He became Minister of Agriculture in the 1974 Labour Government. Matilda Ghez, also from Tunisia, was a woman whose great-heartedness made her an object of love and respect in our party and beyond. She was the embodiment of that rare quality we call 'nobility of spirit'. Back in Tunisia, she had been the leader of WIZO, the women's Zionist organization, and she quickly found her place in public life in Israel too. She was a devoted admirer of Ben-Gurion and transferred her loyalty to me after he died. For years, she endured the suffering of members of her family, and later she too wrestled with pain and illness. But anyone meeting her would assume that she lived a life of perfect bliss, so great was the inner peace she radiated. She never gave any sign of the crushing sorrows that weighed upon her, but rather spread love and hope over all around her. She became one of the most popular women in Israel.

But all in all, only a tiny handful of first-generation North African immigrants rose quickly to national recognition. As time passed, though, young leaders began to make their mark on Israeli politics on the local level, particularly in development towns. They were authentic representatives of the second generation – less religious than the original immigrants, but still deeply traditional, proud of the heritage their community had brought with it. Many second-generation North Africans go to soccer on Saturday afternoon, which is not strictly permitted by the religious law; but they will have attended synagogue in the morning, with their parents and their children, thus upholding tradition while accommodating their habits to modern life.

One often hears about the salient success stories among North African

Jews who immigrated to France – in academic life, in the arts and in commerce. People sometimes compare these careers and those of the mayors of Israeli development towns. I personally believe that these mayors are not one whit inferior to their French counterparts. For the life of a mayor in a small or middle-sized Israeli town is certainly harder than that of a university dean in Paris. The Jewish People has produced its fair share of professors over the years, but it still has a dearth of good mayors and builders of towns. In Israel today, a cadre of town-builders – many of them of North African stock – is growing to maturity. Their towns are growing, too; from Kiryat Shmona in the north to Dimona in the south, they form the backbone of the country.

My own political career has been influenced repeatedly by my sympathy for, and identification with, the North African immigrant – and their tendency to support the Likud Party. As I have mentioned, that tendency was an important factor in the outcome of the 1977 election.

I took over the party leadership in 1977 in a difficult, if not desperate, situation. We were headed for our first electoral defeat ever. I had obviously not sought or expected to find myself in this position in such circumstances. But true to the rabbinic adage, 'Where there are no men, you try to be a man', I plunged into the fray, tackling first the election campaign itself, and then the heartbreaking, thankless task of recon-struction. Having read the histories of Nazism, Bolshevism and fascism, I realized that such movements never win power on their own strength, but rather that they depend upon the weakness and deterioration of liberal and socialist forces in society. I view Mussolini, for instance, more as the product of the failure of socialism in his country than the reflection of any inherent strength in Italian fascism.

In looking at our own case, *mutatis mutandis*, I came to see that we were in a fight for the life of our movement. The dangers were enormous, and our party's resources – both pecuniary and political – were veritably empty. A great pall of silence hung over Labour headquarters in Tel Aviv. After all, who wants to dance with a corpse? In the eyes of many political observers, that is how we were regarded: the remnants of an epoch that was now over.

Very few party members were ready to throw themselves whole-heartedly into the unspectacular task of rebuilding the movement. An exception to this was Haim Bar-Lev, the one-time IDF Chief of Staff (1968–72), who had served as a Minister under Golda and Rabin. He became Labour Secretary-General. Yossi Beilin, a young political reporter for the Histadrut newspaper *Davar*, agreed, not without hesitation, to become party spokesman.

Of course, the old guard leaders were still very much around: Golda; her *éminence grise* Yisrael Galili; Yitzhak Ben-Aharon, the fiery former Histadrut leader; Haim Zadok, the former Minister of Justice; as well as Moshe Baram, Haim Gvati and Yehoshua Rabinowitz, three other Labour veterans who had served as Ministers in the now much-mourned Labour Government. Not all of them were my most ardent admirers; in fact, some of them heartily disliked me. But I was the man who had taken the burden of the reconstruction of the Labour Party on my shoulders, and they all had to concede that and behave accordingly. Perhaps, as some have said, this was indeed my 'finest hour'. I was always conscious of the danger of sinking in the sea of difficulties that threatened to engulf us. But I kept swimming – sometimes butterfly, sometimes the crawl – and kept my head above the waves. I enjoyed loyal support – which I want to put on the record here – from the veteran leadership of Mapam, our sister party, then allied with us in a unified bloc called The Labour Alignment. Meir Yaari, Yaacov Hazan, Meir Talmi, Victor Shemtov and Haika Grossman – the Mapam old guard – were less spoilt than the Labourites, perhaps because they had learned to live with the pain of opposition life in the past. They were more generous towards me than some of the senior figures of my own party.

We had thirty-two seats in the Knesset. (We had won thirty-three, but Moshe Dayan left the party when he became Foreign Minister under Begin.) With these, we tried to organize an effective opposition. In all honesty, though, I cannot deny that we suffered almost physical pangs of jealousy at the sight of Begin's early successes. Why, we asked ourselves, did Sadat have to come to Jerusalem just *now*? I frankly admired Begin's 'Project Renewal' scheme, whereby, with the help of overseas Jewish philanthropy, the Government set about providing much-needed face-lifts for inner-city slum districts and provincial development towns.

Above all, we watched with sadness tinged with jealousy and bitterness as the newly founded Democratic Movement for Change, with its fifteen Knesset seats, joined with Begin and the religious parties in a new coalition. This party, led by Yigael Yadin, ought 'rightfully' to have been solidly allied with us: they had taken our voters, and they advocated, on most key issues, policies similar to our own. Why did men like Yadin, Meir Amit and Aharon Yariv (both former heads of military intelligence), and Amnon Rubinstein (a prominent constitutional lawyer, later a leader of the left–liberal Meretz Bloc), make common cause with the Likud? It was as unintelligible as it was unforgivable. But the fact was that they had, and there is no point in arguing with facts. The Democratic Movement for Change's men themselves argued that they had gone into politics in order to bring about a change of government, which they saw as the prelude to sweeping reforms of the political system and the bureaucracy. They wanted constituency elections instead of the nation-wide proportional system. Yadin was appointed Deputy Prime Minister in charge of domestic affairs, with an ostensibly broad mandate encompassing several key ministries. In the event, the Democratic Movement for Change's platform remained largely unrealized and the various disparate groups that comprised the new party soon began to drift apart.

The problem of the original, massive misunderstanding between the old-timers and the new immigrants from North Africa has hung like a dark shadow over Israeli society. It is impossible truly to understand Israeli politics without comprehending this key factor. Culturally, there was incompatibility – and a failure to seek harmony and coexistence. Economically, there was inequality – an inequality caused chiefly by the time gap between the immigration and absorption of most Ashkenazi Israelis and the arrival of the North Africans.

Indeed, I sometimes feel that the important divisions that cut through Israel are not those between left and right, but rather those demarcating the various layers of immigration. Immigration is the single most potent political factor influencing Israeli society and shaping its democratic institutions. It may now be that the flame of North African protest is finally fading, as the resentments and protests of the new wave of immigration – from the former Soviet Union – grow in intensity. The change of government brought about by the 1992 election, which returned Labour to power after years of Likud dominance, was due, in no small degree, to this new and significant phenomenon.

21 RABBIS' WRATH

The sense of discrimination and the spirit of protest among North African immigrants led to the creation of separate 'ethnic' political parties. The size of the North African community – the largest immigration until the Soviet migration in the late 1980s – made the promise of success realistic and attractive.

Tami, a breakaway from the National Religious Party, was founded by Aharon Abuhatseira in 1981. The Abuhatseira family, headed by notable rabbis, has for generations been held in reverence by Moroccan Jews. The tomb of Rabbi Yaacov Abuhatseira (d. 1880), in Egypt, is still a favourite pilgrimage site today. Rabbi Yisrael Abuhatseira, popularly called 'Baba Sali', settled in the small Negev town of Netivot in the 1960s, and his home and synagogue soon became the centre of a major religious cult. Today, his tomb attracts a constant flow of worshippers. Tens of thousands of Moroccan Israelis assemble there each year on the anniversary of his death. His son, called 'Baba Baruch', runs the yeshiva-and-synagogue complex nearby. Aharon Abuhatseira, a nephew of Baba Sali, made his career in local politics, in the town of Ramle, and later rose to ministerial rank within the NRP. Tami won a very respectable three seats in its first electoral test, but later it waned as an independent party and eventually merged into the Likud.

I have always liked and admired Aharon. He is widely read – his speciality is the Napoleonic Wars – boundlessly inquisitive and endowed with a sharp, precise, analytical mind. For years, I kept up a close, informal dialogue with him, in the hope that he might eventually be persuaded to join the Labour Party. In our conversations, I found him close to our own positions, both in the areas of defence and foreign policy, and of social and economic issues.

Aharon was charged with bribery in a celebrated case in 1980 and acquitted for lack of evidence. Immediately upon his acquittal, new charges of financial irregularities were brought against him, and this time he was convicted and sentenced to three months of community service. The shadow of that episode has dogged him throughout his subsequent career. While he was acquitted in court of the more serious allegations levelled against him, some sections of the public never fully forgave him. Others have never ceased to question the motivation of the officials who arraigned him in the first place. If he had been an Ashkenazi rather than a promising Moroccan politician, they argue, he would never have been brought to court. This view is grounded, among other things, in the fact that among the North African communities charitable funds, run by leading figures like the Abuhatseiras, are an accepted part of community life. The funds will sometimes provide discreet aid to needy families, and in such cases the requirements of proper book-keeping, complete with formal invoices and receipts, are not always adhered to. It is easy, therefore, for personal or political enemies to concoct allegations of misappropriation against the heads of these funds.

I never believed that much good could come from the creation of an avowedly 'ethnic' party — either for the particular community to which the new party was designed to appeal or for the country as a whole. Rather than healing inter-communal wounds, such parties inevitably poured salt on them.

In any event, my hopes of inducing Abuhatseira to throw in his lot with Labour never came to fruition. Within Labour itself, there were widespread if unspoken reservations about his personal and political history. And he could never quite overcome his doubts over whether his political constituency could come to regard the Labour Party as its natural home.

My friendship with Abuhatseira finally laid to rest, as far as I was concerned, the spurious thesis that North African politicians have to be hawks, or that they have to be at least seen to be hawks, in the eyes of their supporters. I came to realize that the Israeli political picture was far more complex than that.

The Labour Party was increasingly dependent on the support of at least part of the North African community, with its strong religious traditionalism. The support of this sector was all the more vital because of the rapid and radical changes — both political and ethnic — taking place in the Ashkenazi religious camp. In the early years of the state, the religious minority was mainly Ashkenazi – at least in the sense that the leaders of the Orthodox parties (the NRP, Agudat Yisrael and Poalei Agudat Yisrael*) were all political moderates, and almost all Ashkenazi. Religious voters were divided fairly evenly between the staunchly Zionist NRP, which had been an active partner in the Zionist movement since the outset, and the non-Zionist Aguda movement. The NRP was allied with Labour in what came to be known as 'the historic alliance', which dated back to the pre-state years. During the formative period of the 1940s and 1950s, a strong personal friendship developed between Ben-Gurion and the NRP leader, Rabbi Yehuda Leib Maimon. Politically, the Labour–NRP axis formed the solid foundation of Labour's coalition governments.

Labour's relations with Aguda were more complex. The closest ties were with Poalei Agudat Yisrael, a quasi-socialist splinter group that had moved nearer to Zionism and set up its own kibbutzim. The main movement, Agudat Yisrael, blew hot and cold. Its political leader, Rabbi Yitzhak Meir Levin, served as a Minister in the first Ben-Gurion Government; but later the party seceded from the coalition, though it continues, intermittently, to support it from the outside.

Aguda draws its strength from two sources: the 'courts' of the Hassidic *rebbes* and the 'Lithuanian-style' yeshivas. Both of these sub-groups within pre-Holocaust Eastern European Orthodoxy have managed to transplant themselves to Israel (and to the United States) and to regenerate their decimated communities. In recent years, the dean of the largest yeshiva, Ponevezh, Rabbi Eliezer Shach, has achieved a pre-eminent position among the *mitnagdim* (opponents), the non-Hassidic stream. Ponevezh produces many of the nation's rabbis and *dayanim* (rabbinical court judges); hence Rabbi Shach's writ runs far beyond its campus, in the all-Orthodox city of Bnei Brak. Well into his nineties, he is an authoritarian figure whose leadership qualities and political acumen are no less formidable than his Talmudic scholarship.

I met Rabbi Shach once, at his request, for a lengthy private conversation in the home of Rabbi Moshe David Tannenbaum (d. 1993), the long-serving Secretary of the Council of Yeshivas. Rabbi Tannenbaum had always gone out of his way to show friendship towards me (and towards Ben-Gurion's other aides, Yitzhak Navon, Teddy Kollek and Haim Yisraeli). This relationship dates back to the first year of the

---

* Lit. The Workers of Agudat Yisrael.

state, when I was instrumental – on Ben-Gurion's instructions – in negotiating the arrangement whereby yeshiva students were exempted from military service. The arrangement – a focus of controversy ever since – followed lengthy negotiations with a number of elderly yeshiva deans, who reminded me of my grandfather. They argued that their yeshivas had existed for centuries, surviving both the Tsars and the Bolsheviks, but that they had been decimated by the Nazis. Now, the few surviving institutions would be doomed to extinction – in the Jewish state of all places – if their students were forced to enlist. The students, they insisted, spent their days and nights in study of the Talmud. It was more than an academic discipline; it was a way of life. To disrupt it by army service, even for a relatively short period, would mean cutting these young men off from their religious and intellectual moorings.

At that time, their demand meant deferring the service of a few hundred young men each year. Our consent was given with the proviso that the exemption applied only to full-time yeshiva students, and that it expired as soon as a student left the yeshiva. Despite the relatively small numbers involved, this was no simple decision. The War of Independence was still raging. Our slogan, 'The whole nation is the army; the whole country is the battlefield', was no mere hyperbole. The yeshiva deferment was politically and socially problematic. On the other hand, the rabbis were saying – and I believed them – that they would move their yeshivas abroad if the concession they asked for was not granted. I remember being particularly moved and influenced by the words of Rabbi Kalman Kahane, a political leader of Poalei Agudat Yisrael and a founding member of one of its kibbutzim. 'I have twelve children,' he said, 'ten of them boys. Nine of the ten serve in the army. I want the tenth to say in the yeshiva – and to pray for the safety of the others.'

We demand that the Orthodox show tolerance towards us, I remember thinking. By the same token, we ought to show tolerance towards them and towards an issue that is obviously of the greatest importance to them. I recommended to Ben-Gurion that we agree to the deferment arrangement for a limited number of yeshiva students, and he concurred.

Thirty years later – by which time the limited number had swelled to many thousands – Rabbi Shach sought me out to thank me. He told me that I had been 'an agent of the Divine will'. Short and slight of build, with short-sighted eyes peering through thick horn-rimmed glasses and sporting a scraggly white beard, he looked like a Chinese mandarin. But he spoke like a tough and determined political leader. In his special style of Hebrew (the modern language liberally spiced with Yiddish phrases and with old-world Ashkenazi pronunciation), he explained his position. 'Other nations, too, have their own independent countries,' he said. 'Other nations, too, have industry and agriculture, armies and parliaments. Those are not the things that make our nation special. What we have, and no one else has, is the Torah. It is the Torah, not the state, that keeps us, and our duty therefore is to keep the Torah. Not to absorb alien cultures. Not to profane the holy sabbath. Not to eat the unkosher foods that the Torah prohibits. Not to raise a nation of ignoramuses – ignorant, that is, of our vast Torah literature.'

In many ways it was remarkable that Rabbi Shach, with his quaint Ashkenazi pronunciation and his rigid adherence to the Lithuanian-Ashkenazi heritage, should have become the spiritual – and political – mentor of a large group of North African immigrant rabbis and yeshiva students. But this is what, in fact, happened during the 1970s, with young Sephardi scholars, at Ponevezh and other yeshivas, increasingly looking to Rabbi Shach for religious and political guidance. At the same time, the Orthodox political parties were becoming increasingly Sephardi in their grass-roots composition, as large numbers of North African immigrants joined their ranks while second- and third-generation Ashkenazi Israelis tended to drift away from Orthodoxy.

This ethnic shift was not reflected in the composition of the *leadership* of the Orthodox parties, however. They remained, with rare exceptions (Aharon Abuhatseira was one), solidly Ashkenazi. This, in turn, spurred resentment among the Sephardi members – among them, the rising generation of scholars affiliated with Agudat Yisrael and loyal to Rabbi Shach. In 1984, an all-Sephardic Orthodox party, Shas, was founded, with the active encouragement of Rabbi Shach, as a breakaway from Agudat Yisrael. It achieved instant success – four Knesset seats – in the elections that year. But it, too, eventually gravitated into the Likud-led camp.

During this time, another important change in the Orthodox section of society was occurring within the NRP, which had traditionally positioned itself at the centre of the political spectrum. The NRP, long regarded as a bridge of moderation and pragmatism between the Orthodox and the secular segments of Israeli society, now moved increasingly towards the political right, until it aligned itself with the Likud. The NRP gave birth to and nurtured Gush Emunim,* a cadre of pioneering

* See pages 168–71.

devotees who became the vanguard of the Jewish settlement movement in the densely populated heartlands of the administered territories.

Emunim's founders were all disciples of Rabbi Zvi Yehuda Kook, son of the first Chief Rabbi of Palestine, Abraham Isaac Kook (d. 1935). I met Rabbi Zvi Yehuda several times, and well remember his vivacious personality. But when the conversation turned to religion and ideology, his outlook was rigid. For him, 'the integrity of the Land' came first, and everything else – all the other commandments and moral precepts – took second place. The two rising leaders of the NRP's young guard during the 1970s, Zevulun Hammer and Yehuda Ben-Meir, led their following – and with it, much of the party – steadily towards the hardline right. They hardly realized how they themselves were being kidnapped, spiritually, psychologically and politically, by the fiery certitudes of Gush Emunim.

Some pockets of opposition within the NRP tried to hold out against this drift to the right. I urged the leaders of these groups to try to manoeuvre between the growing fervour for 'the integrity of the Land' gripping their party, and the natural desire of politicians to compromise so as to preserve the integrity of their party. But the hardliners swept all before them.

The emerging picture in the 1980s, then, showed two concurrent trends, both disturbing for Labour. On the one hand, the religious settlement movement and its political hinterland, largely Ashkenazi, finding political expression in the NRP and various rightist splinter groups, was a natural ally for the Likud. On the other hand, the North African immigrants, still harbouring a sense of grievance, also saw in the Likud an outlet for their political aspirations.

The 1981 election results illustrate these trends. Under my leadership, Labour made a brilliant recovery from its 1977 defeat, winning forty-seven seats, compared to thirty-three. The Democratic Movement for Change under Yigael Yadin had effectively disintegrated by 1981, and most of its voters returned to Labour. The Likud won forty-eight (up from forty-five), so that theoretically both major parties had good prospects of forming a coalition. In practice, though, the Orthodox parties and the ethnic Sephardi party Tami all lined up behind the Likud. In the next election, in 1984, Labour led the Likud by forty-four to forty-one, but again the Orthodox parties sided with the Likud, forcing

Labour and the Likud to form the Government of National Unity*. The same pattern repeated itself in the 1988 election. In all these elections, Labour attracted more Ashkenazi voters than Sephardi, and the Likud more Sephardi voters than Ashkenazi.

A number of sociologists and political scientists were quick to jump to conclusions – which, as it turned out, were quite wrong. They reasoned that with the higher-than-average birth-rate among Orthodox and North African families, Labour was done for. It would never again find the partners necessary to put together a stable coalition. Demography was against it.

But while experts might be able to explain the past, they suffer from the same short-sightedness as the rest of us when it comes to the future. Thus, these would-be prophets of doom failed to foresee the large-scale immigration from the USSR (and its successor states) in the late 1980s and early 1990s, which substantially changed demographic patterns and projections, at least in the short and medium term. Nor did the experts correctly predict the political persuasions of these newcomers, who proved unimpressed by the demagogy of the right or the preachings of the national-religious ideologues. The ex-Soviet immigration includes a remarkably high proportion of university graduates, especially in the sciences. The contrast between them and the state that reared them is glaring: never has such an unintelligent regime produced such an impressive intelligentsia. For Israel, their advent represents the triumph of the Zionist dream over seven decades of hostile communist indoctrination. For the Labour Party, their advent has meant an important new reservoir of moderate political support.

Nor, indeed, were the ostensible experts any more accurate or sensitive in understanding the essence of Shas. This growing movement placed at its head the foremost Sephardi rabbinical figure, Rabbi Ovadia Yosef. Iraqi-born, Yosef completed his term as Sephardi Chief Rabbi of Israel in 1983. He is recognized among Sephardi Jews, in Israel and abroad, as their foremost Talmudic and halachic† authority. There has probably been no other Sephardic sage of his academic stature in our century. On meeting Yosef, one is immediately confronted by his phenomenal mind and memory: he remembers everything he reads. He knows the Bible, the Talmud and all the classical rabbinic literature by heart, and peppers

---

* See pages 231–3.
† That part of the Talmud concerned with religious law.

every speech and conversation with long, relevant – and meticulously accurate – quotations. I will never forget one conversation in particular, in which he rattled off the convoluted ancestry and marital ties of various Hassidic houses in pre-war Poland and Russia, splicing in stories and anecdotes about the qualities and weaknesses of the different *rebbes*. Yet Yosef wears his vast knowledge lightly. He is a pleasant, friendly man; not querulous and sharp-tongued like Rabbi Shach.

As a political leader – or rather as the spiritual mentor of a political party – Rabbi Yosef turned out to be a dedicated moderate. I often spent time with him, holding long conversations partly on religion (his part) and partly on foreign policy (mine). His basic position is that, in Jewish Law, saving human lives by avoiding war is a higher priority than preserving Greater Israel.

In 1990, he made his move: he appeared on Israel Television, in brocaded black robes with a purple turban-like ceremonial hat, to proclaim his support for territorial compromise that could bring peace. This was anathema to the religious right, to the disciples of Rabbi Kook and to most of the Ashkenazi Orthodox establishment.

Yosef's television appearance was intended to presage Shas's parliamentary 'divorce' from the Likud and its entry into a new coalition with Labour. The party's political leader, Minister of the Interior Arye Deri, a young man of exceptional abilities, had been assuring me for months that, as 'Israel's principal statesman', I must try to end the impasse in the peace process by ending the policy-paralysis of Yitzhak Shamir's 'Unity Government'. In March 1990, Shas did indeed vote with Labour to bring down the Likud Government in the Knesset. Days later, Rabbi Yosef went on television to deliver his peace credo. I was buoyed – only to have my hopes shattered when the Shas faction recommended to the President of the State that he entrust the task of forming a new government to Shamir.* Deri explained lamely that he had had to follow Rabbi Shach's orders – and Rabbi Shach eschewed a coalition with 'pig-eating leftists'. Yosef tried to soften the blow by telephoning President Herzog and explaining that, despite Shas's formal support of Shamir, he personally recommended that the President entrust the Prime Ministership to me.

* Under the system then in place – it has since been amended by legislation – the President of the State would consult all of the political parties and then mandate one of their number to try to form a government. The candidate would have up to forty-two days to accomplish his task.

I soldiered on, nevertheless, in the hope of cobbling together a narrow majority with the help of Agudat Yisrael MKs. The result was one of the most awkward, embarrassing and heartbreaking situations of my political career. Two Aguda MKs, whose support I had counted on, backed off at the last moment – leaving me to face a specially convened session of the Knesset without the majority that I thought I had. I needed all my *sang-froid* to emerge from this bitter predicament with a modicum of self-respect.

But in the long run, as it turned out, the false alarm of 1990 did presage Shas's shift, following the 1992 election, into Rabin's Labour-led coalition, which was committed to a peace based on compromise. Moreover, this shift was more than just a parliamentary realignment.

The NRP, like Shas, won six seats, but we could make no headway with them; of their six MKs, three were relatively moderate, but the other three were enthusiastic devotees of Gush Emunim, and the party as a whole was effectively paralysed.

Rabbi Shach's hold on Shas was broken but his was still the most influential voice in Agudat Yisrael, which emerged from the 1992 election with four seats. Aguda refused to join the coalition and, in the crucial Knesset vote on the agreement with the PLO in September 1993, voted with the opposition.

Shas, though formally out of the coalition at this time, abstained – thereby ensuring a solid majority for the Government. Rabbi Yosef gave strict orders that no one in Shas was to vote against peace, and this time his orders were obeyed.

Apart from Shas, the Orthodox movements lined up against the peace agreement. It is hard to know whether this vote reflected the religious parties' positions on the actual agreement, or whether it was, in part at least, an expression of protest against what they regard as the rampant secularism of the left. Party-political considerations were also in play. The NRP, having stayed out of the coalition Government, watched in jealous impotence throughout the previous year as its traditional fief-doms – the Ministry of Education and the Ministry for Religious Affairs – were taken over by Shas. Aguda was also unhappy that the long-established practice of 'special budgeting' for religious institutions was ended.

Aguda made a point of stressing in its public rhetoric the sanctity of the Land of Israel. The party's parliamentary leader, Rabbi Avraham Shapira, asserted in the House that 'the Land has always belonged to the Holy One, Blessed be He – and it always will'. No mortal man had the right, Shapira declared, to transfer the title deeds of the Land. He added, though, that in order to avoid bloodshed it was permissible 'to make certain concessions'. In my view, it was a mistake, when the coalition Government was formed the previous summer, to leave Aguda out. They could have been brought into the Government, or at least into an alliance with the Government, pledging their support in key Knesset votes in return for the Government's support for their various concerns and interests. But my involvement in the formation of that Government was minimal. In fact, it was virtually non-existent.

All this time a police investigation, accompanied by massive media coverage, was being conducted against Deri. In 1993, three years after the inquiry began, he was finally charged with bribery, embezzlement and misappropriation of public funds. Another Shas MK, Rafael Pinhasi, was charged in connection with election funds, but the Knesset refused to waive his parliamentary immunity. As other Shas politicians ran into legal difficulties, a feeling gradually began to grow among its followers that these criminal investigations were truly an anti-Sephardi witch-hunt.

Rabbi Yosef felt alone and isolated: alone among the major rabbinical leaders in his support for the Government's policies, and isolated within the Government camp as his senior political acolyte was – as he saw it – hounded from office. (Deri was required by the High Court to step down as a Minister once the charges were pressed against him.) I had long conversations with Yosef during this period, and was able to see at first hand how heavily his loneliness weighed on him. He feared that without Deri at his side, he would be unable to sustain Shas's growth and dynamism. But he knew that for the foreseeable future Deri's energies and abilities would chiefly be consumed by his legal battle.

My conflict with the other Orthodox movements did not end with the Knesset vote on the agreement with the PLO. A few days after the vote, I became embroiled in a public dispute with Rabbi Shach. I had appeared in New York before the Conference of Presidents of Major American Jewish Organizations and had remarked, in my address, that Judaism, unlike Catholicism, has no concept of the 'apostle of Christ', in the person of the Pope. There is no single authority in Judaism, I explained; every rabbi thus has the right to express his own opinions and interpretations. The sages of the Talmud expressed this belief in a well-known aphorism: 'The Torah has seventy faces.' No rabbi, therefore, has the right to impose his views on other rabbis.

These remarks kindled the wrath of Rabbi Shach, who assumed that I was referring to him. He published the following response in his party newspaper:

... How great is the pain and how deep is the sorrow, when a member of the present Government arises – this Government whose intention is to turn the Nation of Israel into just another nation – and he a man who has neither learned nor studied, who at most has perhaps read the text of the Bible, but has no idea what the Talmud is ... the Talmud whose authors had the power to revive the dead, whose disciples were the greatest of men, who ... taught our nation all that was handed down to Moses at Sinai. Yet this man, who is neither himself a scholar nor ever lived in the midst of scholars, stands up and dismisses all of these generations of Talmudic sages with a sweep of his hand. Can there be any greater chutzpah than this? ... In his words, he has struck at every single Jew – because he has struck at our faith in God's Torah as it was transmitted to us, through the generations, from Moses our Teacher, who received it from the Almighty at Sinai before the eyes of the whole Nation of Israel. I write with grief in my heart ... Eliezer Menachem Shach.

I was not prepared to let this go unanswered and, therefore, published a polite but stern riposte:

The Foreign Minister expresses his astonishment that a rabbi has publicly accused him of insulting the rabbis of Israel and the Torah of Israel without ascertaining the true facts. The Foreign Minister has always respected the rabbis, the Torah and the Orthodox community. He has always done his very best to promote Jewish identity and the preservation of the Jewish heritage which we have inherited from our forefathers. He has always sought to emphasize the uniqueness of our culture.

In his speech the Foreign Minister contended that it was not acceptable for one rabbi to impose his views on other rabbis on any issue. He said that from ancient times, great rabbis were divided on all sorts of issues, and he quoted the Talmudic adage, 'The Torah has seventy faces'.... Far be it from the Minister to strike out against the Torah of Israel.

The Foreign Minister hopes that a rabbi expressing his opinions in public will do so with dignity and accuracy, both in this particular matter and in all matters relating to the weighty issue of peace....

Polemics apart, Rabbi Shach has, in my opinion, led the ultra-Orthodox community down a political blind alley. He has provoked widespread anger and resentment among ordinary Israelis through the virulence of his rhetoric. In a series of speeches over recent years, he has repeatedly attacked the kibbutzim and the labour movement, accusing them of deliberately uprooting Jewish tradition. He has also performed a complete turnabout in his position on peace – from extreme doveishness to hardline hawkishness – just at a time when, after a quarter-century of debates, doves and hawks at last had a tangible peace proposal to consider.

22 THE LONG SEARCH

When a group of young army officers came to power in Egypt in the wake of the anti-royalist revolution of 1952, Ben-Gurion believed that this might be a unique opportunity to talk peace. The regime of King Farouk had been hopelessly corrupt. The revolution, and the rise to power of the relatively young and idealistic officers, seemed like a fresh breeze blowing across the land of the Nile.

Ben-Gurion voiced his hopes both in public statements and in secret overtures to Mohammed Neguib, the officers' leader, and later to his charismatic successor, Gamal Abdel Nasser. I personally initiated one such overture, suggesting that we try to establish a channel to Nasser through the Yugoslav ruler, Josip Broz Tito, with a view to his organizing a meeting between Ben-Gurion and Nasser on the island of Brioni. Ben-Gurion wrote a letter to Tito, which I arranged to have delivered through Shaike Dan, one of our most senior intelligence operatives with high-level contacts in Belgrade. But Nasser rejected our approaches. He claimed that if he attempted to make peace with Israel, he would forfeit his Presidency and probably his life.

When Nasser died in 1970 and was succeeded by Anwar Sadat, we Israelis were all deeply concerned. Sadat was regarded by Israeli analysts as an unimpressive figure, a weak and hesitant man who had attained the Presidency as a compromise candidate. In the light of subsequent events, this was one of the most glaring mistakes in political intelligence ever made by Israel. Sadat, in retrospect, is universally and rightly seen as one of the most important Arab statesmen of this century.

His true qualities should have become clear, to us and to others, when he did what no other Arab leader had ever dared to do: throw the Soviets out of his country. Slowly – perhaps too slowly – it began to dawn on us that beyond all the rumour and ridicule stood a decisive man of action, a leader far different from those with whom we had contended in the past. His decision to go to war in 1973 was a fateful choice for his country – as was his historic decision, four years later, to make peace.

One of Sadat's oldest friends and closest aides was Hassan Tohamey. An intense, almost obsessive man, and a religious zealot, Tohamey was also a zealot for peace. One rarely meets a person embracing such remarkably contradictory traits. As his country's Ambassador to Austria, Tohamey had come under the spell of Bruno Kreisky, who never ceased lecturing him on the need for peace between Israel and the Arabs. Sadat's first secret emissary to Israel, Tohamey met Moshe Dayan twice in Morocco in the autumn of 1977 and was captivated by him.

Dayan spoke so winningly that Tohamey plainly did not attend minutely to what he had been told. In fact, Dayan did not commit himself explicitly to any specific concessions; rather, he created a general impression of commitment. Thus Dayan was able to return home and report that he had not committed himself, while Tohamey could believe – and report – that he had obtained Israel's consent to Egypt's demands. Tohamey's zeal and Dayan's subtlety together laid the foundations for the Israeli–Egyptian peace. This became clear to me when I had the opportunity later to meet Tohamey and to engage him in a lengthy conversation.

Sadat saw himself both as a prophet of peace and as a victorious warrior – a sort of Gandhi and Napoleon rolled into one; as he told me more than once, these were the two figures in modern history whom he most admired. In his long, flowing *galabiya*, in the village of his birth, he assumed the role of Gandhi. Resplendent in his field-marshal's uniform, he was Egypt's Napoleon.

Sadat's policy reflected the same dualism: he was the military strategist who launched the Yom Kippur War, and the apostle of peaceful accommodation who took his message to the Knesset in Jerusalem in the dramatic odyssey of November 1977. Beneath his ostensible naïveté, which worked a magic of its own, were acute instincts that led him to take momentous decisions. Looking back today, I would argue that if it were not for Sadat, there would have been no peace with Egypt. Syria's Hafez Assad is widely acclaimed as a strong and decisive leader – but at the time of writing, more than sixteen years after Sadat's peace initiative, Assad is still finding it hard to undertake an act of courage and vision of the kind that Sadat performed so long ago. Sixteen years in the lives of both nations have been wasted, but the Syrian President is incapable of summoning up the resources of wisdom and flexibility that helped bring stable peace to the Israeli–Egyptian border.

Of course, while Sadat wanted peace, he wanted it his own way. First, he believed that he had to win over America, so that America would persuade Israel of the seriousness of his intentions. Second in his order of priorities was what he called the 'psychological dimension' of peace. He would often remark that 90 per cent of the dispute was in the realm of psychology. It was chiefly to break through the psychological barrier that he took that most historic of steps – his visit to Jerusalem. The third factor facilitating peace was that he was ready to conclude a peace in stages, giving Israel a chance to verify his seriousness and sincerity. And finally, he was willing to make peace on his own, without the other Arab countries. When he saw that Syria was not prepared to join him on the path to peace, he parted company with Syria, in spite of the fact that he had insisted, in the post-1973 disengagement accords, on maintaining a precise symmetry with Syria. Similarly, he informed King Hussein of Jordan in September 1978 that he was going to Camp David, but pointedly did not invite the King to join him on his journey towards peace. He promised to report to the King, but he never did, and that was in effect the last time they spoke to each other. Subsequently, Sadat was to be heard on occasion making unkind comments about King Hussein and his family. Although Sadat insisted at Camp David that there could be no separate peace between Israel and Egypt without a framework agreement on the Israeli–Palestinian conflict, he concluded that framework agreement 'on behalf' of the Palestinians, without the Palestinians being present.

Without these four points, peace would not have been possible. In order to make peace, you have actually to set about making it; merely wanting it in the abstract is not enough. Sadat's approach facilitated the practical conclusion and implementation of a peace treaty between our two countries, to the lasting benefit of us all. To Sadat's great credit, it must be said that all four pillars of his policy seemed impossibly precarious when he began to construct them. His determination and perseverance made them strong.

Could peace have come before the Yom Kippur War? In 1971 and 1972, there was much discussion in Jerusalem of a possible interim agreement with Egypt, involving a partial Israeli withdrawal from Sinai and the reopening of the Suez Canal, which had been blocked since the 1967 war. However, Golda Meir was Prime Minister, and to her Sadat's conditions seemed wholly unacceptable. They were, indeed, very demanding. The main problem was not, as the media depicted it at the time, the deployment of several hundred Egyptian troops or police on the Sinai side of the Canal (though the then Chief of Staff, Lieutenant-General Haim Bar-Lev,* vigorously opposed even that). The problem for Israel was that Sadat demanded that we agree on a six-month timetable for the withdrawal of the IDF from the whole of Sinai, to be followed, six months later, by its withdrawal from the West Bank and Gaza. Golda and her close adviser, Minister without Portfolio Yisrael Galili, rejected these terms outright, and Moshe Dayan's efforts to search for a flexible compromise were not successful. Nor were they widely supported around the Cabinet table.

It is hard to judge today whether peace with Sadat might have been possible at that time on the terms that were eventually agreed to five years later. It would be irresponsible for me to pass judgment from the convenient perspective of hindsight. I do feel, though, as I felt then,† that the tentative proposals for an interim agreement were a beginning. I would have been happier if it had been explored more tenaciously, but I have to admit that the conditions that Sadat put forward at the time virtually forced the Government to reject his advances.

The Yom Kippur War changed the equation in two key respects. It gave Sadat enough of a victory to feel able to negotiate an agreement with Israel based on compromise, and it dealt him enough of a defeat for him to realize that Egypt had no realistic prospect of imposing its will on Israel by military means. Egypt won honour in the war, but neither side won the war: Egypt failed to achieve a military victory and Israel did not attain a political victory.

In Israel, the war ended in a dreadful atmosphere of grief and recrimination. How was it, people asked, that experienced leaders had failed to read the writing on the wall? The Agranat commission of inquiry‡ did

* Bar-Lev retired from the army soon after to become a Cabinet Minister under Golda Meir. He was called back to the army at the height of the Yom Kippur War crisis and given command of the southern front. He served later as Secretary-General of the Labour Party, as a Cabinet Minister during the 1980s, and as Israel's Ambassador to Russia.
† I was a junior Minister at that time and not actively involved in defence and foreign policy.
‡ A five-man commission of inquiry under the then President of the Supreme Court, Justice Shimon Agranat, set up to investigate the intelligence failure that resulted in Israel's being taken by surprise by the Egyptian and Syrian attacks on Yom Kippur. The other commission

not lay the blame on Golda or Dayan, but their prestige and public standing were grievously damaged and eventually both felt forced to resign. Dayan's subsequent efforts to bring off the peace treaty with Sadat were his way of trying to compensate the bereaved families, the nation as a whole, and himself for the cost of the Yom Kippur débâcle.

The 'peace process', as it came to be called, got under way even before the guns fell silent. Henry Kissinger had two major concerns: to ensure that the Russians stayed out, and that the war ended quickly and did not escalate into a global catastrophe. From his standpoint, both of these goals were achieved (though at one stage the Americans resorted to the rare and dramatic measure of declaring a nuclear alert in order to drive home their message to the Russians). By the last phase of the war, Kissinger was actively mediating to relieve the Egyptian Third Army, trapped by the IDF on the western (Egyptian) side of the Suez Canal, and beginning to craft the first disengagement-of-forces agreement between Israel and Egypt.*

The controversy that arose in Washington in the aftermath of the war, over the respective roles played by Henry Kissinger and James Schlesinger during the fighting,† did not sour my own relations with the brilliant Defence Secretary. I met him at the Pentagon for the first time when I was Minister of Defence, in the summer of 1974, and still retain a vivid memory of that encounter. Schlesinger arrived more than an hour late, keeping me and my aides waiting, along with his own retinue of generals and admirals. He mumbled apologies and immediately suggested that we meet alone. Sitting opposite him, I could not help but notice that he was wearing unmatching socks. But my faint bemusement quickly gave way to complete surprise when he posed his first question. I was expecting a pointed inquiry into our missile capacity or our nuclear programme, but instead Schlesinger asked, 'Now looking back, do you

members were Supreme Court Justice Moshe Landau, State Comptroller Yitzhak Nebenzahl, former IDF Chief of Staff Yigael Yadin and Haim Laskov.
* This first agreement was signed on 18 January 1974, in Geneva. It was followed by a disengagement agreement between Israel and Syria, signed on 6 June 1974, also in Geneva. The second, more substantive disengagement agreement between Israel and Egypt was concluded, after much shuttling by Kissinger, in September 1975. See pages 162–4.
† Defence Secretary Schlesinger was accused in certain media accounts of delaying the American military airlift of much-needed equipment and ammunition to Israel. The accusation was attributed to Kissinger. Some commentators suggested that in fact it was Kissinger who had deliberately slowed the re-supply operation, in order to prevent too-crushing an Israeli victory.

think Herzl* was right or not?' I launched into a long explanation of why I thought that Herzl had been right, interrupted frequently by my host's penetrating comments and questions.

By the time of Camp David, in the autumn of 1978, the place of the hyperactive American Secretary of State had been taken by an even more involved and committed American President. Without the unique contribution of Jimmy Carter, there would have been no Camp David agreement; of that I am certain. Carter immersed himself in the most intricate details of the negotiations, in the drafting process and, above all, in persuading the parties to give ground. He became, in effect, the indefatigable go-between as well as the host. Moreover, as host, he engineered the almost total isolation of the negotiators from the outside world, which was itself a vital element in the eventual success of the Camp David conference. That success became his greatest achievement as President.

But the Camp David agreement, in essence, resolved only one of the issues on the agenda: the Israeli–Egyptian peace. The negotiators decided, consciously or subconsciously, to reach for the only agreement that was attainable and to leave the other problems – the Palestinian problem, Jerusalem, peace between Israel and the other Arab states – unresolved.

These other problems were referred to in various cosmetic accords and side-letters. For Sadat, obviously, the agreement had to say something about the Palestinians. The Palestinian autonomy scheme, elaborately detailed in the Camp David Accords, fulfilled that need. But in my view, it was designed less to procure autonomy for the Palestinians than to vindicate Egypt's peace agreement with Israel. Similarly, the Preamble, which defines the Camp David Accords as a paradigm for peace with other Arab countries,† was designed as a necessary sop to Syria rather than as a meaningful commitment.

In the final analysis, Sadat was right to do this. The ancient Jewish rabbis teach that if you grab too much, you get nothing. If Sadat had linked the Israeli–Egyptian peace treaty to agreements with Syria, Jordan and the Palestinians, we would not have reached peace with Egypt. During my many meetings with Sadat, I believe I came to understand

---

* Theodor Herzl (1860–1904), founder of the Zionist movement.
† '... this framework ... is intended ... to constitute a basis for peace not only between Egypt and Israel, but also between Israel and each of its neighbours ...'

his thinking. He knew that if he waited for the rest of the Arab world, neither he nor the Arab world would reach peace. But if he broke ranks and lunged forward alone, others would soon follow in his wake.

Analysing the Camp David Accords from this perspective, we can discern three distinct sections: 1. an explicit framework for peace between Israel and Egypt; 2. cosmetic formulations relating to other parties; and 3. deferral of issues that were felt to have no solution.

As for the first part, in the Accord with Egypt, Begin was forced to concede every last grain of sand in the Sinai Peninsula. He had publicly promised the Israeli settlers of northern Sinai that he would make his home among them when he retired. This pledge was intended both to reassure the settlers and to vie with Ben-Gurion's demonstrative decision to live with the pioneering kibbutzniks of Sde Boker. As it turned out, the pledge was but another of Begin's rhetorical contributions to Israeli politics. The Begin Government removed the last, diehard settlers by force. Perhaps only a right-wing government can take such action. But I am not convinced, to this day, that that traumatic experience was inevitable. I had lengthy conversations with Moshe Dayan on this painful point. Dayan believed that Sadat might have been persuaded to let the settlements stay, at least for twenty-five or thirty years, if Israel stressed their agricultural character. As a village boy himself, Sadat might have been prepared to make concessions for the sake of agriculture. I believe that the Begin Government made a grievous, historic error in this aspect of the negotiations.

As far as the second part was concerned, the Camp David Accords did not provide a true solution to the Palestinian problem. Later, when I tried to interest Sadat in some sort of 'Gaza first' scheme – whether under Egyptian aegis or separate from Egypt – as a way of launching Palestinian autonomy, he wouldn't hear of it. He wanted nothing to do with Gaza. In addition, Begin altered the Hebrew translation for cosmetic purposes. The 'legitimate rights of the Palestinian people' was rendered as 'the legitimate rights of the Arabs of *Eretz Yisrael*', to which transparent ploy Carter, in his capacity as a Hebrew linguist, gave his assent.

The key issue that was sidestepped at Camp David by deferral was, of course, Jerusalem. Three separate letters were attached to the Accords, in which each of the protagonists set out his country's position on Jerusalem. In effect, they agreed to disagree on this fraught subject.

I was always sober and realistic in my appraisal of the Camp David Accords. I knew that they were essentially an agreement between Israel and Egypt. I also knew that when Begin agreed to return every grain of Egyptian sand, that would set the precedent, in the eyes of other potential partners, for any future negotiation. But I recognized that this was a take-it-or-leave-it situation, in terms of both the withdrawal and the settlements. There was no point in fooling ourselves. Each and every one of us had to make a clear-cut decision. Labour was in opposition, but I proposed that we support the entire package, including the dismantling of the settlements. Probably I could have served the party's interests better by taking a more popular position, supporting the 'good' parts of the Accord and balking at the others. But, as I kept saying at the time, we were in opposition to the Government – not to peace.

This was the line I took at a stormy and dramatic session of our central committee. Leading the opposing camp was Yigal Allon, who demanded that Labour not endorse the Accord. The majority supported my position. The Allon group asked for the right to vote according to their conscience in the Knesset, and I supported them on that – once I was sure that there were sufficient supporters of the agreement among Likud and Labour together to ensure its safe passage. Without Labour's votes, the Camp David Accords would not have been endorsed by the House. Looking back, I have no regrets whatever. We acted, I believe, as a serious and responsible opposition. We did not look for the easy way out, voting in favour of the peace but against the withdrawal. Ours was an act of patriotism in the most meaningful sense of that overused word. Our policy was much applauded, in Israel and around the world.

The same dilemmas that existed at the time of the Camp David Accords still affect Middle East peace-making today. Now, as then, to promote simultaneous negotiations with all the Arab parties together is to court deadlock – because the most hesitant and retrogressive among them will always have the power to veto the whole proposal. Similarly, to propose a uniform solution on all fronts is to ignore the differences between individual places and situations. Judea and Samaria (the West Bank) are different from Sinai in so many crucial respects, and the Golan Heights are also governed by different considerations. In a hospital, each patient has his own temperature, caused by his own illness; there is little point in calculating the average temperature of all the patients.

I believed then, and I still believe today, that workable solutions depend upon the resourcefulness and creativity of local statesmen. There are no 'off-the-shelf' solutions that can simply be selected and applied. The great breakthrough in the agreement with Egypt consisted in the fact that this was our first treaty with an Arab country. But the peace with Egypt was also the easiest. Sinai is not the Holy Land, the historic homeland of the Jewish People. Sinai, moreover, is virtually empty; once it is demilitarized by agreement, the question of sovereignty over it becomes less important. The other fronts, I always realized, would be tougher to resolve.

23 JORDANIAN OPTION

I have always thought in terms of the Israel–Jordan–Palestine triangle and the Syria–Lebanon axis. In the triangle, the relatively small dimensions of the territory belie the complexity of the ethnic mélange. East of the river, Jordan is four times the size of Mandatory Palestine – the area to the west of the river which is comprised of Israel, the West Bank and Gaza. But Jordan's population includes a strong Palestinian component. King Hussein has always sought to embrace the Palestinians within Jordanian national identity, but one cannot really know the extent of his success. The Palestinians, at any rate, are dogged by identity problems, whether consciously or subconsciously. Ultimately the question is, who is to rule over whom – Jordan over the Palestinians, or the Palestinians over Jordan? They both speak of the desire for a confederation, but each visualizes the confederation differently. Many Palestinians, for instance, expect the West Bank eventually to gain mastery over the East.

Over many years of pondering the future of our region, I have developed a two-tiered approach to the problem. The people of the region, I firmly believe, will have to build a new Middle East, a region capable of existing and prospering in the twenty-first century. To achieve this end, they will need to set aside ancient conflicts and to make peace among themselves.

The New Middle East, as I envisage it, is neither a pipe-dream nor an expendable luxury. It is a vital necessity without which we shall not be able to raise the living standards of the people of our region. As the standard of living goes up, the level of violence and tension will go down. But living standards cannot be raised solely by begging for foreign aid. The region must take its future in its own hands. It must stop pouring away precious resources on harmful or pointless causes, and must start, instead, to exploit fully its natural advantages. The most harmful and most wasteful of causes, of course, is the never-ending, always growing arms race. Regional expenditure on defence already exceeds $50 billion a year. The arms race could be significantly slowed if all the competitors jointly and simultaneously agreed to reduce its frenetic, punishing pace. One obvious step would be to cut down the size of standing armies.

Similarly, certain countries in our region would do well to recognize that old-style, totalitarian governments, apart from their other defects, cost enormous amounts of money to run. The apparatus of repression – secret police forces, lavish displays of military power, vast machinery to support the personality cult, state organizations dedicated to the stifling of dissent and the fomenting of fear – is hugely expensive. In addition to depriving ordinary people of their liberty and their human rights, these organs of absolutism rob the common folk of the bread that is rightly theirs. Dictatorship, in fact, is becoming so expensive these days that only rich countries can afford it – and even they find themselves eventually bled white by the leech-like imposition of an echelon of parasitical repression on to their societies.

Making peace in our region would not only put an end to the devastating drain of blood and treasure, but it would also promote the enhanced generation of wealth. If oil, gas and water pipelines were laid through countries and across borders not according to strategic fears and political quirks, but rather according to economic good sense, the benefits would soon flow to everyone. The same applies to other key infrastructures: roads, railways, telecommunications – these could all serve the region as a whole, facilitating the smooth and efficient movement of trade and tourism between countries. The creation of a regional 'water bank' could ensure the equitable – and economically profitable – distribution of water resources. Such a 'bank' would also facilitate the development of additional water sources, through desalination and purification, using the most effective available technology. For this is the only way for our region to confront one of its greatest challenges: the advancing deserts that threaten to erode the meagre reserves of arable land which must feed a constantly growing population.

Before laying the foundations of this New Middle East, as before any building project, the ground must first be cleared. In our case, the ground is sown with mines, and these must be painstakingly defused.

I have never doubted that the Palestinian problem is a mine that could trigger any number of others, and that defusing the Israeli–Palestinian conflict is the key to regional peace. That perception became all the more true, and all the more urgent, in the wake of Camp David and the Israeli–Egyptian peace treaty. I constantly searched for new and creative ways of tackling the Palestinian issue – not only for political expediency, but also out of a feeling that this was a moral imperative. The Jewish People were not born to rule over other peoples. 'Who is the strong man?' the Talmud asks. It then answers, 'He who conquers his own evil inclinations.' Throughout history, the true moral destiny of the Jewish People has always remained the conquest of evil inclination.

It was in the context of this pursuit of a peaceful solution that I first met King Hussein – the first of many meetings – in the summer of 1974. There were three of us on the Israeli side: Prime Minister Yitzhak Rabin, Foreign Minister Yigal Allon, and myself, then the Minister of Defence. King Hussein was flanked by his Prime Minister and longtime confidant, Zaid Rifai. They arrived by helicopter at a deserted spot in the Arava Valley, in the south of the country, where we had prepared a discreet but comfortable caravan.

The King made a powerful impression on me. Though short in stature, his ramrod posture and swift, athletic movements radiate a strong presence. His smile is warm and captivating; his manners are impeccable. He seems always in full control of his every muscle, and, as I was to learn with time, is invariably well briefed and on top of the subject under discussion.

Hussein is a national leader who embodies a complex knot of often conflicting interests and concerns. He constitutes the epitome of Hashemite pride. He sees himself as a personification of the Arab destiny. Yet at the same time he is beset by worries over strategic threats posed to his relatively small and weak desert kingdom by its various Arab neighbours. He is also troubled by economic concerns, as Jordan battles for survival and prosperity in an inhospitable climate. As a boy, he was close to his grandfather, King Abdullah, and the old King's assassination, in July 1951, on the Temple Mount in Jerusalem, was a trauma that Hussein has carried with him all his life.

His basic attitude towards Israel is one of admiration. He has always treated Israel with respect – except on that one fateful day, 5 June 1967, when he allowed himself to be duped by Egypt's Nasser into believing that the Egyptian armed forces were beating the IDF in the field.* Hussein's own view of that fateful day is very different. The King's position was – and still is – that Israel fired the first short at Egypt,† and that therefore Jordan, as a member of the Arab League and a part of the Arab Common Defence Pact, was acting in self-defence against an attack.

Despite its relative poverty and all the other objective difficulties, Jordan has flourished under Hussein's rule. It has built up a fairly advanced educational system and an efficient and disciplined army. Jordan has conducted a wise but firm policy towards the Palestinians over the years. When in 1948 the Palestinians were exhorted by the Mufti of Jerusalem to leave the areas that were to become Israel – temporarily, as he promised them – Jordan opened its gates to them. When, in the aftermath of the 1948 war, Jordan unilaterally annexed the West Bank, it awarded its citizenship to the Palestinians living both there and in the East Bank. No other Arab country – neither Syria nor Lebanon, nor even Egypt – dealt in this civilized and humanitarian way with the Palestinian refugees who found themselves living indefinitely within its borders. During the period before 1967, King Hussein deliberately developed the East Bank at a faster pace than the West Bank, with a view to encouraging West Bank Palestinians to make their homes across the river. He believed that Palestinians making this move would quickly adopt a fully Jordanian national identity.

Yet, despite his sympathy for the Palestinians' individual and collective plight, Hussein acted without hesitation when his regime was threatened by the PLO in 1970 ('Black September'),‡ pitting the full fury of his army against them. He felt that he had reached the end of his tether, having tried for over two years to avoid a violent showdown with the myriad paramilitary groups functioning – and often fighting each other – inside his country under the vague aegis of the PLO.

King Hussein's relations with Israel have been similarly complex and delicate. Outwardly, Jordan was always a loyal and orthodox member of

---

* An intercepted telephone conversation between the two Arab rulers, hours after the Six Day War broke out – and after the Egyptian air force had been effectively destroyed by Israel – disclosed how Nasser had persuaded Hussein to join in the war. The result was that Israel drove the Jordanian army out of East Jerusalem and the West Bank.

† In Israel's view, Nasser's closure of the Straits of Tiran was itself an act of war, justifying acts of self-defence on Israel's part. Nasser's insistence, moreover, on the removal of the UN Emergency Force from the Sinai portended further acts of war by Egypt.

‡ See page 164.

the Arab League and, as such, it maintained a state of war with 'the Zionist entity'. In practice, however, especially after the 1956 Sinai–Suez War, the long Israeli–Jordanian border has been mostly peaceful. The two port/resort towns of Eilat and Aqaba nestle cheek-by-jowl on the scenic northern shore of the Red Sea, yet never a shot has been fired from the one at the other. Hussein and his top aides would meet from time to time with Israeli leaders or senior officials to resolve common problems, such as water allocation, and to ward off potential dangers that threatened to disrupt this comfortable tranquillity. At many such meetings the participants would discuss, informally, whether the time had yet come for an effort to negotiate a formal and contractual peace between them.

Before my first meeting with King Hussein, I obtained Rabin's and Allon's approval to put forward my own thoughts on the Palestinian problem. I proposed that a possible solution lay in the creation of three political entities: Israel, Jordan and a Palestinian entity that would be administered by the other two jointly. The Palestinian entity, comprising the West Bank and Gaza, would be wholly demilitarized. It would fall under no single sovereignty; instead, residents carrying Jordanian passports would vote for the Jordanian parliament, and those with Israeli citizenship would vote for the Knesset in Jerusalem. The inhabitants of the Gaza Strip, many of whom were stateless refugees, would receive Jordanian passports. The three entities would form one single economic unit, open to the free movement of goods, of persons and of ideas. Worshippers of all faiths would have free access to their holy places.

The King's reaction was not negative. During a break in the discussion, he told me that he thought my plan was interesting and said he would study it further.

Our basic position was that we opposed the creation of a separate Palestinian state. Such a state, as we saw it, would split Western Palestine down the middle, leaving Israel with an untenable and indefensible narrow waist. True, we had agreed to partition in the past, but that very partition may well have brought on the Six Day War. Moreover, the Jewish settlements that we had built in the Jerusalem area and down the Jordan Valley in the years since the Six Day War would make a re-partitioning of the country dauntingly difficult.

In our view, a Palestinian state, though demilitarized at first, would over time inevitably strive to build up a military strength of its own, and the international community, depending upon massive Second and Third

World support at the United Nations, would do nothing to stop it. That army, eventually, would be deployed at the very gates of Jerusalem and down the entire, narrow length of Israel. It would pose a constant threat to our security and to the peace and stability of the region.

In addition, a Palestinian state, led by the PLO as it then was, would have been dogmatically committed to continuing the fight against Israel. Unlike Hussein's Jordan, which lived alongside Israel in *de facto* peace, the PLO still preached the elimination of the sovereign Jewish state from the region – and it practised what it preached to the fullest extent that its terrorist gangs and border marauders could manage. The PLO's 'Palestine Covenant', the binding charter of the organization, called expressly or implicitly for the elimination of Israel in all but six of its thirty-three paragraphs. The PLO made rejectionism its political dogma. It attacked Israelis and Jews at home and abroad, making itself thoroughly hated by the entire Israeli nation.

A further reason for our opposition to an independent Palestinian state was our longstanding, if oblique, support for Jordan. Jordan was a well-established state with a stable regime, a well-defined constitution and an army. Jordan had taken responsibility for the large majority of Palestinians, granting them its citizenship, which they had eagerly and gratefully accepted. Many of Jordan's Prime Ministers had been West Bankers, mainly from Nablus. The educational curriculum on the West Bank (even in areas under Israeli administration) was wholly Jordanian. Hussein's portrait still appeared on the front page of every text-book. Jordan's status, indeed its very existence, could conceivably be threatened by the rise of a separate Palestinian state.

When I took over as Prime Minister of the Government of National Unity in 1984, I was busy extricating the army from Lebanon and the country from economic crisis. The peace process had been effectively paralysed since the collapse of the Israeli–Egyptian autonomy talks held in the wake of Camp David. The Israeli–Egyptian peace treaty had withstood the strain of the Lebanon War, but relations were soured by an unresolved dispute over Taba, a small stretch of Red Sea coast just south of Eilat, from which Israel had refused to withdraw when it pulled out of the rest of Sinai in April 1982.

President Mubarak insisted that the Taba dispute be submitted to arbitration. Israel, while vigorously asserting its claim to Taba, privately harboured doubts as to the validity of that claim. Apparently the key border-stones had been tampered with at some time since their original placement in 1906. The inner Cabinet, comprised of five Labour members and five members of the Likud, was divided down the middle, and for months on end the Likud Ministers would not budge. Their leader, Foreign Minister Yitzhak Shamir, brought to bear on this relatively minor but bothersome issue of Taba all of his very considerable qualities of stubbornness. Mubarak countered, with unremitting vehemence, that we had returned all the vast expanses of Sinai to Sadat – and should not now deny him the tiny 100-acre patch of Taba.

The arguments went on endlessly in the inner Cabinet. Eventually though, David Levy, the Likud Housing Minister, moved towards our position – as he had done in the debate over withdrawal from Lebanon.*His shift enabled us to refer the Taba dispute to international arbitration before the end of my twenty-five months as Prime Minister in October 1986. The arbiters finally decided in favour of Egypt, and the beach was returned to Egyptian sovereignty. Today, the large resort hotel that comprises most of Taba is Egyptian-run, but it still serves a mainly Israeli clientele, as well as frequently hosting the ongoing peace negotiations, both on the Israeli–Palestinian 'track' and on the broader multilateral plane.

I was determined not to let either our domestic problems or the Taba impasse stand in the way of possible progress with Jordan. We kept in close touch with Amman, both through the Americans and through our own private channels. The American Secretary of State, George Shultz, and his highly knowledgeable and experienced Middle East aide, Dick Murphy, were keenly interested in the prospects of advancing the Israeli–Jordanian relationship, with a view to resolving the Palestinian problem. Another key American player was Tom Pickering, the Ambassador to Israel from January 1986, a wise and diligent professional diplomat with whom we felt distinctly comfortable. Pickering had served previously in Amman and was finely attuned to the aspirations and constraints of the royal court.

Murphy travelled incessantly through the region, seeking to put together a negotiating framework that would embrace Palestinian figures acceptable to us, functioning within a broad Jordanian–Palestinian representation. Separately, I opened a channel to the PLO, sending Israeli emissaries to meet PLO representatives in order to seek out whatever information was available on the fates of Israeli personnel missing in

* See page 234.

action in Lebanon. Shamir knew of these missions: they were discussed in our discreet 'Prime Ministers' troika', which was comprised of Shamir, Rabin and myself. The months rolled by, and my truncated term as Premier★ drew to a close. I had achieved most of my goals: the IDF was out of Lebanon, save for a supervisory presence in the border security zone held by the Israeli-backed SLA; inflation had been brought down, and kept down; Taba had finally been submitted to arbitration, as the Likud reluctantly acknowledged that we were required, under the terms of the treaty, to take this step; and relations with Jordan had been markedly improved, though there had been no tangible breakthrough in the peace process.

Some of my colleagues and friends tried to persuade me not to go through with the rotation with Shamir. My popularity ratings were topping 80 per cent, and there was plainly a broad public appreciation of what I had been able to achieve in the short time allotted to me. Rather, then, these advisers suggested, end the National Unity coalition and bring about early elections. I dismissed such advice, however well-meaning it might have been. As far as I was concerned, honouring the agreement was the paramount consideration. I had given my word, and now I must keep it. Shamir and I duly changed places on the appointed day, but becoming Foreign Minister in no way weakened my urgent sense that the Jordanian opening must continue to be pursued with vigour and determination.

King Hussein's position was that he was prepared to negotiate a peace treaty, but only in the context of an international conference on peace in the Middle East that would bring together the Great Powers and all of the regional protagonists. He was supported in this by the Soviet Union, France, Britain and, with some hesitation, by the United States. Shamir flatly rejected the idea of an international conference. He argued that such a conference would impose a solution on the parties and, given the likely composition of the conference and the known positions of most of its participants, that solution would probably be unacceptable to Israel. Shamir, however, was careful to clothe this rejection in moderate-sounding language whenever Shultz or Murphy flew into the region on yet another shuttling effort.

★ Under the 'rotation' agreement between myself and Shamir, each was to serve as Prime Minister of the Government of National Unity for twenty-five months – half of the statutory term; see page 233.

I too opposed an international conference if it could impose its collective will on the protagonists. But I saw nothing wrong with an international conference that would convene in formal opening session – thus providing the Arabs with the legitimizing fig-leaf they needed – and then split into bilateral working groups. After all, that had been the pattern of the Geneva conference, which had convened soon after the Yom Kippur War. Within the framework of that conference, Israel had negotiated two disengagement agreements with Egypt and one with Syria. It was arguably the success of that procedure that had led, in time, to the Sadat Initiative and the subsequent peace treaty with Egypt.

As the long, frustrating months of diplomacy grew into years, I decided to cut through the complicated and necessarily slow-moving machinery of shuttle diplomacy, and tried to reach a breakthrough by means of a secret summit. I approached a common friend of mine and of King Hussein's, the prominent London attorney Mr (now Lord) Victor Mishcon, who is a model of wisdom, tact and discretion, and asked him to set up a meeting. The time and place were fixed: Saturday, 11 April 1987, at Mishcon's home in central London. I told Shamir what I had arranged, and he gave me his consent. Decked out in a stylish brown wig and wearing my most elegant suit, as befits a royal audience, I accordingly took off for London, aboard a small executive jet. I was accompanied by my loyal aide Dr Yossi Beilin, who was serving as Political Director-General of the Foreign Ministry at this time, and by a senior representative of the Prime Minister's Office.

We were invited to the Mishcons for lunch. The staff had been given the day off, and Joan Mishcon, our gracious host, cooked and served a delicious meal herself. When it was over, King Hussein suggested that the two of us go into the kitchen to help with the washing up.

At 2 p.m., we settled down for our political discussion. It was to continue for seven hours. It began with a *tour d'horizon* in which we reviewed the events of the past year. We dwelt on the Soviet Union, on Iran and Syria, and on the Palestinian situation. The King was in sparkling form, weaving hilarious anecdotes into his pithy political assessments. He told me of a conversation with President Reagan in which he had been asked about fishing in the Dead Sea. He spoke of his wife, Queen Noor, who was in America to celebrate the hundredth birthday of her grandmother, and of his son, who piloted a Cobra helicopter in the Royal Jordanian Air Force. I found that especially poignant: my son was a Cobra pilot in the Israeli air force.

Zaid Rifai had a funny story of his own. On a recent visit to Cairo, he said, he had stayed at an official government guesthouse. Returning late one night, he found his way blocked by sleepy, stolid guards who did not recognize him and were clearly not interested in making his acquaintance at that late hour. Desperate to get to bed, he hit on the idea of proclaiming himself to be Shimon Peres, who he knew had recently visited Cairo and was put up at the same guesthouse. That did the trick; for the Israeli Prime Minister, the gates were opened wide.

The conversation flowed smoothly and pleasantly in this way until we gradually got down to the real issues. Hussein said that he had decided not to visit Washington in the near future, since the administration seemed thoroughly confused as to what it was trying to achieve in our region. Rifai added that a recent offer of American aid to Jordan had been so small as to be insulting.

Hussein continued with sharp and impatient criticism of the PLO leadership. They were ambiguous in their basic political positions, he said, but theirs was not a constructive ambiguity but rather one that reflected vague and indeterminate political thinking. The PLO engaged in terror and effectively rejected all openings for productive negotiations. This mixture, said Hussein, could offer only hopelessness and explosive danger. The King stressed that his vision of an international conference did not, in practice, embrace the PLO − as long as the PLO's rejection of Security Council Resolutions 242 and 338* effectively disqualified the organization from participation. He fully expected the PLO to abrogate its agreement with Jordan on political co-ordination, concluded the previous year. (He was soon to be proved right in this.) In the long term, he predicted, the PLO would lose the support of the main players in the Arab world.

We were clearly on the same wavelength. I reiterated at length why, in my view, neither Israel nor Jordan could regard the PLO, committed by its charter to seek the destruction of Israel, as a partner for peace. Israel certainly did not want to see Yasser Arafat ruling in Amman, I noted pointedly.

On the tactical plane, my proposal was for a Jordanian–Palestinian delegation, which would not include avowed members of the PLO, at peace talks. Arafat, I argued, would have no choice but to acquiesce. (I was to be proved correct when a peace conference eventually convened

* See Appendix I, pages 359–61.

in Madrid, in November 1991.) Here, too, we found a common language. Hussein repeated that the PLO's extremism ruled it out as a party to the proposed conference. But the Palestinians would not want to be left out altogether, and hence they would agree to a joint delegation with Jordan, and would seek to put together a representation that would be acceptable to Israel.

I told the King of my recent meeting with a Soviet envoy who turned up at a Socialist International meeting in Rome specifically to see me. His message was that Moscow accepted the concept of a 'non-coercive' international conference. The five Permanent Members of the Security Council would participate in the conference; they would not dictate solutions, but would merely lay down 'principles' upon which solutions would be based. This too, I told Hussein, was unacceptable to me. I was ready for a conference, but wanted no 'laying down' by anyone. Solutions must evolve out of free, bilateral negotiations between the Middle East parties, and the conference must merely serve as a useful framework under the aegis of the international community.

Hussein observed that Soviet policy-making was clearly undergoing a very real and positive change, even though many of the policy-makers and officials remained unchanged.

Summing up our positions, we found ourselves in agreement on many, though not all, of the key issues relating to an international conference. We agreed that the time was ripe to move towards a resolution of the conflict. We also agreed that an international conference should be convened to launch the process, but should not itself impose solutions. In practice, we agreed that the conference should assemble once, and that every subsequent session would require the prior consent of all the parties. We agreed, too, that there should be a unified Jordanian–Palestinian delegation which would not include members of the PLO. Finally, we agreed that following the opening session the actual negotiating would be done in bilateral, face-to-face groups, with Israelis and their Arab adversaries sitting opposite each other to talk peace. (This procedure was actually adopted several years later at the Madrid peace conference and the subsequent negotiations in Washington.)

The King spoke enthusiastically of this agenda. He stressed the urgency of reaching a comprehensive settlement. His commitment to the peace process was clear and unequivocal, he said. 'This is a holy challenge for me,' he declared, 'a religious duty.' He explained that he understood Israel's reservations about an international conference, 'but the goal is peace, not a conference'. Jordan had no interest in creating a conference in which Israel would feel isolated or victimized. While the Soviet and the Chinese positions were close to those of the Arabs, the United States was closer to Israel, and so were Britain and France, he maintained. Palestinians participating in the conference would be doing so within the confines of the Jordanian delegation. Moreover, they would have to accept explicitly the authority of Resolutions 242 and 338 and to dissociate themselves from terrorism.

Rifai said that he too agreed with the key points that I had articulated. 'Well then,' I replied, 'why don't we try to write down our agreement?'

The King said that he could not do this, as he had another engagement, which would take him one hour. He suggested that, in the meantime, we draft two documents: one detailing the principles and procedures of the proposed international conference, and the other setting out the agreements and understandings between Israel and Jordan.

The King and Rifai left, and we quickly got down to work. When they returned, we had the two papers ready for them. They read them carefully, and Rifai started listing changes he wanted to propose. But Hussein stopped him. The two drafts, he said, accurately reflected the agreements we had reached.★

We decided, therefore, to transmit them to the Americans, with each side separately informing the Americans that these documents summarized the position we had agreed on. We would both ask the United States to adopt the agreement, and to present it, through the Secretary of State, as an *American proposal*. This was in accordance with a prior understanding we had reached with Dick Murphy and Tom Pickering. At that stage, of course, no one anticipated a fully fleshed out and written accord. Our understanding was that if we could reach any substantial – though informal – points of agreement with Jordan, they would be taken up and worked on by the Americans, and eventually presented as American ideas.

We certainly felt, as we prepared to take our leave, that we had achieved a momentous breakthrough. With Jordan, we had agreed on a non-coercive international conference, on a Jordanian–Palestinian joint delegation, on the effective exclusion of the PLO, and on our common determination to advance together towards peace. The King seemed to be both happy and at peace with himself. He had taken the basic, strategic

★ See Appendix II, pages 361–2.

decision to lead the Jordanian–Palestinian camp into a peace process with Israel, and he seemed to be comfortable with that decision. Even Rifai, whose function as Prime Minister had all too often been to pour cold water on any bold move towards peace, appeared to acquiesce in his monarch's brave and far-reaching decision. We flew back to Israel that same night, deeply gratified, and with a sense of eager anticipation.

I had asked Yossi Beilin to fly from London to Helsinki, where I knew that Secretary of State Shultz would be stopping off en route to Moscow. Beilin met Shultz's political aide, Charlie Hill, and reported in detail on the secret meeting with Hussein. He gave the startled American diplomat copies of the two agreed drafts. Hill was unreservedly enthusiastic.

I called Prime Minister Shamir as soon as I got home, early on Sunday morning. We agreed to meet alone, after the weekly Cabinet session. I gave Shamir a full account of my talks with the King and read to him the texts of the two drafts. He asked me to read them again, and I did so. But when he asked me to leave the papers with him, I refused. I told him frankly that I was afraid of leaks, not by him – he was always discreet – but by members of his staff. Anyway, I added, the idea was for the Americans to put these agreements forward as *their* proposal; it would be better, therefore, if he received them from the Americans. Shamir said nothing.

By this time, we in Israel had come full circle in our attitude towards Secretary of State Shultz – from suspicion and trepidation to close trust and confidence. When he was appointed, in July 1982, we were worried because he was serving at that time as the President of Bechtel, a giant construction company that had extensive contracts in Saudi Arabia and other Arab states. I had made his acquaintance earlier, when he had visited Israel as the Secretary of Labour under Richard Nixon. He was accompanied by Irving Shapiro, who was the first-ever Jewish Chairman of Du Pont. After Shultz became Secretary of State, I asked Shapiro to check out discreetly whether Shultz might consider appointing Henry Kissinger as a special peace envoy to the Middle East. The reply I received, through Shapiro, was from Shultz himself. The Secretary had two points to make: firstly, two serious people cannot run the same operation; and secondly, did we really think that someone who was not Jewish could not be a genuine friend of Israel? I was impressed, and indeed it did not take long before all of us in Jerusalem came to recognize Shultz's deep regard for Israel, and his sincere and urgent wish to move the Middle East peace process forward.

During the years of the Government of National Unity, the somewhat strange procedure that evolved – and that was dutifully followed by Shultz, Murphy, and the American Ambassador in Tel Aviv – was to conduct virtually all official meetings in duplicate, once with Shamir and once with me. Shultz would fly in periodically, usually with his wife, O'Bie. I was always moved to see with what loving care and courtesy he would escort her down the steps from the aeroplane. As our mutual confidence grew, we would exchange views with complete frankness and informality. I understood that the personal relationship between Shultz and Shamir was similarly close, though I assumed that on the substantive issues of Middle East peace-making Shultz's views were closer to mine than to Shamir's.

Beilin returned from Helsinki full of optimism. Ambassador Pickering in Tel Aviv was equally enthusiastic, as was Dick Murphy, who said that he could hardly believe his eyes when he read the draft accords. All of us felt that we had made a major breakthrough, and that Shamir's fears would be allayed: the international conference would not have the power to impose any solution, and the PLO would not participate in the negotiations.

We could not have been more wrong. Circumventing his Foreign Minister (me), Shamir sent Minister without Portfolio Moshe Arens★ to Washington, to meet Shultz as soon as he came back from Moscow. Ostensibly, Arens flew to the United States for a series of public appearances on behalf of the State of Israel Bonds organization. I was told nothing of his mission to Shultz.

Speaking for Shamir, Arens informed the Secretary of State that if the United States were to present the Israel–Jordan draft agreements, it would be considered a crass interference in Israel's internal affairs. Surprisingly, Shultz accepted this argument. To our great disappointment, he did not present the drafts.

The breakthrough, full of hope and promise, was asphyxiated at birth. King Hussein's disappointment and disillusionment were boundless – as were my own. I tried desperately to save the situation by proposing to Shultz that an imminent Washington summit between President Reagan and Secretary Gorbachev be worked up into a quasi-international conference, with the two superpower leaders inviting Hussein and Shamir

★ Arens had served as Israeli Ambassador to the United States from 1981 to 1982 and as Minister of Defence from 1983 to 1984.

to join them. Shamir was prepared to consider this, Shultz told me later, but King Hussein had by this time lost faith in the Americans' peace diplomacy.

In the light of all of this, I was amazed to read in Shultz's memoirs★ that 'the foreign minister of Israel's government of national unity was asking me to sell to Israel's prime minister, the head of a rival party, the substance of an agreement made with a foreign head of state ... Peres was informing me, and wanting me to collaborate with him, before going to the prime minister.' Obviously, Shultz was mistaken. I did not ask him to go to Shamir instead of me. I went to Shamir myself. I did not expect Shultz to persuade Shamir instead of me. I had laid out the entire scenario to Shamir in advance, after we had agreed with the United States that an agreement reached between Jordan and Israel would be presented as an American proposal. This device was intended to make it easier for the two sides to reach the agreement.

Shultz also writes in his memoirs that, 'Arens stressed the impropriety of what Peres had done. "I was astounded to learn that Peres negotiated an agreement, even *ad referendum*. This has never happened in Israeli history before," he said.'† But that, too, is unfounded. I had briefed Shamir in advance. And isn't negotiating *ad referendum* what every Foreign Minister does?

In Israel, too, all manner of legends grew up around my London meeting. People said, or wrote, that Shamir had not known about it beforehand, or alternatively that he was not fully informed about its outcome. Both of these allegations are groundless. Shamir knew of and approved of my mission to London, and he was the first to be told of what had been achieved as soon as I got back. Granted, he did not know in advance that King Hussein and I would reach a written agreement. But neither did I. The idea of drafting our agreements and understandings in a formal document evolved during the London meeting.

After the collapse of the London agreement, I seriously considered resigning. The problem was that I could hardly resign without explaining fully to the public the reason for my resignation; but King Hussein and I had agreed to keep our agreement, and indeed our meeting itself, a secret. Neither of us issued any official confirmation that it had even

★ George P. Shultz, *Turmoil and Triumph – My Years as Secretary of State* (Charles Scribner's Sons, New York, 1993), p. 939.
† *Ibid.*, p. 941.

taken place. If I were to resign and to explain why, I would dishonour the commitment I had made to Hussein and embarrass him. His Government would presumably feel forced to issue a denial, which in turn would leave our public in Israel uncertain what to believe.

We all paid a heavy price for the destruction of my milestone agreement with King Hussein. Hundreds of people, Palestinians and Israelis, paid with their lives: within months the Palestinian *intifada* broke out in the West Bank and Gaza, resulting in years of violence and bloodshed. From the heights of hope shared by the few who knew what had been achieved in London, our region was plunged once more into an extended period of despondency and frustration. Indirectly, the 1987 failure led to the break-up of the Government of National Unity in 1990, when the Labour Party under my leadership finally concluded that the only justification for preserving this Government – the hope for progress towards peace – was non-existent as long as Shamir was in power.

24 A CHANGING WORLD

I personally paid a heavy price for this fiasco. After our withdrawal from the Government of National Unity, the Likud and its allies remained in office until the election of June 1992. I stood for re-election as leader of my party and its candidate for Prime Minister, but was defeated by Yitzhak Rabin in a close race. This was an especially painful defeat for me, as I felt that it was caused in large measure by the participation of two other candidates in the contest: Yisrael Kessar, the Secretary-General of the Histadrut, and Ora Namir, a respected Labour Member of the Knesset.* Kessar mobilized the strength of the Histadrut organizational machine behind his campaign. This was particularly effective in the Arab sector; in some Arab villages, nearly 100 per cent of the votes went to Kessar. Kessar ended up with 17 per cent of the overall votes, Namir with 4 per cent, I with 35 per cent and Rabin with 40.5 per cent – just enough to win.

In a second round of primaries, for the party's parliamentary candidates, I was given a massive show of support: more than 100,000 party members – 84 per cent of all those who voted – supported me, and I led the Knesset list after Rabin. We ran on a clear and unequivocal 'peace platform' and we won forty-four seats – hardly a landslide, but sufficient to create a Labour-led coalition (and, together with our allies, to prevent the Likud from forming a viable alternative). I campaigned with the help of a small personal campaign staff. I was well received wherever I appeared; people made a point of saying that they felt I had been hard done by. Relations between Rabin and myself during the campaign were

* Kessar became Minister of Transport in the 1992 Labour-led Government and Namir Minister of Labour and Social Welfare.

strained. At our victory celebration on election night, at a Tel Aviv hotel, party activists gave me a great cheer when I walked in, and milled around me enthusiastically. Someone apparently rushed off to Rabin with the news that the 'Peres camp' was forming again. Rabin thereupon made his own speech in which he stressed that *he* would lead the Government, that *he* would appoint the Ministers, and so forth. The media responded in the days that followed with a splurge of speculation that the old Rabin–Peres rivalry would now burst out again in all its fury. 'Peres', the pundits asserted, on learning that Rabin was offering me the Foreign Ministry, 'is incapable of being Number Two.'

But I resolved now to set aside personal regrets or resentments and to dedicate myself entirely to the cause of peace. I was bitter in my heart over what had happened; I felt that I had earned my party's trust and that I had been unfairly removed from the leadership just when global and regional developments brought peace into prospect. But bitterness is not statesmanship. It was my duty now to prove that I had the strength to accept tough and unpleasant decisions when these were part of the democratic process. I was not entering the new Government, as I told Rabin and everyone else, in order to renew the old rivalry between the two of us. A divided government would quickly lose the public's confidence at home and would be ineffective abroad. To my friends, I pledged that my behaviour would be determined entirely by one criterion: the progress of the peace process. If that progress were satisfactory, I would be the most loyal and disciplined of Rabin's ministers. If, however, the peace process were allowed to grind to a halt, I would not hesitate to raise the banner of rebellion. I was determined – as I have since proved on many occasions – to swallow affronts and ignore insults in the interests of protecting the peace process and of shoring up this Government, which is committed to peace. My sensitivity is focused entirely on the diplomatic arena, searching for any and every new opening.

In time, Rabin grew convinced that this was indeed my sincere and unswerving resolve. On this basis, a close and fruitful working relationship between us evolved. It enabled us – especially during the months of secret negotiations with the PLO – to meet alone, in an atmosphere of confidence and discretion, to discuss and to argue, without the argument becoming personal, and without it leaking out in the next day's press.

At the Foreign Ministry, I decided not to trigger an immediate chain of personnel moves, but rather to start working with the existing team and to institute changes gradually, over time. I had with me Yossi Beilin, who was re-elected to the Knesset on the Labour list and was now Deputy Foreign Minister. We had been working together for fifteen years and were completely comfortable with each other. Beilin is first and foremost a wise young man. He has deep political convictions and considerable organizational skills that he employs discreetly but very effectively. His political positions periodically arouse antagonism within the party, and this threatened to damage his prospects in the 1992 primaries. My party supporters and I campaigned for him across the country. He himself worked unflaggingly. To everyone's delight, he was elected – and to a relatively high spot, at that. (I would have wanted to see him higher still, but we had feared far worse.)

As I have noted, Beilin began working with me in the Knesset soon after our landslide defeat in 1977. He had left his job as a political correspondent for *Davar* to become the party spokesman. At that particular juncture in Labour's changing fortunes there were not all that many people who would have been prepared to break off a promising career in order to represent a crippled and despondent party. He was in his early thirties, and we immediately struck up a close and easy working relationship. In the run-up to the 1984 elections, he chaired an informal think-tank of academics, professionals and businessmen whom we dubbed our '100 days team'. Their task was to prepare policy-papers on the key issues that would face us if we won the election and set up a new government.

Since then, Beilin has moved with me between my various positions and departments. When I became Prime Minister in 1984, he was appointed Cabinet Secretary – a complex task that he performed with distinction. When I moved over to the Foreign Ministry two years later, he became Political Director-General of the Ministry. After the 1988 election, I became Minister of Finance, and Beilin, now a Knesset Member, was made Deputy Minister. We worked together there until I decided to end the unity coalition in March 1990. Now we would be working together again. He was more mature and more experienced, and was naturally determined to make his own mark on our great common enterprise: searching for peace.

Several other gifted young people had worked with me over the years. One was Dr Nimrod Novik, an able political scientist, who proved highly effective and articulate in foreign policy debates. He served as my policy adviser during the 1980s, but left the government service in 1990 to go into business. Another was Uri Savir, a second-generation diplomat, whom I borrowed from the Foreign Ministry to become my spokesman at the Prime Minister's Office, and who then returned with me to the Foreign Ministry, later becoming Consul-General in New York, where he enjoyed considerable success. A brilliant man, he possesses great diplomatic skills – not the least of which is his complete command of half-a-dozen languages – as well as that most rare and precious of qualities: a sense of humour. I earmarked Savir as the next Director-General of the Ministry. For the time being, however, I was working well with the incumbent, Yossi Hadass, whose wide experience and perspicacity I greatly valued. Avi Gil, another young and highly competent diplomat, who had served as a spokesman at the Foreign Ministry in 1987–8, later moved across with me to the Ministry of Finance. He is now my Chief of Bureau. Gil's straightforwardness and cheery disposition make him popular with everyone. He is also blessed with a great sensitivity, seeming to detect problems before they surface.

The three of them – Beilin, Savir and Gil – quickly grew into a closely co-ordinated team, working with me, advising me and dreaming, with me, of peace in the Middle East.

The legacy that the defeated Likud Government left us in the summer of 1992 was a 'peace process' that had proceeded nowhere. It was based, formally, on the structures set up at the Madrid peace conference of November–December 1991. This had created a 'two-track' machinery: bilateral negotiations between Israel and each of the Arab protagonists – Syria, Lebanon, Jordan and the Palestinians, the latter two nominally united in one 'Jordanian–Palestinian' delegation – and a multilateral framework, in which other Arab states and states outside the region joined in discussions on regional development.

Madrid had been an important and promising milestone, a significant achievement for the American administration and for the Likud Government in Israel. James Baker, the US Secretary of State, proved an adept and gifted arm-twister; he exercised precisely the right amount of pressure on all parties to ensure that the conference took place, and that it ended on a positive note. For Yitzhak Shamir, the arm-twisting meant that he now accepted what he had previously resisted – a non-coercive international conference. This, of course, was precisely what I had agreed to with King Hussein back in 1987. Shamir also went to

Madrid knowing that he would be sitting at the same table as a founder of the PLO, Dr Haider abdel-Shafi of Gaza, who headed the Palestinian delegation.*

I particularly welcomed the success of the Madrid conference in bringing a large number of Arab states, not directly involved in the conflict with Israel, to the negotiating table. The multilateral framework seemed especially encouraging; it was a recognition that peace between the conflicting parties must be attended by a much broader assault on the economic problems of all the peoples of the Middle East.

But little progress had been made in the months since Madrid. The 'tracks' created were little more than rocky, unpaved paths when we began setting up our new Government. Rabin and I agreed that he should direct the bilateral negotiations, and that I would participate in the policy-making. I was also to head the multilateral effort, with his participation.†

It seemed clear from the outset that the bilaterals needed more American involvement, while the multilaterals needed broader international input – from the Europeans and the Japanese. It was clear, too, that the bilaterals were to be the more intensive of the two tracks, and the multilaterals the more extensive. Finally, it was clear that there would be no real progress in the multilaterals unless there was progress in the bilaterals.

I told Rabin that I intended to explain to the members of multilaterals that while the bilaterals were primarily a negotiation between parties, and thus dealt with the conflicts of the past, the multilaterals should focus on issues and should thus primarily consider prospects for the Middle East region in the future. I felt that the peace process until now had been based on a misconception: instead of negotiating over the substance of peace and the benefits that would accrue from it – for all the parties – we had been dealing solely with the price to be paid for peace and with the decades-old causes of the conflict. I thought that

* The Likud Government's position was that it would refuse to negotiate with active and official members of the PLO, but that it would negotiate with representatives of the Palestinians living in the administered areas, regardless of their known ties to the PLO, provided that they did not appear at the conference as representatives of the PLO. Dr abdel-Shafi and other Palestinian delegates made no secret, at Madrid or after, of their effective subordination to PLO headquarters in Tunis.
† A second Middle East peace conference, held in Moscow in January 1992, had created four multilateral committees to deal with regional issues: economics, water resources, arms control and environment. A fifth committee on refugees was added later.

unless our people were given a new sense of the situation, it would be hard for them and, therefore, for their leaders to shake loose from the rigid thinking that was still the residue of the old world.

I believed that the world was in the throes of a cataclysmic change. For most of our century we had been living according to rules that had evolved from global confrontations that were now rapidly evaporating. First among these was the confrontation between East and West, between communism and democracy. This was an ideological, political and military stand-off that directly influenced the conflict in our region. The East, in effect, had aligned itself with the Arab cause. Moscow supplied the Arabs with both weapons and diplomatic support. Moscow and its allies provided a steady and reliable source of military hardware, offering both the military and political backing that enabled the Arabs to make war on Israel. Furthermore – and hardly less significant – the communist bloc provided radical Arab regimes with a model for their state structure. Many of them, some deliberately and others almost unwittingly, embraced the Soviet form of centralization.

The collapse of the USSR thus signalled far-reaching changes for our region. The Arabs no longer had a source of arms, generous with supplies and over prices and payments, whose support had been grounded in politics and ideology.

The other old-world confrontation was between North and South – the North, industrialized, developed, technologically advanced, self-confident, mostly white, faced the future with confidence; while the South, poor, backward and mainly non-white, was riddled with discrimination, resentment and disillusionment. On the diplomatic plane, this division produced both blocs and bloc voting. The Third World, or non-aligned bloc, gave their moral, psychological and parliamentary support to the Arab states. Every vote at the United Nations became a landslide against Israel because of this division of the world. The original leaders of this bloc, Nehru, Tito and Nasser, represented three continents.

This bloc, too, has collapsed in recent years. China, a key element, is making huge strides forward economically, and the 'Tigers' of South-East Asia are charging through the dividing line that ostensibly separates rich and poor nations. Nasser was succeeded by Sadat, the man who dared to make peace with Israel. After Tito's death, Yugoslavia disintegrated. And India eventually realized that, in spite of all its professions of solidarity with the Arabs, the Arabs themselves gave their support and solidarity to Muslim Pakistan, in its ongoing rivalry with India.

Economically, moreover, India has also set out upon the road to progress and prosperity. The sweeping 'North–South: rich–poor' generalization is no longer accurate. Latin America, a southern continent whose countries had been part of the non-aligned bloc, is moving impressively towards political and economic democracy. The only one of the southern continents still largely sunk in underdevelopment is Africa. There, AIDS rages while the desert laps at the fertile land.

In this new world, moreover, conflicts within countries are increasingly replacing the old-style conflicts between countries. Wherever a centralized regime – usually communist – tried to mould an amalgam of heterogeneous ethnic groupings into a single nation, repressed ethnic rivalries have broken out anew. In Yugoslavia Tito tried to ignore ethnic divisions and to create new political demarcations. But in politics, as in cooking, you can break eggs and make omelettes, but no one can break the omelettes and make eggs. Wherever 'ethnic omelettes' were created in the past, daunting political difficulties have now come to the surface.

One of the reasons why I believe in the need for political separation between Israelis and Palestinians stems from the example of Yugoslavia. The full lesson to be learned from this and other ethnic disputes is that nations should live separately as political entities, but together as economic units.

From the Israeli perspective, the massive global changes have meant that the source of the almost inexhaustible military support for the Arabs has now dried up, and the source of almost automatic political support for their case has also run low. The old divisions no longer hold. In this new world, the division is between those who still live in the old world and those who have set their sails to be directed by new and more hopeful winds.

In the Middle East, the Gulf War of 1991 swept away another old-world division that had been an unchallengeable fact of political life for decades. No longer were the Arab states inevitably united among themselves, and united against Israel. An Arab state had engaged in naked aggression against a sister state. An international coalition, including Arab states, had been formed to beat back the aggressor. It suddenly became clear to many in the region that the real threat to peace was not from Israel, but rather from ruthless and fanatical leaders of certain states in the region. Khomeini's rise to power in Iran a decade earlier had created a real and deep schism within the Moslem world, between fundamentalists and liberals. The main threat facing many Arab governments came not from Israel and Zionism, but from the Ayatollah in Tehran and other extremists. Increasingly, the Arabs themselves saw that this was the case – and were prepared to admit it, both to themselves and to others. In other words, the Arab–Israeli conflict, which had been the strongest source of Arab unity, ceased to play that role as Arab unity gave way to dangerous divisions.

In Israel, sadly, many political leaders continued to talk as though these great changes had not taken place, and as though our stereotypical conception of the Arabs was somehow stronger than the new realities of the Arab world. We seemed unable to grasp the magnitude of the changes, both global and regional, that were occurring around us. The world has moved beyond having ideological confrontation, and has thus lost one of the principal motivations for military struggle. The world has come to realize that economic opportunity is available for all of mankind, black and white, Southerner and Northerner. Economic rivalries have begun to take the place of military confrontation. The military confrontations required trained armies, fortified borders, constant vigilance and suspicion. Economic advancement requires a very different set of circumstances: open borders, markets that straddle political demarcations, goodwill, good products and constant competition.

The movements of the Jewish national renaissance and the Arab national renaissance met – and clashed – at the same place and time. But times are now changing. Our condition in the 1990s is very different from that which prevailed in the 1950s. The world in which these two movements were born, and grew to fruition, no longer exists. They both now have to seek new and uncharted solutions to their problems.

My basic position, as we set out on our ambitious voyage in the summer of 1992, was clear to my close circle of advisers. Since we had effectively lost the 'Jordanian option', at least for the time being, we had no choice but to develop a Palestinian option. I felt that there was no real prospect of implementing the Palestinian autonomy plan as originally proposed by the Likud Governments as their interpretation of the Camp David agreements in 1978. Negotiations on the basis of the Camp David formula had led nowhere in the past. I believed that genuine implementation would mean in practice negotiating the handover of the entire West Bank and Gaza to Palestinian rule, for which we were not ready. Instead, I supported the idea of an interim agreement. If we could not agree at this stage on a map, at least we could reach an agreement on a timetable, in the hope that time itself would alter the circumstances so that we would eventually be able to agree with the Palestinians on a common map.

The main difficulty, as I saw it, was the West Bank (Judea and Samaria), not the Gaza Strip. Any attempt to draw up an autonomy proposal for the West Bank would immediately run into the seemingly insurmountable problem of Jerusalem. The West Bank, moreover, is home to 120,000 Jewish settlers (compared to only 5,000-odd in Gaza). Any attempt to remove them forcibly could create an irreparable split within the nation. Labour's strategic thinking on the West Bank had undergone various revisions over the years. Influenced by the Allon Plan,* the Labour-led Governments from 1967 to 1977 set up a string of Jewish settlements down the Jordan Valley. Moshe Dayan himself had argued that Israel should broaden its painfully narrow 'waist' by expanding into some of the western sections of Judea and Samaria contiguous with the old border – and hence he encouraged the creation of new settlements just over the 1967 line. The Likud, and especially Ariel Sharon, hoped eventually to annex all or most of the West Bank. Therefore, Likud Governments invested great resources and energy in setting up Jewish settlements all over Judea and Samaria. These three divergent concepts hopelessly confused demography with geography, until it had become effectively impossible to conceive of border-lines that could be acceptable to a solid majority of Israeli opinion, let alone to the Palestinians.

That underlying confusion made the prospects of a negotiated settlement appear increasingly remote. Nevertheless, when we took office, the fact was that Israel was engaged in a negotiation – in the wake of the Madrid conference – with a Jordanian–Palestinian delegation in Washington. That fact could hardly be ignored and we naturally wanted to build on it. Nominally, the Palestinian team did not include PLO members. In practice, several negotiators were past members of the PLO, and the entire delegation took its orders from PLO headquarters in Tunis. After each negotiating session in Washington, several of the Palestinian team would repair to Tunis to report on the progress of the meetings and to receive new instructions. At the negotiating sessions themselves, they were cautious almost to the point of immobility.

Back in 1980, when the Israeli–Egyptian negotiations on Palestinian

* See page 165.

autonomy were going nowhere, I had suggested that we should look at 'Gaza first', and I returned to this concept now. The Gaza Strip presented neither of the daunting problems that we faced on the West Bank. Gaza, I argued, would never be Israel's salvation, and, in addition, we did not have the means to save Gaza from its own grim predicaments: the overcrowding, the poverty, the refugees. The Strip is a tiny area with a population of some 800,000, which had doubled in the last twenty years alone and was continuing to grow. Our presence there merely added more woe to this woe-begotten stretch of land – and gave us nothing at all save a growing, festering sense of shame at our inability to relieve any of its problems. We had neither interest nor business running the life of the Gaza Strip or policing its squalid, teeming streets. Our rule over Gaza was an ongoing, ghastly mistake. I was frankly sorry that we had created any Jewish settlements there at all. It was like robbing the poor; there is so little land there anyway. The settlements contribute nothing to national security, but they tie down large numbers of IDF troops in ensuring their own security.

One of the only Israeli projects in Gaza that we can take some pride in is the industrial area that has developed alongside the Erez checkpoint, the main crossing-point between the Gaza Strip and Israel-proper. This project was initiated by Moshe Dayan, then Minister of Defence, and myself, when I was the Minister in charge of the administered areas, not long after the 1967 war. It was intended as a microcosm of the common market, where Israelis and Arabs could separately or jointly set up workshops and small businesses.

But in all honesty, nobody wanted Gaza. The Egyptians were probably relieved to have lost it; the West Bankers rejected the concept of Gazans coming to live, or even to work, among them. The Gazans were always last in line at airports or train stations around the world because they had no passports, only *laissez-passer* cards. Many Gazans doubtlessly preferred the daily commute to Israel to the dangers of life inside the Strip, where internecine strife between Palestinian groups took a steady toll of lives.

Over the years, I visited Gaza dozens of times. Each time, I came away ashamed anew of the slums and shanty-towns, the desperate poverty, the sprawling, dusty refugee camps. Granted, the educational system worked, offering schooling to every child, and the medical services also improved dramatically during the years of Israeli administration; we also initiated a modern housing programme, offering people free land and easy mortgages, but all of this was a drop in the bucket: the pace of building and of renewal would never match the swelling birth-rate and growing degradation.

The Gazans have many endearing qualities, in spite of the harshness of their lives. They are an intelligent people; their womenfolk, in particular, are feisty and determined. To put to sea with the Gaza fishermen, as I was able to do on two occasions, is both a pleasurable and a memorable experience.

The logical thing to do, it seemed to me, was to place the responsibility for the future of Gaza in the hands of the people who lived there, and to help raise their living standards to a respectable level. I realized that in proposing the idea of 'Gaza first' in the past, I had made two mistakes: firstly, any proposal coming from the Israeli side was virtually bound to be rejected by the Palestinians; and secondly, the Palestinians suspected that our ceding Gaza was intended as the end of the process of re-conciliation rather than the beginning.

I transmitted a message to the Egyptians – first to Osama el-Baz, Mubarak's top political aide, and later to Foreign Minister Amru Mussa and to the President himself – urging them to persuade the Palestinians to reconsider their objections to 'Gaza first'. This, I contended, could break the ice that had formed over the desultory negotiations in Wash-ington. The Egyptians saw the logic of my argument and began to act. I added a hint to the effect that it might be possible to extend 'Gaza first' to something more – so long as Jerusalem and the settlements were not involved.

My Cabinet colleagues, including the Prime Minister, believed that the indigenous Palestinian leadership who comprised the negotiating team in Washington would gradually gain stature and independence and be able to negotiate without the close and stifling supervision of the PLO. I believed that they were mistaken. But they felt that I was wrong and were concerned that it would be impossible to negotiate with Arafat. In August 1992, in a private conversation with Rabin, I suggested that Israel should reconsider its position on negotiating with Arafat. But there was no agreement between us.

In January 1993, in another private meeting with the Premier, I told him again that, in my view, we must take bold steps towards negotiations with the PLO. As long as Arafat remained in Tunis, I argued, he rep-resented the 'outsiders', the Palestinian diaspora, and would do his best to slow down the peace talks. I suggested that we propose to Arafat and his staff that they move to Gaza. Once there, they would have the right to vote and to stand in elections; and if elected, they would represent the Palestinians directly in negotiations with Israel. My criticism of the Washington talks was that we were trying to reach a declaration of principles without any reference to specific territorial issues. The way to succeed, I believed, was to link a declaration of principles to a tangible concept of 'Gaza first plus'.

I made no secret of my positions. They were known to my close aides at the Foreign Ministry – and to several key figures in the PLO. They knew, too, that I strongly believed in the economic dimension of peace-making. To construct a political staircase without economic banisters is to take the risk that people will begin to climb, only to fall off before they reach the top.

It was against this backdrop that I learned from Yossi Beilin that two academics who were working with him with my knowledge, had been told by the PLO, during talks in Oslo early in 1993, that the organization was now prepared to adopt the 'Gaza first' approach, together with a 'mini-Marshall Plan' for economic development in the territories. Their interlocutor and the man who delivered this message was Abu Ala'a (whose full name is Ahmed Suleiman Khoury), a veteran member of the PLO leadership and confidant of Chairman Arafat.

25 OSLO BACK-CHANNEL

The turning point was finally at hand. The time had come for us to make good on our campaign commitments. Rabin had pledged to implement the Palestinian autonomy plan within nine months of our taking office, and that deadline was now approaching. I, too, was impatient to move forward. The window of opportunity was there, but it took tenacity, good fortune and assistance from an unexpected quarter to open it.

FAFO, or the 'Forskningsstiftelsen for Studier av Arbeidsliv, Fagbevegelse og Offentlig Politikk', is a Norwegian research organization that was engaged in field work in the territories during the summer of 1992, when its director, Terje Rod Larsen, became acquainted with Yossi Beilin. Soon afterwards, Beilin became Deputy Foreign Minister, and the FAFO research project attracted the attention of the Norwegian Government. In September, the Norwegian Minister of State, visiting Israel in connection with the project, suggested to Beilin that Norway could help set up a discreet back-channel between Israel and the PLO.

Beilin, responding cautiously, put Larsen in contact with two academics not formally connected with the Government, Dr Yair Hirschfeld, a Haifa University political scientist who had worked with FAFO in the past, and Dr Ron Pundak. In December 1992, Hirschfeld received an approach, through a relative in London, from the PLO's 'minister of finance', Abu Ala'a. The two men agreed to attend a seminar on human resources to be held by FAFO in a secluded villa at Sarpsborg, near Oslo.

The 'seminar' took place on 20–22 January. There were only five participants: Hirschfeld and Pundak on the Israeli side; Abu Ala'a, Maher el-Kurd and Hassan Asfour representing the Palestinians. Abu Ala'a, plainly intending his message to be conveyed to the Government in Jerusalem, outlined a three-point proposal:

1 A 'Gaza first' option, whereby Israel would commit itself to withdrawing from the Gaza Strip 'within two or three years'. The Strip would then become a trusteeship, under Egypt or under a multinational mandate, for a limited period. Meanwhile, negotiations would continue on an interim autonomy scheme for the West Bank, which, once agreed, would be put in place there.
2 A 'mini-Marshall Plan' for the West Bank and Gaza, in which the international community would undertake, through aid and investment, to invigorate and massively expand the economies of the territories.
3 Intensive economic co-operation between Israel and the Palestinian interim authorities.

These ideas bore out my own basic approach – 'Gaza first' and a major focus on the economic aspects of peace-making. There was to be a declaration of principles of fairly vague content, and an initial transfer of autonomous powers – 'early empowerment' as it was termed in the negotiators' jargon – was to begin upon the signing of this document.★

One key element in the Palestinian proposal, the trusteeship, seemed doubtful from the start. Nevertheless, I met Rabin alone on 9 February for another frank and thorough discussion of our Palestinian policy. I repeated my firm opinion that we should try to induce Arafat to leave Tunisia and to return to the territories. I listed the advantages in the Abu Ala'a proposal as I saw them:

1 Israel would announce that it intended to withdraw from Gaza within a fixed period of two or three years.
2 The 'mini-Marshall Plan' for the Gaza Strip would get under way.
3 These developments would not prejudice the ongoing bilateral negotiations in Washington for a full-scale autonomy agreement with the Palestinians.
4 Meanwhile, we could simultaneously draw up plans for long-term economic co-operation between Israel and the Gaza Strip.
5 Desalination plants could be built in the Strip, as well as tourism

★ The Israeli and Palestinian negotiators in Washington were working during this time – without much success – on a declaration of principles and on 'early empowerment'.

facilities, a harbour and an oil pipeline terminal, all of which would help boost its economy.

6 The talks on this proposal would proceed discreetly, without the official Palestinian negotiators knowing about them.

Rabin asked me to suspend the talks until after a visit to the region by Warren Christopher, the American Secretary of State, later in February. I sent word to our two unofficial emissaries that they might carry on their discussions along the general lines that I had approved, explaining that we would review the situation after Secretary Christopher's trip.

The five 'seminarists' met again in Sarpsborg on 11–12 February and quickly got down to work on drafts of a declaration of principles, which they resolved to produce, together with a paper setting out 'Guidelines for a Regional Marshall Plan' and an Israeli–Palestinian 'Co-operation and Working Programme'. After this meeting, Hirschfeld sent me a long and detailed account of the sessions and an assessment of their significance. The talks on the Declaration of Principles, he wrote, had run into trouble on four issues (which were to continue to dog the negotiators through the coming months):

1 Jurisdiction – how to define the geographical and legal ambit of Palestinian autonomy;

2 Jerusalem – whether East Jerusalem Palestinians would be entitled to stand as candidates and/or vote in the elections for the self-government Council;

3 Arbitration – how to set up a mutually agreeable machinery for resolving disputes; and

4 Security – the extent to which Israel would retain control of security in the territories during the interim period.

It is important to note, in light of what finally emerged, that the initial discussion in Oslo of 'Gaza first' envisioned an Israeli withdrawal only in two years' time, but it also envisioned a withdrawal from all of the Strip, including the Jewish settlements. The settlements, Abu Ala'a suggested, could become joint Israeli–Palestinian co-operation projects. Abu Ala's said that he and his colleagues spoke for Chairman Arafat, for Abu Mazen and for Farouk Kaddumi. The PLO, he said, was not insisting on an overt role for itself in the peace process at this time. If the Oslo discussion eventually produced an agreement, the PLO leadership in

Tunis could instruct the Palestinian negotiators in Washington to endorse it.

By the third meeting, on 20–22 March, the two sides were reaching for solutions to some of the thorny issues. On the issue of voting in Jerusalem, for instance, the suggestion put forward was that East Jerusalemites cast their ballots in the Holy Places – the Moslems at the Mosque of al-Aksa and the Christians at the Church of the Holy Sepulchre. Hirschfeld and Pundak felt that this could be acceptable to Israel, as it could claim that its concession on this point was linked somehow to the Palestinians' religious rights at the Holy Places – and did not signify a direct political nexus between Jerusalem and the autonomy.

It was at this session that the idea first surfaced that the United States might 'adopt' the Israeli–PLO accord – assuming an accord was indeed reached through the Oslo back-channel. The Americans would then 'propose' the substance of the accord at the Washington talks, as though they came from their own initiative. This continued to be the stated assumption of both sides throughout the negotiation, but in the end the Americans themselves rejected it.

Meanwhile, we were growing steadily more disenchanted by the performance of the Palestinian negotiating team in Washington, where the bilateral talks, launched at the Madrid peace conference, had been dragging on desultorily for many months. The team was led by an eminent Gazan doctor, Haider abdel-Shafi, and was composed – at Israel's insistence – exclusively of West Bank and Gaza residents. Our impatience mounted as the Israeli negotiators reported that the Palestinian team was disorganized and incapable of taking even the most minor decision without referring first to Arafat in Tunis for instructions.

This situation came to a head in April 1993, when the Palestinian delegation proclaimed a boycott of the Washington talks, in response to Israel's expulsion of some 400 fundamentalist Islamic activists from the West Bank and Gaza. The talks seemed doomed to indefinite stagnation, and would indeed have been so doomed had it not been for Arafat's vigorous insistence that they resume.

In Oslo, meanwhile, unbeknown to the Washington negotiators, Abu Ala'a's discussions with Hirschfeld and Pundak continued, uninterrupted by the crisis surrounding the mass deportation. The atmosphere, naturally, was affected by the crisis, but the two sides' determination to hammer out an agreement was not.

In their reports to me, the two Israeli academics stressed that Arafat's eventual instructions that the Palestinian delegation return to Washington were attributable, in large measure, to the existence of the Oslo back-channel. They also noted that Abu Ala'a, who co-ordinated the Palestinian teams in the various multilateral negotiations, had quietly removed a delegate to whom Israel objected from one of their teams.★ I formed the distinct impression that Abu Ala'a was a man of his word, a man with whom we could do business.

The reports from Oslo indicated that the PLO was in serious difficulties, both financial and political, and that the time, therefore, was right for Israel to clinch a deal with the organization. Hirschfeld added that Dan Kurtzer, one of the US State Department's top Middle East specialists, had been briefed on the Oslo talks and had reacted most favourably. 'Kurtzer regards the results of our meetings as a major step forward,' Hirschfeld reported. 'He sees our talks as complementing the Washington negotiations.' Kurtzer had enthusiastically encouraged the Israeli academics to continue their efforts, pledging to come up with American compromise proposals 'if you run into problems'.

The Norwegians told Hirschfeld that Secretary of State Warren Christopher had asked their Foreign Minister, Johan Jorgen Holst, to come personally to Washington to report on this novel, and obviously significant, Israeli–Palestinian dialogue.

I decided that it was time to go back to Rabin. We met alone on 14 May. I reviewed the story so far, stressing that Kurtzer was in the picture and that he was extremely supportive. In a series of lengthy consultations, I stressed that the PLO men in Oslo were more flexible, more imaginative and more authoritative than the West Bank–Gaza team negotiating in Washington. In Oslo, interesting proposals had been made to define the jurisdiction of the autonomy and to establish Israel's residual status and powers during the interim period – two issues that had long been deadlocked in Washington. Moreover, the 'Gaza first' concept, I stressed to Rabin, was most definitely in the interest of Israel: an overwhelming majority of Israelis wanted to get out of the teeming, terror-ridden Gaza Strip. In the evolving Oslo agreement, I also pointed out, the five-year interim period was to begin at once. In the 1978 Camp David agreement,

★ Israel's position at that stage was that it would not negotiate with any avowed PLO official; Yussef Sayigh was a member of the Palestine National Council, the PLO's parliament-in-exile. I contacted Egyptian Foreign Minister Amru Mussa, and also asked Hirschfeld to raise the matter with Abu Ala'a. Abu Ala'a promptly dealt with it.

by contrast, the five-year clock was to start ticking only after all the details of the autonomy had been agreed and put in place. The Camp David process had an end, but no definite beginning; it set up the target, but failed to provide the bow and arrows to shoot at it.

In the dramatic weeks that followed, Rabin, by disposition always cautious, moved slowly and warily. He was sceptical about the Oslo talks; sometimes he wholly disbelieved in them. When asked later why he did not share the secret with any of his close aides, he replied frankly that he doubted anything would come of Oslo. None the less he gave me, and the talks, a chance. And ultimately, when the final goal became attainable, he did not draw back.

I suggested to Rabin that perhaps I should go to Oslo to negotiate personally with Abu Ala'a, but he vetoed this because he felt that this would commit the Cabinet, which was entirely unaware of this back-channel to the PLO. Yet the time had come to start a more formal negotiation, entailing greater commitment by Israel. I decided to send Uri Savir, the Director-General of the Foreign Ministry, to the fifth round of the Oslo talks. His presence made an immediate and dramatic impact, because of his rank and his personal brilliance. Though he was only forty, I had appointed him Director-General some months before, overruling doubts and criticism from others in the Ministry. Youth can be a handicap, but it need not be. I myself had been entrusted with the Director-Generalship of the Defence Ministry at the age of twenty-nine. Intellectual gifts, diligence and commitment can make up for a lack of experience. (Despite his years, Savir had in fact amassed a good deal of diplomatic experience.)

Abu Ala'a did not hide his pleasure at Savir's appearance; he saw this – correctly – as palpable proof that Israel was taking the Oslo channel seriously. Our condition for Savir's participation was that it remain totally secret. Minister Holst and his aides, for their part, informed us that they had received an enthusiastic green light both from Christopher and from Kurtzer to press ahead with the Oslo talks.

The secrecy surrounding the Oslo talks was also rigidly maintained in Jerusalem. Apart from the negotiators, only Rabin, myself, Yossi Beilin, my political aid Avi Gil and Beilin's aide Shlomo Gur were aware of what was happening. At many key moments during these months, Rabin and I dispensed with even this close circle of aides, discussing tactics just between ourselves and not sharing our thoughts with anyone else.

Savir must have surprised the Palestinians by indicating that 'Gaza first', in the Israeli view, need not necessarily mean a commitment now and implementation only after many months, or even years. Could it not mean, he asked, a handover of Gaza within three or four months of the signing of a declaration of principles, even *before* a detailed agreement on interim self-government for the West Bank had been concluded? The trusteeship of the Gaza Strip, in Savir's hypothetical scenario, would be run jointly by the Palestinians, the Egyptians and the Jordanians, in full co-operation with Israel.

By this time, 'Gaza first' had begun to evolve into 'Gaza and Jericho first'. I had hinted to the Egyptians some time before that we were prepared to consider a 'Gaza-plus' proposal, and that Jericho might be the 'plus'. In April, Rabin went to Ismailiya for talks with Mubarak. The Egyptian President presented him with a proposed map of a 'Gaza and Jericho first' scenario, in which the Palestinian self-governing district of Jericho incorporated the Allenby Bridge, one of the two bridges★ over the River Jordan that link the Kingdom of Jordan with the West Bank. Rabin was taken aback. I had discussed with him the idea of transferring Jericho to the Palestinians, but we did not mention the bridges. He flatly rejected Mubarak's map. When he returned, I told him that I believed we could exclude the bridge from the plan. Furthermore, I said, we should insist that Jericho – and not Jerusalem – become the administrative centre for the entire West Bank–Gaza self-governing body that would eventually be created.

In Oslo in May, Abu Ala'a suggested that a joint Israeli–Palestinian police force could patrol the Allenby Bridge, adding that 'real control' of the bridge would stay in Israel's hands. My initial instruction to Uri Savir was to reject the whole Jericho idea since I felt that I must first co-ordinate our position fully and clearly with Rabin. Savir, in his report, stressed the major importance of the idea for the Palestinians. Their internal opposition, he reported, was gnawing at Arafat with the sceptical assertion that 'Gaza first' would become 'Gaza first and last'.

Arafat himself was to make this same point to Johan Holst when the two men met in Tunis in July, at a critical and delicate stage of the negotiations. Gaza, the PLO leader observed, has no religious significance for the Israelis. To withdraw solely from Gaza would be construed, he said, as signifying that Israel intended to hold on to all the areas that *do* have religious significance for Judaism – in other words, the entire West

★ The other is the Adam Bridge.

Bank. Holst felt that what Arafat was saying was that even if the true import of 'Gaza first' was not 'Gaza first and last', the PLO Chairman would find it impossible to convince his people of that. 'He would be confronted', Holst advised me, 'with an impossible sales problem.'

In my talks with Rabin, we eventually agreed on 'Gaza and Jericho first' – but without the bridges, and with the specific proviso that Jericho would become the administrative centre of the autonomous Palestinian territory. Abu Ala'a raised the subject again in Oslo in mid-June, proposing 'a symbolic withdrawal from Jericho, or another place on the West Bank'. The PLO's point, plainly, was that the first phase of the agreement must signal in tangible terms that the self-government would be taking effect on the West Bank and not just in Gaza. In any case, as Abu Ala'a himself added, once the interim self-government scheme was fully in place, there would be no difference between the status of Jericho and the rest of the West Bank.

Jerusalem, in Israel's view – all of Jerusalem – is sovereign Israeli territory and the capital of our state. East Jerusalem was formally annexed to Israel by Knesset legislation shortly after the 1967 war. We recognized in Oslo – as did Menachem Begin in the Camp David negotiations – that this position was disputed by the other side, hence our proposal that the entire issue of Jerusalem be expressly deferred till the permanent status negotiations, which are to begin in the third year of the five-year interim period.

Thus, the Declaration of Principles as it was eventually signed provides that the jurisdiction of the Palestinian self-governing Council 'will cover the West Bank and Gaza Strip territory, except for issues that will be negotiated in the permanent status negotiations' (Article IV), which will 'cover remaining issues, including Jerusalem, refugees, [and] settlements ... (Article V, 3).

Throughout the Oslo process, we were determined not to make any political concessions on Jerusalem. Savir drove the point home during his very first meeting with Abu Ala'a. If the Palestinian side insisted on dealing with Jerusalem in the Declaration of Principles, he warned, they would kill the whole negotiation. I voiced the same warning during a meeting with Holst's aide, Mona Juul, and Terje Larsen (they are husband and wife) in a Jerusalem hotel in July.

The Palestinians, however, did not give up without a fight. As their opening position, they demanded that the seat of the autonomous self-government be in Jerusalem. And they clung doggedly to their demand that East Jerusalemites be eligible both to stand and to vote in the election for the self-governing Council. In the end, the wording of Annex I to the Declaration of Principles provided that 'Palestinians of Jerusalem who live there will have the right to participate in the election process, according to an agreement between the two sides'. The Labour Party's position in the past, as Abu Ala'a and his colleagues well knew, was that East Jerusalemites should be barred from standing as candidates – since they would not be subject to the autonomous self-government – but that they should be able to vote in the election, though at polling stations located outside the city limits. We proposed polling stations in Ramallah or Bethlehem; the Palestinians proposed them in the Moslem and Christian Holy Places in the Old City of Jerusalem. The Palestinian negotiators knew, however, that the issue of candidacy and residency could be finessed by a would-be candidate setting up a second home, for registration purposes, outside Jerusalem.

As 'Gaza and Jericho first' gradually took shape as the shared goal of the Oslo negotiation and the first practical provision of the Declaration of Principles, we began to revise our positions on other basic ideas, notably that of trusteeship. My close aides, delving into legal precedents, suggested that international trusteeships in recent history were almost always established as a phase in decolonization, designed to lead eventually to full independence. Israel's declared position was that it opposed the creation of an independent Palestinian state following the interim period of self-government. Certainly we were not prepared to commit ourselves at the outset of the interim period to accepting the Palestinians' demand for eventual independence.

Our choices were succinctly spelled out in June by the newest member of our peace team, Yoel Singer, an able attorney who had served for many years in the legal department of the IDF and was involved in that capacity in the peace talks with Egypt after Camp David. Both Rabin and I knew him well and trusted his judgment. Singer was engaged in private practice in Washington when he received our 'summons' from Jerusalem to join the Oslo talks. For several weeks, he shuttled between the three cities, winding up his affairs in Washington, preparing to take up his new post as Legal Adviser to the Foreign Ministry in Jerusalem, and negotiating alongside Savir in Oslo.

In a memorandum addressed to Rabin and me, Singer listed three alternatives:

1 Some form of trusteeship for Gaza and Jericho;
2 For Gaza and Jericho to become parts of a Jordanian–Palestinian confederation;
3 For Gaza and Jericho to become the first components of the Palestinian interim self-government, with the IDF remaining in certain parts of the Gaza Strip in order to protect the Jewish settlements, which would stay there undisturbed.

Singer recommended the third alternative, which was in fact already evolving as the basic Israeli policy-position. Rabin, meeting with Beilin, Singer and me on 10 June, laid great stress on the need to ensure that the IDF's redeployment, first in Gaza and Jericho and later in the whole West Bank, be clearly defined in the Declaration of Principles as a matter for Israel's sole discretion. The Declaration could include a requirement for 'consultation' with the Palestinians, the Prime Minister said, but not for 'agreement' with them. The detailed deployment of Israeli troops for strategic defence or for the protection of Israeli settlements and Israeli civilians would not be conditional on the other party's agreement.

At the next meeting in Oslo, on 14 June, Savir and Singer faithfully followed these instructions, and were pleased to find that Abu Ala'a was open to the suggestion. The draft that the Palestinians had brought to this meeting made no mention of the IDF's role in ensuring external defence and the security of Israelis, but Abu Ala'a signalled that he was prepared to be flexible. 'My instructions', the PLO official disclosed, 'are that in matters of security I am to be open to your suggestions.' Israel would define its own security locations. 'But please,' he added, smiling, 'don't declare the entire West Bank a security area!'

It was at this session that our delegation finally laid to rest the trusteeship proposal. 'Is it feasible from your point of view', Savir asked Abu Ala'a, 'to do without it?' 'It's your choice,' the affable but shrewd Palestinian replied. Savir said that the Palestinians should think in terms of taking over Gaza and Jericho within three or four months of the signing of the Declaration of Principles.

Savir and Singer dwelt, during this meeting, on another and recurring key Israeli concern: whether the self-governing Council was to be comprised of one body or two. The point was one of principle. In the Palestinians' view, the interim self-government authority should include the three classic branches of democratic rule – executive, legislative and judicial. Hence, Abu Ala'a and his team demanded, the Council should comprise a quasi-parliament, with the right and power to make laws, and a quasi-cabinet of department heads, charged with running the day-to-day affairs of the self-government. The Israeli side, in keeping with its narrower view of the self-government scheme, sought to restrict the Council to one single body – intended as an executive body – and to limit this body's legislative functions to by-laws and regulations, to the exclusion of primary legislation. Such legislation, the Israeli negotiators argued, was the hallmark of a sovereign state.

This dispute was linked to several others also stemming from the Palestinians' desire to extend the ambit of the self-government so that it would inexorably lead to full sovereignty, and the Israelis' concern to limit it so that the permanent status of the territories was not prejudiced by the terms of the interim agreement. Thus the Palestinian negotiators pressed repeatedly for the wording, 'mutual legitimate, national and political rights' in the preamble to the Declaration of Principles. We eventually agreed, reluctantly, to 'political', but refused to accept 'national'. It was omitted. I did agree, after consultation with Rabin, to the declaration (in Article I) that 'the interim arrangements are an integral part of the whole peace process and that the negotiations on the permanent status will lead to the implementation of Security Council Resolutions 242 and 338'.

Similarly, the Palestinians demanded that the Declaration of Principles provide (Article VII) that 'after the inauguration of the Council, the Israeli Civil Administration and military government will be dissolved'. We countered that while the Civil Administration would be 'dissolved' once the autonomy was in place, the military government could only be 'withdrawn', not 'dissolved' – because legally the military government would remain the source of authority in the territories. The Palestinians agreed, in the end, to that distinction.

As for the composition of the Council, Singer insisted that the Council must be one single body. Abu Ala'a, always the resourceful negotiator, drew a diagram on a sheet of paper to illustrate, as he claimed, the essentially unitary nature of the Palestinians' concept: they, too, envisaged one single body, but divided within itself into legislative and executive organs:

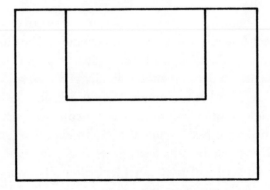

In the end, after much pulling to and fro, the Declaration of Principles, as signed, did not resolve this dispute, but rather left it to further negotiations. Article VII (3) of the Declaration provided that 'the Interim Agreement shall . . . specify the Council's executive authority and legislative authority, in accordance with Article IX below and independent Palestinian judicial organs'. Article IX provides that 'the Council will be empowered to legislate in accordance with the Interim Agreement, within all authorities transferred to it'.

26 PEACE TAKES SHAPE

The understanding reached in the early summer that Gaza and Jericho were to become Palestinian self-government enclaves (and not an international trusteeship) obviously suggested that Yasser Arafat and the PLO leadership would visit, and probably settle there, soon. I fully understood the tremendous political and emotional significance for the PLO of such a 'return', but I was convinced that this was the right step. I was determined to negotiate carefully so as to achieve a balanced accord, beneficial to both sides.

My strategic goal was to obtain, in return for the 'return', an undertaking from the PLO to recognize Israel, to forswear terrorism finally and irrevocably, and to abrogate those provisions of its charter – the 'Palestine National Covenant' – which committed the organization to fight for the destruction of the Jewish state. Tactically, my purpose was to defer this aspect of the negotiation until as late as possible, knowing how important it was to the other side. And indeed, the talks on mutual recognition between Israel and the PLO gathered momentum only towards the end of the negotiations on the Declaration of Principles, and reached their climax only after the Declaration had been initialled.

For the purposes of the Declaration of Principles' discussions, however, one point had to be cleared up immediately. Arafat could not arrive in Gaza and Jericho as 'President of Palestine', the rank which he had arrogated to himself when the PLO had proclaimed their 'State of Palestine' in 1989. We put forward our position unequivocally to the Palestinians, and reiterated it to the Norwegians, intending them to reflect our opinion in their own conversations with Arafat.

Less clear – but deliberately so – was the geographical definition of Jericho. Abu Ala'a, predictably enough, produced British Mandatory maps in which the 'Jericho District' extended most of the way from the River Jordan to Jerusalem. This was the situation too, he told our team, under Jordan (1948–67). Our side demurred, but not too vigorously – since it was apparent from his presentation that he knew he was 'trying this on', and would be prepared to settle for far less than the Mandatory dimensions of the ancient biblical city and its environs. The issue was left for the subsequent detailed negotiations, which began during October at the Egyptian Red Sea resort of Taba. Predictably, the two sides began with diametrically polar positions: the Palestinians with their Mandatory maps and Israel with a definition of Jericho that barely extended beyond the town centre.

Another question addressed but not resolved was the size of the Palestinian police force that would be established to maintain 'internal security and public order' (Annex II) in Gaza and Jericho upon the withdrawal of the IDF. At a session in Oslo at the end of June, the Palestinians asked our side for a 'professional assessment' of how many policemen would be required to do the job in the Gaza Strip. At a later meeting, Abu Ala'a told Singer and Savir that the PLO wanted 'at least 16,000 people' to police Gaza. Of these, he said, 6,000 would be Palestinians and another 10,000 members of the 'temporary international or foreign presence, as agreed upon' (Annex II).

The size and nature of this foreign presence was another matter much discussed but never nailed down in Oslo. Abu Ala'a said at one point that he thought the Americans would be prepared to contribute troops, which Singer thought far-fetched. I myself suggested to Holst's aides, only half in jest, that perhaps we could invite Singapore to send troops. After all, Singapore was being increasingly held up – by me, among others – as the paradigm of a rags-to-riches economic miracle which Gaza, at peace and with large-scale overseas investments, could try to emulate.

The issue of the temporary foreign presence should not be confused with that of the foreign observers who have been invited to monitor the elections for the self-government Council – a subject of much discussion and dispute during the Oslo process. The Palestinians proposed that the Declaration of Principles (Article III) should provide for 'international supervision' of the elections. Singer countered with 'agreed supervision and international observation', to which Abu Ala'a replied with 'international supervision to be agreed upon'. In the end, the Palestinians accepted Singer's proposal for 'agreed supervision and international observation'. But, at their insistence, the paragraph continues: 'while the Palestinian police will ensure public order'.

The fact is that there were various hints issued during the Oslo process that the elections might be deferred or might not be held at all. I did not see them as necessarily a condition. I do not believe that democracy can be imposed artificially on another society, though I do believe that the Palestinians could potentially become the first truly democratic Arab society, and that nothing would be a greater boon to Arab life than true democracy. The approach laid down by the Declaration of Principles in this respect was clear:

1 The 'Gaza and Jericho first' plan goes into effect quickly and independently of any other conditions;
2 In the rest of the West Bank, key areas of civilian life are also to be transferred by Israel to Palestinian control *before* the election and inauguration of the Council, and regardless of whether the full Interim Agreement has been concluded. This 'early empowerment' is to include five spheres: education and culture, health, social welfare, direct taxation and tourism, as well as 'additional powers and responsibilities, as agreed upon';
3 The five-year interim period begins upon the withdrawal from Gaza and Jericho – and continues regardless of whether the projected election takes place and the Council is inaugurated. The permanent status negotiations are to commence, as provided in Article v, 'not later than the beginning of the third year of the interim period, between the Government of Israel and the Palestinian people's representatives'. The Declaration pointedly does not say who these 'representatives' will be. It does not state specifically that they must be the members of the elected Council.

Camp David, by contrast, provided that 'When the self-governing authority (administrative council) in the West Bank and Gaza is established and inaugurated, the transitional period of five years will begin.' It specified, too, that the permanent status negotiations must be conducted between 'Egypt, Israel, Jordan and the elected representatives of the inhabitants of the West Bank and Gaza'. In practice, no agreement was reached on the elections or on the ambit of the self-governing authority; hence the authority was never 'established and inaugurated' – and thus, fifteen years after Camp David, the five-year transitional period has not yet begun.

Another important issue left to subsequent negotiations was that of the 'passages' or crossing-points between Gaza and Egypt and between Jericho and Jordan. Despite Abu Ala'a's unofficial hint, early in the talks, that the PLO was prepared to acquiesce to our controlling these passages, the formal PLO position remained fairly rigid. In a draft Declaration of Principles presented to the Oslo forum on 12 July, the PLO proposed that both the Gaza and the Jericho passages be 'under the responsibility of the Palestinian authorities, with international supervision and in co-operation with Israel'. Even that formulation, though wholly unacceptable from our point of view, was something of a concession. At the previous meeting, the Palestinians had demanded exclusive control over the Jericho–Jordan passage – that is, the Allenby Bridge – explaining that Israel could set up its own checkpoints west of the Jericho district.

A more substantive softening of the PLO position occurred early in August. Singer reported from Oslo that Abu Ala'a was now prepared to agree to wording that would clearly give Israel the responsibility for the Jordan passage, in co-ordination with the Palestinian authorities and with an agreed-upon international presence. This was still not good enough. In maintaining our firm position on this issue, we were motivated not only by our own direct and obvious security interests, but also by those of Jordan. Our earnest wish was that the Jordanians, completely in the dark about this evolving agreement, eventually be brought round not only to accepting it, but also to participating actively in the development of a new political and economic order encompassing both sides of the River Jordan. King Hussein and his key advisers knew that joint Israeli–Jordanian control of the River Jordan bridges had prevented potentially hostile or disruptive elements from crossing into the kingdom. The Jordanians were sure to want this discreet but effective screening to continue – and would not thus want the bridges to be left to the fledgling Palestinian authorities.*

Also much debated at Oslo, but not resolved by the time the Declaration of Principles was signed on 19 August, was the issue of Palestinian traffic between the two self-governing areas, Gaza and Jericho. In their 12 July draft, the Palestinians proposed 'a passage' between the two areas 'guaranteeing freedom of mobility'. They were thinking in terms of a

---

* This dispute with the PLO over control of the passages from Egypt and Jordan featured prominently in the subsequent negotiations between Israel and the PLO on the Gaza–Jericho phase. It was one of the key obstacles that delayed the scheduled implementation until well into 1994.

special road and air corridor. We could hardly countenance such extra-territorial routes bisecting the country, but we understood the Palestinians' desire for free movement between the two parts of the self-governing territory. We had agreed to the Palestinians' demand that the Declaration declare that 'the two sides view the West Bank and the Gaza Strip as a single territorial unit, whose integrity will be preserved during the interim period'.

When the Norwegian Foreign Minister, Johan Holst, met Arafat in Tunis on 20 July, he tried to persuade the PLO leader 'to think in terms of guaranteed access' rather than of a physical corridor. Arafat replied that he was not out 'to cut Israel in two'. He was not demanding an international corridor, he said, but rather designated roads and Israeli guarantees of access on those roads.

Arafat's first open and direct intervention in the Oslo process had come a week earlier, with a carefully composed letter addressed to 'the meeting', which Abu Ala'a handed out to all the participants at the start of a negotiating round. Representing Israel were Savir and Singer, with Hirschfeld and Pundak; the Palestinian side comprised Abu Ala'a, Hassan Asfour and Mohammed abu-Kash. 'We deal with this special channel in full seriousness,' Arafat wrote, 'and we think that through a direct and frank manner we will be able to find a temporary and satisfactory interim solution. . . .'

He continued pointedly: 'Our need for this step is apparent to you, and your need to take this step is also clear to us.' On Jerusalem he wrote that he was

aware of its sensitivity for both parties . . . but we cannot sidestep it in the interim period completely, and there are arrangements on the table, concerning the right to participate as voters and candidates in elections . . . that will not harm the position of both sides, pending the final status negotiations.

We regarded Arafat's letter as a timely and positive contribution. It seemed to reflect qualities of moderation and responsible statesmanship that were by no means always apparent in the PLO Chairman's public performances, nor indeed in his diplomatic encounters.

Johan Holst had also got through to 'the other Arafat' during his visit to Tunis, though only when he met him in private sessions. In a larger forum, the PLO chief was at his vague and blustering worst. The visit was semi-secret, in that it was ostensibly an official trip to Tunisia by the

Norwegian Foreign Minister, and meetings with Arafat were added to the schedule as 'extras'. But those meetings, of course, were the real purpose of Holst's mission. He sent Mona Juul and Terje Larsen to Jerusalem with a handwritten report to me. He had been friendly but firm with Arafat, he wrote. He had pointed out that the Oslo negotiators had already exchanged five drafts of the Declaration of Principles and still there was no complete agreement. On some of the disputed issues, moreover, the PLO was now 'deviating from the substance of realistic proposals'. Holst urged Arafat that 'the PLO can never achieve a better deal than now'. Arafat's response, Holst recorded, was 'firm and thoughtful'.

I met with Larsen and Juul (together with Savir, Hirschfeld, Pundak, Avi Gil and Shlomo Gur). I felt that the negotiations were now at a critical stage, and I wanted to give them a first-hand sense of our positions. But above all, I wanted to inject a sense of urgency into the Oslo process. 'Let's wrap it up fast,' I said. 'Don't let the Oslo track become like chewing-gum – like the Washington track has become.'

The key sticking-points for us, I said, were Jerusalem, security and the jurisdiction question. We were not prepared to accept that East Jerusalemites stand in the elections, 'but I don't see elections happening so soon. . . . It would be silly to force a crisis now over that problem and endanger the whole agreement.'

According to Holst, the PLO Chairman was equally anxious to press ahead. 'He made an impassioned reference to the deteriorating living conditions in Gaza,' Holst reported. 'He said that delay could mean both Israel and the PLO losing control.' Holst had accordingly suggested to Arafat that the two sides try to finalize the Declaration of Principles at their next session in Oslo. But the next session proved frustrating. Holst was briefed by Abu Ala'a when it ended, on 27 July, and wrote to me the same day, noting that the results of the round seemed

somewhat unclear. . . . I asked [Abu Ala'a] whether the Palestinians were very concerned with being tricked, warning of the alleged danger of Israeli cleverness. He responded affirmatively . . . and expressed the view that the Israelis did not seem to be acting independently, and that they appeared to reflect American interests. The implication was that the US remains irrevocably hostile to the PLO.

After studying our own negotiators' reports of the round and consulting with Rabin, I wrote back to Holst:

... Your incisive and in–depth analysis ... is of great value to us – both to Prime Minister Rabin and to myself – in evaluating the very intricate dynamics of this unique channel and opportunity.... The limits of manoeuvrability have been tested. Now, the time is ripe for decisions.... The biggest risk of all is the inability to take any risks.

I intended my Norwegian colleague and friend to convey the substance of my letter in his own parallel contacts with Arafat, and thus I continued:

I must share with you my honest concern that again they [the PLO] may opt to aspire for a too-perfect solution.... The vacuum may be filled by opposing forces, or with other initiatives, including the possibility of desired progress between Israel and Syria. Secretary Christopher is at this very moment visiting our region....

I had transmitted a similar message of urgency two weeks earlier, through the good offices of President Mubarak of Egypt. While visiting Cairo, I sought to persuade Mubarak, as I urged Holst, that the nego-tiations had exhausted themselves and that it was now time for decisions. Arafat, I was told, wanted to meet me. But this was not the time to meet, I explained to the Egyptian leader. This was the time to cut through the remaining obstacles and to conclude the agreement. Then the time would come for meetings.

Throughout these months, we had initiated no direct contact with the Americans regarding the Oslo process, nor they with us. We knew from Holst – as did Arafat – that he had briefed Secretary Christopher in person, and, as we have seen, that earlier Hirschfeld had spoken to one of the Secretary's Middle East aides, Dan Kurtzer, and received his warm encouragement. Beyond that, nothing. I assumed Christopher's silence was grounded in a healthy blend of diplomatic discretion and scepticism.

Given the intimacy of our relations with Washington, this situation was strange. But I was not particularly disturbed by it. As I told Holst's aides, Juul and Larsen, 'We want the Americans to get all the credit – after the agreement is concluded.' I recalled my still fresh and searing memory of how the Americans had ruined my agreement with King Hussein in 1987 by listening to Shamir. We must try to have the agreement signed in Washington as the crowning act of a long-term American diplomatic effort, I said. The Norwegians were sceptical.

The full story would inevitably leak out, they said. As it turned out, Christopher shared their view, rejecting the notion that the agreement could be passed off as the product of American mediation.

27 NEW DAWN

'We must hurry,' I told our Norwegian friends, 'or we may end up with a peace treaty but no government to sign it.' We were in Stockholm on 17 August, almost a month after Johan Holst's visit to Tunis. Our coalition looked shakier than ever. The High Court of Justice had ruled that the Shas Party leader, Arye Deri, who was facing charges of financial wrongdoing, must give up his Cabinet seat, even before the Knesset had decided on whether to remove his parliamentary immunity. Meanwhile, further negotiations in Oslo, in the wake of Holst's intervention in Tunis, had whittled down the differences with the Palestinians to just three points. 'Let's try to wrap it up now,' I urged Holst, 'while I'm here in Scandinavia.'

As good fortune would have it, I was on an official visit to the Scandinavian countries, which had been scheduled long before and was entirely unconnected with the secret negotiations in Oslo. But the visit enabled me now to maintain close and constant contact with our negotiators.

I was due to fly from Sweden to Norway the following evening, but, in the meantime, Holst had discreetly flown into Stockholm at my request, with Mona Juul and Terje Larsen, to see if we could expedite matters. We told our curious Swedish hosts that the Norwegians wanted to settle, before my arrival in their country, the vexed issue of a heavy water consignment that we had obtained from them years ago, allegedly by complicated means. They seemed to accept that explanation of the neighbouring statesman's unannounced arrival.

Larsen said that the Palestinians 'love drama', and he therefore proposed to telephone them in Tunis to tell them that Shimon Peres was right there with him – ready to negotiate the final points. I said that if he thought my presence added to the drama, he could refer to it. But he was to transmit our unwavering insistence that the Council of the autonomous territories – the Palestinian Authority, as it was to be known – must have its seat in Jericho. That, for us, was an integral part of the logic of 'Gaza and Jericho first', and we were not prepared to countenance their setting up their institutions anywhere else.

On the tactical plane, I suggested that Larsen hint to the Palestinians that Israel might yet go for a quick deal with Syria instead of concluding the accord with the PLO. Damascus, I said – and this was quite true – had been putting out markedly favourable signals of late. Israel would not want to leap forward on both tracks simultaneously; it would have to choose one or the other.

Holst remarked that the Palestinians believed Israel was super-sophisticated and that they therefore looked for traps between every line of the draft articles. 'If they only knew . . .', I laughed. Mona also laughed and recounted how our Ambassador in Sweden had sat there that very afternoon, explaining why I would never negotiate with the PLO and never deviate from the Madrid conference framework. Technically, he was right.

Meanwhile, Larsen was trying, without success, to track down Abu Ala'a in Tunis. Finally, he gave up and placed a call to Arafat himself. The Chairman, Larsen reported, confirmed that we were 'very close' to completion, but he said that Abu Ala's must do the final negotiating.

At 1.15 a.m., Larsen reached him at last. 'I've got the two fathers here with me,' he said. 'My father wants to talk to you.' Holst took the phone and began reading through the outstanding paragraphs. In the interests of security, he also tried to veil his references, but he kept forgetting himself and saying 'Israel'. Eventually, he decided to say 'Blurp' for 'Israel', which had the rest of us doubled up with laughter. Abu Ala's said that he was 'with my father, and we need ninety minutes alone together before we get back to you'. The conversation resumed at 2.25, then again at 2.45, at 3.00, then at 4.00 and finally at 4.20. By this time, I had gone to bed, only to be awakened by Avi Gil and Yoel Singer each time a new formula was reached.

By the final call, the excitement in Arafat's office was discernible over the line. When the last point was declared settled, we could hear them cheering and weeping, and we knew that they were hugging one another.

'Only Fellini could have dreamed up a set like this,' said Avi Gil. How right he was. Two days had passed, and we were now in Norway on the next leg of our Scandinavian trip. We had been put up in the official government guesthouse, a three-storey building in the suburbs of Oslo, with an elegant dining-room and reception-room on the top floors and bedrooms on the ground floor.

At 10.30 p.m., the official dinner drew to a close. The entire Israeli delegation was present, together with twenty Norwegian guests, among them the Parliamentary Speaker, Jo Benkow, a much respected figure throughout Norway and a proud Jew. He had recently decided to retire from public life, and members of parliament from all parties grouped together to plant a forest in his honour in Israel.

Johan Holst made the appropriate after-dinner speech, and I duly gave a reply. As soon as people started getting up to go, I made a show of being tired and announced that I was going to bed.

I actually got into bed, but I couldn't even pretend to sleep. In two hours, we were to sign the first peace agreement between Israel and the Palestinians. Even I, an inveterate napper, could not stop thinking about the approaching drama.

I had begun my day in Stockholm with a song in my heart. But this mood of jubilation was soon darkened by the news from Israel that seven of our soldiers had been killed by a roadside bomb in south Lebanon. A real tragedy, and doubly disastrous because of the timing. I phoned Rabin to commiserate. He briefed me on the details of the attack. I reported to him in dry, businesslike tones that the Palestinians had agreed to our formula on Jericho and that, therefore, we would be signing the agreement tonight. He made no comment.

Now, at last, the great moment was at hand. The officials accompanying me on this Scandinavian tour were all in bed, apart from Gil. Our Ambassador to Norway, Yoel Allon, one of our best professional diplomats, had gone home, unaware of what was about to take place in his bailiwick. One by one, the lights went out on the ground floor. At midnight, I got up, dressed again and quietly slipped upstairs. Larsen had organized three rooms: one for the Palestinians, one for the Israelis and one for the Norwegians. The negotiating teams, headed by Savir and Abu Ala'a, had been working together secretly in a downtown Oslo hotel, putting the finishing touches to the Declaration of Principles, haggling over the last words and phrases, right down to the wire. They were brought separately to the guesthouse by the Norwegian secret service and 'smuggled' inside through a back entrance.

The Israelis and the Palestinians were each to gather in our respective rooms and then to proceed to the Norwegian room, where the ceremony would take place. The Norwegians were setting out bottles of champagne when I arrived. I asked them to dispense with the champagne, explaining that my heart was heavy with the loss of our seven young men. While I was as excited as anyone by the imminent signing, I did not feel like champagne. We all hoped, I added, that the agreement we were about to sign would prevent such pointless killing of young people in the future. But that was in the hopeful future and, meanwhile, we were in the painful present. Hope and pain, I said, were mingled in our minds.

The Norwegian secret service had set up video cameras to record the event for posterity. They also provided a still photographer. We had agreed in advance that the photographs would be made available only with the express consent of all the parties.

The Norwegians proposed that the proceedings begin with Johan Holst and me standing together to receive the members of the two delegations. We were to shake hands with each of them in turn. Then, the delegations would take their places at the table for the signing. In a particularly moving touch, our hosts had arranged that the signing take place on the historic table on which Norway's agreement of secession from Sweden had been signed in 1905. The two sides would sign, and then Holst would affix his own signature as witness. Someone suggested that I stand behind the Israeli delegation during the signing and then say a few words afterwards. But I explained that I could not formally participate in the signing (apart from a brief posed picture), nor make a speech, because the agreement had not yet been submitted to the Cabinet for approval. It had to remain 'deniable', in case, God forbid, the need to deny it should still arise. However, I was prepared to be present in the room during the signing, sitting on the side with Mrs Holst.

I decided that Uri Savir and Yoel Singer should sign for Israel, with Yair Hirschfeld and Ron Pundak standing behind them. The signatories on the Palestinian side were to be Abu Ala'a and his young aide, Hassan Asfour, who is said to be a rising star in the PLO.

Holst told me that Abu Ala'a wanted to meet me alone, and I agreed.

As the minutes ticked by, the electric excitement in the air grew almost palpable. Finally, at 2.30 a.m., we took our places in the 'receiving line': Johan Holst, Mrs Holst and myself. The three members of the Palestinian delegation filed in, we shook their hands, and then the four Israelis followed. Abu Ala'a shook my hand with visible emotion.

An expectant silence settled over the room as the delegations took their seats. It was disturbed only by the whirring and clicking of the cameras – and then by the blessed sound of pens on paper. The agreements had been prepared in three folders bound in red leather – one for each of the parties and one for the witness.

With the signing over, the speeches began. Holst spoke in praise of peace, brimming with pride over the major role that his modest-sized country had played in bringing an end to so deep-rooted a conflict which so many others had tried and failed to resolve.

Abu Ala'a spoke next. In one hand, he held his prepared text, and in the other a large handkerchief. He waged an unequal struggle with his tears. No sooner had he begun speaking than he began crying, and so he continued, speaking and crying, crying and speaking. (Larsen told me later that Abu Ala'a had asked the Norwegians for an English-language secretary to whom he wanted to dictate his speech, since his command of English, he maintained, was not good enough for him to write by himself what was after all an historic document.)

And indeed for Abu Ala'a, as the representative of the Palestinian people, this was a supremely historic moment: it was the climax of the Palestinians' history as a people. He thanked Norway. He thanked the Israeli delegation. He noted that the agreement was the best possible birthday present for me, as my seventieth birthday fell on that day. The intensity of his emotion affected everyone in the room.

Savir was the final speaker. He delivered a polished address – perhaps a little too polished for the occasion – referring to the tragedy, for both our nations, that would now come to an end as a result of this agreement. The Promised Land, he concluded, could now become a land of promise again.

With this, the ceremony came to an end, and I retired with Abu Ala'a to another room for the private conversation he had sought. Once again, he thanked me effusively, in his own name and in the name of Chairman Arafat, for the part I had personally played in making this night come about. He assured me that all the major figures in the PLO leadership would be comfortable with the agreement. He indicated that they had inducted Farouk Kaddumi in the Oslo process, though Feisal Husseini and Hanan Ashrawi knew nothing thus far. The PLO, said Abu Ala'a, trusted that I would continue helping them in the future. Virtually everything depended on us, he asserted.

For my part, I stressed that we were entirely sincere when we said that

349

we had no wish to rule over the Palestinian people. Rabin and I had taken an enormous risk. We had needed total secrecy for the success of the whole venture – and we still needed that secrecy until we submitted the agreement to our Cabinet and until we told the Americans. I said that, like the Palestinians, we too had a direct interest, both political and economic, in the success of the agreement. 'The fate of Gaza can be like that of Singapore,' I asserted. 'From poverty to prosperity in one sustained leap.'

He said that he had closely followed my efforts for peace. Just recently, he had shown Arafat the text of my address to the European Parliament, in which I had called for substantial economic aid for the Palestinians in the territories. Arafat said that he was not surprised: he knew, he explained, that I was capable of saying things and doing things on behalf of the Palestinians that many Arab states would neither say nor do.

We spoke of the need to build up a new Middle East, and he professed much enthusiasm for my hopes and visions – which warmed my heart. Abu Ala'a, short, balding, incisive and excitable, had handled the negotiations with consummate skill. Now, he was tasting the first fruits of his labours.

What a night! For me, this was the second time that I had brought my country to the threshold of peace. The first time had been six years earlier, in London, with King Hussein. Our agreement could have become the basis for a comprehensive settlement. Had that happened, many lives would have been saved and much misery avoided. But Shultz backed away, because of Shamir's pressure on him, and the opportunity was wasted. This time, I resolved, I must try to ensure that nothing like that happened.

How strange it is, I found myself thinking, that we Israelis are now the ones granting the Palestinians what the British had granted us more than seventy years ago, a 'homeland in Palestine', in the words of the Balfour Declaration of November 1917.

I didn't even try to fall asleep that night, but lay waiting for the dawn of the new day.

No sooner had we all sat down than Warren Christopher was on his feet again, pouring drinks. I jumped up too, exclaiming, 'Hey, I'm from a kibbutz! You mustn't serve me.'

That melted any unbroken ice, and we quickly settled into a serious conversation. It was ten days after that momentous night in Oslo, and now Johan Holst and I were on another secret rendezvous, this time in California, with the American Secretary of State, Warren Christopher, and his top Middle East adviser, Dennis Ross.

When I had returned hom from Scandinavia, Rabin and I agreed that we must now urgently inform the Americans of what was afoot. We could hardly proceed to negotiate a mutual recognition agreement with the PLO while Washington still maintained its strict diplomatic boycott of the Organization. 'Either you should go to Clinton,' I suggested, 'or I should go to Christopher.' Rabin preferred that I go. I had made tentative plans with Holst, and we now arranged to fly over together. Christopher, vacationing on the West Coast, arranged to receive us at a naval air base near Santa Barbara, and we arrived with our close aides aboard an executive jet.

We had worked out in advance a sort of sales-pitch-cum-agenda. I was to open with a review of the Oslo agreement before moving on to the current negotiations on mutual recognition between Israel and the PLO. Holst would then take over, stressing the American role in the overall peace process and reminding Christopher of how he had briefed him about the Oslo negotiations. I was to put forward the idea that the United States 'adopt' the Declaration of Principles as its own initiative and 'submit' it to the parties in the Washington talks.

Holst and I suggested, and Christopher immediately agreed, that after the tripartite session there should be separate meetings between Americans and Israelis and between Americans and Norwegians. Then the three teams would meet briefly to sum up, and, finally, the three Ministers should confer together without aides. Holst had 'budgeted' ninety minutes for the whole process. In fact, we spent four-and-a-half hours in intensive – and enjoyable – talks.

I began by pointing out that the PLO had made significant concessions which the Palestinian delegation had consistently rejected in the Washington talks. I stressed that we had not yet wrapped up the seven-point accord on mutual recognition, because we were very much aware of the administration's commitment to Congress not to reopen official contacts between the US and the PLO, and we wanted to talk it through with the Secretary first. Thus far, only Rabin and I knew of the agreement that had been initialled in Oslo, and of the ongoing negotiation over mutual recognition. The fact that this had not leaked out was incredible. 'Keeping secrets is not usually one of our national characteristics,' I observed.

Holst now reminded Christopher of their meeting back in May, when he had reported to the Secretary on what was beginning to evolve in Oslo. 'Your visit to the Middle East [early in August] clearly had a strong impact', Holst continued enthusiastically, 'both on these negotiations and on the multilateral talks.'

Alone with Christopher and Dennis Ross, I adopted a more intimate and more sombre tone. 'I learned my lesson from the London agreement,' I said, not mincing my words. 'Shultz got cold feet at the last moment. Shamir sent Moshe Arens to Shultz to stop him from coming out to the region – and everything was destroyed.' The point was plain enough, and I didn't need to drive it home.

'King Hussein has never really abandoned his interest in the West Bank,' I continued. 'Even when he proclaimed that he was out of the game, he didn't fully mean it. He expected to be called back. That didn't happen, and meanwhile we in Israel want to rid ourselves of the burden of occupying the Palestinians.'

I went on: 'There are two ways of dealing with the PLO: by force, or by political wisdom. And I'm frankly not sure that force is a workable option.' The Palestinians probably still harboured hopes of taking over Jordan one day, while in Israel people feared an independent Palestinian state. In the long run, therefore, only a Jordanian–Palestinian accord could overcome these fears and ensure stability.

I predicted confidently that the broad majority of the Israeli public would welcome the autonomy agreement, despite the settlers' inevitable efforts to depict it as a disaster. The Likud, I said, would find it hard to oppose the withdrawal from Gaza and Jericho. We would argue that the agreement had saved Jerusalem. The city was explicitly excluded from the ambit of the proposed self-government authority; its status was consigned to the permanent status negotiations.

I told Christopher that we had been working closely with President Mubarak, who had brought his Foreign Minister Amru Mussa and his close aide Osama el-Baz into the picture. The Palestinian side too had confided in the Egyptians and had also kept the Tunisians informed. Ross asked whether King Hussein knew what was happening. I said that we had not filled him in.

As for mutual recognition and the seven-point accord, if the United States agreed in principle, we could conduct an intensive week of negotiations in Washington* with the Palestinians, and produce an

---

* In the event, the talks that clinched the Israeli–PLO mutual recognition accord were held in Paris.

agreement that would be hailed by the whole world as a success for American diplomacy and as a bright beginning for the Middle East. The United States after all, had insisted unwaveringly for years on the very concessions which we proposed to secure from the PLO in the seven-point agreement.

'Shimon,' Christopher asked with the utmost frankness, 'what do the seven points mean for the United States?'

I explained that Secretary Shultz had begun an official dialogue with the PLO at the end of 1988, after Arafat had publicly fulfilled the longstanding American conditions that he forswear terrorism, accept Security Council Resolutions 242 and 338, and recognize Israel's right to exist in peace. Subsequently, a sea-borne PLO unit attacked an Israeli beach, and his successor, Secretary Baker, had suspended the dialogue. 'The seven points cover your conditions,' I assured the Secretary.

'You've done a tremendous job,' Christopher said. 'My initial response to these developments is very, very positive.'

I assured him that Rabin and I were ready to continue with serious negotiations with Syria. I wanted to allay any unspoken concern that we were concluding a 'separate peace' with the PLO and would leave the other tracks of the Washington talks to stagnate. 'We believe that the progress with the Palestinians will help to spur the Syrians towards progress too.' With the Palestinians, the choice had been to make a great leap forward or to remain bogged down. I quoted Churchill's line about not crossing a chasm in two steps. 'The way to a deal with Syria, on the other hand, is by a phased, step-by-step approach,' I said.

'Are you sure Arafat will live up to his commitments?' Ross asked.

'Yes,' I replied. 'He conceded on Jerusalem because he wants Gaza.' I acknowledged that some of the senior PLO people were contemptuous of Arafat. 'But they need him. They know they can't succeed without him.' In Scandinavia, I added wryly, I had found myself 'doing a UJA* job for the Palestinians!' I also told Christopher that we had briefed two top American Jewish leaders on the terms of the agreement, without telling them, though, that it had actually been initialled. The two, Lester Pollack and Malcolm Hoenline, the Chairman and Executive Director respectively of the Conference of Presidents of American Jewish Organizations, had both responded enthusiastically. The same was true, I said, of Arye Deri, the leader of the Shas Party, whose support was so

---

* United Jewish Appeal: the main fundraising organization for Israel in America.

important to us at home. The Secretary and Ross listened with interest.

When the three teams reassembled, Christopher, though still wholly positive in his attitude to the agreement, made it clear that he was not prepared to 'adopt' it as an American initiative. That was just not a credible option, he said. The press would quickly dig up the full story of how the agreement had evolved. I suggested that our line should be that the United States was closely involved from the start and that Norway 'helped bridge the gaps'.

On the seven points, the Secretary was totally supportive. 'If you reach an agreement on them,' he said, 'we will allow a PLO representative to come to Washington for the signing.' Ross suggested that we insist that the PLO undertake not only to renounce terrorism but also to discipline member-groups that continued to engage in acts of terrorism. This important point was eventually incorporated into the Israeli–PLO accord.

Holst and I urged Christopher to approach a number of Arab moderates – among them Morocco, Tunisia, Kuwait, Oman and Jordan – with an American proposal that they publicly proclaim a state of peace with Israel. I encouraged the Secretary to think in terms of a major signing ceremony in Washington, with foreign governments and the media in full attendance. We agreed immediately to inform François Mitterrand, Helmut Kohl and John Major of what was happening, and to begin building with them, together with the Japanese and others, an international financial framework that would provide vital aid for Palestinian economic development.

EPILOGUE

I was born an optimist and have remained one throughout my life. Pessimism has always seemed to me a useless frame of mind. I have been blessed, too, with good health, except for one near brush with death in 1989, when I was suddenly taken ill with a rare type of blood poisoning. According to my mother, I went through childhood without contracting any of the usual childhood illnesses. Now, in my seventies, as I look back over my life, a phrase comes to mind that was coined by Gabriel García Márquez in one of his stories: 'an unpaid dreamer'.

My life's work is not yet done. The final, crowning chapters of my biography are still being written at this time. They deal with the subject closest to my heart – peace. We are ending a decades-long history dominated by war, and embarking on an era in which the guns will stay silent while dreams flourish. I feel that I have earned the right to dream. So much that I dreamed in the past was dismissed as fantasy, but has now become thriving reality. Peace in our region is no longer part of a dream-world; it has built a permanent place for itself in the realm of reality. Since concluding this text, I have visited Amman and signed with King Hussein a draft agreement* that furnished the basis for the Israel–Jordan 'Washington Declaration'.† I have visited Yasser Arafat at his office in Gaza and seen the new reality there beginning to take shape. As I write these closing words, I am preparing for a major economic conference in Casablanca, Morocco, where statesmen and businessmen from the region and the world will discuss the economic underpinnings of the new Middle East.

---

* On 3 November 1993.
† Of July 1994; see Appendix IV, pages 379–83.

The world into which I was born no longer exists, but I have been fortunate to be present at the birth of a new world – sometimes as an onlooker, sometimes as an active participant in the act of creation.

But even now I am not inclined to give up dreaming. Two dreams in particular take up much of my waking thoughts. One concerns the future of the Jewish People, the other the future of the Middle East.

In the new era which the world has now entered, the wealth and power of nations depend more on the development of intellectual resources than on the possession of natural resources. Quality is the key criterion rather than quantity, universalism is superseding nationalism. All this poses new problems that nations and their leaders have not had to grapple with before. In the past, a nation's identity was moulded from its people's special characteristics, the geography of its land, and the unique properties of its language and culture. Today, science has no national identity, technology no homeland, information no passport. A country's intellectual standard is more significant than its size. The productivity of its arable land counts for more than its acreage.

Modern man speaks two languages: the language of verbal communication and the language of computers. National cultures and heritages must compete for man's attention with the mind-absorbing advances of universal science.

The Jewish People's challenge in today's world is to defend its unique heritage. This is no less demanding a task than was the previous national challenge – the physical defence of the homeland. Preserving the Hebrew language in the world of today and tomorrow is as much a strategic undertaking as guarding the borders has been until now. The test is how to ensure that our children remain Jewish – Jewish not merely by their ethnic origins, but by their self-identity and sense of mission.

In history, Judaism has been far more successful than the Jews themselves. Jews were frequently persecuted, exiled, plundered and murdered. The Jewish People remained small and weak, but the Jewish spirit went on from strength to strength. The Bible is to be found in hundreds of millions of homes throughout the monotheistic world. The moral majesty of the Book of Books has been undefeated by the vicissitudes of history. On the contrary, time and again history has succumbed to the Bible's immortal ideas. The message that the one, invisible God created Man in his image, and that there are therefore no higher and lower orders of man, has fused with the realization that morality is the highest form of wisdom – and perhaps of beauty and of courage, too. It is that which distinguishes man from beast. Slings and arrows and gas chambers can annihilate men, but they cannot destroy human values, dignity and freedom.

Jewish history presents an encouraging lesson for mankind. For nearly four thousand years a small nation carried a great message. For part of this period the nation dwelt on its own land; later, it wandered in exile. This small nation swam against the tides and was repeatedly beaten, banished and downtrodden. There is no example in all of history – neither among the great empires nor among their colonies and dependencies – of a nation, after so long a saga of tragedy and misfortune, rising up again, shaking itself free, gathering together its dispersed remnants, and setting out anew on its national adventure, defeating doubters within and enemies without, reviving its land and its language, rebuilding its identity, and reaching towards new heights of distinction and excellence. The message of the Jewish People to mankind is that faith can triumph over all adversity.

The Jews are traditionally the People of the Book, but in today's world the book must fight to hold its own against the screen. The depth of the book must compete against the speed of the screen. Man's natural image, as portrayed in print, must vie with his made-up face as it appears on camera. The screen, of course, has clear advantages in this struggle: it is accessible, ubiquitous, absorbed without effort. It amuses and entertains us. But the screen, ultimately, distorts our image.

The conflicts shaping up as our century nears its close will be over the content of civilizations, not over the territory they occupy. Jewish culture has lived over many centuries on alien soil. Now, it has taken root again it its own soil. For the first time in history, some five million people speak Hebrew as their native language. That is both a lot and a little: a lot, because there have never been so many Hebrew-speakers before; but a little, because a culture based on five million people can hardly withstand the pervasive, corrosive effects of the global television culture.

In the five decades of Israel's existence, our efforts have been focused on re-establishing our territorial centre. In the future, we shall have to devote our main effort to re-establishing our spiritual centre. The Jewish People is neither a nation nor a religion in the accepted sense of those terms. Its essence is a message rather than a political structure; a faith rather than an ecclesiastical hierarchy. The Jewish People and the Jewish religion are one and the same. Judaism – or Jewishness – is a fusion of belief, history, land and language. Being Jewish means belonging to a people that is both a chosen people and a universal people. My greatest dream is that our children, like our forefathers, do not make do with the transient and the sham, but continue to plow the historic Jewish furrow in the field of the human spirit. My hope is that Israel will become the centre and source of our heritage, not merely a homeland for our people; that the Jewish People will not need to depend on others, but will give of itself to others.

As for our region, the Middle East, Israel's role is to contribute to the region's great and sustained revival. It will be a Middle East without wars, without fronts, without enemies, without ballistic missiles and without nuclear warheads. A Middle East in which people, goods and services can move freely from place to place without the need for customs clearance and police licences. A Middle East in which every believer will be free to pray in his own language, Arabic or Hebrew or Latin or whatever language he chooses, and in which his prayers will reach their destination without censorship, without interference and without offending anyone. A Middle East in which nations strive for economic equality, but encourage cultural pluralism. A Middle East in which every young man and woman can attain university education. A Middle East in which living standards are in no way inferior to those in the most advanced countries of the world. A Middle East in which waters flow to slake thirst, to made crops grow and deserts bloom, in which no hostile borders bring death, hunger and despair on the peoples of the region. A Middle East of competition, not of domination. A Middle East in which men are their neighbours' allies, not their hostages. A Middle East that is not a killing field, but a field of creativity and growth. A Middle East that honours its past history so deeply that it strives to add new, noble chapters to that history.

This book is my personal testimony to the fact that it is permissible for a man to dream – not just any dreams, but great dreams.

APPENDICES

I   United Nations Security Council Resolutions 242 and 338

Resolution 242, 22 November 1967:

Having failed to take any decision, the General Assembly on 21 July voted to adjourn and to refer the discussion on the Middle East crisis back to the Security Council. Although the Middle East was also the subject of many of the speeches heard during the regular session of the General Assembly in September 1967, the Security Council continued its debates and was presented with draft Resolutions by Britain, the Soviet Union and the United States. On 22 November 1967, it unanimously adopted Resolution 242, which formed the terms of reference for the mission of Ambassador Gunnar Jarring. The Resolution was formulated by the British Ambassador to the United Nations, Lord Caradon; it established provisions and principles which, it was hoped, would lead to an agreement.

The Security Council

Expressing its continuing concern with the grave situation in the Middle East,

Emphasizing the inadmissibility of the acquisition of territory by war and the need to work for a just and lasting peace in which every state in the area can live in security,

Emphasizing further that all member states in their acceptance of the Charter of the United Nations have undertaken a commitment to act in accordance with Article 2 of the Charter,

1 **Affirms** that the fulfilment of Charter principles requires the establishment of a just and lasting peace in the Middle East which should include the application of both the following principles:

(i) Withdrawal of Israeli armed forces from territories occupied in the recent conflict;

(ii) Termination of all claims or states of belligerency and respect for and acknowledgment of the sovereignty, territorial integrity and political independence of every state in the area and their right to live in peace within secure and recognized boundaries free from threats or acts of force;

2 **Affirms further** the necessity

(a) for guaranteeing freedom of navigation through international waterways in the area;

(b) for achieving a just settlement of the refugee problem;

(c) for guaranteeing the territorial inviolability and political independence of every state in the area, through measures including the establishment of demilitarized zones;

3 **Requests** the Secretary-General to designate a special representative to proceed to the Middle East to establish and maintain contacts with the states concerned in order to promote agreement and assist efforts to achieve a peaceful and accepted settlement in accordance with the provisions and principles in this resolution;

4 **Requests** the Secretary-General to report to the Security Council on the progress of the efforts of the special representative as soon as possible.

Resolution 338, 22 October 1973:

Following the recovery of the Golan Heights and the occupation of a bulge inside Syria, and the extension of the Israeli presence in the west bank of the Suez Canal, international efforts to stop the war were intensified. United States Secretary of State Dr Kissinger flew to Moscow on 20 October and, together with the Soviet Government, the United States proposed a ceasefire Resolution. The Security Council met on 21 October at the urgent request of the US and the USSR. By fourteen votes to none and no abstentions (China did not participate in the vote), the Council adopted the following Resolution:

The Security Council.

1 Calls upon all parties to the present fighting to cease all firing and terminate all military activity immediately, no later than 12 hours after the moment of the adoption of this decision, in the positions they now occupy;

2 Calls upon the parties concerned to start immediately after the cease-fire the implementation of Security Council Resolution 242 (1967) in all of its parts;

3 Decides that immediately and concurrently with the cease-fire, negotiations start between the parties concerned under appropriate auspices aimed at establishing a just and durable peace in the Middle East.

II   The Peres–Hussein London Agreement, 11 April 1987

A three part understanding between Jordan and Israel

A   Invitation by UN Secretary-General.

B   Resolutions of the international conference.

C   The modalities agreed upon by Jordan–Israel.

A   The Secretary-General will issue invitations to the five permanent members of the Security Council and the parties involved in the Arab–Israeli conflict in order to negotiate a peaceful settlement based on Resolutions 242 and 338, with the objects of bringing a comprehensive peace to the area, security to its states, and to respond to the legitimate rights of the Palestinian people.

B   The participants in the conference agree that the purpose of the negotiations is the peaceful solution of the Arab–Israeli conflict based on Resolutions 242 and 338 and a peaceful solution of the Palestinian problem in all its aspects. The conference invites the parties to form geographical bilateral committees to negotiate mutual issues.

C Jordan and Israel have agreed that:

   1 The international conference will not impose any solution or veto
      any agreement arrived at between the parties.

   2 The negotiations will be conducted in bilateral committees directly.

   3 The Palestinian issue will be dealt with in the committee of the
      Jordanian–Palestinian and Israeli delegations.

   4 The Palestinians' representatives will be included in the Jordanian–
      Palestinian delegation.

   5 Participation in the conference will be based on the parties'
      acceptance of Resolutions 242 and 338 and the renunciation of
      violence and terrorism.

   6 Each committee will negotiate independently.

   7 Other issues will be decided by mutual agreement between Jordan
      and Israel.

The above understanding is subject to approval of the respective
governments of Israel and Jordan.

The text of this paper will be shown and suggested to the USA.

III   The Israeli–Palestinian Declaration of Principles, September 1993

The Government of the State of Israel and the PLO team (in the
Jordanian–Palestinian delegation to the Middle East Peace Conference)
(the 'Palestinian Delegation'), representing the Palestinian people, agree
that it is time to put an end to decades of confrontation and conflict,
recognize their mutual legitimate and political rights, and strive to live
in peaceful coexistence and mutual dignity and security and achieve a just,
lasting and comprehensive peace settlement and historic reconciliation
through the agreed political process. Accordingly, the two sides agree to
the following principles:

Article I

AIM OF THE NEGOTIATIONS

The aim of the Israeli–Palestinian negotiations within the current Middle East peace process is, among other things, to establish a Palestinian Interim Self-Government Authority, the elected Council (the 'Council'), for the Palestinian people in the West Bank and the Gaza Strip, for a transitional period not exceeding five years, leading to a permanent settlement based on Security Council Resolutions 242 and 338.

It is understood that the interim arrangements are an integral part of the whole peace process and that the negotiations on the permanent status will lead to the implementation of Security Council Resolutions 242 and 338.

Article II

FRAMEWORK FOR THE INTERIM PERIOD

The agreed framework for the interim period is set forth in this Declaration of Principles.

Article III

ELECTIONS

1 In order that the Palestinian people in the West Bank and Gaza Strip may govern themselves according to democratic principles, direct, free and general political elections will be held for the Council under agreed supervision and international observation, while the Palestinian police will ensure public order.

2 An agreement will be concluded on the exact mode and conditions of the elections in accordance with the protocol attached as Annex I, with the goal of holding the elections not later than nine months after the entry into force of this Declaration of Principles.

3 These elections will constitute a significant interim preparatory step toward the realization of the legitimate rights of the Palestinian people and their just requirements.

Article IV

JURISDICTION

Jurisdiction of the Council will cover West Bank and Gaza Strip territory, except for issues that will be negotiated in the permanent status negotiations. The two sides view the West Bank and the Gaza Strip as a single territorial unit, whose integrity will be preserved during the interim period.

Article V

TRANSITIONAL PERIOD AND PERMANENT STATUS NEGOTIATIONS

1 The five-year transitional period will begin upon the withdrawal from the Gaza Strip and Jericho area.

2 Permanent status negotiations will commence as soon as possible, but not later than the beginning of the third year of the interim period, between the Government of Israel and the Palestinian people representatives.

3 It is understood that these negotiations shall cover remaining issues, including: Jerusalem, refugees, settlements, security arrangements, borders, relations and cooperation with other neighbors, and other issues of common interest.

4 The two parties agree that the outcome of the permanent status negotiations should not be prejudiced or preempted by agreements reached for the interim period.

Article VI

PREPARATORY TRANSFER OF POWERS AND RESPONSIBILITIES

1 Upon the entry into force of this Declaration of Principles and the withdrawal from the Gaza Strip and the Jericho area, a transfer of authority from the Israeli military government and its Civil Administration to the authorized Palestinians for this task, as detailed herein, will commence. This transfer of authority will be of a preparatory nature until the inauguration of the Council.

2 Immediately after the entry into force of this Declaration of Principles

and the withdrawal from the Gaza Strip and Jericho area, with the view to promoting economic development in the West Bank and Gaza Strip, authority will be transferred to the Palestinians on the following spheres: education and culture, health, social welfare, direct taxation, and tourism. The Palestinian side will commence in building the Palestinian police force, as agreed upon. Pending the inauguration of the Council, the two parties may negotiate the transfer of additional powers and responsibilities, as agreed upon.

Article VII

INTERIM AGREEMENT

1 The Israeli and Palestinian delegations will negotiate an agreement on the interim period (the 'Interim Agreement').

2 The Interim Agreement shall specify, among other things, the structure of the Council, the number of its members, and the transfer of powers and responsibilities from the Israeli military government and its Civil Administration to the Council. The Interim Agreement shall also specify the Council's executive authority, legislative authority in accordance with Article IX below, and the independent Palestinian judicial organs.

3 The Interim Agreement shall include arrangements, to be implemented upon the inauguration of the Council, for the assumption by the Council of all of the powers and responsibilities transferred previously in accordance with Article VI above.

4 In order to enable the Council to promote economic growth, upon its inauguration, the Council will establish, among other things, a Palestinian Electricity Authority, a Gaza Sea Port Authority, a Palestinian Development Bank, a Palestinian Export Promotion Board, a Palestinian Environmental Authority, a Palestinian Land Authority and a Palestinian Water Administration Authority, and any other Authorities agreed upon, in accordance with the Interim Agreement that will specify their powers and responsibilities.

5 After the inauguration of the Council, the Civil Administration will be dissolved, and the Israeli military government will be withdrawn.

Article VIII

PUBLIC ORDER AND SECURITY

In order to guarantee public order and internal security for the Palestinians of the West Bank and the Gaza Strip, the Council will establish a strong police force, while Israel will continue to carry the responsibility for defending against external threats, as well as the responsibility for overall security of Israelis for the purpose of safeguarding their internal security and public order.

Article IX

LAWS AND MILITARY ORDERS

1 The Council will be empowered to legislate, in accordance with the Interim Agreement, within all authorities transferred to it.

2 Both parties will review jointly laws and military orders presently in force in remaining spheres.

Article X

JOINT ISRAELI–PALESTINIAN LIAISON COMMITTEE

In order to provide for a smooth implementation of this Declaration of Principles and any subsequent agreements pertaining to the interim period, upon the entry into force of this Declaration of Principles, a Joint Israeli–Palestinian Liaison Committee will be established in order to deal with issues requiring coordination, other issues of common interest, and disputes.

Article XI

ISRAELI–PALESTINIAN COOPERATION IN ECONOMIC FIELDS

Recognizing the mutual benefit of cooperation in promoting the development of the West Bank, the Gaza Strip and Israel, upon the entry into force of this Declaration of Principles, an Israeli–Palestinian Economic Cooperation Committee will be established in order to develop and implement in a cooperative manner the programs identified in the protocols attached as Annex III and Annex IV.

Article XII

LIAISON AND COOPERATION WITH JORDAN AND EGYPT

The two parties will invite the Governments of Jordan and Egypt to participate in establishing further liaison and cooperation arrangements between the Government of Israel and the Palestinian representatives, on the one hand, and the Governments of Jordan and Egypt, on the other hand, to promote cooperation between them. These arrangements will include the constitution of a Continuing Committee that will decide by agreement on the modalities of admission of persons displaced from the West Bank and Gaza Strip in 1967, together with necessary measures to prevent disruption and disorder. Other matters of common concern will be dealt with by this Committee.

Article XIII

REDEPLOYMENT OF ISRAELI FORCES

1 After the entry into force of this Declaration of Principles, and not later than the eve of elections for the Council, a redeployment of Israeli military forces in the West Bank and the Gaza Strip will take place, in addition to withdrawal of Israeli forces carried out in accordance with Article XIV.

2 In redeploying its military forces, Israel will be guided by the principle that its military forces should be redeployed outside populated areas.

3 Further redeployments to specified locations will be gradually implemented commensurate with the assumption of responsibility for public order and internal security by the Palestinian police force pursuant to Article VIII above.

Article XIV

ISRAELI WITHDRAWAL FROM THE GAZA STRIP AND JERICHO AREA

Israel will withdraw from the Gaza Strip and Jericho area, as detailed in the protocol attached as Annex II.

Article XV

RESOLUTION OF DISPUTES

1 Disputes arising out of the application or interpretation of this Declaration of Principles, or any subsequent agreements pertaining to the interim period, shall be resolved by negotiations through the Joint Liaison Committee to be established pursuant to Article X above.

2 Disputes which cannot be settled by negotiations may be resolved by a mechanism of conciliation to be agreed upon by the parties.

3 The parties may agree to submit to arbitration disputes relating to the interim period, which cannot be settled through conciliation. To this end, upon the agreement of both parties, the parties will establish an Arbitration Committee.

Article XVI

ISRAELI–PALESTINIAN COOPERATION CONCERNING REGIONAL PROGRAMS

Both parties view the multilateral working groups as an appropriate instrument for promoting a 'Marshall Plan', the regional programs and other programs, including special programs for the West Bank and Gaza Strip, as indicated in the protocol attached as Annex IV.

Article XVII

MISCELLANEOUS PROVISIONS

1 This Declaration of Principles will enter into force one month after its signing.

2 All protocols annexed to this Declaration of Principles and Agreed Minutes pertaining thereto shall be regarded as an integral part hereof.

Done at Washington, DC, this thirteenth day of September 1993.

For the Government of Israel

Shimon Peres

For the P L O

Witnessed By:

The United States of America

Warren Christopher

The Russian Federation

ANNEX I

PROTOCOL ON THE MODE AND CONDITIONS OF ELECTIONS

1 Palestinians of Jerusalem who live there will have the right to participate in the election process, according to an agreement between the two sides.

2 In addition, the election agreement should cover, among other things, the following issues:

  a the system of elections;

  b the mode of the agreed supervision and international observation and their personal composition; and

  c rules and regulations regarding election campaign, including agreed arrangements for the organizing of mass media, and the possibility of licensing a broadcasting and TV station.

3 The future status of displaced Palestinians who were registered on 4 June 1967 will not be prejudiced because they are unable to participate in the election process due to practical reasons.

ANNEX II

PROTOCOL ON WITHDRAWAL OF ISRAELI FORCES FROM THE GAZA STRIP AND JERICHO AREA

1 The two sides will conclude and sign within two months from the date of entry into force of this Declaration of Principles, an agreement on the withdrawal of Israeli military forces from the Gaza Strip and Jericho area. This agreement will include comprehensive arrangements to apply in the Gaza Strip and the Jericho area subsequent to the Israeli withdrawal.

2 Israel will implement an accelerated and scheduled withdrawal of Israeli military forces from the Gaza Strip and Jericho area, beginning immediately with the signing of the agreement on the Gaza Strip and Jericho area and to be completed within a period not exceeding four months after the signing of this agreement.

3 The above agreement will include, among other things:

a Arrangements for a smooth and peaceful transfer of authority from the Israeli military government and its Civil Administration to the Palestinian representatives.

b Structure, powers and responsibilities of the Palestinian authority in these areas, except: external security, settlements, Israelis, foreign relations, and other mutually agreed matters.

c Arrangements for the assumption of internal security and public order by the Palestinian police force consisting of police officers recruited locally and from abroad (holding Jordanian passports and Palestinian documents issued by Egypt). Those who will participate in the Palestinian police force coming from abroad should be trained as police and police officers.

d A temporary international or foreign presence, as agreed upon.

e Establishment of a joint Palestinian–Israeli Coordination and Cooperation Committee for mutual security purposes.

f An economic development and stabilization program, including the establishment of an Emergency Fund, to encourage foreign investment, and financial and economic support. Both sides will coordinate and cooperate jointly and unilaterally with regional and international parties to support these aims.

g Arrangements for a safe passage for persons and transportation between the Gaza Strip and Jericho area.

4 The above agreement will include arrangements for coordination between both parties regarding passages:

a Gaza — Egypt; and

b Jericho — Jordan.

5 The offices responsible for carrying out the powers and responsibilities of the Palestinian authority under this Annex II and Article VI of the Declaration of Principles will be located in the Gaza Strip and in the Jericho area pending the inauguration of the Council.

6 Other than these agreed arrangements, the status of the Gaza Strip and Jericho area will continue to be an integral part of the West Bank and Gaza Strip, and will not be changed in the interim period.

ANNEX III

PROTOCOL ON ISRAELI–PALESTINIAN COOPERATION IN ECONOMIC AND DEVELOPMENT PROGRAMS

The two sides agree to establish an Israeli–Palestinian Continuing Committee for Economic Cooperation, focusing, among other things, on the following:

1 Cooperation in the field of water, including a Water Development Program prepared by experts from both sides, which will also specify the mode of cooperation in the management of water resources in the West Bank and Gaza Strip, and will include proposals for studies and plans on water rights of each party, as well as on the equitable utilization of joint water resources for implementation in and beyond the interim period.

2 Cooperation in the field of electricity, including an Electricity Development Program, which will also specify the mode of cooperation for the production, maintenance, purchase and sale of electricity resources.

3 Cooperation in the field of energy, including an Energy Development Program, which will provide for the exploitation of oil and gas for industrial purposes, particularly in the Gaza Strip and in the Negev, and will encourage further joint exploitation of other energy resources. This Program may also provide for the construction of a Petrochemical industrial complex in the Gaza Strip and the construction of oil and gas pipelines.

4 Cooperation in the field of finance, including a Financial Development and Action Program for the encouragement of international investment in the West Bank and the Gaza Strip, and in Israel, as well as the establishment of a Palestinian Development Bank.

5 Cooperation in the field of transport and communications, including a Program, which will define guidelines for the establishment of a Gaza Sea Port Area, and will provide for the establishing of transport and communications lines to and from the West Bank and the Gaza Strip to Israel and to other countries. In addition, this Program will provide for carrying out the necessary construction of roads, railways, communications lines, etc.

6 Cooperation in the field of trade, including studies, and Trade Promotion Programs, which will encourage local, regional and inter-regional trade, as well as a feasibility study of creating free trade zones in the Gaza Strip and in Israel, mutual access to these zones, and cooperation in other areas related to trade and commerce.

7 Cooperation in the field of industry, including Industrial Development Programs, which will provide for the establishment of joint Israeli–Palestinian Industrial Research and Development Centers, will promote Palestinian–Israeli joint ventures, and provide guidelines for cooperation in the textile, food, pharmaceutical, electronics, diamonds, computer and science-based industries.

8 A program for cooperation in, and regulation of, labor relations and cooperation in social welfare issues.

9 A Human Resources Development and Cooperation Plan, providing for joint Israeli–Palestinian workshops and seminars, and for the establishment of joint vocational training centers, research institutes and data banks.

10 An Environmental Protection Plan, providing for joint and/or coordinated measures in this sphere.

11 A program for developing coordination and cooperation in the field of communication and media.

12 Any other programs of mutual interest.

PROTOCOL ON ISRAELI–PALESTINIAN COOPERATION CONCERNING
REGIONAL DEVELOPMENT PROGRAMS

1 The two sides will cooperate in the context of the multilateral peace efforts in promoting a Development Program for the region, including the West Bank and the Gaza Strip, to be initiated by the G-7. The parties will request the G-7 to seek the participation in this program of other interested states, such as members of the Organization for Economic Cooperation and Development, regional Arab states and institutions, as well as members of the private sector.

2 The Development Program will consist of two elements:

a An Economic Development Program for the West Bank and the Gaza Strip.

b A Regional Economic Development Program.

A The Economic Development Program for the West Bank and the Gaza Strip will consist of the following elements:

(1) A Social Rehabilitation Program, including a Housing and Construction Program.

(2) A Small and Medium Business Development Plan.

(3) An Infrastructure Development Program (water, electricity, transportation and communications, etc.).

(4) A Human Resources Plan.

(5) Other Programs.

B The Regional Economic Development Program may consist of the following elements:

(1) The establishment of a Middle East Development Fund, as a first step, and a Middle East Development Bank, as a second step.

(2) The development of a joint Israeli–Palestinian–Jordanian Plan for coordinated exploitation of the Dead Sea area.

(3) The Mediterranean Sea (Gaza) – Dead Sea Canal.

(4) Regional Desalinization and other water development projects.

(5) A regional plan for agricultural development, including a coordinated regional effort for the prevention of desertification.

(6) Interconnection of electricity grids.

(7) Regional cooperation for the transfer, distribution and industrial exploitation of gas, oil and other energy resources.

(8) A Regional Tourism, Transportation and Telecommunications Development Plan.

(9) Regional cooperation in other spheres.

3 The two sides will encourage the multilateral working groups, and will coordinate towards their success. The two parties will encourage intersessional activities, as well as pre-feasibility and feasibility studies, within the various multilateral working groups.

Agreed Minutes to the Declaration of Principles on Interim Self-Government Arrangements

Any powers and responsibilities transferred to the Palestinians pursuant to the Declaration of Principles prior to the inauguration of the Council will be subject to the same principles pertaining to Article IV, as set out in these Agreed Minutes below.

B. SPECIFIC UNDERSTANDINGS AND AGREEMENTS

Article IV

It is understood that:

1 Jurisdiction of the Council will cover West Bank and Gaza Strip

territory, except for issues that will be negotiated in the permanent status negotiations: Jerusalem, settlements, military locations, and Israelis.

2 The Council's jurisdiction will apply with regard to the agreed powers, responsibilities, spheres and authorities transferred to it.

Article VI (2)

It is agreed that the transfer of authority will be as follows:

(1) The Palestinian side will inform the Israeli side of the names of the authorized Palestinians who will assume the powers, authorities and responsibilities that will be transferred to the Palestinians according to the Declaration of Principles in the following fields: education and culture, health, social welfare, direct taxation, tourism, and any other authorities agreed upon.

(2) It is understood that the rights and obligations of these offices will not be affected.

(3) Each of the spheres described above will continue to enjoy existing budgetary allocations in accordance with arrangements to be mutually agreed upon. These arrangements also will provide for the necessary adjustments required in order to take into account the taxes collected by the direct taxation office.

(4) Upon the execution of the Declaration of Principles, the Israeli and Palestinian delegations will immediately commence negotiations on a detailed plan for the transfer of authority on the above offices in accordance with the above understandings.

Article VII (2)

The Interim Agreement will also include arrangements for coordination and cooperation.

Article VII (5)

The withdrawal of the military government will not prevent Israel from exercising the powers and responsibilities not transferred to the Council.

Article VIII

It is understood that the Interim Agreement will include arrangements for cooperation and coordination between the two parties in this regard. It is also agreed that the transfer of powers and responsibilities to the Palestinian police will be accomplished in a phased manner, as agreed in the Interim Agreement.

Article X

It is agreed that, upon the entry into force of the Declaration of Principles, the Israeli and Palestinian delegations will exchange the names of the individuals designated by them as members of the Joint Israeli–Palestinian Liaison Committee.

It is further agreed that each side will have an equal number of members in the Joint Committee. The Joint Committee will reach decisions by agreement. The Joint Committee may add other technicians and experts, as necessary. The Joint Committee will decide on the frequency and place or places of its meetings.

ANNEX II

It is understood that, subsequent to the Israeli withdrawal, Israel will continue to be responsible for external security, and for internal security and public order of settlements and Israelis. Israeli military forces and civilians may continue to use roads freely within the Gaza Strip and the Jericho area.

Done at Washington, DC, this thirteenth day of September, 1993.

For the Government of Israel   For the PLO

Witnessed By:

The United States of America

[signature: Warren Christopher]

The Russian Federation

[signature]

September 9, 1993

Mr Prime Minister,

The signing of the Declaration of Principles marks a new era in the history of the Middle East. In firm conviction thereof, I would like to confirm the following PLO commitments:

The PLO recognizes the right of the State of Israel to exist in peace and security.

The PLO accepts United Nations Security Council Resolutions 242 and 338.

The PLO commits itself to the Middle East peace process, and to a peaceful resolution of the conflict between the two sides and declares that all outstanding issues relating to permanent status will be resolved through negotiations.

The PLO considers that the signing of the Declaration of Principles constitutes a historic event, inaugurating a new epoch of peaceful coexistence, free from violence and all other acts which endanger peace and stability. Accordingly, the PLO renounces the use of terrorism and other acts of violence and will assume responsibility over all PLO elements and personnel in order to assure their compliance, prevent violations and discipline violators.

In view of the promise of a new era and the signing of the Declaration of Principles and based on Palestinian acceptance of Security Council Resolutions 242 and 338, the PLO affirms that those articles of the Palestinian Covenant which deny Israel's right to exist, and the provisions of the Covenant which are inconsistent with the commitments of this letter are now inoperative and no longer valid. Consequently, the PLO undertakes to submit to the

Palestinian National Council for formal approval the necessary changes in regard to the Palestinian Covenant.

Sincerely,

Yasser Arafat
Chairman
The Palestine Liberation Organization

9 9 93

Yitzhak Rabin
Prime Minister of Israel

September 9, 1993

Mr Chairman,

In response to your letter of September 9, 1993, I wish to confirm to you that, in light of the PLO commitments included in your letter, the Government of Israel has decided to recognize the PLO as the representative of the Palestinian people and commence negotiations with the PLO within the Middle East peace process.

Yitzhak Rabin
Prime Minister of Israel

10.9.93

Yasser Arafat
Chairman
The Palestinian Liberation Organization

September 9, 1993

Dear Minister Holst,

I would like to confirm to you that, upon the signing of the

Declaration of Principles, I will include the following positions in my public statements:

In light of the new era marked by the signing of the Declaration of Principles, the PLO encourages and calls upon the Palestinian people in the West Bank and Gaza Strip to take part in the steps leading to the normalization of life, rejecting violence and terrorism, contributing to peace and stability and participating actively in shaping reconstruction, economic development and cooperation.

Sincerely,

Yasser Arafat
Chairman
The Palestine Liberation Organization
9 9 93

His Excellency
Johan Jørgen Holst
Foreign Minister of Norway

IV   The Israel–Jordan Washington Declaration, 25 July 1994

A   After generations of hostility, blood and tears and in the wake of years of pain and wars, His Majesty King Hussein and Prime Minister Yitzhak Rabin are determined to bring an end to bloodshed and sorrow. It is in this spirit that His Majesty King Hussein of the Hashemite Kingdom of Jordan and Prime Minister and Minister of Defence, Mr Yitzhak Rabin of Israel, met in Washington today at the invitation of President William J. Clinton of the United States of America. This initiative of President William J. Clinton constitutes an historic landmark in the United States' untiring efforts in promoting peace and stability in the Middle East. The personal involvement of the President has made it possible to realize agreement on the content of this historic declaration.

The signing of this declaration bears testimony to the President's vision and devotion to the cause of peace.

B In their meeting, His Majesty King Hussein and Prime Minister Yitzhak Rabin have jointly reaffirmed the five underlying principles of their understanding on an Agreed Common Agenda designed to reach the goal of a just, lasting and comprehensive peace between the Arab States and the Palestinians, with Israel.

   1 Jordan and Israel aim at the achievement of just, lasting and comprehensive peace between Israel and its neighbours and at the conclusion of a Treaty of Peace between both countries.

   2 The two countries will vigorously continue their negotiations to arrive at a state of peace, based on Security Council Resolutions 242 and 338 in all their aspects, and founded on freedom, equality and justice.

   3 Israel respects the present special role of the Hashemite Kingdom of Jordan in Muslim Holy shrines in Jerusalem. When negotiations on the permanent status will take place, Israel will give high priority to the Jordanian historic role in these shrines. In addition the two sides have agreed to act together to promote interfaith relations among the three monotheistic religions.

   4 The two countries recognize their right and obligation to live in peace with each other as well as with all states within secure and recognized boundaries. The two states affirmed their respect for and acknowledgment of the sovereignty, territorial integrity and political independence of every state in the area.

   5 The two countries desire to develop good neighbourly relations of cooperation between them to ensure lasting security and to avoid threats and the use of force between them.

C The long conflict between the two states is now coming to an end.

In this spirit the state of belligerency between Jordan and Israel has been terminated.

D Following this declaration and in keeping with the Agreed Common Agenda, both countries will refrain from actions or activities by either side that may adversely affect the security of the other or may prejudice the final outcome of negotiations. Neither side will threaten the other by use of force, weapons, or any other means, against each other, and both sides will thwart threats to security resulting from all kinds of terrorism.

E His Majesty King Hussein and Prime Minister Yitzhak Rabin took note of the progress made in the bilateral negotiations within the Jordan–Israel track last week on the steps decided to implement the sub-agendas on borders, territorial matters, security, water, energy, environment and the Jordan Rift Valley.

In this framework, mindful of items of the Agreed Common Agenda (borders and territorial matters) they noted that the boundary sub-commission has reached agreement in July 1994 in fulfilment of part of the role entrusted to it in the sub-agenda. They also noted that the sub-commission for water, environment and energy agreed to mutually recognize, as the role of their negotiations, the rightful allocations of the two sides in Jordan River and Yarmouk River waters and to fully respect and comply with the negotiated rightful allocations, in accordance with agreed acceptable principles with mutually acceptable quality. Similarly, His Majesty King Hussein and Prime Minister Yitzhak Rabin expressed their deep satisfaction and pride in the work of the trilateral commission in its meeting held in Jordan on Wednesday, July 20 1994, hosted by the Jordanian Prime Minister, Dr Abdessalam al-Majali, and attended by Secretary of State Warren Christopher and Foreign Minister Shimon Peres. They voiced their pleasure at the association and commitment of the United States in this endeavour.

F His Majesty King Hussein and Prime Minister Yitzhak Rabin believe that steps must be taken both to overcome psychological barriers and to break with the legacy of war. By working with optimism towards the dividends of peace for all the people in the region, Jordan and Israel are determined to shoulder their responsibilities towards the human dimension of peace making. They recognize imbalances and disparities are a root cause of extremism which thrives on poverty and unemployment and the degradation of human dignity. In this spirit, His Majesty King Hussein and Prime Minister Yitzhak Rabin have today approved a series of steps to symbolize the new era which is now at hand:

1 Direct telephone links will be opened between Jordan and Israel.
2 The electricity grids of Jordan and Israel will be linked as part of a regional concept.
3 Two new border crossings will be opened between Jordan and Israel – one at the southern tip of Aqaba–Eilat and the other at a mutually agreed point in the north.
4 In principle, free access will be given to third country tourists travelling between Jordan and Israel.
5 Negotiations will be accelerated on opening an international air corridor between both countries.
6 The police forces of Jordan and Israel will cooperate in combating crime, with emphasis on smuggling and particularly drug smuggling. The United States will be invited to participate in this joint endeavour.
7 Negotiations on economic matters will continue in order to prepare for future bilateral cooperation including the abolition of all economic boycotts.

All these steps are being implemented within the framework of regional infrastructural development plans and in conjunction with the Jordan–Israel bilaterals on boundaries, security, water and related issues and without prejudice to the final outcome of the negotiations on the items included in the Agreed Common Agenda between Jordan and Israel.

G His Majesty King Hussein and Prime Minister Yitzhak Rabin have agreed to meet periodically or whenever they feel necessary to review the progress of the negotiations and express their firm intention to shepherd and direct the process in its entirety.

H In conclusion, His Majesty King Hussein and Prime Minister Yitzhak Rabin wish to express once again their profound thanks and appreciation to President William J. Clinton and his Administration for their untiring efforts in furthering the cause of peace, justice and prosperity for all the peoples of the region. They wish to thank the President personally for his warm welcome and hospitality. In recognition of their appreciation to the President, His Majesty King Hussein and Prime Minister Yitzhak Rabin have asked President William J. Clinton to sign this document as a witness and as a host to their meeting.

His Majesty King Hussein   Prime Minister Yitzhak Rabin

President William J. Clinton

INDEX